XSLT and XPath On The Edge, Unlimited Edition™

XSLT and XPath On The Edge, Unlimited Edition™

Jeni Tennison

M&T Books

An imprint of Hungry Minds, Inc.

New York, NY • Cleveland, OH • Indianapolis, IN

XSLT and XPath On The Edge, Unlimited Edition™

Published by
M&T Books
An imprint of Hungry Minds, Inc.
909 Third Avenue
New York, NY 10022
www.hungryminds.com

Library of Congress Control Number: 2001089354

ISBN: 0-7645-4776-3

Printed in the United States of America

10 9 8 7 6 5 4 3 2 1

1B/SR/QZ/QR/IN

Distributed in the United States by Hungry Minds, Inc.

Distributed by CDG Books Canada Inc. for Canada; by Transworld Publishers Limited in the United Kingdom; by IDG Norge Books for Norway; by IDG Sweden Books for Sweden; by IDG Books Australia Publishing Corporation Pty. Ltd. for Australia and New Zealand; by TransQuest Publishers Pte Ltd. for Singapore, Malaysia, Thailand, Indonesia, and Hong Kong; by Gotop Information Inc. for Taiwan; by ICG Muse, Inc. for Japan; by Intersoft for South Africa; by Eyrolles for France; by International Thomson Publishing for Germany, Austria, and Switzerland; by Distribuidora Cuspide for Argentina; by LR International for Brazil; by Galileo Libros for Chile; by Ediciones ZETA S.C.R. Ltda. for Peru; by WS Computer Publishing Corporation, Inc., for the Philippines; by Contemporanea de Ediciones for Venezuela; by Express Computer Distributors for the Caribbean and West Indies; by Micronesia Media Distributor, Inc. for Micronesia; by Chips Computadoras S.A. de C.V. for Mexico; by Editorial Norma de Panama S.A. for Panama; by American Bookshops for Finland.

For general information on Hungry Minds' products and services please contact our Customer Care department within the U.S. at 800-762-2974, outside the U.S. at 317-572-3993 or fax 317-572-4002.

For sales inquiries and reseller information, including discounts, premium and bulk quantity sales, and foreign-language translations, please contact our Customer Care department at 800-434-3422, fax 317-572-4002 or write to Hungry Minds, Inc., Attn: Customer Care Department, 10475 Crosspoint Boulevard, Indianapolis, IN 46256.

For information on licensing foreign or domestic rights, please contact our Sub-Rights Customer Care department at 212-884-5000.

For information on using Hungry Minds' products and services in the classroom or for ordering examination copies, please contact our Educational Sales department at 800-434-2086 or fax 317-572-4005.

For press review copies, author interviews, or other publicity information, please contact our Public Relations department at 317-572-3168 or fax 317-572-4168.

For authorization to photocopy items for corporate, personal, or educational use, please contact Copyright Clearance Center, 222 Rosewood Drive, Danvers, MA 01923, or fax 978-750-4470.

Library of Congress Cataloging-in-Publication Data

 Hungry Minds™ is a trademark of Hungry Minds, Inc.

 is a trademark of Hungry Minds, Inc.

About the Author

Jeni Tennison, a leading XSLT specialist and a regular and verbose contributor to XSL-List (http://www.mulberrytech.com/xsl/xsl-list), is one of the maintainers of the EXSLT initiative (http://www.exslt.org) and the implementer of XSLTDoc, an XSLT-based application for browsing XSLT applications (http://www.jenitennison.com/xslt/utilities).

Jeni has a knowledge-engineering background and is currently working as a freelance XML and XSLT consultant. She teaches courses on various XML-related topics, including XSLT, and has worked on several real-world XML and XSLT projects.

Jeni lives with her partner, two cats, and a vast Lego collection in Nottingham, England.

Credits

ACQUISITIONS EDITOR
Grace Buechlein

PROJECT EDITOR
Chandani Thapa

TECHNICAL EDITOR
David Carlisle

COPY EDITORS
Roxane Marini
Luann Rouff

EDITORIAL MANAGER
Colleen Totz

PROJECT COORDINATOR
Maridee Ennis

GRAPHICS AND PRODUCTION SPECIALISTS
Sean Decker, Brian Drumm,
Kelly Hardestry, Joyce Haughey,
Jackie Nicholas, Kendra Span,
Brian Torwelle, Jeremy Unger

QUALITY CONTROL TECHNICIANS
John Greenough,
Andy Hollandbeck,
Carl Pierce, Linda Quigley

PROOFREADING AND INDEXING
TECHBOOKS Production Services

Preface

This book is intended for people who are already familiar with XML and have used XSLT and XPath. Thus, this book is designed for those who have acquired an understanding of the basics but who have not yet acquired an understanding of all the ins and outs of putting together a complex stylesheet. In the Introduction, I cover things that you should already know, partly to jar your memory and partly to introduce you to the terms that are used throughout the book.

This is not a book for beginners. After the Introduction, I launch directly into a discussion about using XSLT to address real problems. In addition, this book focuses on *how* you can achieve your goals within your XSLT stylesheet. It does not focus on explaining the syntax of XSLT elements or XPath functions. If you are looking for a reference book, I recommend Mike Kay's *XSLT Programmer's Reference* from Wrox Press.

The goal of each chapter is to provide solutions to common problems — to discuss these issues thoroughly enough so that you may learn new techniques to use with XSLT in the process. Although you may not read this book from cover to cover, you will find that it provides you with several methods of doing things when you need to do something in XSLT and don't know how to approach it. In addition, it also provides advice about which method is best to use in which situation.

Book Outline

The body of the book is split into five parts. In the first part, I look at various low-level tasks that you might need to do in XSLT, and I construct a number of utility templates to help you accomplish them. The chapters in this section address topics such as reformatting numbers, searching and replacing in text, and manipulating and analyzing data in XML.

The second part of this book examines higher-level tasks within a stylesheet and discusses how to approach them, including filtering XML, doing translations between XML vocabularies, sorting, numbering and grouping information, and creating summary information such as indexes and tables of contents.

The third part takes an even wider view and looks at the issues involved with creating XSLT applications. I discuss ways of separating style from format and breaking up your stylesheet into functional and physical modules to make it easier to maintain and reuse. Also, I outline how to create dynamic applications using client-side transformation with MSXML and server-side transformation with Cocoon.

In the fourth part, the discussion focuses on how to put the finishing touches on your stylesheet — how to make it create the exact output that you're after and how to make it perform more efficiently.

In the final part, I examine the various extensions that are available for XSLT in the major XSLT processors (Saxon, Xalan, and MSXML) and how to use them.

Special Unlimited Edition

One of the best features about this book is that it doesn't end with the last page. As the owner of this book, you have access to the Unlimited Edition Web site (`http://unlimited-edition.com`).

For up to a year after the book is published (and until a new edition becomes available), new material is posted to the Web site to discuss the most recent or expanded XSLT and XPath topics. Also, you have access to every chapter of this book from this site. You can download chapters in PDF format so you can look through them offline as well.

Conventions Used in This Book

This book uses a number of styles to highlight particular types of words or text:

Construct	Format	Example
XSLT element/attribute name	bold monospace	`xsl:template`, `select`
Function	monospace with parentheses	`normalize-space()`
Axis	monospace	`preceding-sibling`
Node test	monospace	`node()`, `*`
XPath	monospace	`transactions/transaction`
Element/attribute name	monospace	`transaction`, `date`
Literal values	monospace	`16`, `true`, `NaN`
String	monospace with single quotes	`'TV license'`
URL	monospace	`http://www.w3.org/XSL`

When a section is supplementary to the main text, I use one of the following icons:

 A Note highlights or expands on something I've just talked about.

> ## What Is a Sidebar?
> Sidebars discuss larger topics that are tangentially related to the main text.

 A Caution indicates something that you should watch out for.

 A Cross-Reference provides a link to another chapter in the book or to a resource where you can learn more.

 A tip provides a hint that should help you write better XSLT or XPaths.

When I discuss a piece of code, I often highlight parts of that code using bold text to indicate places that have changed or that are particularly noteworthy. For example, in the following snippet, I've highlighted the li element:

```
<xsl:template match="transaction">
   <li><xsl:apply-templates /></li>
</xsl:template>
```

Contacting the Author

If you have any comments or questions on any aspect of this book, please get in touch with me at mail@jenitennison.com. You may find my Web site http://www.jenitennison.com helpful, as well as the Web site associated with this book, www.unlimited-edition.com. For general XSLT queries, though, I recommend XSL-List — see http://www.mulberrytech.com/xsl/xsl-list.

Acknowledgments

I'd very much like to thank David Carlisle for his insightful comments on this book. I'm also very grateful to Gert Bultman of Xi advies bv for giving me a detailed audience-eye critique and to Jarno Elovirta for all his suggestions. Also, thanks to Tony Graham for his early comments.

I would also like to thank the team at Hungry Minds — Grace Buechlein, Chandani Thapa, Roxane Marini, Luann Rouff, and Gus Miklos — for guiding me through my first book.

And many thanks to all those on the XSL-List who have given me this expertise by asking difficult questions, and to all those who have encouraged me to write it down somewhere, particularly Dave Pawson, Chris Bayes, and John Simpson. Also, I would like to thank the various experts — but most especially Mike Kay, David Carlisle (again), and Steve Muench — who have tirelessly given their time to answer my (and many others') naïve queries. And many thanks to the members of the XSL WG who have invested so much effort in making XSLT a language worth getting excited about.

Finally, of course, my thanks to the friends, family, and furry ginger creatures, who supported me while I wrote this book. But mainly to Bill, whose understanding, generosity, and penchant for shoot-em-ups never cease to amaze me.

Contents at a Glance

Contents

Introduction

This book is aimed at people who already have some experience using XSLT. You should be familiar with most XSLT elements and XPath functions; understand the concepts of node trees, node sets, and result tree fragments; and know how to use various XSLT processors from the command line, within Internet Explorer, or using Cocoon.

This Introduction gives you a whistle-stop tour of XPath and XSLT that goes over the things that you should already know. You may want to read it simply to come to grips with the terminology that you'll see in the rest of the book, but it also provides pointers to the chapters that address particular issues.

XPath BasicsXPaths lie at the heart of XSLT — they're used to select and match nodes, to test conditions, and to calculate values. Getting comfortable with using XPaths enables you to take full advantage of XSLT and stands you in good stead with other XML-based applications, such as XML Schema, XPointer and XQuery, which take advantage of them. I'll be using XPaths in various ways throughout this book. Here, I'm going to cover the basics. Meanwhile, a reference section in Appendix A covers them as well.

 The XPath Recommendation is available at `http://www.w3.org/TR/ xpath` if you want additional technical details.

Value Types

There are four value types in XPath, and two that are introduced by XSLT. The four basic value types are as follows:

- **Boolean:** True or false

- **Number:** A floating point number, `NaN` (not a number), `Infinity` and `-Infinity`

- **String:** A piece of text; none of the characters within a string have any particular significance in XPath

- **Node set:** An unordered group of nodes

The two value types that XSLT introduces are as follows:

◆ **Result tree fragment:** A portion of a result tree that is very similar to a mini node tree with a single root node; it cannot be indexed in the same way as a node tree.

◆ **External objects:** Objects created and used by extension functions; they do not fall into one of the other value types.

 It's likely that the distinction between result tree fragments and node sets will disappear in XSLT 2.0.

 I give some examples of external objects in Chapter 18, where I talk about extension functions.

Nodes and Node Trees

When an application wants to operate on an XML document (such as an XSLT processor running an XSLT stylesheet over an XML document), it builds an internal model of what the document looks like. In general, this model is known as a *document object model* or *DOM*. In XPath and XSLT, it's called a *node tree*.

 The standard type of DOM is the *W3C DOM*. But there are lots of different ways to represent an XML document internally, and applications won't necessarily use the W3C DOM. The W3C DOM is somewhat different from the DOM that's used in XPath.

Nodes are the abstract components that make up a node tree. Many different kinds of nodes exist, and each type represents a different kind of component in an XML document. The following node types are significant in XSLT:

◆ **Root nodes:** The top of the node tree

◆ **Element nodes:** XML elements

- ◆ **Attribute nodes:** XML attributes
- ◆ **Text nodes:** Textual content in XML elements
- ◆ **Comment nodes:** XML comments
- ◆ **Processing instruction nodes:** XML processing instructions
- ◆ **Namespace nodes:** The in-scope namespaces on an element

Some of the text nodes may consist purely of whitespace because they're used to indent and format parts of the document. These are known as *white-space-only text nodes*.

The node tree reflects the *logical* form of the document rather than its *physical* form, which means that node trees don't contain nodes representing things such as the XML declaration, the DOCTYPE declaration, CDATA sections, or entities within the document.

A discussion on controlling the physical features of a document that you create with XSLT can be found in Chapter 16.

For example, take the following XML document:

```
<?xml version="1.0"?>
<!DOCTYPE collection SYSTEM "collection.dtd">
<?xml-stylesheet type="text/xsl" href="collection.xsl"?>
<collection>
   <DVD rating="15">
      <title>plunkett &amp; macleane</title>
      <director>Jake Scott</director>
   </DVD>
   <!-- insert other films -->
</collection>
```

This document is parsed into the node tree shown in Figure I-1.

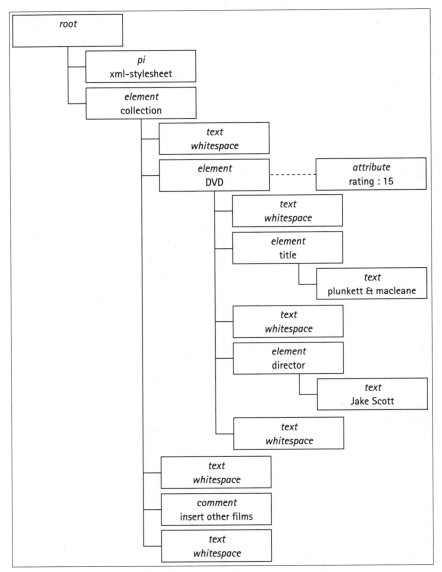

Figure I-1: An example node tree

Most of these types of nodes have a *name* (such as the name of an element or an attribute), and they all have a *string value* that is used when comparing nodes with each other. Each node also has a *base URI*, which is usually the URI of the document or entity that it comes from.

The top node of any node tree is the *root node*. The top-most element in a document is called the *document element*. In a well-formed XML document, only one document element ever exists. The nodes that appear within a node in a node tree are known as its *children*. As you might expect, then, every node except for the very top node has a *parent*. In most instances, a node's parent is an element node, with the only exception to this being nodes that are directly under the root node (the document element and any top-level processing instructions or comments).

 Attributes and namespace nodes fit into the node tree at an odd angle. Their parent is the element that they're associated with, but they are not counted as children of that element.

XPaths

There are two types of XPaths: *expressions* and *patterns*. Expressions return a value, which might be a node set that is processed or a string that is output. Patterns either match a particular node or don't match that node.

XPATH EXPRESSIONS
The three main ways in which XPath expressions are used within XSLT are to select nodes for processing, to test whether a condition is true or not, and to return a value.

NODE SET EXPRESSIONS The most common way that XSLT uses XPaths is to select node sets either for processing immediately or to assign to a variable and process later. These XPaths usually occur within a `select` attribute, for example on `xsl:for-each` or `xsl:apply-templates`, and are known as *location paths*.

The purpose of location paths is to select *node sets* from a node tree. As with directory paths, location paths can be *absolute* or *relative*. Absolute location paths start from a known location such as the root node or a particular element identified by an ID or a key. Relative location paths start from the *context node*. You can get the context node with the following expression:

The Current Node and Current Node List

In XSLT, there's also the concept of a *current node list* and a *current node*. The current node list is a list of the nodes that are currently being processed within the XSLT stylesheet, and the current node is the node that is being processed *right now*.

The current node and the context node start out being the same node at the beginning of an XPath. And while the context node changes within an XPath, the current node always remains the same. You can get the current node with the `current()` function.

```
self::node()
```

This can be abbreviated to simply:

.

A location path is made up of a number of *steps*. Each step takes you from a node to a node set. Each step is separated from the one before it with a /. When you put steps together, each of the nodes that are selected from one step are used as starting points for the node set generated by the next step.

Every step is made up of an *axis* and a *node test*. The axis specifies the direction that the step is taken in, whereas the node test specifies the kinds of nodes that should be collected in that direction. Within a step, the axis and the node test are separated by a double colon (::).

The default axis is the child axis. This takes you from the context node to the children of that node. The second important axis is the attribute axis. This takes you from the context node to the attributes of that node. This is quite a useful axis, so there is a shorthand for specifying it, namely an @. The final essential axis is the parent axis. This takes you from the context node to the parent of that node. The shortcut that you can use to get to the parent of the context node is ... The other axes are as follows:

- descendant — Takes you to the descendants of the context node.
- descendant-or-self — Takes you to the descendants of the context node and the context node itself.
- ancestor — Takes you to the ancestors of the context node.
- ancestor-or-self — Takes you to the ancestors of the context node and the context node itself.
- preceding-sibling — Takes you to the siblings (children of the same parent) of the context node that occur before it in document order.
- following-sibling — Takes you to the siblings of the context node that occur after it in document order.
- preceding — Takes you to the nodes that occur before the context node in document order, but that aren't its ancestors.
- following — Takes you to the nodes that occur after the context node in document order, but that aren't its descendants.
- namespace — Takes you to the namespaces associated with the context node.
- self — Takes you to the context node itself.

The second part of a step is the node test, which tests each node available along an axis to see whether it should be part of the node set returned by the step. Each axis has a *principal node type*. The principal node type is the type of node that you expect to find along an axis. For most axes, the principal node type is elements; if the `attribute` axis is used, then the principal node type is attributes, and if the `namespace` axis is used, it's namespace nodes. You can also select *all* nodes of the principal node type with the node test *. Using a name as a node test selects nodes of the principal node type that have that name. You can test for nodes of types other than the principal node type using different kinds of node tests:

◆ `node()` — Tests whether the node is a node (always true, so collects all nodes along the axis)

◆ `text()` — Tests whether the node is a text node

◆ `processing-instruction()` — Tests whether the node is a processing instruction

◆ `comment()` — Tests whether the node is a comment

PREDICATES   *Predicates* act as filters on node sets. They test the nodes in a node set: when the test is false, the node is filtered out of the node set. Predicates are placed in square brackets either at the end of a step or at the end of a location path. Predicate placement is important because predicates often test nodes according to their position in the *context node list*.

Positional predicates test the position of a node in the context node list against a number. For example, the following path selects the third `transaction` child element of the context node:

`transaction[3]`

Other predicates can be used to test just about any other feature of a node that you care to mention. Within a predicate, the context node is the node that you're currently testing, so all location paths are resolved relative to that node. For example, the following path selects the `transaction` element whose `type` attribute is equal to `'CR'`:

`transaction[@type = 'CR']`

You can have any number of predicates following each other. The context node list for each predicate contains the nodes that are still in the node set after it's been filtered by the previous predicates. Predicates can be used at any point in a location path, but they only apply to the immediately preceding step.

You can combine node sets by creating a union using the | operator. If there were any nodes that occurred in both node sets, the union only holds one copy of them. You can use predicates on the result of a union, just as you can on any node set.

TEST EXPRESSIONS   XPaths that are used to test whether something is true or not usually occur in a `test` attribute. XPaths that are used to test things are interpreted in the same way as predicates: they are treated as Boolean values. As such, they often involve logical operators such as and, or and the `not()` function and comparative operators such as =, !=, <, <=, > or >=.

The Context Node List

The context node list is a list of nodes that is currently being looked at; the context node is the one node in this list that is being looked at *right now*. The order of the context node list depends on the position of the predicate. If the predicate is at the end of a location path, then the context node list is always arranged in *document order*. However, if the predicate is at the end of a step, then the order of the context node list depends on the axis that was used in the step. Usually it's document order again, but when you use a reverse axis such as ancestor or preceding-sibling, it will be in *reverse document order*.

You can find out two things about the context node list: how long it is, using the last() function; and what position the context node is at within it, using the position() function.

If you use an expression in a test attribute that doesn't return a Boolean value, then the value of the expression is coerced to a Boolean. Empty node sets, empty strings, 0 and NaN all give the value false and everything else returns true.

VALUE EXPRESSIONS   XPaths are often used in XSLT to select values that are interpreted as strings. This type of XPath can occur:

◆ Within attribute value templates

◆ In the select attribute on xsl:value-of

◆ In the use attribute on xsl:key

◆ In the select attribute on xsl:sort

The value given by XPaths used in these situations is just as if you used the string() function to turn them into a string. If the value you give is a string or a number, that value is added to the output. If it's a Boolean value, either 'true' or 'false' is added to the output. If the value you select is a node set, on the other hand, as it is above, the string value of only the first node in the node set (in document order) is added to the output.

These XPaths usually involve some XPath functions, which are summarized in the reference section in Appendix A. They may also involve mathematical operators such as +, -, *, div and mod.

XPATH PATTERNS

Patterns are introduced in XSLT as a way of testing nodes to see whether they fulfill certain criteria. Patterns usually occur in match attributes, such as those on xsl:template and xsl:key. Patterns resemble location paths, but they work in a different way and have a restricted syntax.

When a processor evaluates a pattern, it already has a node in mind, and it's just trying to check whether the node it's looking at matches that particular pattern. Thus, patterns are evaluated backwards – testing the node against the last step in the pattern, and then testing its parent against the previous step, and so on. If all the tests return true then the node matches the pattern, which might mean that the template is activated or that the node is stored in the key, as appropriate.

Another way of working out whether a node matches a pattern is to see whether there is any ancestor of that node such that evaluating the pattern as a location path from that ancestor results in a node set that contains the node. If the node has an ancestor for which this would be true, then the node matches the pattern.

XSLT Basics

XSLT is part of a larger initiative within the World Wide Web Consortium (W3C) to define a way of presenting XML documents. This initiative is known as XSL (Extensible Stylesheet Language), and has the following two parts:

- XSLT – XSL Transformations, which deals with restructuring documents
- XSL-FO – XSL formatting objects, which deals with laying out information for presentation

XSLT is an XML vocabulary that's used to define a transformation between an XML document and a result document, which might be in another XML vocabulary, in HTML, or a text document. XSL-FO is just one of the XML vocabularies that can be produced by XSLT, and it doesn't have any particular prominence in this book.

Elements and attributes that are part of XSLT are placed in the XSLT namespace. Conventionally, and within this book, these elements are indicated with the prefix 'xsl', but you can use any prefix that you prefer. The namespace for XSLT elements is:

```
http://www.w3.org/1999/XSL/Transform
```

There is another namespace that sometimes masquerades as XSLT:

`http://www.w3.org/TR/WD-xsl`

This namespace can only be used with old versions of MSXML; it is very restricted and very different from XSLT. You should not use this namespace. See the MSXML FAQ at `http://www.netcrucible.com/xslt/msxml-faq.htm`.

XSLT transformations are defined in XSLT *stylesheets* – this nomenclature is used despite the fact that XSLT might not have anything to do with the styling of the XSLT. An XSLT stylesheet operates on a *source node tree*, which may be held in a file or may only ever exist in memory. When the XSLT stylesheet runs, it produces a *result node tree*. As with the source node tree, the result node tree may exist purely in memory. It may also be output in various ways, depending on the instructions given to the processor with the xsl:output element.

You can find a detailed discussion on controlling the output of a result node tree in Chapter 16.

Templates

An XSLT stylesheet is comprised of a number of *templates* that define a particular part of the process. Templates are defined with xsl:template elements, each of which holds a sequence of XSLT instructions that are carried out when the template is used.

The two ways of using templates are by *calling* them and by *applying* them. If an xsl:template element has a name attribute, it defines a *named template*, and you can use it by calling it with xsl:call-template. If an xsl:template element has a match attribute, it defines a *matching template*, and you can apply it by applying templates to a node that it matches using xsl:apply-templates.

A template is both a named template and a matching template when the xsl:template that defines it has both a name attribute and a match attribute.

BUILT-IN TEMPLATES

Several built-in templates are designed to assist you by providing default processing for different kinds of nodes. These templates have the following effects:

◆ The content of the root node is processed.

◆ Elements are ignored, but their contents are processed.

◆ Any text in the source is copied to the result.

◆ All other nodes are ignored.

When the processor starts processing the stylesheet, it begins by taking the root node of the source node tree and trying to find a template to apply to it. If you create an XSLT stylesheet without any templates in it, the processor processes the content of the root node, which includes the document element. Then, it processes the content of the document element, which may include other elements, and so on, recursively down the node tree. When it encounters a text node, it outputs that text node. The effect of this is that if you have a stylesheet that doesn't contain any templates then you will get all the text in the source XML as output.

MODES

If an `xsl:template` element has a `mode` attribute, it defines a *moded template*. Moded templates are matching templates, which will only be applied when templates are applied in the mode specified by their `mode` attribute. You apply templates in a particular mode by specifying that mode in the `mode` attribute of `xsl:apply-templates`. Templates can only be applied in one mode at a time. Applying templates without specifying a mode means that only those templates without a mode can be applied.

 You can use modes to break up a stylesheet into functional modules. This is discussed in Chapter 12.

TEMPLATE PRIORITY

When a processor is told to apply templates to a node set, it goes through the nodes one by one and tries to find a matching template that matches each node. When it finds one, it uses that template to process the node. There might be more than one template that matches the node. Templates with a higher import priority override templates that are imported.

If multiple templates remain after discounting ones that have been imported, then the processor assigns a priority to each template. The priority of a template can be set explicitly with the `priority` attribute on `xsl:template`. Otherwise, the priority is based on the pattern in the `match` attribute, from lowest to highest as follows:

◆ Patterns that match all nodes of a particular type (e.g. all elements)

◆ Patterns that match nodes in a particular namespace (e.g. all XHTML elements)

◆ Patterns that match nodes by name (e.g. all p elements)

◆ Patterns that include additional tests through predicates or through additional steps (e.g. all p elements that are descendents of a `table` element)

If more than one template matches a node, and they have the same priority, the processor uses the last template defined in the stylesheet.

The Result Tree

Templates' main role is to generate sections of the result tree. Within a template, any element that is not in the XSLT namespace causes a copy of that element to be added to the result tree, and the original element's content is processed to provide the copy's content in the result tree. These elements are known as *literal result elements*.

The attributes of literal result elements are also added to the result tree. Their values can be computed dynamically using *attribute value templates*. Within an attribute value template, anything within curly braces ({}) is evaluated as an XPath expression, and the result of the evaluation is inserted in the attribute value. Attribute value templates are also used in some attributes on XSLT instructions.

Any text within a stylesheet is added to the result tree automatically, unless it consists purely of whitespace. You can add whitespace to the result tree by placing it within xsl:text — any text within xsl:text is added to the result tree literally. You can use xsl:value-of to add calculated values to the result tree, or xsl:number to insert numbers in it.

Elements can also be generated with the xsl:element instruction, and attributes with the xsl:attribute instruction. Similarly, comments can be created with xsl:comment and processing instructions with xsl:processing-instruction. Any node can be added to the result tree by copying it. You can create a shallow copy with xsl:copy, which just copies the current node, or a deep copy with xsl:copy-of, which copies the selected nodes and all their descendants.

You can find a discussion of the various ways of creating nodes in the result tree and the advantages and disadvantages of the different methods in Chapter 6.

Controlling Flow

You can go through a set of nodes one by one, iterating over those nodes, by applying templates to them with xsl:apply-templates. You can also iterate over a set of nodes using xsl:for-each. As a result, the content of the xsl:for-each is processed with each of the nodes as the current node. With both instructions, the nodes are usually processed in document order, but you can change the order using xsl:sort.

Various ways of changing the order of nodes in the output are examined in Chapter 7.

XSLT has two conditional constructs doing different things according to some tests: xsl:if and xsl:choose. The content of the xsl:if element is only processed when the expression held in its test attribute evaluates as true. Each xsl:choose contains one or more xsl:when elements and may contain an xsl:otherwise. The content of the first xsl:when whose test attribute evaluates as true is processed. If none of the tests evaluate as true, then the content of the xsl:otherwise, when there is one, is processed.

Variables and Parameters

Variables are declared with xsl:variable. The two types of variables are *local variables*, which are defined within templates and only accessible within that template, and *global variables*, which are defined at the top level of the stylesheet and are accessible anywhere. A local variable cannot have its value reassigned, but global variables can be overridden by local variables.

Variables can be set in two ways. First, they can be set through the select attribute. Second, they can be set through content of xsl:variable. Setting a variable through its content always sets it to a result tree fragment. The select attribute can set a variable to any value type.

Parameters are defined by xsl:param and work in much the same way as variables, except that the value of a parameter may be overridden by having another value passed to it. The value defined by the select attribute or content of xsl:param is the default value of the parameter, and is used when no other value is passed to it from outside.

Parameters that are defined within templates must occur before anything else within the template. These *local parameters* can be overridden when the template is applied or called using xsl:with-param within xsl:apply-templates or xsl:call-template. Parameters are passed by name — the name attribute of xsl:with-param indicates the parameter that it defines the value of. As with variables and default parameter values, the xsl:with-param element can set a value either through the select attribute or through its content.

Parameters that are defined at the top level of the stylesheet are *global parameters*. The XSLT Recommendation doesn't say anything about how global parameters are given values — each XSLT processor sets global parameters in a different way.

Chapter 14 shows how to set parameters with client-side processing in MSXML and Chapter 15 shows how to set parameters when using Cocoon.

Keys

Keys create a hashtable that enables you to access nodes quickly. They are defined by xsl:key at the top level of the stylesheet. When a key is created, the processor works through the current document, finding all the nodes that match the pattern given in the match attribute of the xsl:key. Each of these nodes is stored in a hashtable and indexed by one or more *key values*. The key values are identified by evaluating the expression held in the use attribute of the xsl:key for the node as a string. However, if this expression returns a node set, the node is indexed by the string values of each of the nodes, rather than by just the first node in the node set.

Using keys can greatly add to the efficiency of your stylesheet, as is discussed in Chapter 17. They are also a vital component of some methods for grouping, which is talked about in Chapter 9.

Combining Stylesheets

Stylesheets can be combined together using xsl:include or xsl:import, both of which occur at the top level of the stylesheet. Including a stylesheet means that its contents are used just as if the contents were defined within the including stylesheet. Importing a stylesheet makes its contents available, enabling you to override the constructs it defines within the importing stylesheet.

You can find a detailed discussion about importing and including stylesheets in Chapter 13.

XSLT Processing Basics

An XSLT stylesheet is interpreted and run by an XSLT processor. The XSLT processor takes the XML document and turns it into a node tree and does the same with the XSLT stylesheet. The XSLT processor then works through the source node tree, following the instructions in the stylesheet, to generate the result tree.

XSLT compilers such as XSLTC from Sun Microsystems read in the XSLT stylesheet and construct compiled code to enact the instructions contained in the stylesheet. These compiled stylesheets, or translets, can be faster than normal XSLT processors because they don't have to interpret the stylesheet each time.

The three basic models for using an XSLT process or an XML document with XSLT are described here in terms of XML documents being transformed into viewable HTML, but the paradigms also apply to XML-XML transformation for business-to-business systems.

◆ **Client-side transformation:** Ship the XML and the XSLT stylesheet to the client computer and let it do the processing.

◆ **Server-side transformation:** Accept requests for XML documents, transform these documents on the server, and ship the result to the client computer.

◆ **Batch transformation:** Process the XML document with the stylesheet at the command line, and accept requests for the result of that transformation.

Client-side transformation is supported by XSLT processors embedded in browsers, such as MSXML in Internet Explorer or the Transformiix module for Netscape. Client-side transformation has the advantage that you can spread the processing overhead onto the client machines. However, it means you are dependent on the client browser dealing correctly with the XSLT. Client-side transformation usually means using the `xml-stylesheet` processing instruction at the top of the XML document, which takes the following form:

```
<?xml-stylesheet type="text/xsl" href="stylesheet.xsl" ?>
```

In Chapter 14, you can find a discussion on creating dynamic client-side XSLT applications.

Server-side transformation is supported by XSLT processors, which can act as servlets or which are embedded within publishing frameworks such as Cocoon from the Apache project or XSQL Pages from Oracle. Server-side transformation has the advantage that the served pages are automatically updated when the XML or the XSLT stylesheets change. However, it can add a processing overhead to the server.

In Chapter 15, I talk about creating dynamic server-side XSLT applications.

Batch transformation is supported by XSLT processors that can be accessed from the command line, so most XSLT processors can be used for batch transformations. Batch transformation isn't particularly easy to use because you have to remember to retransform your XML when it or the stylesheet changes, and it prevents dynamic applications. However, it may be the only option available when you cannot guarantee the capabilities of the client machines, and you do not have access to a server-side publishing framework.

Part I

Building Utility Templates

Chapter 1

Manipulating Numbers

IN THIS CHAPTER

◆ Localizing numbers

◆ Handling long numbers

◆ Spelling out numbers for voice processing

◆ Interpret alphanumeric strings as numbers

◆ Changing the base of numbers

THIS CHAPTER LOOKS AT how to manipulate numbers in various ways, in particular how to transform them from one numbering style into another. The templates that you see during this and the next few chapters are useful utilities on their own, but also demonstrate some important principles about constructing *recursive templates* — templates that call themselves. Recursive templates are the bedrock of programming in XSLT because it is a declarative or functional programming language rather than a procedural one, so it's important for you to get a grip on how to create them.

This chapter concentrates on numbers as one of the principal types of information that you will need to handle within a stylesheet. Numbers can come directly from the data held in the XML source document, from analysis of that data or from information about the position of the nodes that you're looking at in the source node tree or in the list that the stylesheet is currently processing. Wherever they come from, you will usually need to format them for the output of the stylesheet.

Formatting Numbers as Strings

Most of the processing that you do in XSLT involves creating strings because the output that you're after usually involves lots of them — that's how you get information to the consumer of the new document that you create. This section looks at how to turn numbers into strings in different formats using XSLT. XML often holds numbers — it's one of the most basic types of information that there is. Presenting those numbers to people involves formatting them so that they're easier to read, and transforming them for different markup languages might involve altering them to fit that language. You might want to format prices, populations, readings, statistics, any number of numbers, but the principles are the same.

Formatting Decimal Numbers

As you're probably already aware, getting different formats for decimal numbers is controlled by the `format-number()` function and the `xsl:decimal-format` element. The syntax of the `format-number()` function is as follows:

```
format-number(number, pattern, format?)
```

 The `format-number()` function and `xsl:decimal-format` are based on similar functionality in Java's DecimalFormat class.

The pattern used as the second argument of `format-number()` and the decimal format referred to by the third argument must match each other — the decimal format defines the meaning of the characters in the pattern string. The decimal format is designed to help you to localize the formatting of numbers for particular regions.

This section looks at using `format-number()` and `xsl:decimal-format` in detail, especially at how to deal with localizing numbers.

LOCALIZING NUMBERS

Localizing the formatting of a number involves altering both the pattern used for the format and the decimal format used to define the meaning of the characters in the string. The first step is to define a number of decimal formats for each language or region that you intend to use in your application using the `xsl:decimal-format` element. Each decimal format should be given a distinct name with extra information specified through other attributes:

- The decimal separator (`decimal-separator`) and grouping separator (`grouping-separator`)

- The strings used for infinity (`infinity`) and not a number (`NaN`)

- The characters used for the minus sign (`minus-sign`), percent sign (`percent`), per-mille sign (`per-mille`) and zero digit (`zero-digit`)

- Characters to represent digits (`digit`) and the positive and negative pattern separators (`pattern-separator`), if necessary

For example, you can generate different decimal formats for different European countries:

```
<xsl:decimal-format name="UK"
   decimal-separator="." grouping-separator=","
   infinity="Infinity" NaN="NaN" />
```

```
<xsl:decimal-format name="France"
   decimal-separator="," grouping-separator=" "
   infinity="Infinità" NaN="PdN" />
<xsl:decimal-format name="Italy"
   decimal-separator="," grouping-separator="."
   infinity="Infinite" NaN="NaN" />
```

Once these decimal formats are defined, you can generate pattern strings that correspond to these decimal formats. You may well find it helpful to hold these pattern strings in a separate XML structure (perhaps embedded in your stylesheet), each identified with the same name as you used for the decimal format. The following pattern strings, for example, give the method of formatting currencies in the three countries:

```
<format region="UK">&#163;#,##0.00</format>
<format region="France"># ##0,00 F</format>
<format region="Italy">L'.' #.##0</format>
```

With these defined within a `$formats` variable and given a region specified in the `$region` parameter, you can format a number with the function call:

```
format-number(., $formats[@region = $region], $region)
```

You can also use the `translate()` function if you need to convert from a number of Arabic numerals into a different base-10 numbering scheme or vice versa. Simply translate each Arabic numeral into the corresponding character in the numbering scheme. For example, if you had a phone number that you wanted to translate into Japanese, then with the appropriate entity definitions, you could use:

```
translate($phone,
          '&jp0;&jp1;&jp2;&jp3;&jp4;&jp5;&jp6;&jp7;&jp8;&jp9;',
          '0123456789')
```

FORMATTING PATTERNS

The patterns used in `format-number()` provide lots of control over the format of a decimal number:

◆ **Number of decimal places:** Use zero digits (0) after the decimal separator to indicate the minimum number of decimal places; use digit characters (#) to indicate the maximum. For example:

```
format-number($reading, '0.0##')
```

Keeping Stylesheet Information in XML

As you no doubt already know, XML is a great way to hold information, and you can take full advantage by getting it to hold the static information that you use in your stylesheets.

One way to do this is to embed the XML that you use inside your stylesheet. As long as you use a namespace (other than XSLT) for this XML, the XSLT processor will ignore it, and you can get at it using the document() function. For example, you could include the formats in your stylesheet with:

```
<utl:formats xmlns:utl="http://www.mycompany.com/utilities">
    <utl:format region="UK">&#163;#,##0.00</utl:format>
    <utl:format region="France"># ##0,00 F</utl:format>
    <utl:format region="Italy">L'.' #.##0</utl:format>

</utl:formats>
```

You can then access the utl:format elements and place them into a $formats variable with:

```
<xsl:variable name="formats"

            select="document('')/utl:formats/utl:format" />
```

If you have a lot of information, it's often worth separating it out into a separate XML document that you again access using the document() function. This saves you from cluttering your stylesheet and makes the namespaces a little easier to handle.

Another method for creating XML variables is to use the node-set() extension function, which is available in most processors, as you'll see in Chapter 18. You can declare the XML directly as a result tree fragment in a variable as follows:

```
<xsl:variable name="formats-rtf">
    <format region="UK">&#163;#,##0.00</format>
    <format region="France"># ##0,00 F</format>
    <format region="Italy">L'.' #.##0</format>

</xsl:variable>
```

You can then convert the result tree fragment into a node set to access it:

```
<xsl:variable name="formats"

            select="exsl:node-set($formats-rtf)/format" />
```

Using an extension function is convenient, but it means that your stylesheet is less portable. Using the EXSLT version of the node-set() function as above, for example, means that, at time of writing, the stylesheet will only work in the three XSLT processors Saxon, 4XSLT and jd.xslt.

Certain processors, such as Saxon and jd.xslt, support the XSLT 1.1 Working Draft in which there are no such things as result tree fragments. If you are using these processors, then you don't have to use the `node-set()` extension function, and can instead assign the variable as follows:

```
<xsl:variable name="formats"
              select="$formats-rtf/format" />
```

This way of creating XML variables is likely to become the norm in XSLT 2.0.

This formats the reading with a minimum of one decimal place and a maximum of three. If a number has more decimal digits that the maximum you specify, then the number is rounded (as using the `round()` function) to give that maximum.

◆ **Number of digits in a group:** Use a digit character (#), then the grouping separator (,), and then a number of digit or zero-digit characters to indicate the number of digits in a group. For example:

```
format-number($light-years, '#,##0')
```

This formats the number of light years in groups of three digits.

There's no point in specifying the size of groups prior to the last one (for example, giving a pattern such as '#,###,##0').Only the last group in the pattern string is used to determine the size of the groups in the output.

◆ **Percent and per-mille:** Use a percent sign (%) at the end of the format to multiply the number by 100 and add the percent sign; the per-mille sign (‰) does the same but multiplies by 1,000 and adds the per-mille sign. For example:

```
format-number(0.175, '0.0%')
```

This produces the formatted number `17.5%`.

You can add any extra text that you want around the formatted number, such as currency characters (as demonstrated previously), by including them within the pattern. Just be certain to quote any of the meaningful characters that you use in the decimal format and that appear in the string. For example, previously I used the pattern:

```
L'.' #.##0,0#
```

The period after the L has to be quoted to stop the XSLT processor interpreting it as a grouping separator.

INTERPRETING LOCALIZED NUMBERS

Some numerical strings can be converted back to numbers fairly easily, but usually converting numbers with format-number() is a one-way process. This is because the formatting process often gets rid of information, and, more importantly, the number() function (which turns a string into a number) can only cope with numbers that don't have any text around them and that don't use grouping separators. If the number is in a format such as the following:

```
12.345,67 F
```

The number() function will then return the value NaN. To return the number you want (12345.67), you first have to strip the string to contain just numbers, perhaps using substring-before() or substring-after(). You then need to turn the number into one that will be recognized, with no grouping separator and using a period as the decimal separator. You can do this with the translate() function, with the second argument consisting of a string holding the decimal separator followed by the grouping separator and the third argument being just a period:

```
translate('12.345,67', ',.', '.')
```

This replaces the decimal separator with a period and deletes all grouping-separator characters from the string. Thus, it gives a string that has a format that the number() function can interpret as a number.

Formatting Integers

You can use format-number() for integers as well as decimals. However, the format-number() function can only format a number with digits — it can't convert the number to other numbering schemes, such as alphabetical or Roman numbering. If you want to convert numbers to one of these schemes, then you should look at xsl:number.

Chapter 8 examines using xsl:number to generate numbers, rather than simply to format them.

Numbering Schemes

The numbering schemes that you can use depend on the XSLT processor that you're using. Check the documentation for the processor to find out which numbering schemes it supports. The formats that have guaranteed support across processors are Western numbering (1, 2, 3, 4, 5), upper and lowercase letters (A, B, C, D, E and a, b, c, d, e) and upper and lowercase Roman numbering (I, II, III, IV, V and i, ii, iii, iv, v).

Other numbering schemes may use different values for the `lang` and `letter-value` attributes of `xsl:number`. The `lang` attribute indicates the language the numbering scheme should use and the `letter-value` attribute distinguishes between alphabetical (a, b, c) and traditional (i, ii, iii) numbering schemes where necessary.

When some processors see a character that is part of (but doesn't start) an alphanumeric numbering scheme, they adopt that numbering scheme but start the numbering from that character. For example, some processors, given the instruction

```
<xsl:number value="5" format="d" />
```

will give the letter h (the fifth lowercase character after d).

Processors may also support more complex numbering schemes such as spelled-out numbers (one, two, three). However, you shouldn't rely on the availability of these numbering schemes.

The main purpose of `xsl:number` is to number nodes within a node tree. However, you can use it to format any number by giving that number as the value of the `value` attribute. For example, you could format the number 17 as a lowercase letter with the following code:

```
<xsl:number value="17" format="a" />
```

The `xsl:number` element gives you control over the grouping separator and grouping size through separate attributes (`grouping-separator` and `grouping-size`) rather than the format string method that's used in `format-number()`.

The format pattern is held in the `format` attribute and works slightly differently from the one used in `format-number()`. You use the first character in a particular alphanumeric numbering scheme to represent a number (which could be multiple digits long) in that format. Any characters that aren't recognized as being part of any alphanumeric numbering scheme (for example, punctuation characters) are included literally, but everything else is used to format the number. That means you can't include letters in the format string, although you can include characters such as periods and brackets.

All the attributes that influence the numbering scheme used by `xsl:number` are attribute value templates, so that you can determine them dynamically. If you are dealing with several numbering schemes, you may find it helpful to create XML to hold the information about the different schemes and to refer to these to complete the various attributes of xsl:number (see sidebar, "Numbering Schemes"). For example, you might use the following:

```
<format region="Western">A</format>
<format region="Russian">&#x410;</format>
<format region="Japanese">&#x30A2;</format>
```

Given that the $region parameter holds one of these regions and the $formats variable holds the format elements from the this XML, you could then get different formats for the different regions with the following:

```
<xsl:number value="17" format="{$formats[@region = $region]}" />
```

FORMATTING LONG INTEGERS

XML documents often involve long numbers that can be treated as integers, such as customer numbers, credit card numbers, or bank sort codes. If these need to be formatted with a regular grouping pattern, then you can use either format-number() or xsl:number to do it. For example, you could format a bank sort code (which consists of three groups of two digits, separated by hyphens) either by defining a decimal format that uses a hyphen as a grouping separator:

```
<xsl:decimal-format name="sort-code" grouping-separator="-" />
```

and then using that decimal format:

```
format-number($sortCode, '#-##', 'sort-code')
```

or by setting the group size and separator on xsl:number:

```
<xsl:number value="$sortCode"
   grouping-size="2" grouping-separator="-" />
```

You do have to take care, though, that the numbers that you're formatting aren't over the maximum number size in XSLT (technically "double-precision 64-bit format IEEE 754 values"). If you're using numbers that are over 16 digits long, you'll start running into problems. When formatting numbers that are this size, it's better to convert them to strings and divide them up that way. For example, you could format credit card numbers (which are 16 digits long) with the following to create groups of four digits separated by spaces:

```
concat(substring($cardNo, 1, 4), ' ', substring($cardNo, 5, 4), ' ',
       substring($cardNo, 9, 4), ' ', substring($cardNo, 13))
```

You will also need to use string-manipulation functions to format numbers that don't have a regular structure — if they involve groups of different sizes or use different separators between different groups, for example.

INTERPRETING ALPHANUMERIC STRINGS

Just as formatting a decimal number is usually a one-way operation, so is using `xsl:number` to give an alphanumeric representation of a number. However, there are ways to get back to a number from an alphanumeric representation, as this section describes.

There are two kinds of alphanumeric strings: ones that use alphabetic numbering schemes (a, b, c) and ones that use traditional numbering schemes (i, ii, iii). Each needs to be approached in a different way.

ALPHABETIC NUMBERING   Let's first look at alphabetic representations — a, b, c . . . aa, ab, ac, and so on. This is the kind of numbering that you get when you format numbers with alphabetic numbering schemes using `xsl:number` or from columns in spreadsheets. The first step is to deal with numbers that are less than the number of letters in the representation (26 in the case of the English alphabet). To get the number of a letter, you need a method of identifying the position of the letter in the alphabet. Because the alphabet consists of single characters, the easiest way to do this is to define a string variable to hold the alphabet:

```
<xsl:variable name="alphabet"
              select="'abcdefghijklmnopqrstuvwxyz'" />
```

Now, given a character, you can work out what number it represents by looking at the length of the string that appears before the character and adding 1 to it:

```
string-length(substring-before($alphabet, $char)) + 1
```

If you have an alphanumeric made up of several letters, then you need to work through it one letter at a time. For example, the alphanumeric string `xslt` equates to:

```
the position of x (24) multiplied by the length of the alphabet (26) cubed
plus
the position of s (19) multiplied by the length of the alphabet (26) squared
plus
the position of l (12) multiplied by the length of the alphabet (26)
plus
the position of t (20)
```

There's a recursive pattern here. If you take the first character of an alphanumeric string, the value it represents is the value of the character (as determined by its position in the alphabet) multiplied by the length of the alphabet to the power of the length of the remaining string. The value of that character needs to be added recursively to the value of the rest of the string.

Calculating the Power of a Number

Unfortunately, there's no way to calculate a number to the power of something in XSLT, so you need a separate template to do that. It must take two parameters: the number that is to be raised to the power and the power that it needs to be raised to:

```
<xsl:template name="power">
   <xsl:param name="number" select="0" />
   <xsl:param name="power" select="1" />
   ...

</xsl:template>
```

This is recursive template: it performs its calculation by calling itself recursively, adjusting the values of the parameters used in each call. The template has to stop calling itself when the power that the number is to be raised to is 0, in which case the template needs to produce 1. Otherwise, the result is the multiplication of the number by the result of calling the template with the number and the power minus 1 as the two parameters:

```
<xsl:template name="power">
   <xsl:param name="number" select="0" />
   <xsl:param name="power" select="1" />
   <xsl:choose>
      <xsl:when test="$power = 0">1</xsl:when>
      <xsl:otherwise>
         <xsl:variable name="multiple">
            <xsl:call-template name="power">
               <xsl:with-param name="number" select="$number"
/>
               <xsl:with-param name="power" select="$power - 1"
/>
            </xsl:call-template>
         </xsl:variable>
         <xsl:value-of select="$number * $multiple" />
      </xsl:otherwise>
   </xsl:choose>
</xsl:template>
```

To make the power template robust, you must add code to make sure that $power is not negative, test that $power is an integer, and test that both $number and $power can be interpreted as numbers. As you'll see later in this section, you may also want to increase its efficiency by making it tail recursive.

Chapter 13 goes into detail about how to make utility templates robust.

With the power template in place, you can put together the recursive conversion of the alphanumeric string. This will be a recursive template that takes a single value as a parameter, so it's a good idea to define both a match and a name for the template. Making it a matching, moded template means that it's easy to convert a particular alphanumeric node into a number—you can just use xsl:apply-templates on an alphanumeric attribute to get its decimal number. Making it a named template supports the recursion that you need to do and means that it's possible to apply it in other circumstances, for example if characters need to be stripped from the value of the node before it's converted.

The template first calculates the value of the first character in the string, and then the power to which the number of letters in the alphabet needs to be raised to get the multiplier for this value. The template then calculates the result of calling itself on the rest of the string, but only if there is a rest of the string to call itself on. (It's vital that the test on the rest of the string is included, otherwise the template would recurse endlessly on an empty string.) Once all these values have been calculated, the template puts them together to give the return value:

```xsl
<xsl:template match="node()|@*" mode="alphanumeric-to-number"
              name="alphanumeric-to-number">
  <xsl:param name="string" select="string(.)" />
  <xsl:variable name="char-value"
     select="string-length(substring-before($alphabet,
                                      substring($string, 1, 1))) + 1" />
  <xsl:variable name="power" select="string-length($string) - 1" />
  <xsl:variable name="multiple">
     <xsl:call-template name="power">
        <xsl:with-param name="number" select="string-length($alphabet)" />
        <xsl:with-param name="power" select="$power" />
     </xsl:call-template>
  </xsl:variable>
  <xsl:variable name="rest-value">
     <xsl:choose>
        <xsl:when test="$power > 0">
           <xsl:call-template name="alphanumeric-to-number">
              <xsl:with-param name="string" select="substring($string, 2)" />
           </xsl:call-template>
        </xsl:when>
        <xsl:otherwise>0</xsl:otherwise>
     </xsl:choose>
  </xsl:variable>
  <xsl:value-of select="($char-value * $multiple) + $rest-value" />

</xsl:template>
```

To make the `alphanumeric-to-number` template robust, you need to test that `$string` isn't empty and that the character you're trying to convert is actually in the alphabet. You should also add a warning when a Boolean value is passed as the string — it's fairly unlikely that users will want to know the numerical value of `'true'` or `'false'`.

You can see that this template steps through the characters in the string one by one, from the start to the end, mirroring the original description of the calculation involved:

```
the position of x (24) multiplied by the length of the alphabet (26) cubed
plus
the position of s (19) multiplied by the length of the alphabet (26) squared
plus
the position of l (12) multiplied by the length of the alphabet (26)
plus
the position of t (20)
```

But there is another way of characterizing the same calculation:

```
the position of t (20) plus
  the length of the alphabet (26) multiplied by
  the position of l (12) plus
    the length of the alphabet (26) multiplied by
    the position of s (19) plus
      the length of the alphabet (26) multiplied by
      the position of x (24)
```

This characterization leads to a different template, where you work through the string backwards, starting at the last character and adding its numerical value to the result of applying templates to the rest of the string, multiplied by 26. This template is as follows:

```
<xsl:template match="node()|@*" mode="alphanumeric-to-number"
              name="alphanumeric-to-number">
  <xsl:param name="string" select="string(.)" />
  <xsl:variable name="string-length" select="string-length($string)" />
  <xsl:variable name="char-value"
     select="string-length(
                substring-before($alphabet,
                                   substring($string, $string-length))) + 1" />
  <xsl:variable name="rest-value">
    <xsl:choose>
```

```
        <xsl:when test="$string-length > 1">
           <xsl:call-template name="alphanumeric-to-number">
              <xsl:with-param name="string"
                 select="substring($string, 1, $string-length - 1)" />
           </xsl:call-template>
        </xsl:when>
        <xsl:otherwise>0</xsl:otherwise>
     </xsl:choose>
  </xsl:variable>
  <xsl:value-of select="$char-value +
                     (string-length($alphabet) * $rest-value)" />
</xsl:template>
```

You should add the same kind of checks to this template as to the previous one to make it robust.

This template involves significantly fewer calculations and fewer template calls because you don't have to use the power template to work out what to multiply the value of a particular character by. As you can see, it's also a lot shorter. The way in which you think about a recursive calculation can have a marked effect on the templates that you generate.

There is a final template to look at that tackles this problem. This template follows the same characterization of the calculation as the last one, but works through the string from the start to the end and keeps track of the running total through a parameter that is only ever used during the recursion. On each recursion, the template passes a new total that's calculated by adding the value of the current character to the old total multiplied by 26 (the length of the alphabet). The template looks as follows:

```
<xsl:template match="node()|@*" mode="alphanumeric-to-number"
             name="alphanumeric-to-number">
  <xsl:param name="string" select="string(.)" />
  <xsl:param name="total" select="0" />
  <xsl:variable name="char-value"
     select="string-length(substring-before($alphabet,
                                       substring($string, 1, 1))) + 1" />
  <xsl:variable name="new-total"
             select="($total * string-length($alphabet)) + $char-value" />
  <xsl:choose>
     <xsl:when test="string-length($string) = 1">
        <xsl:value-of select="$new-total" />
```

```
    </xsl:when>
    <xsl:otherwise>
        <xsl:call-template name="alphanumeric-to-number">
            <xsl:with-param name="string" select="substring($string, 2)" />
            <xsl:with-param name="total" select="$new-total" />
        </xsl:call-template>
    </xsl:otherwise>
  </xsl:choose>
</xsl:template>
```

This template has one big advantage: it uses *tail recursion*. Tail recursion is recursion in which the last thing that a template does is call itself. Tail recursion is particularly important because processors can optimize processors that use it by changing the recursion into an iteration (a loop). This increases the speed of the template and it means that the processor doesn't run into problems with deep recursion — it doesn't matter how many times the template is called. If you can, you should make all your templates use tail recursion as this will increase the speed of your stylesheet.

Redefining the $alphabet variable to give a different sequence of characters enables this approach to be used with any alphanumeric numbering scheme that uses single characters for numbers. As you'll see later in this chapter, a variation on it can be used to convert to hexadecimal, for example.

TRADITIONAL NUMBERING   The second common type of alphanumeric numbering scheme uses Roman numerals. Converting numbers that use this numbering scheme involves stepping through the string one character at a time and adding (or taking away) the value of that character to (or from) the value of the rest of the string. Again, this requires a recursive template.

In this template, though, you must know two things about a particular Roman numeral — its value and its relationship with the numeral that occurs next in the string. (If the next numeral has a higher value than this one — for example the i in the string iv — then the value of this numeral needs to be taken away from the value of the rest of the string.) It's possible to calculate both a numeral's value and its relationship with the next numeral from the position of the numeral in a string (i.e. 'ivxlcdm'), but doing so is a little tedious in XSLT, mainly because there's no way in XPath to raise a number to the power of something, so you'd have to use the power template again.

For this reason, you use an XML notation to hold the information about the numerals instead, setting up a $roman-nums variable to hold the following XML using one of the techniques discussed earlier in this chapter:

```
<num value="1"   >i</num>
<num value="5"   >v</num>
<num value="10"  >x</num>
<num value="50"  >l</num>
<num value="100" >c</num>
```

```
<num value="500" >d</num>
<num value="1000">m</num>
```

Now you can get the value of the first character in the string by looking at the num element within $roman-nums that has a string value equal to the numeral:

```
$roman-nums/num[. = substring($string, 1, 1)]
```

Given this num element, you can also test whether the second numeral in the string has a higher value by testing whether there is a following sibling to the num element whose string value is equal to the second character:

```
$num/following-sibling::num = substring($string, 2, 1)
```

The rest of the template follows the same kind of pattern as the tail-recursive alphanumeric-to-number template earlier in this chapter:

```
<xsl:template match="node()|@*" mode="roman-to-number" name="roman-to-number">
   <xsl:param name="string" select="string(.)" />
   <xsl:param name="total" select="0" />
   <xsl:variable name="roman-num"
                 select="$roman-nums/num[. = substring($string, 1, 1)]" />
   <xsl:variable name="new-total">
      <xsl:choose>
         <xsl:when test="$roman-num/following-sibling::num =
                         substring($string, 2, 1)">
            <xsl:value-of select="$total - $roman-num/@value" />
         </xsl:when>
         <xsl:otherwise>
            <xsl:value-of select="$total + $roman-num/@value" />
         </xsl:otherwise>
      </xsl:choose>
   </xsl:variable>
   <xsl:choose>
      <xsl:when test="string-length($string) = 1">
         <xsl:value-of select="$new-total" />
      </xsl:when>
      <xsl:when test="string-length($string) > 1">
         <xsl:call-template name="roman-to-number">
            <xsl:with-param name="string" select="substring($string, 2)" />
            <xsl:with-param name="total" select="$new-total" />
         </xsl:call-template>
      </xsl:when>
   </xsl:choose>
</xsl:template>
```

To make the `roman-to-number` template robust, you need to test that `$string` isn't empty and that the character you're trying to convert is a Roman numeral. You should also test that the value being passed isn't a number or a Boolean — these never have string values that are valid Roman numbers.

I go into detail about creating utility templates in Chapter 13.

Turning Numbers into Ordinals

The `format-number()` function and the `xsl:number` element are great for simple formatting of numbers, but turning numbers into a word is another matter.

Generating an ordinal number (for example, 1st, 2nd, 3rd) from a number involves looking only at the last digit of the number and deciding what to do on the basis of that digit. There are two ways of getting the last digit of a number. You can convert it to a string and then take the last character in that string:

```
substring($number, string-length($number) - 1)
```

The variable `$number` in the preceding code is converted to a string implicitly within both the `substring()` and `string-length()` functions.

Alternatively, you can use the remainder after dividing the number by 10:

```
$number mod 10
```

For most numbers, adding the ordinal indicators is simply a matter of looking at this final digit and seeing if it is 1, 2, 3 or another number. However, with English numbering schemes there are special cases for 11, 12 and 13 (11th, 12th and 13th) — again you can find these using either the substring or mod technique:

```
<xsl:value-of select="$number" />
<xsl:choose>
```

```
    <xsl:when test="$number mod 100 = 11 or
                     $number mod 100 = 12 or
                     $number mod 100 = 13">th</xsl:when>
  <xsl:when test="$number mod 10 = 1">st</xsl:when>
  <xsl:when test="$number mod 10 = 2">nd</xsl:when>
  <xsl:when test="$number mod 10 = 3">rd</xsl:when>
  <xsl:otherwise>th</xsl:otherwise>
</xsl:choose>
```

It's worth making a point about using variables here. When most numbers are processed by this code, they will have six calculations performed on them: working out the number mod 100 and the number mod 10 three times each. The same calculation is being carried out on the same number three times, and each calculation takes time, so it's worth using variables to hold the result of the calculations and then using that for the comparisons:

```
<xsl:variable name="tens" select="$number mod 100" />
<xsl:variable name="ones" select="$number mod 10" />
<xsl:value-of select="$number" />
<xsl:choose>
  <xsl:when test="$tens = 11 or
                   $tens = 12 or
                   $tens = 13">th</xsl:when>
  <xsl:when test="$ones = 1">st</xsl:when>
  <xsl:when test="$ones = 2">nd</xsl:when>
  <xsl:when test="$ones = 3">rd</xsl:when>
  <xsl:otherwise>th</xsl:otherwise>
</xsl:choose>
```

Spelling Out Numbers

You can do two general kinds of recursion with numbers: recursion based on their numerical value (which I show in action in converting decimal to hexadecimal numbers) and recursion based on the position of digits within a numerical string. You've already seen a couple of examples of using the position of digits in a numerical string in converting alphanumeric numbering schemes into numbers. Another example is spelling out numbers: taking the number 123 and generating the string 'one hundred and twenty three'.

I'm only going to deal with numbers up to 999 with this template. Going beyond that is left as an exercise for the reader, though I'll provide you with a couple of pointers that might help.

In this template, you take a number and give a spelled-out string for it. Again, you define this template as both a moded and a named template to make it easier to call. The basic shape for the template involves giving the spelled-out value for the first digit in the numeric string, and then recursing over the rest of the string to give the spelled-out value for that. The stopping condition is if the remainder of the string consists only of zeros. You can find that out by deleting all the zeros in the remaining string (using the `translate()` function) and seeing whether that string has anything left in it:

```
<xsl:template match="node()|@*" mode="spell-out" name="spell-out">
   <xsl:param name="number" select="number(.)" />
   <xsl:variable name="first" select="substring($number, 1, 1)" />
   <xsl:variable name="rest" select="substring($number, 2)" />
   ...
   <xsl:if test="translate($rest, '0', '')">
      <xsl:call-template name="spell-out">
         <xsl:with-param name="number" select="$rest" />
      </xsl:call-template>
   </xsl:if>
</xsl:template>
```

The way in which a particular digit is spelled out depends on its position within the string — how many other digits are there? Ones (one digit) and hundreds (three digits) both use the same string for the number (hundreds have the string `hundred` afterwards) whereas tens (two digits) have a different string.

To make these strings easy to access, you store them as XML, here assigned to the variable `$digits`:

```
<num ones="one" tens="ten" />
<num ones="two" tens="twenty" />
<num ones="three" tens="thirty" />
<num ones="four" tens="forty" />
<num ones="five" tens="fifty" />
<num ones="six" tens="sixty" />
<num ones="seven" tens="seventy" />
<num ones="eight" tens="eighty" />
<num ones="nine" tens="ninety" />
```

TIP If you're trying to put together a function that goes beyond 999, use the remainder after dividing the number of digits by three to work out what category (ones or tens) the number is in. Use the `mod` operator.

You can get the num element that corresponds to the digit that you're considering with a location path that indexes into the num elements held in the $digits variable according to its position in the XML with a positional predicate:

```
$digits/num[number($digit)]
```

The $digit variable is a string because it was created by the substring() function, which returns strings. Therefore, you have to explicitly convert the $digit variable to a number using the number() function. If you don't convert it to a number, then it will be interpreted as a Boolean value, which will be true as long as there's a first digit (that is to say, most of the time), and you'll just get a node set of all the num elements. Alternatively, you could use an explicit comparison between the position of the num element and the $digit variable:

```
$digits/num[position() = $digit]
```

You could use xml:lang on the num elements to indicate the language of the spelled-out digits and retrieve the ones in the required language using a construct like:

```
$digits/num[lang($lang)][number($digit)]
```

However you should be aware that some other languages use different patterns when spelling out numbers, so you may also have to change the way that the template works.

Adding this to the template skeleton that you created earlier, your function now looks like the following:

```xsl
<xsl:template match="node()|@*" mode="spell-out" name="spell-out">
   <xsl:param name="number" select="number(.)" />
   <xsl:variable name="first" select="substring($number, 1, 1)" />
   <xsl:variable name="rest" select="substring($number, 2)" />
   <xsl:variable name="num" select="$digits/num[number($first)]" />
   <xsl:variable name="ndigits" select="string-length($number)" />
   <xsl:choose>
      <xsl:when test="$ndigits = 2">
         <xsl:value-of select="$num/@tens" />
      </xsl:when>
      <xsl:otherwise>
```

```
        <xsl:value-of select="$num/@ones" />
        <xsl:if test="$num and $ndigits = 3"> hundred</xsl:if>
    </xsl:otherwise>
</xsl:choose>
<xsl:if test="translate($rest, '0', '')">
    <xsl:call-template name="spell-out">
        <xsl:with-param name="number" select="$rest" />
    </xsl:call-template>
</xsl:if>
</xsl:template>
```

When this template is applied to a node, it converts the string value of the node to a number with the number() function to get the number used in the rest of the code. This ensures that nodes that don't have numeric values are always treated as NaN.

This function works fine (well, it gives one long string without any spaces, but I'll get to that later) aside from the number 0 and anything between 11 and 19. These are special cases: if the number is 0 then the template should give the string zero; if the number is between 11 and 19 then it should give the spelled-out version of that number and stop recursing since it's come to the end of the string. The latter case is the more complex. First, you need to have another variable ($teens) that gives the values of those numbers, again holding XML:

```
<num>eleven</num>
<num>twelve</num>
<num>thirteen</num>
<num>fourteen</num>
<num>fifteen</num>
<num>sixteen</num>
<num>seventeen</num>
<num>eighteen</num>
<num>nineteen</num>
```

Now, these numbers all fall into the "tens" category so you could make this part of the "tens" condition within xsl:choose. However, you have to also change the way the recursion works: if the number is between 11 and 19, then you don't want to recurse onto the next digit because that will already have been spelled out. Unlike a procedural language, you can't break the template at any point, so the only way of avoiding the recursion is to test that the number isn't between 11 and 19 (again) before recursing or to have a higher-level xsl:choose for conditions that avoid recursion. In this case, you should do the latter because there's nothing else in the "tens" part of the template that you want to reuse for the "teens".

With these tests, the template now looks like the following:

```
<xsl:template match="node()|@*" mode="spell-out" name="spell-out">
   <xsl:param name="number" select="number(.)" />
   <xsl:variable name="first" select="substring($number, 1, 1)" />
   <xsl:variable name="rest" select="substring($number, 2)" />
   <xsl:choose>
      <xsl:when test="$number = 0">zero</xsl:when>
      <xsl:when test="$number > 10 and $number &lt; 20">
         <xsl:value-of select="$teens/num[$number - 10]" />
      </xsl:when>
      <xsl:otherwise>
         <xsl:variable name="num" select="$digits/num[number($first)]" />
         <xsl:variable name="ndigits" select="string-length($number)" />
         <xsl:choose>
            <xsl:when test="$ndigits = 2">
               <xsl:value-of select="$num/@tens" />
            </xsl:when>
            <xsl:otherwise>
               <xsl:value-of select="$num/@ones" />
               <xsl:if test="$num and $ndigits = 3"> hundred</xsl:if>
            </xsl:otherwise>
         </xsl:choose>
         <xsl:if test="translate($rest, '0', '')">
            <xsl:call-template name="spell-out">
               <xsl:with-param name="number" select="$rest" />
            </xsl:call-template>
         </xsl:if>
      </xsl:otherwise>
   </xsl:choose>
</xsl:template>
```

Now, a little bit of formatting is in order. At the moment, you just get a long string, with no spaces in it, that gives the spelled out number, so the number 123 comes out as string 'onehundredtwentythree'. You only need to add spaces if you're continuing to recurse, so you can add the spaces within the xsl:if element surrounding the recursion. Also, you only need to add anything if you've output something during this recursion — if there's been a digit to work with. If you've just given the string 'hundred' then you need to append ' and '; otherwise you need to append just a space:

```
<xsl:template match="node()|@*" mode="spell-out" name="spell-out">
   <xsl:param name="number" select="number(.)" />
   <xsl:variable name="first" select="substring($number, 1, 1)" />
   <xsl:variable name="rest" select="substring($number, 2)" />
```

```
<xsl:choose>
    ...
    <xsl:otherwise>
        <xsl:variable name="num" select="$digits/num[number($first)]" />
        <xsl:variable name="ndigits" select="string-length($number)" />
        ...
        <xsl:if test="translate($rest, '0', '')">
            <xsl:if test="$num">
                <xsl:choose>
                    <xsl:when test="$ndigits = 3"> and </xsl:when>
                    <xsl:otherwise><xsl:text> </xsl:text></xsl:otherwise>
                </xsl:choose>
            </xsl:if>
            <xsl:call-template name="spell-out">
                <xsl:with-param name="number" select="$rest" />
            </xsl:call-template>
        </xsl:if>
    </xsl:otherwise>
</xsl:choose>
</xsl:template>
```

To make the `spell-out` template robust, you need to test that `$number` is actually a number and doesn't have more than three digits in it, unless you develop it to handle numbers over 999, of course.

Changing the Base of Numbers

Changing the base of a number involves recursing through it by its value (as opposed to recursing through it by its digits as you did to spell out a number). Converting between decimal and hexadecimal representations of a number can be particularly useful, especially if you're dealing with color specifications.

Most vocabularies, such as SVG or XSL-FO, allow you to specify colors in either hexadecimal notation or in functional notation where the red, green and blue colors are declared as decimal numbers or percentages, so usually you will not have to convert color notations. If you are using the various attributes in HTML that deal with colors, then ideally you should stop using those attributes and use Cascading Style Sheets (CSS) (which accepts decimal and hexadecimal notations) instead, but if you are producing web pages for use with older browsers then this may not be possible.

Converting from Hexadecimal to Decimal

Converting a hexadecimal number to a decimal number involves a very similar process as outlined previously for translating from an alphabetic notation to a decimal one. However, there are a couple of important changes to make. Firstly, the alphabet consists of the hexadecimal characters rather than the English alphabet:

```
<xsl:variable name="alphabet" select="'0123456789ABCDEF'" />
```

Secondly, hexadecimal notations work slightly differently from alphabetic numbering because they number from 0 rather than from 1. An alphabetic numbering scheme goes a, b, c, ..., x, y, z, aa, ab, ac and so on; whereas hexadecimals go 0, 1, 2, 3, ..., D, E, F, 10, 11, 12 and so on. All this means is that the alphabet must include this zero character and that you don't need to add one when working out a character's value from the alphabet string. The adjusted template is as follows:

```
<xsl:template match="node()|@*" mode="hexadecimal-to-decimal"
            name="hexadecimal-to-decimal">
  <xsl:param name="string" select="string(.)" />
  <xsl:param name="total" select="0" />
  <xsl:variable name="char-value"
     select="string-length(substring-before($alphabet,
                                    substring($string, 1, 1)))" />
  <xsl:variable name="new-total"
              select="($total * string-length($alphabet)) + $char-value" />
  <xsl:choose>
     <xsl:when test="string-length($string) = 1">
        <xsl:value-of select="$new-total" />
     </xsl:when>
     <xsl:otherwise>
        <xsl:call-template name="hexadecimal-to-decimal">
           <xsl:with-param name="string" select="substring($string, 2)" />
           <xsl:with-param name="total" select="$new-total" />
        </xsl:call-template>
     </xsl:otherwise>
  </xsl:choose>
</xsl:template>
```

Converting from Decimal to Hexadecimal

For an example of the problems faced in using colors with just HTML (without the CSS that would make coloring easier to manage), let's consider a situation in which an XML specification of an interface is converted to an HTML form. The XML specification looks like the following:

```
<form>
   <control type="panel" red="255" green="255" blue="255">
      <control type="label" red="236" green="124" blue="124">
         First Name:
      </control>
      <control type="textField" />
   </control>
</form>
```

This XML specifies that the form consists of a panel, which contains a label and a text field. You need to convert the panel into a table with the indicated background color, and the label needs to be some text in the color indicated. In HTML, this means creating a table element with a bgcolor attribute and a font element with a color attribute, both of which use a hexadecimal color notation.

There's no automatic way of converting from decimal to hexadecimal in XPath or XSLT; to do so, you need a recursive template. As usual with recursive templates, you define both a match and a name for the template. Making it a matching, moded template means that it's easy to get the value of a particular node in hexadecimal — you can just use xsl:apply-templates on the red attribute in that decimal-to-hex mode to get its value in hexadecimal. Making it a named template supports the recursion that you need to do and means that it's possible to apply it in other circumstances, for example if the hexadecimal number is actually a substring of the value of a node. The bare bones of the decimal-to-hex template is therefore as follows:

```
<xsl:template match="node()|@*" mode="decimal-to-hex"
              name="decimal-to-hex">
   <xsl:param name="decimalNumber" select="number(.)" />
   ...
</xsl:template>
```

You must first get the general structure for the template. What is the stopping condition — the minimal value that will be passed to the template, at which point the template needs to stop to prevent it from recursing forever — and how should that be processed? In this case, the minimal value is a decimal number under 16 — any number of that kind can be converted directly to a single hexadecimal digit. How is the recursive result built up? In this case, the result is a string — if the number is 16 or over, then the result of the recursion on the rest of the number converts to hexadecimal digits that appear before this one. This characterization of the problem gives the basic structure of the template:

```
<xsl:template match="node()|@*" mode="decimal-to-hex"
              name="decimal-to-hex">
```

```
    <xsl:param name="decimalNumber" select="number(.)" />
    <xsl:if test="$decimalNumber >= 16">
      <xsl:call-template name="decimal-to-hex">
        <xsl:with-param name="decimalNumber" select="..." />
      </xsl:call-template>
    </xsl:if>
    <xsl:value-of select="..." />
</xsl:template>
```

 Looking at this template, you can see that the last thing that happens in the template is a value being output. Earlier in the chapter, you saw the advantages of using a tail-recursive template, in which the last thing that happens is the template calling itself. You could make this template tail recursive if you need to make it more efficient.

Now you must determine how to split the current number into the part that should be processed during this recursion and the part that should be left for the next recursion. The number to be dealt with has to be less than 16 — in fact it's the remainder after dividing the number by 16 (the number mod 16). The rest of the number is the result of dividing the number by 16, rounded down to the nearest integer. It is this number that the recursion should be applied to, as shown in the following code:

```
<xsl:template match="node()|@*" mode="decimal-to-hex"
              name="decimal-to-hex">
    <xsl:param name="decimalNumber" select="number(.)" />
    <xsl:if test="$decimalNumber > 16">
        <xsl:call-template name="decimal-to-hex">
          <xsl:with-param name="decimalNumber"
                          select="floor($decimalNumber div 16)" />
        </xsl:call-template>
    </xsl:if>
    <xsl:value-of select="...$decimalNumber mod 16..." />
</xsl:template>
```

Now you need to convert a number under 16 into the equivalent hexadecimal digit. Because all the hexadecimal digits are one character long, you can create a string made up of the digits in order, which you can then index into. The following instruction assigns the string of hexadecimal digits to the $hexDigits variable:

```
<xsl:variable name="hexDigits" select="'0123456789ABCDEF'" />
```

The equivalent hexadecimal digit for a number under 16 is the digit at that position within the string plus 1. So the number 0 translates into the first digit in the string, the number 1 to the second digit, and so on. It's easiest to get at that character using the substring() function, as follows:

```
<xsl:template match="node()|@*" mode="decimal-to-hex"
            name="decimal-to-hex">
  <xsl:param name="decimalNumber" select="number(.)" />
  <xsl:if test="$decimalNumber >= 16">
    <xsl:call-template name="decimal-to-hex">
      <xsl:with-param name="decimalNumber"
                      select="floor($decimalNumber div 16)" />
    </xsl:call-template>
  </xsl:if>
  <xsl:value-of
      select="substring($hexDigits,
                        ($decimalNumber mod 16) + 1, 1)" />
</xsl:template>
```

To make this template robust, you need to check that the number that's passed to it is actually a number. You may also want to use the following to check that it isn't a Boolean value being interpreted as a number:

```
number($decimalNumber) and
(string($decimalNumber) = 'true' or
 string($decimalNumber) = 'false')
```

The hexadecimal numbers that color specifications in HTML use have to be two hexadecimal digits long. Of course, this template doesn't know that the numbers have to be two characters long, so you also need to do a bit of padding to make sure that there are two digits for each. You can do this with the following code:

```
<xsl:if test="string-length($redHex) = 1">0</xsl:if>
<xsl:value-of select="$redHex" />
```

You can find more information about adding padding and conditional strings in Chapter 2, and see that an alternative one-liner would be:

```
concat(substring('0', string-length($redHex)), $redHex)
```

The final template that converts the red, green, and blue attributes into a hexadecimal color string is as follows:

```
<xsl:template match="*" mode="color">
   <xsl:variable name="R">
      <xsl:apply-templates select="@red" mode="decimal-to-hex" />
   </xsl:variable>
   <xsl:variable name="G">
      <xsl:apply-templates select="@green" mode="decimal-to-hex" />
   </xsl:variable>
   <xsl:variable name="B">
      <xsl:apply-templates select="@blue" mode="decimal-to-hex" />
   </xsl:variable>
   <xsl:text>#</xsl:text>
   <xsl:if test="string-length($R) = 1">0</xsl:if>
   <xsl:value-of select="$R" />
   <xsl:if test="string-length($G) = 1">0</xsl:if>
   <xsl:value-of select="$G" />
   <xsl:if test="string-length($R) = 1">0</xsl:if>
   <xsl:value-of select="$B" />
</xsl:template>
```

Summary

In this chapter, you've learned how to use `format-number()` (in combination with `xsl:decimal-format`) and `xsl:number` to format numbers, and in particular how to format numbers according to a specific locale. I also showed you how to use these methods to format large integers, but pointed out that you need to use string functions to handle really large numbers because of the limits on numbers in XPath.

You also examined various ways of recursing over numbers and numeric strings. You've seen five utility templates:

- `power` — Takes a number and raises it to a power

- `alphanumeric-to-number` — Takes an alphanumeric string and turns it into a number (and can be used to convert a hexadecimal number into a decimal number)

- `roman-to-number` — Takes a Roman number and turns it into a decimal number

- `spell-out` — Takes a number up to 1,000 and turns it into a spelled-out string of that number

- `decimal-to-hex` — Takes a decimal number and turns it into a hexadecimal number

These templates demonstrate two major ways of recursing over numbers: digit by digit (as in the spell-out template) or by some derivative of their values (as in the power and decimal-to-hex templates). They also show some of the ways that numbers can be combined in recursive templates: by multiplication (in the power template), addition (in the alphanumeric-to-number and roman-to-number templates), and by concatenation (in the decimal-to-hex template).

You also saw that how you characterize a problem can make a big difference to the type of recursive templates that you develop. These differences can make a template more efficient, especially if they make a template tail recursive, so it's always worth trying to approach a problem from a different angle to see if there's a better way to tackle it.

Chapter 2

Reformatting Strings and Text

IN THIS CHAPTER

◆ Adding padding to strings

◆ Aligning strings

◆ Splitting strings into elements

◆ Searching and replacing within strings

CHAPTER 1 FOCUSED ON creating templates for displaying and manipulating numbers and looked at various ways of recursing over numbers. This chapter also covers low-level processing, but this time looks at manipulating strings rather than numbers.

Detailed string manipulation is particularly useful when creating text output, such as generating comma-delimited or fixed-format files for import into spreadsheets or databases. It is also handy when interpreting strings that use internal formatting conventions rather than XML, perhaps because they are exported from other applications or because the XML designer wanted to limit the size of the XML files.

XPath has quite a bit of support for basic string manipulation in a range of functions:

◆ `string()` and `format-number()` for creating strings

◆ `starts-with()`, `contains()` and `string-length()` for testing strings

◆ `substring()`, `substring-before()` and `substring-after()` for getting substrings

◆ `translate()` and `normalize-space()` for changing strings

However, once you get beyond basic string manipulation, you have to combine these functions with XSLT to achieve the functionality you want. In this chapter, I'm going to look at how to do some more complex string manipulation and how to design recursive templates that deal with strings.

Adding Padding

Padding involves adding spaces, other characters or even images to some text to align it on a page. If you're using XSLT to output a display format such as HTML or XSL-FO, you probably won't care much about padding: all the alignment and whitespace normalization is done for you by the viewer application. However, if you're using XSLT to produce text files or if you're using it to get complex formats such as tree representations, then you need to start using it to create indents.

Padding Numerical Strings

You can use the `format-number()` function to pad numerical strings, as long as you don't mind the string being padded with the zero digit. When you use the zero digit in a pattern string, it specifies the minimum length of the number, either before or after the decimal point and the processor pads the number with zeros to create a string of that length when the number isn't long enough. So, for example, you can pad a number to five characters with:

```
format-number($number, '00000')
```

You could use another character for the zero digit by setting the `zero-digit` attribute on the `xsl:decimal-format` you use. For example, you could pad a number to five characters with hyphens by defining a decimal format that used a hyphen as the zero character:

```
<xsl:decimal-format name="hyphens" zero-digit="-" />
```

and then referencing that decimal format in the call to `format-number()` as in the following:

```
format-number($number, '-----', 'hyphens')
```

Alternatively, you can replace all the occurrences of the zero digit with another character after formatting with the `translate()` function as follows:

```
translate(format-number($number, '00000'), '0', '-')
```

However, both these approaches run into problems if the number contains a zero. Instead, simply convert the number to a string and pad it with one of the following techniques.

Padding Strings with Characters

Padding strings with characters involves concatenating the string with a padding string consisting of the requisite number of characters. The number of characters needed to pad a string is the total number of characters you want, minus the number of characters in the string that you're padding. To right align a string, padding with periods, to make something ten characters long, for example, you could use the following:

```
concat(substring('..........', 1, 10 - string-length($string)),
       $string)
```

This is almost exactly the same as the following:

```
concat(substring('..........', string-length($string) + 1),
       $string)
```

The difference is that the preceding code takes the padding characters from the end of the string rather than the start, which makes a difference when you use a string that doesn't just consist of the same character repeated over and over again, for example:

```
concat(substring('1234567890',
                 string-length('foo') + 1), 'foo')
```

then you get the string '4567890foo' rather than '1234567foo'.

Left aligning a string is even easier: you can concatenate the string and its padding, and then take the number of characters that you want from it:

```
substring(concat($string, '..........'), 1, 10)
```

One feature of this is that if the string is longer than the number of characters that you want, it is truncated — whether that's something you want to happen depends on your application.

Centering a string involves placing half the padding to its left and half the padding to its right. The length of one of the halves should be rounded down using floor() and the other rounded up using ceiling():

```
concat(substring('..........',
                 ceiling((string-length($string) + 10) div 2) + 1),
       $string,
       substring('..........',
                 floor((string-length($string) + 10) div 2) + 1))
```

Putting these three possibilities together, you can create a template that aligns a string given that string and a padding string. Because it's likely that this template is to be used on nodes, you can make it a matching template as well as a named one, so that it's possible to apply it or call it. If it's applied to a node, use the normalized string value of that node as the string — you don't want to have spurious spaces surrounding the string:

```
<xsl:template match="node()|@*" mode="align" name="align">
   <xsl:param name="padding" />
   <xsl:param name="align" select="'left'" />
   <xsl:param name="string" select="normalize-space(.)" />
   <xsl:variable name="lstring" select="string-length($string)" />
   <xsl:variable name="lpadding" select="string-length($padding)" />
   <xsl:choose>
      <xsl:when test="$lstring >= $lpadding">
         <xsl:value-of select="substring($string, 1, $lpadding)" />
      </xsl:when>
      <xsl:when test="$align = 'right'">
         <xsl:value-of select="concat(
                                 substring($padding, 1, $lpadding - $lstring),
                                 $string)" />
      </xsl:when>
      <xsl:when test="$align = 'center'">
         <xsl:variable name="half-lstring" select="$lstring div 2" />
         <xsl:variable name="half-lpadding" select="$lpadding div 2" />
         <xsl:value-of
            select="concat(
                      substring($padding, 1,
                               floor($half-lpadding - $half-lstring)),
                      $string,
                      substring($padding,
                               floor($half-lstring + $half-lpadding) + 1))" />
      </xsl:when>
      <xsl:otherwise>
         <xsl:value-of select="substring(concat($string, $padding),
                                         1, $lpadding)" />
      </xsl:otherwise>
   </xsl:choose>
</xsl:template>
```

This template defaults to left alignment if no value is specified for the $align parameter or if the value of $align isn't 'right' or 'center'. To make this template more robust, you should check whether the $align is actually 'left' within the xsl:otherwise, giving a message when it isn't, and that the padding string has some characters in it.

One of the troubles with the template as previously defined is that it requires whoever uses it to pass in a padding string. It would be nice if there were also a way of passing in a padding character (or a string of padding characters) and the total length of the required string. You could just change the `align` template so that it worked in that way, but to give maximum flexibility, it might be worth adding a separate template that calls the `align` template, but constructs the padding string for the user:

```
<xsl:template match="node()|@*" mode="align-with" name="align-with">
   <xsl:param name="align" select="'left'" />
   <xsl:param name="string" select="normalize-space()" />
   <xsl:param name="pad-chars" select="' '"/>
   <xsl:param name="pad-length" select="string-length($string)" />
   <xsl:variable name="padding">
      ...
   </xsl:variable>
   <xsl:call-template name="align">
      <xsl:with-param name="string" select="$string" />
      <xsl:with-param name="align" select="$align" />
      <xsl:with-param name="padding" select="$padding" />
   </xsl:call-template>
</xsl:template>
```

Now it's a matter of constructing the padding string. The padding string needs to be the length specified by $pad-length and consist of the characters specified by $pad-chars. In a procedural programming language, you could use a for or while loop to repeatedly add strings to a variable until it was the right length. With XSLT, though, you need to use recursion to produce the same effect.

You need a template that, given a string of characters and a padding length, gives you a padding string of that length, made up of the characters. On each recursion, if the string of padding characters is shorter than the padding you need, you need to return that padding string followed by the result of calling the same template with a padding length that's shorter by the length of the padding string. If the string of padding characters is longer than or the same length as the padding you need, you can just return the (truncated if need be) padding string. Here is a basic version of such a template.

```
<xsl:template name="padding">
   <xsl:param name="pad-chars" select="' '" />
   <xsl:param name="pad-length" select="1" />
   <xsl:variable name="lpad-chars" select="string-length($pad-chars)" />
   <xsl:choose>
      <xsl:when test="$lpad-chars >= $pad-length">
         <xsl:value-of select="substring($pad-chars, 1, $pad-length)" />
      </xsl:when>
```

```
      <xsl:otherwise>
         <xsl:value-of select="$pad-chars" />
         <xsl:call-template name="padding">
            <xsl:with-param name="pad-chars" select="$pad-chars" />
            <xsl:with-param name="pad-length"
                            select="$pad-length - $lpad-chars" />
         </xsl:call-template>
      </xsl:otherwise>
   </xsl:choose>
</xsl:template>
```

 To make the `align-with` template robust, you need to ensure that `$pad-chars` is not an empty string and that `$pad-length` is a number and not Infinity — in either case, you can get infinite recursion. You should also test whether `$pad-length` is a negative number, or whether `$pad-chars` is a Boolean. If so, issue warnings as it's unlikely that a user wants to pass those kinds of values to the template.

Now that you have a template that can generate a padding string, you just need to slot in a call to the template within the `align-with` template:

```
<xsl:template match="node()|@*" mode="align-with" name="align-with">
   <xsl:param name="align" select="'left'" />
   <xsl:param name="string" select="normalize-space()" />
   <xsl:param name="pad-chars" select="' '"/>
   <xsl:param name="pad-length" select="string-length($string)" />
   <xsl:variable name="padding">
      <xsl:call-template name="padding">
         <xsl:with-param name="pad-chars" select="$pad-chars" />
         <xsl:with-param name="pad-length" select="$pad-length" />
      </xsl:call-template>
   </xsl:variable>
   <xsl:call-template name="align">
      <xsl:with-param name="string" select="$string" />
      <xsl:with-param name="align" select="$align" />
      <xsl:with-param name="padding" select="$padding" />
   </xsl:call-template>
</xsl:template>
```

Minimizing the Depth and Number of Recursions

One of the big problems with recursive templates is that a deep recursive stack can cause some XSLT processors (especially those that don't optimize tail recursion) to crash. Also, all the instructions that you place in a recursive template will be processed on each recursion, which can mean that the template takes a long time to run and can use a lot of memory.

In the padding template, it's likely that the recursion is going to be quite deep — the majority of cases involve passing a string consisting of a single character (for example, ' . ') and could involve a fairly large $pad-length (for example, 20).

One of the ways of minimizing the depth of recursion is to divide the processing into two each time. The padding template, rather than calling itself just once, could call itself twice, each time dealing with half the padding length (one rounded down, the other rounded up). This would involve the following changes to the code:

```
<xsl:template name="padding">
   <xsl:param name="pad-chars" select="' '" />
   <xsl:param name="pad-length" select="1" />
   <xsl:variable name="lpad-chars" select="string-length($pad-chars)" />
   <xsl:choose>
      <xsl:when test="$lpad-chars >= $pad-length">
         <xsl:value-of select="substring($pad-chars, 1, $pad-length)" />
      </xsl:when>
      <xsl:otherwise>
         <xsl:variable name="lremaining" select="$pad-length - $lpad-chars" />
         <xsl:value-of select="$pad-chars" />
         <xsl:if test="$lremaining > 1">
            <xsl:call-template name="padding">
               <xsl:with-param name="pad-chars" select="$pad-chars" />
               <xsl:with-param name="pad-length"
                            select="floor($lremaining div 2)" />
            </xsl:call-template>
         </xsl:if>
         <xsl:call-template name="padding">
            <xsl:with-param name="pad-chars" select="$pad-chars" />
            <xsl:with-param name="pad-length"
                         select="ceiling($lremaining div 2)" />
         </xsl:call-template>
      </xsl:otherwise>
   </xsl:choose>
</xsl:template>
```

Continued

Minimizing the Depth and Number of Recursions *(Continued)*

With this template, the depth of the recursion for getting a padding string 20 characters long made up of a single character repeating itself is 4 rather than 19. However, it has no effect on the number of recursions that are carried out in total, and in some ways makes it worse because the template involves extra tests and calculations. It also has the disadvantage that it stops the template from being tail recursive because the template calls itself in two places rather than just once at the end of the template. So while this change can help processors that don't detect tail recursion, it makes those that optimize it less efficient.

Another way of reducing the depth of the recursion that will work in this padding template is to lengthen the padding string using the concat() function, which is more efficient than recursion, and pass this lengthened string through to the next recursion. This reduces the depth of the recursion and reduces the number of times the template is called. Adding this technique, the template now looks like:

```
<xsl:template name="padding">
   <xsl:param name="pad-chars" select="' '" />
   <xsl:param name="pad-length" select="1" />
   <xsl:variable name="pad-string"
      select="concat($pad-chars, $pad-chars, $pad-chars, $pad-chars,
                     $pad-chars, $pad-chars, $pad-chars, $pad-chars,
                     $pad-chars, $pad-chars, $pad-chars, $pad-chars)" />
   <xsl:variable name="lpad-string" select="string-length($pad-string)" />
   <xsl:choose>
      <xsl:when test="$lpad-string >= $pad-length">
         <xsl:value-of select="substring($pad-string, 1, $pad-length)" />
      </xsl:when>
      <xsl:otherwise>
         <xsl:value-of select="$pad-string" />
         <xsl:call-template name="padding">
            <xsl:with-param name="pad-chars" select="$pad-string" />
            <xsl:with-param name="pad-length"
                            select="$pad-length - $lpad-string" />
         </xsl:call-template>
      </xsl:otherwise>
   </xsl:choose>
</xsl:template>
```

This template simply calls other templates to do its dirty work, so there's no need to test the values that are passed into it — the testing can all take place in the templates that actually use them.

Padding Strings with Elements

You've learned about how to pad strings with characters, but often, especially when converting to HTML, you want to pad strings with elements, such as the following spacer image:

```
<img src="spacer.gif" alt="  " />
```

Here, the padding works slightly differently — the element is similar to a single character that needs to be repeated a number of times. You can adjust the padding template so that it deals with nodes rather than strings:

```
<xsl:template name="node-padding">
   <xsl:param name="pad-nodes" select="' '" />
   <xsl:param name="repeat" select="1" />
   <xsl:copy-of select="$pad-nodes" />
   <xsl:if test="$repeat > 1">
      <xsl:call-template name="node-padding">
         <xsl:with-param name="pad-nodes" select="$pad-nodes" />
         <xsl:with-param name="repeat"
                         select="$pad-length - 1" />
      </xsl:call-template>
   </xsl:if>
</xsl:template>
```

Your aim here is for the value passed in the $pad-nodes parameter to be repeated exactly the number of times indicated by $repeat. For example, with $repeat equal to 20, the string '1234567890' would be repeated 20 times rather than twice (to create a string 20 characters long) as it would be with the padding template.

Repetition with the Piez Method

The Piez method, named after Wendell Piez, is another way of repeating a string or a node set multiple times rather than using recursion. The Piez method uses an `xsl:for-each` instruction to iterate, but fixes the length of the node set that's iterated over to the number of times that the content should be repeated.

The first step is to set up a node set that is guaranteed to be larger than the maximum number of repetitions that you need. One good way of doing that is to use the nodes from the stylesheet's own node tree. Gathering all the nodes in the stylesheet tree is almost always sufficient:

```
document('')//node() | document('')//*/@* | document('')//*/namespace::*
```

Of course, it's better to collect fewer nodes (if you can get away with it) just to prevent the processor from having to collate that huge node set. For example, you can often drop the namespace and attribute nodes, and might be able to just use the element nodes, depending on the complexity of your stylesheet. You can store these nodes in a variable such as:

```
<xsl:variable name="random-node-set"
              select="document('')/*" />
```

Now, to iterate a certain number of times, you just need to pick that number of nodes from the node set. You can do this by testing whether the `position()` of the node is less than or equal to the number of nodes you want. So, an alternative to the recursive solution to create the padding would be:

```
<xsl:for-each select="$random-node-set[position() &lt;= $pad-length]">
  <xsl:copy-of select="$pad-nodes" />

</xsl:for-each>
```

Of course, this technique can be used to repeat anything a certain number of times. It's not necessarily to create padding only. It's major drawback is that there is a limit to the number of repetitions it can create, which is determined by the number of nodes you can collect to iterate over.

Splitting Strings into Elements

It's often a lot easier to process information with XSLT (and other XML-based applications) if it's stored as a set of elements rather than as a single string. While most transformations for presentation involve creating strings rather than splitting them up, the first conversion effort of an XML initiative often involves processing existing information to give it a different structure, and transformations between similar XML vocabularies can also involve generating structure where there was none before.

Dividing a Poem into Lines

One common case involves breaking up some structured text according to a character. In these cases, you need to recurse over the string, breaking it at the character and putting that text within an element. As an example, take the following poem:

```
<poem>
Three wise men of Gotham
Went to sea in a bowl;
If the bowl had been stronger,
My song would have been longer.
</poem>
```

You want to split this into lines:

```
<poem>
<line>Three wise men of Gotham</line>
   <line>Went to sea in a bowl;</line>
   <line>If the bowl had been stronger,</line>
   <line>My song would have been longer.</line>
</poem>
```

To do this, you need a recursive template that splits a string into lines. You make this a matching template (so that you can just apply templates to the poem element) and a named template (so that you can do the recursion). The recursion splits the string into the string before the first line break and the string after the line break, on which the template is called recursively. You only want to create a line element for the string before the first line break if there's something other than whitespace in it. This gives you the template:

```
<xsl:template match="node()|@*" mode="split" name="split">
   <xsl:param name="string" select="string()" />
   <xsl:variable name="break" select="'&#xA;'" />
   <xsl:variable name="multiline" select="contains($string, $break)" />
   <xsl:variable name="line">
      <xsl:choose>
         <xsl:when test="$multiline">
            <xsl:value-of
               select="normalize-space(substring-before($string, $break))" />
         </xsl:when>
         <xsl:otherwise>
            <xsl:value-of select="normalize-space($string)" />
         </xsl:otherwise>
      </xsl:choose>
   </xsl:variable>
```

```
<xsl:if test="string($line)">
  <line><xsl:value-of select="$line" /></line>
</xsl:if>
<xsl:if test="$multiline">
  <xsl:call-template name="split">
    <xsl:with-param name="string"
                    select="substring-after($string, $break)" />
  </xsl:call-template>
</xsl:if>
</xsl:template>
```

Tokenizing a String

Dividing a poem into lines is a specific example of a more general problem known as tokenization: splitting a string up at a particular character or combination of characters. To make the split template into a more general tokenize template, turn the $break variable into a parameter so that it can be set by the calling template, and change the elements that are produced so that they are tokens rather than lines:

```
<xsl:template match="node()|@*" mode="tokenize" name="tokenize">
  <xsl:param name="string" select="string()" />
  <xsl:param name="break" select="'&#xA;'" />
  <xsl:variable name="multitoken" select="contains($string, $break)" />
  <xsl:variable name="token">
    <xsl:choose>
      <xsl:when test="$multitoken">
        <xsl:value-of
          select="normalize-space(substring-before($string, $break))" />
      </xsl:when>
      <xsl:otherwise>
        <xsl:value-of select="normalize-space($string)" />
      </xsl:otherwise>
    </xsl:choose>
  </xsl:variable>
  <xsl:if test="string($token)">
    <token><xsl:value-of select="$token" /></token>
  </xsl:if>
  <xsl:if test="$multitoken">
    <xsl:call-template name="tokenize">
      <xsl:with-param name="string"
```

```
                  select="substring-after($string, $break)" />
        <xsl:with-param name="break" select="$break" />
      </xsl:call-template>
   </xsl:if>
</xsl:template>
```

Splitting a String at Elements

Another way the poem could have been formatted is:

```
<poem>
Three wise men of Gotham<br />
Went to sea in a bowl;<br />
If the bowl had been stronger,<br />
My song would have been longer.<br />

</poem>
```

Here, the lines of the poem are divided up by br elements. In fact, to the XSLT processor, the preceding poem element looks like:

```
+-(element) poem
   +- (text) &#xA;Three wise men of Gotham
   +- (element) br
   +- (text) &#xA;Went to sea in a bowl;
   +- (element) br
   +- (text) &#xA;If the bowl had been stronger,
   +- (element) br
   +- (text) &#xA;My song would have been longer.
   +- (element) br

   +- (text) &#xA;
```

The lines of the poem are thus (the normalized value of) all the text nodes within the poem element except the last, which contains just whitespace. The template for the poem element can simply iterate over these nodes to get the following lines:

```
<xsl:template match="poem">
   <poem>
      <xsl:for-each select="text()[position() != last()]">
         <line><xsl:value-of select="normalize-space()" /></line>
      </xsl:for-each>
   </poem>

</xsl:template>
```

TIP Some strings use multiple token delimiters. For example, date-times in the format:

```
2001-03-09T15:05:00
```

In these cases, you can substitute all the token delimiters for spaces using the `translate()` function and use the `tokenize` template given previously to split up the string at spaces:

```
<xsl:call-template name="tokenise">
   <xsl:with-param name="string"
          select="translate($date, '-T:', '   ')" />
   <xsl:with-param name="break" select="' '" />
</xsl:call-template>
```

Wrapping Lines

Another kind of tokenization simply involves splitting up a string to produce tokens a certain number of characters long. For example, you might want to split up a paragraph into lines up to 80 characters long.

The first step is to tokenize the string into lines 80 characters long, regardless of when the splits in the lines occur. For this, as usual, you need a matching and a named template that, as with the `tokenize` template, uses recursion to iterate over a string. However, this time the recursion needs to use the `substring()` function to split the string into the number of characters that are required:

```
<xsl:template match="node()|@*" mode="wrap" name="wrap">
   <xsl:param name="string" select="normalize-space()" />
   <xsl:param name="line-length" select="80" />
   <xsl:variable name="line" select="substring($string, 1, $line-length)" />
   <xsl:variable name="rest" select="substring($string, $line-length + 1)" />
   <xsl:if test="$line">
      <xsl:value-of select="$line" />
      <xsl:text>&#xA;</xsl:text>
   </xsl:if>
   <xsl:if test="$rest">
      <xsl:call-template name="wrap">
         <xsl:with-param name="string" select="$rest" />
         <xsl:with-param name="line-length" select="$line-length" />
      </xsl:call-template>
   </xsl:if>
</xsl:template>
```

Now you need to address lines breaking in the middle of words. The easiest way to do this is to check whether the last character of the line is a space. If it is, that's fine, but if it isn't, you only want the line up to the last space. This is more difficult than it appears because the `substring-after()` and `substring-before()` functions operate on the *first* occurrence of a character in a string rather than the last occurrence of that character. You need to create a template to get the substring before the last occurrence of a space in a string.

The `substring-before-last` template needs to get the substring before the last occurrence of a character (or string) in a string. This involves recursing through the string until the remaining string doesn't hold the character any more.

```
<xsl:template name="substring-before-last">
   <xsl:param name="string" />
   <xsl:param name="char" select="' '" />
   <xsl:if test="contains($string, $char)">
      <xsl:value-of select="substring-before($string, $char)" />
      <xsl:variable name="rest" select="substring-after($string, $char)" />
      <xsl:if test="contains($rest, $char)">
         <xsl:value-of select="$char" />
         <xsl:call-template name="substring-before-last">
            <xsl:with-param name="string" select="$rest" />
            <xsl:with-param name="char" select="$char" />
         </xsl:call-template>
      </xsl:if>
   </xsl:if>
</xsl:template>
```

With the `substring-before-last` template in place, it's now a matter of amending your definition of the "line" and of the "rest of the string". If the string is longer than your desired line length, you need to get the string up to the last space in the first 80 characters of the line. (If the string is already less than the length of the line, you can just give the string itself.) The "rest of the string", used in the next recursion, is then a substring of the original string, starting from the character after the end of the line you've just identified, plus one character (for the space):

```
<xsl:template match="node()|@*" mode="wrap" name="wrap">
   <xsl:param name="string" select="normalize-space()" />
   <xsl:param name="line-length" select="80" />
   <xsl:variable name="line">
      <xsl:choose>
         <xsl:when test="string-length($string) > $line-length">
            <xsl:call-template name="substring-before-last">
               <xsl:with-param name="string"
                               select="substring($string, 1, $line-length)" />
               <xsl:with-param name="char" select="' '" />
            </xsl:call-template>
         </xsl:when>
         <xsl:otherwise><xsl:value-of select="$string" /></xsl:otherwise>
```

```
      </xsl:choose>
   </xsl:variable>
   <xsl:variable name="rest"
                 select="substring($string, string-length($line) + 2)" />

   ...
</xsl:template>
```

 Here, I've shown how to wrap a line with a new line character. Of course, you could use an element instead to insert delimiters, or you could wrap each line in its own element, as you require.

Gradual Tokenization

If you graduate to tokenizing strings that are more complex than these, you should consider using another language, in particular one that has support for regular expressions. While it's possible to write complex tokenizers in XSLT, it's seldom worthwhile doing so, unless you enjoy the intellectual exercise.

In general, it's a lot easier to manipulate elements than strings in XSLT, so your first step should be to replace all the meaningful characters in the string into elements that can represent them. For example, rather than:

```
<expression>substring($string, string-length($line) + 2)</expression>
```

it would be easier to manipulate the following mixed content:

```
<expression>
   substring<open-br /><dollar />string<comma />
   string-length<open-br /><dollar />line<close-br /> <plus /> 2<close-br />
</expression>
```

You can then use grouping techniques on a structure, like the one above, to build up a nested structure for the string, to eventually make it:

```
<function name="substring">
   <arg><variable name="string" /></arg>
   <arg>
      <plus>
         <function name="string-length">
            <arg><variable name="line" /></arg>
         </function>
         <number>2</number>
      </plus>
   </arg>
</function>
```

Replacing characters or strings is discussed in the next section.

 Grouping techniques are discussed in Chapter 9.

Searching and Replacing

Searching and replacing characters and strings has many applications in XSLT. One particular place in which searching and replacing is useful is in escaping significant characters in code. For example, JavaScript strings can't include new line characters — if you're producing a JavaScript string with XSLT then the new line characters in the source text need to be replaced with the string '\n'. It's also sometimes useful to pick out particular words in some text so that you can create links from them or highlight them.

Searching and Replacing Characters

XPath gives lots of support for searching and replacing characters, most importantly through the translate() function. You can use the translate() function to replace characters with other characters, for example to change a string from lowercase to uppercase:

```
translate($string,
          'abcdefghijklmnopqrstuvwxyz',
          'ABCDEFGHIJKLMNOPQRSTUVWXYZ')
```

The translate() function can also delete all the occurrences of particular characters from a string, for example to remove all the digits from a string:

```
translate($string, '0123456789', '')
```

You can also use the translate() function to count the number of occurrences of a character in a string by deleting all the characters in the string that you are *not* interested in, and then by checking the length of the remaining string:

```
string-length(translate($string, other-characters, ''))
```

Getting a string that contains all the "other" characters in the string involves deleting the character that you *are* interested in from the string:

```
string-length(translate($string, translate($string, character, ''), ''))
```

Searching and Replacing Strings

XPath doesn't have as much support for searching and replacing strings as it has for characters. And there is no support for sophisticated searching and replacing using regular expressions.

You can use the `contains()` (or `starts-with()`) function to check whether one string contains another. To do case-insensitive searching, convert all the lowercase characters in the two strings into uppercase, and then compare the strings:

```
contains(translate($string1, $lowercase, $uppercase),
         translate($string2, $lowercase, $uppercase))
```

The danger of using the `translate()` function to give case insensitivity is that both the `$lowercase` and `$uppercase` strings must contain all the characters in the string that you're converting. If you want to check whether all the characters in the string are covered, you can check whether anything remains after deleting all the lowercase and uppercase characters from the string:

```
translate($string, concat($lowercase, $uppercase), '')
```

SEARCHING FOR WHOLE WORDS

If you want to search for whole words, you need a template that checks the characters just before and just after the word you're looking for: a `contains-word` template. The `contains-word` template works through the string recursively looking for the word. It's a Boolean template, which means that it either returns something or nothing at all. You'll use this template to pull out the word from the string, so it's useful to have the template return the two characters on either side of the word (if there are any) as well as the word itself.

```
<xsl:template match="node()|@*" mode="contains-word" name="contains-word">
   <xsl:param name="string" select="string()" />
   <xsl:param name="word" />
   <xsl:if test="contains($string, $word)">
      <xsl:variable name="before" select="substring-before($string, $word)" />
      <xsl:variable name="after" select="substring-after($string, $word)" />
      <xsl:variable name="char-before"
                    select="substring($before, string-length($before))" />
      <xsl:variable name="char-after" select="substring($after, 1)" />
      <xsl:choose>
         <xsl:when test="...">
            <xsl:value-of select="$char-before" />
            <xsl:value-of select="$word" />
```

```
            <xsl:value-of select="$char-after" />
         </xsl:when>
         <xsl:otherwise>
            <xsl:call-template name="contains-word">
               <xsl:with-param name="string" select="$after" />
               <xsl:with-param name="word" select="$word" />
            </xsl:call-template>
         </xsl:otherwise>
      </xsl:choose>
   </xsl:if>
</xsl:template>
```

The testing of the characters immediately before and after the word needs to check whether they are word delimiters — whitespace, punctuation, or nothing at all. Whitespace and nothing at all can be checked using the `normalize-space()` function — if nothing is left after normalizing the spaces in the characters, they're either whitespace or there weren't any characters in the first place. Testing punctuation involves specifying punctuation characters in a string variable and then seeing if the character is part of that set of punctuation characters:

```
<xsl:template match="node()|@*" mode="contains-word" name="contains-word">
   <xsl:param name="string" select="string()" />
   <xsl:param name="word" />
   <xsl:if test="contains($string, $word)">
      <xsl:variable name="before" select="substring-before($string, $word)" />
      <xsl:variable name="after" select="substring-after($string, $word)" />
      <xsl:variable name="char-before"
                    select="substring($before, string-length($before))" />
      <xsl:variable name="char-after" select="substring($after, 1, 1)" />
      <xsl:variable name="punctuation"
                    select="concat('..,;:?!@#=+-_*&amp;^%$|\/&lt;>{}()[]&quot;',
                                   &quot;&apos;&quot;)" />
      <xsl:choose>
         <xsl:when test="(not(normalize-space($char-before)) or
                          contains($punctuation, $char-before)) and
                          (not(normalize-space($char-after)) or
                          contains($punctuation, $char-after))">
            <xsl:value-of select="$char-before" />
            <xsl:value-of select="$word" />
            <xsl:value-of select="$char-after" />
         </xsl:when>
         ...
      </xsl:choose>
   </xsl:if>
</xsl:template>
```

> **TIP** You could make this template optionally case insensitive by adding a para-
> meter and translating both the string and the word during the match if it is
> passed a true value. But to get the most use out of this template, make sure
> that the string that you return is the word as it appears in the string — to
> accomplish this, use the following:
>
> ```
> substring($string, string-length($before) + 1,
>                 string-length($word))
> ```

REPLACING STRINGS

You can't use the `translate()` function to replace occurrences of a character with a string or element, or occurrences of a string with anything at all. Instead, you need a recursive template that works over the string, doing the replacement:

```xsl
<xsl:template match="replace" mode="replace-nodes">
   <xsl:param name="string" />
   <xsl:variable name="next" select="following-
sibling::replace[contains($string, from)][1]" />
   <xsl:choose>
     <xsl:when test="contains($string, from)">
        <xsl:choose>
          <xsl:when test="$next">
            <xsl:apply-templates select="$next" mode="replace-nodes">
              <xsl:with-param name="string"
                           select="substring-before($string, from)" />
            </xsl:apply-templates>
          </xsl:when>
          <xsl:otherwise>
            <xsl:value-of select="substring-before($string, from)" />
          </xsl:otherwise>
        </xsl:choose>
        <xsl:copy-of select="to/node()" />
        <xsl:apply-templates select="." mode="replace-nodes">
          <xsl:with-param name="string"
                       select="substring-after($string, from)" />
        </xsl:apply-templates>
     </xsl:when>
     <xsl:when test="$next">
        <xsl:apply-templates select="$next" mode="replace-nodes">
          <xsl:with-param name="string" select="$string" />
        </xsl:apply-templates>
     </xsl:when>
     <xsl:otherwise>
```

```
            <xsl:value-of select="$string" />
        </xsl:otherwise>
    </xsl:choose>
</xsl:template>
```

 The replacement value is copied rather than its value being taken, so that strings or characters can be replaced by elements.

You could expand the replace template to enable it to find and replace whole words by calling the contains-word template to find the word as it is actually found within the string. Make sure that the word-delimiting characters that are included in the found word are given in the output. Here's the complete template:

```
<xsl:template match="node()|@*" mode="replace" name="replace">
    <xsl:param name="string" select="string()" />
    <xsl:param name="find" />
    <xsl:param name="replace" />
    <xsl:variable name="found-word">
        <xsl:call-template name="contains-word">
            <xsl:with-param name="string" select="$string" />
            <xsl:with-param name="word" select="$find" />
        </xsl:call-template>
    </xsl:variable>
    <xsl:choose>
        <xsl:when test="string($found-word)">
            <xsl:value-of select="substring-before($string, $found-word)" />
            <xsl:if test="substring($found-word, 1, 1) != substring($find, 1, 1)">
                <xsl:value-of select="substring($found-word, 1, 1)" />
            </xsl:if>
            <xsl:value-of select="$replace" />
            <xsl:call-template name="replace">
                <xsl:with-param name="string">
                    <xsl:if test="substring($found-word, string-length($found-word))
                                 != substring($find, string-length($find))">
                        <xsl:value-of
                            select="substring($found-word,
                                      string-length($found-word))" />
                    </xsl:if>
                    <xsl:value-of select="substring-after($string, $found-word)" />
                </xsl:with-param>
                <xsl:with-param name="find" select="$find" />
                <xsl:with-param name="replace" select="$replace" />
```

```
      </xsl:call-template>
    </xsl:when>
    <xsl:otherwise>
      <xsl:value-of select="$string" />
    </xsl:otherwise>
  </xsl:choose>
</xsl:template>
```

The `replace` template is fine if you are only concerned about replacing one string at a time, but often there's more than one string that needs replacing. For example, escaping characters in JavaScript involves replacing single and double quotes and new line characters with escaped versions. One way of doing this is to have a large `xsl:choose` statement that tests for each of the characters to be replaced. If you use this, remember to call the template recursively on the string *before* the character being replaced as well as on the string *after* that character; otherwise, only the first tested character is replaced.

An example of this in action is included in Chapter 14.

A more extensible method is to set up a piece of XML that describes the search and replace strings. For example, to escape JavaScript, you could use the XML:

```
<replace><from xml:space="preserve">&#xA;</from><to>\n</to></replace>
<replace><from>&apos;</from><to>\&apos;</to></replace>
<replace><from>&quot;</from><to>\&quot;</to></replace>
<replace><from>\</from><to>\\</to></replace>
```

Set the `xml:space` attribute to the string `'preserve'` if an element contains significant whitespace, especially if the element is in a stylesheet in which most whitespace-only text nodes are stripped using `xsl:strip-space`.

With `replace` elements defined in this way, you could have a recursive template (`replace-nodes`) that worked over the set of `replace` elements. The stylesheet would call the `replace` template with the `from` and `to` child elements of each `replace` element. The string passed to the `replace` template is the result of calling the `replace-nodes` template on the rest of the `replace` elements (if there are any):

```
<xsl:template match="node()|@*" mode="replace-nodes" name="replace-nodes">
   <xsl:param name="string" select="string()" />
   <xsl:param name="nodes" />
   <xsl:variable name="first" select="$nodes[1]" />
   <xsl:variable name="rest" select="$nodes[position() > 1]" />
   <xsl:choose>
      <xsl:when test="$first">
         <xsl:call-template name="replace">
            <xsl:with-param name="string">
               <xsl:call-template name="replace-nodes">
                  <xsl:with-param name="string" select="$string" />
                  <xsl:with-param name="nodes" select="$rest" />
               </xsl:call-template>
            </xsl:with-param>
            <xsl:with-param name="find" select="from" />
            <xsl:with-param name="replace" select="to" />
         </xsl:call-template>
      </xsl:when>
      <xsl:otherwise>
         <xsl:value-of select="$string" />
      </xsl:otherwise>
   </xsl:choose>
</xsl:template>
```

The `replace-nodes` template expects the `$nodes` parameter to be passed a node set of `replace` elements. You can create this node set using one of the methods for defining variables with XML values described in Chapter 1.

This template works fine when you're replacing strings with strings, but if you replace strings with elements then the elements are lost due to the fact that the `replace` template takes substrings to identify the parts before and after the search string. If you need to do multiple replacements and replace strings with elements, then you need a template that recurses in two places: on the substring *before* the search string as well as the substring after it.

```
<xsl:template match="node()|@*" mode="replace-nodes" name="replace-nodes">
   <xsl:param name="string" select="string()" />
   <xsl:param name="nodes" />
   <xsl:variable name="first" select="$nodes[1]" />
   <xsl:variable name="rest" select="$nodes[position() > 1]" />
   <xsl:choose>
      <xsl:when test="$first and $string">
```

```
            <xsl:choose>
                <xsl:when test="contains($string, $first/from)">
                    <xsl:call-template name="replace-nodes">
                        <xsl:with-param name="string"
                            select="substring-before($string, $first/from)" />
                        <xsl:with-param name="nodes" select="$rest" />
                    </xsl:call-template>
                    <xsl:copy-of select="$first/to" />
                    <xsl:call-template name="replace-nodes">
                        <xsl:with-param name="string"
                            select="substring-after($string, $first/from)" />
                        <xsl:with-param name="nodes" select="$nodes" />
                    </xsl:call-template>
                </xsl:when>
                <xsl:otherwise>
                    <xsl:call-template name="replace-nodes">
                        <xsl:with-param name="string" select="$string" />
                        <xsl:with-param name="nodes" select="$rest" />
                    </xsl:call-template>
                </xsl:otherwise>
            </xsl:choose>
        </xsl:when>
        <xsl:otherwise>
            <xsl:value-of select="$string" />
        </xsl:otherwise>
    </xsl:choose>
</xsl:template>
```

In these cases, though, the `replace` elements are all siblings, so you could equally recurse through them by applying templates to one at a time, with the template for one applying templates to its following sibling:

```
<xsl:template match="replace" mode="replace-nodes">
    <xsl:param name="string" />
    <xsl:variable name="next"
        select="following-sibling::replace[contains($string, from)][1]" />
    <xsl:choose>
        <xsl:when test="$next">
            <xsl:apply-templates select="$next" mode="replace-nodes">
                <xsl:with-param name="string"
                        select="substring-before($string, from)" />
            </xsl:apply-templates>
        </xsl:when>
        <xsl:otherwise>
            <xsl:value-of select="substring-before($string, from)" />
```

```
          </xsl:otherwise>
      </xsl:choose>
      <xsl:copy-of select="to" />
      <xsl:apply-templates select="." mode="replace-nodes">
          <xsl:with-param name="string"
                          select="substring-after($string, to)" />
      </xsl:apply-templates>
  </xsl:template>
```

> Rather than always going to the next sibling, this template goes to the first following sibling whose from string is contained in the string; that is, it moves on to the next replace element that involves a string that needs replacing. This reduces the number of recursions when some of the strings that should be replaced don't occur in the string, but it means that the template assumes that the string contains the search string.

This template is a bit harder to apply. You have to apply templates to the first replace element whose from child element is contained in the string, and if there isn't one, you have to return the string as it is. This template will usually be called with the following XSLT snippet:

```
<xsl:variable name="replacement"
              select="$replacements[contains($string, from)" />
<xsl:choose>
   <xsl:when test="$replacement">
      <xsl:apply-templates select="$replacement" mode="replace-nodes">
         <xsl:with-param name="string" select="$string" />
      </xsl:apply-templates>
   </xsl:when>
   <xsl:otherwise>
      <xsl:value-of select="$string" />
   </xsl:otherwise>
</xsl:choose>
```

Summary

I've talked about three types of string manipulation in this chapter: adding padding to strings, splitting up strings, and searching and replacing within strings. Along the way, I've introduced several useful techniques that are applicable in other situations as well:

◆ Ways of minimizing the depth and number of recursions

◆ Using the Piez method to iterate a number of times

◆ Comparing strings case insensitively

◆ Using the `xml:space` attribute to manage whitespace

Within this chapter, I've developed several utility templates:

◆ `align` — Aligns a string within another string

◆ `align-with` — Aligns a string within a string made up of a number of padding characters, to make a string that's a specified length in total

◆ `padding` — Creates a padding string based on padding characters and the length of the padding required

◆ `node-padding` — Repeats nodes (or a string) a specified number of times to produce some padding

◆ `split` — Divides a string into separate lines at new line characters

◆ `tokenize` — Divides a string into tokens at a string or character delimiter

◆ `wrap` — Wraps a string to make lines of a specified length

◆ `substring-before-last` — Gets the substring of a string that occurs before the last occurrence of a character of string within it

◆ `contains-word` — Returns the whole word (plus leading and trailing characters) as it's contained in a string

◆ `replace` — Replaces an occurrence of a character or a string in a string with another character or string (or nothing at all)

◆ `replace-nodes` — Does a batch search and replace on a string based on a dictionary held in XML format

These templates have demonstrated the two main ways of recursing through strings: by taking the `substring-before()` and `substring-after()` a string, and by taking a substring of a certain length, and then the remainder of the string. If what you need to do with a string isn't exactly covered by one of the templates in this chapter, then you should at least be able to use one of these more general recursive patterns.

Chapter 3

Turning XML into Text

IN THIS CHAPTER

- ◆ Converting XML lists into string lists
- ◆ Creating trees from XML hierarchies
- ◆ Serializing XML
- ◆ Creating conditional strings

IN THIS CHAPTER, YOU learn about generating text from XML. Of course, it's easy to get the value of a particular XML node using `xsl:value-of` and to concatenate strings together using the `concat()` function. You've also already seen how to manipulate numerical and textual values in Chapters 1 and 2.

In this chapter, I focus on how to draw information out of the structure of the source XML that you're using. As in the last two chapters, this involves recursive templates, but this time working through XML nodes rather than numbers or strings.

Turning XML Lists into String Lists

In Chapter 2, I showed how to split up strings containing several items separated by a character. Good XML structures often separate list items into individual XML elements so that they're easier to access than they would be in a character-delimited string. But in some applications, particularly for presentation, you want to put those strings back together again.

For example, the options that an applicant wants on a bank account might look like the following:

```
<options>
   <option>Servicecard</option>
   <option>Check book pictures</option>
   <option>Paying in book</option>
</options>
```

Node Positions

When you're dealing with node positions, for example when iterating over a set of options, you need to make sure that the positions that are being assigned to each node are the positions that you are interested in. The position of a node is based on its position in the current node list — the list of nodes that are being processed. In an xsl:for-each, it's easy to work out which nodes are being processed because the expression selecting them is right there in the select attribute. However, if you're applying templates, it's a different story.

Rather than use an xsl:for-each, you can apply templates to the option elements:

```
<xsl:apply-templates select="option" />
```

and use a template that tests the position of the current option element to decide what to do:

```
<xsl:template match="option">
   <xsl:value-of select="." />
   <xsl:choose>
      <xsl:when test="position() = last() - 1"> and </xsl:when>
      <xsl:when test="position() != last()">, </xsl:when>
   </xsl:choose>
</xsl:template>
```

However, the position that is being tested here is the position of the option element within the list of nodes having templates applied to them. You might later (accidentally) have the xsl:apply-templates apply templates to *all* children of the options element:

```
<xsl:apply-templates />
```

Now the position of the option element is within *all* the children of the options element. Often that includes whitespace text nodes, with the following result:

```
Servicecard, Check book pictures, Paying in book and
```

You can also translate the xsl:for-each into three templates, one template for each of the three types of positions that an option element might have:

```
<!-- the default case - add a comma -->
<xsl:template match="option">
   <xsl:value-of select="." />, <xsl:text />
</xsl:template>

<!-- the penultimate option - add an 'and' -->
<xsl:template match="option[last() - 1]">
   <xsl:value-of select="." /> and <xsl:text />
```

```
</xsl:template>

<!-- the last option - add nothing -->
<xsl:template match="option[last()]">
   <xsl:value-of select="." />

</xsl:template>
```

Here, it doesn't matter if you apply templates to all the children of the `options` element. The positions that are tested with predicates in match patterns are the positions of the nodes (in document order) within the set of nodes that match the node test. So the second template will always match the `option` element that is the last but one `option` element child of its parent.

Trouble arises here, however, if you change the order in which the nodes are processed, for example by sorting the options alphabetically:

```
<xsl:apply-templates select="option">
   <xsl:sort />

</xsl:apply-templates>
```

The match patterns for the templates assess the `option` elements by their position in document order, not in the order that they're being processed. The result is as follows:

```
Check book pictures and Paying in bookServicecard,
```

As a general rule, then, if you have a piece of XSLT in a template that uses the position of the current node, you should make sure that templates are being applied to the set of nodes that you expect and in the order that you expect. You may find it easier just to use `xsl:for-each` rather than templates in these situations.

Rather than put these in a bulleted list, you might want to write out a string list:

```
Servicecard, Checkbook pictures and Paying in book
```

Writing this English list involves iterating over the list, adding a comma after each option aside from the last two — the last but one has an "and" instead, and the final one has nothing:

```
<xsl:for-each select="option">
   <xsl:value-of select="." />
   <xsl:choose>
      <xsl:when test="position() = last() - 1"> and </xsl:when>
      <xsl:when test="position() != last()">, </xsl:when>
   </xsl:choose>
</xsl:for-each>
```

You can extend this xsl:for-each into a general template (and a default moded template) that can output an English list version of any set of nodes:

```
<xsl:template name="english-list">
   <xsl:param name="items" select="/.." />
   <xsl:param name="separator" select="', '" />
   <xsl:param name="final-separator" select="$separator" />
   <xsl:for-each select="$items">
      <xsl:apply-templates select="." mode="english-list-item" />
      <xsl:choose>
         <xsl:when test="position() = last() - 1">
            <xsl:copy-of select="$final-separator" />
         </xsl:when>
         <xsl:when test="position() != last()">
            <xsl:copy-of select="$separator" />
         </xsl:when>
      </xsl:choose>
   </xsl:for-each>
</xsl:template>

<xsl:template match="node()|@*" mode="english-list-item">
   <xsl:value-of select="." />
</xsl:template>
```

This template demonstrates a couple of principles for authoring extensible utility templates. The first principle is that rather than simply giving the value of each node, you apply templates to it in english-list-item mode. This means that if the string that should be added to the list for a particular node is something more than its string value, you can add templates to reflect it. For example, assume one of the options was an overdraft, with a level attribute indicating the level of the overdraft, as follows:

```
<option level="300">Overdraft</option>
```

You could add a template that detected the level attribute and added this in brackets to the string put in the list:

```
<xsl:template match="option[@level]" mode="english-list-item">
   <xsl:value-of select="." />
   <xsl:text /> (<xsl:value-of select="@level" />)<xsl:text />
</xsl:template>
```

Rather than just having the entry Overdraft in the list, you would now have one saying Overdraft (300).

The second way in which the template gives some level of extensibility is that rather than giving the value of the parameters that you expect to be strings, you copy them. This means that if someone passes in a node set or result tree fragment value for the separators, then those are copied rather than their string values being given. For example, you could separate all the options by line breaks in HTML with the following:

```
<xsl:call-template name="english-list">
   <xsl:with-param name="items" select="option" />
   <xsl:with-param name="separator"><br /></xsl:with-param>
</xsl:call-template>
```

I cover the principles for authoring extensible utility templates in more detail in Chapter 13.

Creating a Tree

One common representation for hierarchical information is a tree-like representation in which each level is indented comparative to the previous level. For example, the following XML shows a section hierarchy for the first chapter of this book:

```
<section>
   <title>Chapter 1: Manipulating Numbers</title>
   <section>
      <title>Formatting numbers as strings</title>
      <section>
         <title>Formatting decimal numbers</title>
         <section><title>Localizing numbers</title></section>
         <section><title>Formatting patterns</title></section>
         <section><title>Interpreting localized numbers</title></section>
      </section>
      <section>
         <title>Formatting integers</title>
         <section><title>Formatting long integers</title></section>
         <section><title>Interpreting alphanumeric strings</title></section>
      </section>
      <section><title>Turning numbers into ordinals</title></section>
      <section><title>Spelling out numbers</title></section>
   </section>
   <section>
```

```
      <title>Changing the Base of Numbers</title>
      <section><title>Converting from hexadecimal to decimal</title></section>
      <section><title>Converting from decimal to hexadecimal</title></section>
   </section>
</section>
```

Say you want to use this hierarchy to give an indented tree-like overview of the chapter. For each section, you want to give the title of the section, indented by three non-breaking spaces per level, so the title "Formatting numbers as strings" is indented by three non-breaking spaces, "Formatting decimal numbers" by six, and "Localizing numbers" by nine.

To do this, you need to create a certain amount of padding. The length of the padding depends on the depth of the section within the hierarchy. You can get the depth of a node by counting how many ancestors it has — in this case, you can tell how deep a `section` element is by counting how many `section` element ancestors it has. The length of the padding you need is just this depth multiplied by three:

```
<xsl:template match="section">
   <xsl:variable name="depth" select="count(ancestor::section)" />
   <xsl:call-template name="padding">
      <xsl:with-param name="pad-chars" select="' '" />
      <xsl:with-param name="pad-length" select="$depth * 3" />
   </xsl:call-template>
   <xsl:value-of select="title" /><br />
   <xsl:apply-templates select="section" />
</xsl:template>
```

The preceding template uses the `padding` template from Chapter 2 to create the padding for the sections.

This template generates the following HTML:

```
Chapter 1: Manipulating Numbers<br>
   Formatting numbers as strings<br>
      Formatting decimal numbers<br>
         Localizing numbers<br>
         Formatting patterns<br>
         Interpreting localized
                                             numbers<br>
      Formatting integers<br>
         Formatting long
                                             integers<br>
```

```
         Interpreting alphanumeric
                                        strings<br>
      Turning numbers into ordinals<br>
      Spelling out numbers<br>
   Changing the Base of Numbers<br>
      Converting from hexadecimal to decimal<br>
      Converting from decimal to hexadecimal<br>
```

An alternative method of generating this tree would be to pass the padding as a parameter from each section to its child sections, as follows:

```
<xsl:template match="section">
  <xsl:param name="padding" />
  <xsl:value-of select="title" /><br />
  <xsl:apply-templates select="section">
    <xsl:with-param name="padding"
        select="concat($padding,
                       '   ')" />
  </xsl:apply-templates>
</xsl:template>
```

While an indented tree such as this has a certain simplistic appeal, it would be much clearer if there were lines and symbols that gave more of an idea of the structure of the hierarchy, in the same way as the Folders bar in Windows Explorer. You can start with ASCII art to make things a bit easier — you want to get an output that looks like:

```
o-[*] Chapter 1: Manipulating Numbers
   o-[*] Formatting numbers as strings
   |  o-[*] Formatting decimal numbers
   |  |  +-[*] Localizing numbers
   |  |  +-[*] Formatting patterns
   |  |  '-[*] Interpreting localized numbers
   |  o-[*] Formatting integers
   |  |  +-[*] Formatting long integers
   |  |  '-[*] Interpreting alphanumeric strings
   |  +-[*] Turning numbers into ordinals
   |  '-[*] Spelling out numbers
   o-[*] Changing the Base of Numbers
      +-[*] Converting from hexadecimal to decimal
      '-[*] Converting from decimal to hexadecimal
```

The o character indicates a section that has subsections; the ' character indicates those that don't have any following siblings. Using the template as a starting point, you need, for each section, to give a relevant symbol dependant on its children and its following siblings, and then give its title, followed by line break, before moving on to the next section:

```
<xsl:template match="section">
   ...
   <xsl:choose>
      <xsl:when test="section"> o-</xsl:when>
      <xsl:when test="following-sibling::section"> +-</xsl:when>
      <xsl:otherwise> '-</xsl:otherwise>
   </xsl:choose>
   <xsl:text/>[*] <xsl:value-of select="title" />
   <xsl:text>&#xA;</xsl:text>
   <xsl:apply-templates select="section" />
</xsl:template>
```

The real difference here, though, is that the padding before each section's title may contain the lines that link up sibling sections. It's easy to see the pattern if you split up the padding into parts, each linked to a particular section element. If that section element has a following sibling within the hierarchy, a line needs to link it to that following sibling. If it doesn't, no line is needed. So the required padding can be added by iterating over the ancestors of the current section, adding a line if the ancestor has a following sibling section and no line if it doesn't:

```
<xsl:template match="section">
   <xsl:for-each select="ancestor::section">
      <xsl:choose>
         <xsl:when test="following-sibling::section"> | </xsl:when>
         <xsl:otherwise><xsl:text>    </xsl:text></xsl:otherwise>
      </xsl:choose>
   </xsl:for-each>
   <xsl:choose>
      <xsl:when test="section"> o-</xsl:when>
      <xsl:when test="following-sibling::section"> +-</xsl:when>
      <xsl:otherwise> '-</xsl:otherwise>
   </xsl:choose>
   <xsl:text />[*] <xsl:value-of select="title" />
   <xsl:text>&#xA;</xsl:text>
   <xsl:apply-templates select="section" />
</xsl:template>
```

You can collapse parts of the tree that don't contain the section that you're interested in by adding a test around the application of templates to child sections. For example, if the title of the relevant section is held in the `$current-title` variable, you could use:

```
<xsl:if test=".//section[title = $current-title]">
   <xsl:apply-templates select="section" />
</xsl:if>
```

You can change this template to output HTML rather than ASCII art by changing each portion of text with an appropriate image as follows:

```
<xsl:template match="section">
   <xsl:for-each select="ancestor::section">
      <xsl:choose>
         <xsl:when test="following-sibling::section">
            <img src="line.gif" />
         </xsl:when>
         <xsl:otherwise><img src="space.gif" /></xsl:otherwise>
      </xsl:choose>
   </xsl:for-each>
   <xsl:choose>
      <xsl:when test="section"><img src="branch.gif" /></xsl:when>
      <xsl:when test="following-sibling::section">
         <img src="leaf.gif" />
      </xsl:when>
      <xsl:otherwise><img src="final-leaf.gif" /></xsl:otherwise>
   </xsl:choose>
   <img src="section.gif" />
   <xsl:value-of select="title" /><br />
   <xsl:apply-templates select="section" />
</xsl:template>
```

It's a little harder, but not impossible, to create a tree structure with structures that aren't nested. You need to apply templates to the "children" of a node in the hierarchy to iterate over the "ancestors" of a node, and to be able to work out whether a node has a "following sibling" or not. You may find it easier, though, to create a nested structure first, from which you create the tree.

See the discussion of grouping in Chapter 9 to learn how to create a nested structure from various starting points.

Serializing XML

Giving a serialized version of the XML that you're using can be surprisingly useful. You can use it to help debug your stylesheets, for example, by indicating within comments the source XML that led to a particular piece of output. It can also help if you're creating a dynamic application that uses node set parameters by letting you construct the XML for the parameter, or if you want to display some XML within an HTML page.

See Chapter 14 for information on node set parameters.

Serializing XML involves writing out the characters that make up XML syntax as text. For example, consider the following XML element:

```
<transaction type="DD" payee="British Gas">&#163;24.50</transaction>
```

If you included this XML element within an XML or HTML document, it would be interpreted as an element. If you don't want it to be interpreted as an element, you need to escape the meaningful characters – the less-than signs with < and the ampersand with & – so that the XML parser doesn't interpret them as the start of tags or entities:

```
&lt;transaction type="DD" payee="British Gas">&amp;#163;24.50&lt;/transaction>
```

Alternatively, you can wrap it within a CDATA section so that the characters are no longer meaningful. CDATA sections are a special construct in XML. Within a CDATA section, the characters that are normally special in XML markup (like less-than signs and ampersands) are ignored, so you don't have to escape them individually:

```
<![CDATA[<transaction type="DD" payee="British Gas">&#163;24.50</transaction>]]>
```

This gives exactly the same text as the escaped version that precedes it, but is easier to read. You can control whether a CDATA section is wrapped around the textual content of an element using the `cdata-section-elements` attribute on `xsl:output`.

See Chapter 16 for detailed examples of using CDATA sections.

Comments act in a similar way to CDATA sections except, of course, that the text that they hold is not counted as text within the document and may be lost by the XML parser:

```
<!--<transaction type="DD" payee="British Gas">&#163;24.50</transaction>-->
```

You've now seen three ways that a result XML document can hold serialized XML elements without them being interpreted as XML elements. How can you get that output in your result?

Creating XML Strings

One means of getting some serialized XML in your result is to create some text that serializes the XML that you want to output. You can't simply copy the elements that you want to serialize — the XSLT processor will add the elements to the result tree as elements whereas you want them added as text.

The first step is to generate templates for each node type that give a serialized version of that node type. Comments and processing instructions are easy:

```
<xsl:template match="comment()" mode="serialize">
   <xsl:value-of select="concat('&lt;--', ., '-->')" />
</xsl:template>

<xsl:template match="processing-instruction()" mode="serialize">
   <xsl:value-of select="concat('&lt;?', name(), ' ', ., '?>')" />
</xsl:template>
```

Text nodes are fairly straightforward aside from the fact that some characters within a text node, namely ampersands and less-than signs, need to be escaped. For this, you can use the `replace-nodes` template that was created in Chapter 2. With the variable $text-escapes holding the following XML:

```
<replace><from>&lt;</from><to>&amp;lt;</to></replace>
<replace><from>&amp;</from><to>&amp;amp;</to></replace>
<replace><from>]]&gt;</from><to>]]&amp;gt;</to></replace>
```

you can call the `replace-nodes` template as follows:

```
<xsl:template match="text()" mode="serialize">
   <xsl:call-template name="replace-nodes">
      <xsl:with-param name="string" select="." />
      <xsl:with-param name="nodes" select="$text-escapes" />
   </xsl:call-template>
</xsl:template>
```

Finally, then, you need to serialize elements. Mostly, elements are fairly straightforward. You can tell whether an element is empty (and can therefore be serialized with an empty element tag) by checking whether it has any child nodes. Attribute values need to be escaped in much the same way as text nodes, but you also need to escape any quotes within the attribute value. Set up the $attr-escapes variable to hold the following XML:

```
<replace><from>&lt;</from><to>&amp;lt;</to></replace>
<replace><from>&amp;</from><to>&amp;amp;</to></replace>
<replace><from>&quot;</from><to>]]&amp;quot;</to></replace>
```

The template for serializing elements is then:

```
<xsl:template match="*" mode="serialize">
   <xsl:text />&lt;<xsl:value-of select="name()" />
   <xsl:for-each select="@*">
      <xsl:value-of select="concat(' ', name(), '=&quot;')" />
      <xsl:call-template name="replace-nodes">
         <xsl:with-param name="string" select="." />
         <xsl:with-param name="nodes" select="$attr-escapes" />
      </xsl:call-template>
      <xsl:text>"</xsl:text>
   </xsl:for-each>
   <xsl:choose>
```

```
    <xsl:when test="node()">
       <xsl:text>></xsl:text>
       <xsl:apply-templates mode="serialize" />
       <xsl:value-of select="concat('&lt;/', name(), '>')" />
    </xsl:when>
    <xsl:otherwise /></xsl:otherwise>
  </xsl:choose>
</xsl:template>
```

There are various ways of creating variables that hold XML. These are covered in Chapter 1.

The tricky thing about elements is outputting namespace declarations. Every element has associated with it namespace nodes for all the namespaces declared on it and on all its ancestors, plus the namespace declaration for the XML namespace that is built in to namespace-aware applications. However, you don't want to clutter the XML serialization with repeated namespace declarations and instead only want to include those that are new to the particular element. The relevant namespace declarations for an element are those in which there is no namespace node on its parent element that has the same name (namespace prefix) and string value (namespace URI). So you can include this test to add serialized namespace declarations to the element:

```
<xsl:template match="*" mode="serialize">
   <xsl:text />&lt;<xsl:value-of select="name()" />
   <xsl:for-each select="namespace::*[name() != 'xml']">
      <xsl:if test="not(../../namespace::*[name() = name(current()) and
                                     . = current()])">
         <xsl:text>xmlns</xsl:text>
         <xsl:if test="name()">
            <xsl:text />:<xsl:value-of select="name()" />
         </xsl:if>
         <xsl:value-of select="concat('=&quot;', ., '&quot;')" />
      </xsl:if>
   </xsl:for-each>
   <xsl:for-each select="@*">
      ...
   </xsl:for-each>
   ...
</xsl:template>
```

If you are using the release version of MSXML3, rather than MSXML3sp1, then you will have to use `local-name()` to find the prefix for the namespace rather than `name()`, since with MSXML3 the `name()` function returns `xmlns:prefix` rather than just the namespace prefix.

With these templates in place, you can show the source XML that led to a particular part of a document by applying templates to the source nodes in `serialize` mode. For example, you can add comments holding the source XML for a `transaction` element before a row giving its HTML output:

```
<xsl:template match="transaction">
   <xsl:comment>Source XML:</xsl:comment>
   <xsl:comment>
      <xsl:apply-templates select="." mode="serialize" />
   </xsl:comment>
   <tr>
      <!-- table cells giving details of the transaction -->
   </tr>
</xsl:template>
```

Disabling Output Escaping

You can also output serialized XML by disabling output escaping. Disabling output escaping gives you absolute control over the output of the XSLT processor — anything that you output with output escaping disabled is given in the output exactly as you specified.

In general, disabling output escaping is very ill advised. The controls that XSLT gives you over the output should be enough to create what you want, and reverting to disabling output escaping is often a sign that you've missed the "XSLT way" of doing something — trying to open an element in one template and close it elsewhere, for example, constructing tags sequentially rather than building a result tree. It is also dangerous for portability reasons to rely on disabling output escaping — XSLT processors are not required to support it and if they don't, then they escape your output just as they normally would.

Having said that, serializing XML is a situation in which disabling output escaping can make your life a lot easier and make processing a lot more efficient. For example, if you place a copy of the current node within a comment to help debugging, it would be ideal if the XSLT processor took care of doing all the serialization, especially working out what characters need to be escaped and where. All you really want to do is add the characters `<!--` before the copy and the characters `-->` after the copy. Well, you can do this by disabling output escaping and outputting those characters:

```
<xsl:text disable-output-escaping="yes">&lt;!-- </xsl:text>
<xsl:copy-of select="." />
<xsl:text disable-output-escaping="yes"> --></xsl:text>
```

Similarly, as long as you're generating XML, you could place a serialized version of some XML within your text with the following:

```
<xsl:text disable-output-escaping="yes">&lt;![CDATA[ </xsl:text>
<xsl:copy-of select="." />
<xsl:text disable-output-escaping="yes"> ]]></xsl:text>
```

Either of these methods is a little dangerous — comments cannot contain the string -- and CDATA sections cannot contain the string]]>, and simply copying the nodes gives you no control over the content of the comments and CDATA sections that you produce. But as these situations are fairly rare; the preceding code will work much of the time.

 Using disabling output escaping to produce CDATA sections or comments may not work if the result of your transformation is piped straight on to a SAX or DOM process rather than being written to a file. Wrapping some text in CDATA also won't work if the processor that reads the output of the transformation doesn't understand CDATA sections. Thus you can only use this method if you're outputting an XML file, not if you're outputting HTML (although CDATA sections come from SGML, and HTML is SGML, CDATA sections are not supported by most web browsers). Also, if you want XML code to be included within text output then you have to use the XML serialization templates outlined previously as elements are not output by the processor when using the text output method.

Creating Conditional Strings

The basic XSLT method for creating different strings based on some condition is to use xsl:if or xsl:choose: xsl:if to indicate pieces of strings that should only occur under certain conditions and xsl:choose to indicate those that change under different circumstances. However, there are situations in which using these conditional constructs is too much work or stops you from doing what you need to do, in particular within the match attribute of xsl:key and xsl:template (in which variables are banned) or in the use attribute of xsl:key or the select attribute of xsl:sort (which need string values based on the context node). For these cases, you need another technique.

Rather than using a complex XPath such as the ones described in this section, you may be able to create your own extension function to generate the string. Authoring extension functions is discussed in Chapter 20.

Decoding Enumerated Values

One situation in which you need a conditional string is when decoding a value that is one of a fixed set of codes. This is essentially a translation from some information in the XML into a predictable string. So, for example, you can output a string giving the type of a transaction with the following:

```
<xsl:choose>
   <xsl:when test="@type = 'CR'">credit</xsl:when>
   <xsl:otherwise>
      <xsl:text>debit</xsl:text>
      <xsl:choose>
         <xsl:when test="@type = 'SO'"> (standing order)</xsl:when>
         <xsl:when test="@type = 'DD'"> (direct debit)</xsl:when>
         <xsl:when test="@type = 'WD'"> (withdrawal)</xsl:when>
      </xsl:choose>
   </xsl:otherwise>
</xsl:choose>
```

However, as the number of codes gets larger and larger, it's often more economical to use an XML structure to store the information that you want and then access the values from that XML structure. For example, you could represent the information that's used in the preceding code within an XML structure:

```
<type code="CR">credit</type>
<type code="SO">debit (standing order)</type>
<type code="DD">debit (direct debit)</type>
<type code="WD">debit (withdrawal)</type>
```

If these type elements were stored within the $types variable, then building the relevant string simply involves finding the type element within $types whose code attribute is the same as the type attribute of the current transaction element:

```
<xsl:value-of select="$types/type[@code = current()/@type]" />
```

Using Keys to Access Values

If you have lots and lots of possible codes, then you may find it more efficient to use a key to access them rather than a basic XPath. Taking the example of transaction types, you could define a key that indexed into the type elements by their code attribute:

```
<xsl:key name="types-by-code" match="type" use="@code" />
```

You could then use the key() function to access the relevant type element simply with:

```
key('types-by-code', @type)
```

Watch out, though — the nodes that you want to access with the key() function have to be in the same node tree as the current node. So in the example, unless the type elements are defined within the same document as the transaction elements that you're trying to transform, the key won't find them. If you want to search in another document, you need to change the current node and use the key() function within this new context. For example, if you've stored the type elements within types.xml, then you need to use the following:

```
<xsl:variable name="type" select="@type" />
<xsl:for-each select="document('types.xml')">
   <xsl:value-of select="key('types-by-code', $type)" />

</xsl:for-each>
```

Unfortunately, this means, for example, that you can't use keys to access values to sort by as there is no way of changing the current node within an XPath expression.

You can combine values to create the key for a node by concatenating values within the use attribute of xsl:key. So you could index the type elements by code *and* language with the following:

```
<xsl:key name="types-by-code-and-lang"
        match="type"

        use="concat(@code, ':', @xml:lang)" />
```

With this definition, you could get the relevant string for a particular code and a particular language with:

```
key('types-by-code-and-lang', concat(@type, ':', $lang))
```

Note here, though, that the type elements will be indexed by the literal value of their xml:lang attribute, whereas the lang() function uses the inherited language of the XML element, ignores any case differences, and behaves appropriately with language subsets. Therefore, it's usually better to take advantage of this sophisticated language code processing and thus use:

```
key('types-by-code', @type)[lang($lang)]
```

Chapter 1 covers creating variables that hold XML information.

Storing the text associated with particular codes in a separate structure is useful because it enables you to add text for different languages into your application later, if you need to add multilingual support to the application. You can add an `xml:lang` attribute to the `type` elements, and use the `lang()` function to select only those `type` elements that are in the language that you desire (passed into the stylesheet as the `$lang` parameter):

```
<xsl:value-of select="$types/type[@code = current()/@type]
                      [lang($lang)]" />
```

A bigger advantage, however, is that you no longer need XSLT code to access the string that you want — all the conditions are wrapped up within the XPath.

Accessing the conditional strings with an XPath expression rather than with XSLT instructions means that you can use the string to sort on, for example, as I illustrate in Chapter 7.

Conditions with Computed Values

In the previous section, you saw how to use XML to get fixed strings from coded values. You can't use XML to decode a code if the string that you're after is one that's constructed from other values in the source XML rather than being fixed. For example, for a bank statement application, some accounts are joint accounts. If they are, then you need to insert the name of both the main and joint account holders, with an and in between. The source XML looks as follows:

```
<accountHolders>
   <main>
      <name>...</name>
   </main>
   <joint>
      <name>...</name>
   </joint>
   ...
</accountHolders>
```

You can use the following XML to give the names of the account holders, assuming that the current node is the `accountHolders` element:

```
<xsl:value-of select="main/name" />
<xsl:if test="joint"> and <xsl:value-of select="joint/name" /></xsl:if>
```

There are times when cramming this conditional string into a single XPath expression can be useful for sorting. There are also times when the match pattern of a template or a key, or the key value for a node, needs to contain a conditional string. And it has to be said that XSLT is particularly verbose when it comes to simple conditions, and sometimes you just want to use an XPath to save yourself from typing all that XSLT! But XPath doesn't have a conditional operator, so you need to resort to trickery.

One of the requirements for XPath 2.0 is that it must provide a conditional operator, so future versions of XSLT will not have this limitation.

CONDITIONAL NODE SETS

Conditional node sets are the easiest conditional XPath to use. Any test that you can place in an `xsl:if` or `xsl:when` can be placed in the predicate on an XPath. So you can choose whether or not to display the details of the account holders based on whether the parameter `$show-details` is true with the following:

```
<xsl:apply-templates select="accountHolders[$show-details]" />
```

If `$show-details` is false, then no nodes will be selected by the location path because for no `accountHolders` element is it true that `$show-details` is true. If it is true, on the other hand, then the `accountHolders` element will be selected. Thus the preceding XSLT does exactly the same thing as:

```
<xsl:if test="$show-details">
   <xsl:apply-templates select="accountHolders" />
</xsl:if>
```

CONDITIONAL NUMBERS

Let's look at conditional numbers because knowing how to get conditional numbers will help with getting conditional strings. Let's say that you want to return the number 2 if `$test` is true and the number 5 if `$test` is false. Here, you can use the fact that converting Boolean true to a number gives the value 1 whereas converting Boolean false to a number gives the value 0, so you just need a mathematical formula that converts 0 to 5 and 1 to 2:

```
5 + $test * -3
```

or, equivalently:

```
2 + not($test) * 3
```

The general pattern is as follows:

```
false-value + test * (true-value - false-value)
```

Of course if you know what the true and false values are going to be in advance (as you did in the preceding example), then you can do the last bit of the calculation yourself. Also, if the false value is zero (0), then the pattern is simply:

```
test * true-value
```

CONDITIONAL STRINGS

You can get different strings based on some condition by using the `substring()` function to pick different parts of a string. It's perhaps easiest to start with either getting a whole string or getting none of the string, for example to choose whether to add the ' and ' to the string giving the account holder names. In this case, if `joint` is true (if there's a `joint` element child of the context node) then you want the string ' and '; if it isn't, then you don't. So the substring that you want starts from the first character if `joint` is true and after the last character if `joint` is false. Here, you need a function that maps 0 to `Infinity` (no string can be longer than that!) and 1 to 1:

```
substring(' and ', 1 div boolean(joint))
```

It's important to make sure that the test you use results in a Boolean value. Without the call to the `boolean()` function in the preceding code, you would have gotten the string value of the `joint` element.

Given this insight, it's fairly straightforward to move on to conditional strings that involve both a true and a false value. If you concatenate the two values together (first true and then false) then when the test is true you want the number of characters in the true value string, starting from the first character, whereas when the test is false you want the number of characters in the false string, starting from the first character after the true string. The pattern is thus:

```
substring(concat(true-string, false-string),
        1 + not(test) * string-length(true-string),
        string-length(true-string) +
          not(test) * (string-length(false-string) -
                        string-length(true-string)))
```

This looks very complicated, but it's a lot more approachable if you know what the strings that you're after are. For example to return `'main'` or `'joint'` depending on whether the context node is a `main` element or not you can use the following:

```
substring('mainjoint', 1 + not(self::main) * 4, 4 + not(self::main))
```

If you don't know what the strings are that you're after in advance, then just plug the relevant strings into the preceding pattern and hope for the best!

Getting more than two strings conditionally involves concatenating together the result of several conditional strings, but you have to make sure that the conditions are mutually exclusive. For example, you can translate the abbreviations of a day of the week to its full string with the following:

```
concat(substring(concat($abbrev, 'day'),
                1 div ($abbrev = 'Mon' or $abbrev = 'Fri' or $abbrev = 'Sun')),
        substring('Tuesday', 1 div ($abbrev = 'Tue')),
        substring('Wednesday', 1 div ($abbrev = 'Wed')),
        substring('Thursday', 1 div ($abbrev = 'Thu')),
        substring('Saturday', 1 div ($abbrev = 'Sat')))
```

The general pattern for getting these conditional strings is:

```
concat(substring(string1, 1 div test1),
        substring(string2, 1 div test2),
        ...
        substring(stringN, 1 div testN))
```

 This last method of generating conditional strings is known as the Becker Method, after Oliver Becker.

Summary

In this chapter, you've looked at some of the trickier aspects of pulling information out of XML using XSLT. I've shown you how to create string lists from XML by iterating over the nodes that make up the list, and pointed out some of the pitfalls of doing so using the `position()` function.

I've described how to create pretty trees from XML hierarchies with both ASCII art and HTML images. If you want to use trees to summarize information, you should incorporate the techniques discussed in Chapter 10 as well.

I've also discussed issues concerning serializing XML and shown you how to disable output escaping in order to get some XML emitted as a CDATA section or within a comment. You'll see this in action again in later chapters, notably Chapter 14 when you look at dynamic client-side XML applications.

Finally, you've learned about generating conditional strings. It may seem very theoretical at the moment, but you're going to be using them quite a bit in the following chapters, most notably in Chapter 7 on sorting.

Chapter 4

Analyzing Data in XML

IN THIS CHAPTER

- ◆ Getting totals
- ◆ Counting items
- ◆ Calculating averages
- ◆ Finding minima and maxima

IN THIS CHAPTER, I focus on how to analyze data that's held in XML structures — how to draw out information held across nodes or within strings. XML often holds the minimal amount of information that it needs to, leaving the XSLT application that deals with the XML to calculate and compute any additional information that might need to be displayed. For example, an XML document for a purchase order might list all the items, their unit price and the number of items, but not hold subtotals or calculate the tax due.

XSLT and XPath offer very few built-in functions for analyzing and summarizing data within an XML document, really only providing the following:

- ◆ `sum()` — Sums the values of all the nodes in a node set
- ◆ `count()` — Counts how many nodes there are in a node set

For anything more complex, you need support from utility templates. In this chapter, I examine how to achieve several types of analysis and calculation from information distributed within an XML document. Some of these templates are similar to those in Chapter 3, in that they recurse through nodes, but they involve numerical calculations rather than generating strings or XML. Others perform analysis on values kept in space-separated or comma-delimited strings; these use the same patterns of recursion as you saw in Chapter 2.

Getting Totals

Often, you can simply use the `sum()` function to get totals — as long as you can construct an XPath to get the nodes with the values that you want to sum. For example, if the transactions on a bank account were given using `transaction` elements in a list such as this:

```
<transactions>
   <transaction type="DD" currency="GBP">13.99</transaction>
   <transaction type="CR" currency="USD">125.00</transaction>
   <transaction type="WD" currency="GBP">50.00</transaction>
   ...
</transactions>
```

You could get the total value of the transactions within a bank statement (assuming that the current node is the `transactions` element) by summing the values of the `transaction` elements with the following:

```
sum(transaction)
```

However, this just gives the cash flow through the account, not the overall credit to the account. As this example shows, `sum()` can't be used if you need to calculate the values to be summed within the XSLT. In this example, the transaction with the type `CR` is a credit to the account, whereas those with other types (for example, `DD` and `WD`) are debits. Also, the amounts need to be converted according to the exchange rate between the pound and the dollar. With the preceding XPath, you get the sum:

```
13.99 + 125.00 + 50.00
```

whereas what you actually want is:

```
-13.99 + (125.00 * 0.6) + -50.00
```

There are three ways to achieve this: adding subtotals, building an intermediate node set or writing a recursive function. The following sections addresses each of these in turn.

Summing by Adding Subtotals

In the preceding example, there are four kinds of transactions, each of which need to be added to the total in a different way:

◆ Credits in pounds: add to the total

◆ Credits in US dollars: multiply by 0.6 and add to the total

◆ Debits in pounds: subtract from the total

◆ Debits in US dollars: multiply by 0.6 and subtract from the total

One way of calculating the total credit to the account is to create subtotals for each of the four types of transactions and then add them together appropriately. The `transaction` elements that belong to each of the four groups can be identified through separate paths:

```
transaction[@type = 'CR' and @currency = 'GBP']
transaction[@type = 'CR' and @currency = 'USD']
transaction[@type != 'CR' and @currency = 'GBP']
transaction[@type != 'CR' and @currency = 'USD']
```

You can sum the values of the transaction elements collected by each of these paths. Those in US dollars need to be multiplied by 0.6 before being added to the total, while those that aren't credits need to be subtracted from the total. The resulting calculation is as follows:

```
sum(transaction[@type = 'CR' and @currency = 'GBP'])
+ (sum(transaction[@type = 'CR' and @currency = 'USD']) * 0.6)
- sum(transaction[@type != 'CR' and @currency = 'GBP'])
- (sum(transaction[@type != 'CR' and @currency = 'USD']) * 0.6)
```

As you can see, the expression to calculate the total is a little unwieldy. It also relies on the fact that multiplying a sum of a set of numbers by 0.6 is the same as summing the result of multiplying each of the numbers by 0.6. This equivalence may not hold true for other sums, so it is not always practical to sum calculated values by adding subtotals.

This example and the rest in the section hard-code the value 0.6 as the exchange rate between the dollar and the pound. In real applications, you should make this into a stylesheet parameter or retrieve the exchange rate from elsewhere rather than fixing it within the stylesheet.

Summing by Building an Intermediate Node Set

As XPath provides the `sum()` function to add the values of nodes together, you may as well take advantage of it. One way to sum a set of calculated values, then, is to create a node set in which the values of the nodes are the values that you actually want to sum. In this case, you can create a variable that creates `value` elements for each of the `transaction` elements, each holding the calculated value:

```
<xsl:variable name="values-rtf">
   <xsl:for-each select="transaction">
      <xsl:variable name="converted-value">
         <xsl:choose>
```

```
            <xsl:when test="@currency = 'USD'">
                <xsl:value-of select=". * 0.6" />
            </xsl:when>
            <xsl:otherwise><xsl:value-of select="." /></xsl:otherwise>
        </xsl:choose>
    </xsl:variable>
    <value>
        <xsl:choose>
            <xsl:when test="@type = 'CR'">
                <xsl:value-of select="$converted-value" />
            </xsl:when>
            <xsl:otherwise>
                <xsl:value-of select="-$converted-value" />
            </xsl:otherwise>
        </xsl:choose>
    </value>
  </xsl:for-each>
</xsl:variable>
```

With this variable constructed, you can then sum the value elements within it. To use the sum() function, you need to be able to access the value elements as a node set. You can do this in two ways. First, you can use a two-step transformation, in which you create the node set within the first stylesheet, and then sum them within a second stylesheet. Second, you can use an extension function to convert the $values-rtf result tree fragment into a node set. In either case, you can calculate the sum using the following expression, assuming that the $values variable holds a node that has the value elements as children:

```
sum($values/value)
```

See Chapter 18 for more information about converting result tree fragments to node sets using extension functions.

You can also use this method to sum values that are held in a string. For example, the transactions element might instead hold a string of space-separated values, one for each transaction:

```
<transactions>-13.99 125.00 -50.00</transactions>
```

Here, the node set held by the $nodes variable must be constructed by recursively pulling apart the string to split it into tokens. This is covered in depth in

Chapter 2. You can use the `tokenize` template developed in that chapter to construct a number of `token` elements:

```
<xsl:variable name="values-rtf">
   <xsl:apply-templates select="." mode="tokenize">
      <xsl:with-param name="break" select="' '" />
   </xsl:apply-templates>
</xsl:variable>
```

Note now that the values to be summed are held in `token` rather than `value` elements, since those are the elements generated by the `tokenize` template, so the sum is calculated with the following expression:

```
sum($values/token)
```

Summing with a Recursive Template

A recursive template for summing the required values for the `transaction` elements uses the same XSLT as previously for calculating the value of the transaction, taking into account its currency and type. As the transaction elements are siblings, the recursive template can recurse over the `transaction` elements from sibling to sibling. A `$subtotal` parameter keeps track of the sum so far; if there are no more `transaction` elements then the result is this subtotal added to the value for the current `transaction` element, otherwise this sum is passed on to the next transaction. The following template uses this pattern:

```
<xsl:template match="transaction" mode="sum">
   <xsl:param name="subtotal" select="0" />
   <xsl:variable name="value">
      <xsl:variable name="converted-value">
         <xsl:choose>
            <xsl:when test="@currency = 'USD'">
               <xsl:value-of select=". * 0.6" />
            </xsl:when>
            <xsl:otherwise><xsl:value-of select="." /></xsl:otherwise>
         </xsl:choose>
      </xsl:variable>
      <xsl:choose>
         <xsl:when test="@type = 'CR'">
            <xsl:value-of select="$converted-value" />
         </xsl:when>
         <xsl:otherwise>
            <xsl:value-of select="-$converted-value" />
         </xsl:otherwise>
```

```
      </xsl:choose>
    </xsl:variable>
    <xsl:variable name="next" select="following-sibling::transaction[1]" />
    <xsl:choose>
      <xsl:when test="$next">
        <xsl:apply-templates select="$next">
          <xsl:with-param name="subtotal" select="$subtotal + $value" />
        </xsl:apply-templates>
      </xsl:when>
      <xsl:otherwise>
        <xsl:value-of select="$subtotal + $value" />
      </xsl:otherwise>
    </xsl:choose>
  </xsl:template>
```

With this template, you can sum the transaction elements by applying templates to the first transaction element in sum mode:

```
<xsl:apply-templates select="transaction[1]" mode="sum" />
```

An alternative design is a named template that is passed the set of transaction elements as a parameter, with each recursion calculating the value for the first node in that node set. In this case, because you know that each transaction element can be easily reached from the previous one (using one step along the following-sibling axis), you use a matching template instead as this makes "calling" the template easier — you don't have to specify any parameters when you do so.

For a general utility summing template, however, you need to adopt the alternative design:

```
<xsl:template name="sum">
  <xsl:param name="node-set" select="/.." />
  <xsl:param name="subtotal" select="0" />
  <xsl:choose>
    <xsl:when test="not($node-set)">
      <xsl:value-of select="$subtotal" />
    </xsl:when>
    <xsl:otherwise>
      <xsl:variable name="value-of-first">
        <xsl:apply-templates select="$node-set[1]"
                             mode="sum-value" />
      </xsl:variable>
      <xsl:call-template name="sum">
        <xsl:with-param name="node-set"
                        select="$node-set[position() > 1]" />
        <xsl:with-param name="subtotal"
```

```
                                        select="$subtotal + $value-of-first" />
                </xsl:call-template>
            </xsl:otherwise>
        </xsl:choose>
    </xsl:template>

    <xsl:template match="node()|@*" mode="sum-value">
        <xsl:value-of select="." />
    </xsl:template>
```

TIP To finalize this template, you should test whether the value of the $node-set parameter is actually a node set and issue a warning message using xsl:message if it isn't, returning NaN or 0. If you're dealing with large node sets and you're stuck using a processor that doesn't optimize tail recursion, you may also want to decrease the depth of the recursion by dividing the node sets in half, calling the template on those two halves, and then adding the results together instead. You can see this kind of approach in action later in this chapter with the min template.

You can sum the transaction elements by calling the sum template, passing the set of transaction elements as the value of the $node-set parameter:

```
<xsl:call-template name="sum">
    <xsl:with-param name="node-set" select="transaction" />
</xsl:call-template>
```

The values must be calculated in a helper template that matches the transaction elements in sum-value mode:

```
<xsl:template match="transaction" mode="sum-value">
    <xsl:variable name="converted-value">
        <xsl:choose>
            <xsl:when test="@currency = 'USD'">
                <xsl:value-of select=". * 0.6" />
            </xsl:when>
            <xsl:otherwise><xsl:value-of select="." /></xsl:otherwise>
        </xsl:choose>
    </xsl:variable>
    <xsl:choose>
        <xsl:when test="@type = 'CR'">
            <xsl:value-of select="$converted-value" />
        </xsl:when>
```

```
      <xsl:otherwise>
         <xsl:value-of select="-$converted-value" />
      </xsl:otherwise>
   </xsl:choose>
</xsl:template>
```

You can sum space-separated or comma-delimited values in a string in a similar way, this time working through the string using substring-before() and substring-after(). Of course, with a string there is no need to calculate the values to be summed, but you do need to know the delimiter that's being used to separate them. The template looks as follows:

```
<xsl:template match="node()|@*" mode="sum-string" name="sum-string">
   <xsl:param name="string" select="string(.)" />
   <xsl:param name="delimiter" select="' '" />
   <xsl:param name="subtotal" select="0" />
   <xsl:choose>
      <xsl:when test="not(normalize-space(translate($string, $delimiter, '')))">
         <xsl:value-of select="$subtotal" />
      </xsl:when>
      <xsl:otherwise>
         <xsl:variable name="value-of-first">
            <xsl:choose>
               <xsl:when test="contains($string, $delimiter)">
                  <xsl:value-of
                     select="substring-before($string, $delimiter)" />
               </xsl:when>
               <xsl:otherwise><xsl:value-of select="$string" /></xsl:otherwise>
            </xsl:choose>
         </xsl:variable>
         <xsl:call-template name="sum-string">
            <xsl:with-param name="string"
                            select="substring-after($string, $delimiter)" />
            <xsl:with-param name="delimiter" select="$delimiter" />
            <xsl:with-param name="subtotal"
                            select="$subtotal + $value-of-first" />
         </xsl:call-template>
      </xsl:otherwise>
   </xsl:choose>
</xsl:template>
```

The first xsl:when in the preceding template tests whether there is anything but whitespace left in the string when all the delimiters are deleted from it. If there aren't, then there are no values in that string.

To finalize this template, you should test whether the value of the $string parameter is actually a string. If it isn't, you should issue a warning message and return NaN or 0. Chapter 13 discusses how to carry out these tests and design robust utility templates.

Counting Items

Counting nodes involves simply passing the nodes that you want to count as the argument to the count() function. Counting items in a string is a little more complicated, although *how* complicated depends on the delimiters used between the items in the string.

Counting Character-Separated Items

Items that are separated by a single delimiting character can be counted by getting rid of all the text that *isn't* that character, and then looking at the length of the remaining string to count how many delimiters there are. If there's a delimiter at the end or beginning of the string, you need to take those into account — or you can make sure that there aren't by stripping them before deleting the non-delimiter characters. Without delimiters at the beginning or end of the string, the number of items is the number of delimiters plus one.

I covered how to delete all but certain characters from a string in Chapter 2. If you remember, the pattern was:

```
translate($string, translate($string, character, ''),
'')
```

Stripping the first and last characters from a string involves getting the substring from the second character, which is the length of the original string minus two:

```
substring($string, 2, string-length($string) - 2)
```

If you pass the result of removing all the non-delimiter characters from the string as the argument to the `string-length()` function, you can use it to count the occurrences of a particular character in a string. The pattern for counting character-separated items in a string is thus:

```
string-length(
   translate($stripped-string,
             translate($string, delimiter, ''), ''))
+ 1
```

If there are multiple delimiters, each of which is a single character, you can either change them all into the same character before using the `translate()` function again, or give all the delimiters in the delimiter string. For example, to count the number of colons or commas in a string, you could use:

```
string-length(
   translate($stripped-string,
             translate($string, ':,', ''), ''))
+ 1
```

Counting Word-Separated Items

You can count items that are separated by a multi-character delimiter by tokenizing the string with the `tokenize` template developed in Chapter 2, and then counting the number of tokens that are generated with the `count()` function. However, this involves converting the result tree fragment from the `tokenize` template into a node set, either by having a two-pass transformation or by using an extension function.

The other option is to recurse through the string using `substring-before()` and `substring-after()` and add one for each recursion:

```
<xsl:template match="node()|@*" mode="count-items" name="count-items">
   <xsl:param name="string" select="string(.)" />
   <xsl:param name="delimiter" select="' '" />
   <xsl:param name="subtotal" select="1" />
   <xsl:choose>
      <xsl:when test="contains($string, $delimiter)">
         <xsl:call-template name="count-items">
```

```
      <xsl:with-param name="string"
                      select="substring-after($string, $delimiter)" />
      <xsl:with-param name="delimiter" select="$delimiter" />
      <xsl:with-param name="subtotal" select="$subtotal + 1" />
    </xsl:call-template>
  </xsl:when>
  <xsl:otherwise><xsl:value-of select="$subtotal" /></xsl:otherwise>
</xsl:choose>
</xsl:template>
```

To finalize this template, you should check whether the values passed for the $string and $delimiter parameters are actually strings, and issue warning messages if they're not.

You can use this method to count how many occurrences of a particular word there are in a string: you can think of the word as the delimiter, with the result being the same as the preceding template gives, minus one. Of course, if you want to check that the delimiting string is present as a whole word rather than as part of a word, you need to do some extra checking.

See the discussion of searching for and replacing words in Chapter 2 for more on how to identify a whole word within a string.

Calculating Averages

As statisticians will tell you, there are three kinds of averages:

1. **Mean:** What's normally thought of as the average; the sum of values divided by the number of values

2. **Median:** The value of the middle value in the set, ranked in order

3. **Mode:** The value that has most occurrences in the set of values

If you can sum a set of values and count them, then calculating the mean of the set is easy. I've covered in detail how to do both summing and counting in the previous two sections of this chapter. The others require different handling.

Calculating the Median

Calculating the median value from a set of nodes requires that you sort them in order and then pick the middle one. Sorting the nodes in order involves iterating over them using xsl:for-each, with an xsl:sort to sort the nodes. Remember that the nodes are numerical, so the data-type attribute on xsl:sort needs to be number. The following template takes the nodes as a $nodes parameter. It calculates the position of the middle node in the set by taking the ceiling of the number of nodes in the node set divided by two. It cycles through all the nodes in order, and only gives a value for the one that's positioned in the middle of this sorted list.

```
<xsl:template name="median">
   <xsl:param name="nodes" select="/.." />
   <xsl:variable name="midpoint"
                 select="ceiling(count($nodes) div 2)" />
   <xsl:for-each select="$nodes">
      <xsl:sort data-type="number" />
      <xsl:if test="position() = $middle">
         <xsl:value-of select="." />
      </xsl:if>
   </xsl:for-each>
</xsl:template>
```

Actually, getting the median is a little more complicated than this. If the number of nodes is even, you need the mean of the two middle nodes. You can test whether the number of nodes is even or odd by looking at the the count of nodes, mod 2:

```
<xsl:template name="median">
   <xsl:param name="nodes" select="/.." />
   <xsl:variable name="nnodes" select="count($nodes)" />
   <xsl:variable name="odd" select="$nnodes mod 2" />
   ...
</xsl:template>
```

Within the xsl:for-each you can test whether a particular node is one of the middle pair, but it's trickier to take the mean of those values. In fact, when you find the first of the pair, you have to sort the node set again to identify the second, because you are still interested in the node's position within the sorted list rather than in document order:

```
<xsl:template name="median">
   <xsl:param name="nodes" select="/.." />
   <xsl:variable name="nnodes" select="count($nodes)" />
   <xsl:variable name="odd" select="$nnodes mod 2" />
   <xsl:variable name="midpoint" select="ceiling($nnodes div 2)" />
```

```
<xsl:for-each select="$nodes">
   <xsl:sort data-type="number" />
   <xsl:if test="position() = $midpoint">
      <xsl:choose>
         <xsl:when test="$odd">
            <xsl:value-of select="." />
         </xsl:when>
         <xsl:otherwise>
            <xsl:variable name="next-value">
               <xsl:for-each select="$nodes">
                  <xsl:sort data-type="number" />
                  <xsl:if test="position() = $midpoint + 1">
                     <xsl:value-of select="." />
                  </xsl:if>
               </xsl:for-each>
            </xsl:variable>
            <xsl:value-of select="(. + $next-value) div 2" />
         </xsl:otherwise>
      </xsl:choose>
   </xsl:if>
</xsl:for-each>
</xsl:template>
```

TIP To complete this template, check that the value passed as the $nodes parameter is a node set, and that it's not empty. If it's empty, you need to return NaN.

This template relies on the various values being passed in separate nodes. If the values are held within a string, then you need to tokenize the string (see Chapter 2) and pass the resulting node set into the template.

Another approach, if you are happy to use extension functions, is to copy the middle node(s) into a new node set stored within a variable and then give the average of these nodes:

```
<xsl:template name="median">
   <xsl:param name="nodes" select="/.." />
   <xsl:variable name="nnodes" select="count($nodes)" />
   <xsl:variable name="midpoint" select="ceiling($nnodes div 2)" />
   <xsl:variable name="odd" select="$nnodes mod 2" />
   <xsl:variable name="middle-nodes-rtf">
      <xsl:for-each select="$nodes">
         <xsl:sort data-type="number" />
         <xsl:if test="($odd and position() = $midpoint) or
```

```
                           (not($odd) and (position() = $midpoint or
                                           position() = $midpoint + 1))">
            <xsl:copy-of select="." />
         </xsl:if>
      </xsl:for-each>
   </xsl:variable>
   <xsl:variable name="middle-nodes"
                 select="exsl:node-set($middle-nodes-rtf)" />
   <xsl:value-of select="sum($middle-nodes/node()) div
                         count($middle-nodes/node())" />
</xsl:template>
```

This has the advantage of only iterating through the node set once, but the disadvantage of limiting the portability of your stylesheet because you rely on an extension function.

 You can learn more about support for various `node-set()` extension functions in Chapter 18.

Calculating the Mode

The mode of a set of values is the value that appears most often within that set. The values don't have to be numbers; indeed, usually it makes more sense to get the mode of something if they're not numbers. For example, you could try to get the mode of a set of transaction types. Which occurs most frequently: withdrawals, direct debits, standing orders, or credits to the account? Of course, it might be that two or more values occur the same number of times, so there might be more than one mode. Because of this, a template that gives the mode needs to return a result tree fragment rather than a single value.

The mode(s) of a set of values are those values that occur more frequently than any other value. Working out which values these are is similar to calculating the maximum of a set of values. Take the following set of transactions as an example:

```
<transaction date="2001-03-01" type="DD">8.91</transaction>
<transaction date="2001-03-01" type="DD">22.00</transaction>
<transaction date="2001-03-03" type="CR">400.00</transaction>
<transaction date="2001-03-09" type="SO">633.00</transaction>
<transaction date="2001-03-10" type="WD">50.00</transaction>
<transaction date="2001-03-15" type="CR">0.58</transaction>
```

The most common types of transactions are direct debits and credits — there are two of each of them. You can work out the modes in two steps. Firstly, you need to find the maximum number of times that any value appears, which you can do by finding the maximum "value" of the transactions, where a transaction's "value" is the number of transactions of that type. There's no function to get the maximum value in a node set, let alone when that value is calculated dynamically, so you need to call a utility template to do it for you. The following code shows a call to a template named max which takes a $nodes parameter holding the nodes:

```
<xsl:template name="mode">
   <xsl:param name="transactions" select="/.." />
   <xsl:variable name="max">
      <xsl:call-template name="max">
         <xsl:with-param name="nodes" select="$transactions" />
      </xsl:call-template>
   </xsl:variable>
   ...
</xsl:template>
```

I discuss the details of how the max utility template works in the next section. To work out the "value" of each node, it applies templates to the node in max-value mode. By default, applying templates in this mode gives the numerical value of the node, but in this case you want it to return the count of the transactions that have the same type as the current transaction. The max-value mode template looks as follows:

```
<xsl:template match="transaction" mode="max-value">
   <xsl:value-of select="count(../transaction[@type = current()/@type])" />
</xsl:template>
```

The second step is to find those transactions types that occur that number of times. However, there will be more than one transaction element of each of these types. You want only the unique ones — the first transaction element that appears in the list with that particular type. You can do this by checking whether there are any preceding siblings of the transaction element that have the same type. If there are, then it's not the first of that type, but if there aren't, then it is. The final template looks like the following:

```
<xsl:template name="mode">
   <xsl:param name="transactions" select="/.." />
   <xsl:variable name="max">
      <xsl:call-template name="max">
         <xsl:with-param name="nodes" select="$transactions" />
      </xsl:call-template>
   </xsl:variable>
   <xsl:for-each
     select="$transactions[not(preceding-sibling::transaction/@type = @type)]">
      <xsl:if test="count($transactions[@type = current()/@type]) = $max">
```

```
            <xsl:apply-templates select="." mode="mode-result" />
        </xsl:if>
    </xsl:for-each>
</xsl:template>
```

The preceding template applies templates in mode-result mode to the modes in the transaction list; the template in that mode could output any level of detail about the relevant transactions.

This template is tied very closely to the structure of the data that's used because of the requirement to identify the first node with a particular value within the set, and to identify those nodes that have a "value" that occurs a certain number of times. A more general template could assume that the "value" of a node was its string value, and that all the nodes passed were siblings. This general template would look as follows:

```
<xsl:template name="mode">
    <xsl:param name="nodes" select="/.." />
    <xsl:variable name="max">
        <xsl:call-template name="max">
            <xsl:with-param name="nodes" select="$nodes" />
        </xsl:call-template>
    </xsl:variable>
    <xsl:for-each select="$nodes[not(preceding-sibling::node = .)]">
        <xsl:if test="count($nodes[. = current()]) = $max">
            <xsl:apply-templates select="." mode="mode-result" />
        </xsl:if>
    </xsl:for-each>
</xsl:template>
```

Finding Minima and Maxima

There are three main ways of finding minima and maxima using XSLT:

1. With an XPath expression

2. By sorting and picking

3. By recursion

There is a fourth way of calculating minima and maxima — using an extension function. Chapter 18 describes the various extension functions for calculating minima and maxima.

Finding Minima and Maxima with an Expression

You can find the set of nodes that have a minimum value by choosing all the nodes for which there are no nodes with a value less than their value. This translates to the location path:

```
$nodes[not($nodes &lt; .)]
```

Similarly, you can find the set of nodes that have the maximum value by choosing those nodes for which there are no nodes with a value *more than* its value:

```
$nodes[not($nodes > .)]
```

These paths give all the nodes with the minimum or maximum value. These node sets can be converted to a number using the number() function to give the minimum or maximum; both give the result NaN if there are no nodes in the node set or if the node set contains a node with a non-numerical value.

There are two problems with this solution. The first is that you can't use it to get the minimum value of a node if the "value" of the node is something that's calculated dynamically, for example the currency-converted values of the transaction elements that you saw earlier in the chapter.

You can get around this limitation by creating an intermediate node set to hold the calculated values of the nodes before finding their minimum or maximum. However, doing so involves using one of the node-set() extension functions, which are discussed in Chapter 18.

The second problem is that the larger the set of nodes, the more inefficient the expression becomes. Each time the expression is processed, each node is visited once for each node in the set. If there are two nodes there are four visits, if there are three nodes there are nine visits, and so on. More sophisticated processors might optimize expressions like these so that they actually use a more efficient algorithm, but it's best not to rely on that.

Finding Minima and Maxima by Sorting and Picking

A second way of finding minimum and maximum values is to sort the list of values according to their value (in ascending order to get the minimum and descending order to get the maximum) and then pick the first of the nodes from this sorted list. So, to get the minimum, you would use the following:

```
<xsl:for-each select="$nodes">
   <xsl:sort data-type="number" />
   <xsl:if test="position() = 1">
      <xsl:value-of select="." />
   </xsl:if>
</xsl:for-each>
```

And to get the maximum, you would use the following:

```
<xsl:for-each select="$nodes">
   <xsl:sort data-type="number" select="descending" />
   <xsl:if test="position() = 1">
      <xsl:value-of select="." />
   </xsl:if>
</xsl:for-each>
```

 These both give no value if there aren't any nodes in $nodes; converting that to a number will give the value NaN. Non-numerical values are sorted before numerical values in ascending order and after numerical values in descending order, so the xsl:for-each to get the minimum will give NaN if the node set contains a non-numerical value, whereas the xsl:for-each to get the maximum will give the maximum of the numerical values.

To a certain extent, the sort-and-select method counters the disadvantages of just using an XPath. As long as you can calculate the value of a node within an XPath, you can use this method to get it. For example, you can use this method to find the largest debit from a bank account, taking into account the conversion between dollars and pounds:

```
<xsl:for-each select="transaction[@type != 'CR']">
   <xsl:sort select=". * (1 - (@currency = 'USD') * 0.4)"
             data-type="number" select="descending" />
   <xsl:if test="position() = 1">
      <xsl:value-of select=". * (1 - (@currency = 'USD') * 0.4)" />
```

```
    </xsl:if>
</xsl:for-each>
```

As you can see, this is one of the places where the conditional XPaths discussed at the end of Chapter 3 come into their own.

The sort-and-select method also has the advantage over the XPath expression method in terms of its efficiency as the number of nodes that it involves increases. The processor is likely to have a good method of sorting nodes built into it, so this leads to better performance overall. However, it's still not perfect — it's likely that some nodes will be visited more than once during the sort.

Unlike in a procedural programming language, it is impossible to break out of an xsl:for-each. The body of the xsl:for-each will be processed for each of the nodes in the node set; there's no way to stop after the first one.

Finding Minima and Maxima by Recursion

The final method for finding minimum and maximum nodes is by recursing through the node set. This template keeps track of the minimum value found so far, and this is returned if there are no nodes left in the node set. Otherwise, the template recurses with the $minimum parameter holding the value of the first node in the node set if it's less than the minimum so far, or the minimum so far if not. So, you can get the minimum value with the following:

```
<xsl:template name="min">
   <xsl:param name="nodes" select="/.." />
   <xsl:param name="minimum" select="number(NaN)" />
   <xsl:choose>
      <xsl:when test="not($nodes)">
         <xsl:value-of select="$minimum" />
      </xsl:when>
      <xsl:otherwise>
         <xsl:variable name="value-of-first">
            <xsl:apply-templates select="$nodes[1]" mode="min-value" />
         </xsl:variable>
         <xsl:call-template name="min">
            <xsl:with-param name="nodes" select="$nodes[position() > 1]" />
```

```
      <xsl:with-param name="minimum">
        <xsl:choose>
          <xsl:when test="$value-of-first &lt; $minimum or
                          string($minimum) = 'NaN'">
            <xsl:value-of select="$value-of-first" />
          </xsl:when>
          <xsl:otherwise>
            <xsl:value-of select="$minimum" />
          </xsl:otherwise>
        </xsl:choose>
      </xsl:with-param>
    </xsl:call-template>
  </xsl:otherwise>
</xsl:choose>
</xsl:template>

<xsl:template match="node()|@*" mode="min-value">
  <xsl:value-of select="." />
</xsl:template>
```

and use similar templates to get the maximum value of the node set.

To finalize this template, you should check that the value being passed for the $nodes parameter is actually a node set, and generate an error if it isn't. You should also add checks to make sure that the nodes have numerical values. Chapter 13 discusses how to carry out these tests and design robust utility templates.

This recursive approach builds on the advantages of the preceding sort-and-select approach. You can calculate the value for the node in whatever way you like. In the previous template, you apply templates to the node in min-value mode so that the stylesheet author using the template can add his or her own template for a particular node type that calculates the value of that node. So for example, you could use the following template to give the value for a transaction:

```
<xsl:template match="transaction" mode="min-value">
  <xsl:variable name="converted-value">
    <xsl:choose>
      <xsl:when test="@currency = 'USD'">
        <xsl:value-of select=". * 0.6" />
      </xsl:when>
      <xsl:otherwise><xsl:value-of select="." /></xsl:otherwise>
```

```
        </xsl:choose>
    </xsl:variable>
    <xsl:choose>
        <xsl:when test="@type = 'CR'">
            <xsl:value-of select="$converted-value" />
        </xsl:when>
        <xsl:otherwise>
            <xsl:value-of select="-$converted-value" />
        </xsl:otherwise>
    </xsl:choose>
</xsl:template>
```

In addition, this is the most efficient way of calculating the minimum or maximum of a node set because each node is visited only once. So for large node sets, using this approach will often be a lot faster and use less memory than the other two approaches.

The big disadvantage of the preceding template is that it is very deeply recursive – the recursive depth of the template is equal to the number of nodes in the node set. If you are using a processor that doesn't optimize tail recursion then you could reduce the depth of the recursion by changing the template so that it splits the node set in two each time, and compares the minima for the two halves:

```
<xsl:template name="min">
    <xsl:param name="nodes" select="/.." />
    <xsl:variable name="nnodes" select="count($nodes)" />
    <xsl:choose>
        <xsl:when test="$nnodes &lt;= 1">
            <xsl:apply-templates select="$nodes[1]" mode="min-value" />
        </xsl:when>
        <xsl:otherwise>
            <xsl:variable name="midpoint" select="$nnodes div 2" />
            <xsl:variable name="min-of-first-half">
                <xsl:call-template name="min">
                    <xsl:with-param name="nodes"
                                    select="$nodes[position() &lt;= $midpoint]" />
                </xsl:call-template>
            </xsl:variable>
            <xsl:variable name="min-of-second-half">
                <xsl:call-template name="min">
                    <xsl:with-param name="nodes"
                                    select="$nodes[position() > $midpoint]" />
                </xsl:call-template>
            </xsl:variable>
            <xsl:choose>
                <xsl:when test="$min-of-first-half &lt; $min-of-second-half">
```

```
                <xsl:value-of select="$min-of-first-half" />
            </xsl:when>
            <xsl:otherwise>
              <xsl:value-of select="$min-of-second-half" />
            </xsl:otherwise>
          </xsl:choose>
      </xsl:otherwise>
    </xsl:choose>
</xsl:template>
```

Another approach is to recurse through the nodes individually, moving from one node to the next node that has a lower value. If you assume that the nodes are siblings, moving from one node to the next simply involves finding the immediately following sibling that has a lower value than the current one:

```
<xsl:template match="node()" mode="min">
    <xsl:variable name="value" select="." />
    <xsl:variable name="next"
                  select="following-sibling::node()[. &lt; $value][1]" />
    <xsl:choose>
      <xsl:when test="$next">
        <xsl:apply-templates select="$next" mode="min" />
      </xsl:when>
      <xsl:otherwise><xsl:value-of select="$value" /></xsl:otherwise>
    </xsl:choose>
</xsl:template>
```

Like the other recursive templates, this template is more efficient than using the sort-and-select method because it will only visit each node once, at least in processors that optimize location paths that use a positional parameter. These processors stop searching when they find the node with that position. So in the preceding template, an optimized processor will stop once it finds the first node with a value less than the value of the current node.

The recursive depth of finding the minimum with this template depends on the ordering of the nodes in the source. If the nodes are ordered in descending order, such that the minimum is the last node, the recursive depth will be equal to the number of nodes. On the other hand, if they are ordered in ascending order, there will be no recursion at all. So this method can be better than the other recursive templates, unless you're unlucky with the ordering of the source XML.

The disadvantage of this method, as with the sort-and-select method, is that you can only use it if the values for the nodes can be calculated with a single XPath. A similar template that always gets the value of the next node can be used instead, but the template will suffer from being deeply recursive as it always visits every node in the list:

```
<xsl:template match="node()" mode="min">
   <xsl:variable name="value">
      <xsl:apply-templates select="." mode="min-value" />
   </xsl:variable>
   <xsl:variable name="next" select="following-sibling::node()[1]" />
   <xsl:choose>
      <xsl:when test="$next">
         <xsl:variable name="min-of-rest">
            <xsl:apply-templates select="$next" mode="min" />
         </xsl:variable>
         <xsl:choose>
            <xsl:when test="$value &lt; $min-of-rest">
               <xsl:value-of select="$value" />
            </xsl:when>
            <xsl:otherwise>
               <xsl:value-of select="$min-of-rest" />
            </xsl:otherwise>
         </xsl:choose>
      </xsl:when>
      <xsl:otherwise><xsl:value-of select="$value" /></xsl:otherwise>
   </xsl:choose>
</xsl:template>
```

Basically, it comes down to first choosing the methods that make it *possible* for you to calculate the minima or maxima that you need to calculate and then, from that set of methods, choosing the method that is most efficient on your particular platform, with your particular processor and with your particular source XML. There isn't a one-size-fits-all solution – it might be that you're using a processor that optimizes tail recursion and the depth of recursion therefore doesn't matter. Or it might be that you have so few nodes that a recursive template is overkill and you are happy using a simple select-and-sort method. You have to try the various methods and then choose the one that works best in the particular situation.

 The various `min` templates can easily be altered to become a `max` template instead, by using greater-than rather than less-than.

Summary

In this chapter, you learned various ways to analyze the data within your source XML. You looked at two ways of getting totals when `sum()` can't cut it – building an intermediate node set to use `sum()` on, or summing using recursion. I discussed how to count items in a string, whether they're separated by character delimiters or by words. I examined how to calculate averages, focusing on the difficult averages — medians and modes. Finally, I looked at three ways of calculating minima and maxima: through an XPath expression, with a sort-and-select method, and using recursion.

During the course of this chapter, I developed several utility templates:

◆ `sum` — Sums calculated values with a sum mode template as a helper

◆ `sum-string` — Sums the values in a string that are separated by a delimiter

◆ `count-items` — Counts the number of items, separated by a delimiter, in a string

◆ `median` — Calculates the median value of a set of nodes

◆ `mode` — Calculates the mode value of a set of sibling nodes

◆ `min` — Calculates the minimum value of a set of nodes

You actually saw several implementations of the `min` template, each of which had different properties. Which one is most appropriate depends on your requirements.

Part II

Performing Your Transformation

Chapter 5

Filtering XML

IN THIS CHAPTER, I look at one of the basic types of transformation that you might want to perform: filtering. I start off by looking at the basic principles of doing filtering transformations in XSLT, and look particularly at filtering based on subsections within the document, the namespaces that elements take and the languages assigned to the elements in multilingual documents.

The chapter then goes on to describe some of the ways of carrying out multiple transformations in sequence. Multi-pass transformations can be very useful in simplifying a complex transformation by decomposing it into a number of easy steps, for example calculating a total based on computed values by computing the values in the first step and summing in the second. Sequential transformations are often particularly useful when filtering XML, either filtering on different properties on different steps or filtering first to make consequent transformation more straightforward.

Filtering Principles

Basically, filtering XML involves copying some parts of its structure and content and leaving out others. Filtering doesn't involve restructuring anything, so it's best to use the *push* method – let the source XML drive the transformation, apply templates to everything and use template matches to determine what to do with particular parts of the XML.

If you're doing push transformations, you'll often want to filter out white-space-only text nodes and get the processor to indent the result nicely, so that the XML you get as an output is easy to read:

```
<xsl:output indent="yes" />
<xsl:strip-space elements="*" />
```

Basic Templates

The basis for filtering transformations is the identity transformation, which simply copies everything. There are several combinations of templates that you can use to perform an identity transformation, but the simplest is the one found in the XSLT Recommendation. This matches all kinds of nodes, including attribute nodes, copies the matched node using xsl:copy and adds content by applying templates to the attributes and children of the node recursively:

```
<xsl:template match="@*|node()">
  <xsl:copy>
    <xsl:apply-templates select="@*|node()"/>
  </xsl:copy>
</xsl:template>
```

However, there are two general types of filtering transformations:

1. **Filtering out:** Copy most things, but leave out specific parts

2. **Filtering in:** Leave out most things, but copy specific parts

Of course filters can be described in both ways, but often they lean toward one pole or the other. If you are filtering things out of the source XML, the identity transformation should be the default template that you use, and the specific parts to be filtered out should be matched by templates that don't copy the node, but do go on to try to process its children:

```
<xsl:template match="excluded-nodes">
   <xsl:apply-templates />
</xsl:template>
```

On the other hand, if you're generally ignoring everything but the parts you're interested in, you should use an adapted version of the built-in templates as the default (they need to be adapted so that the values of text nodes don't appear in your output):

Filtering with SAX Filters

With transformations as simple as filtering, it's arguable whether XSLT is the best tool for the job. Filters don't require large changes to the ordering or structure of documents, and they seldom require information involving the structure of the source XML, such as the ancestry or (more importantly) children of elements.

Generally, filtering should occur as soon as possible within the overall process. If the information that you're dealing with is held within a database and then serialized into XML for processing, then rather than filtering the XML that comes out of the database, you should filter the data that goes into the XML. Of course there's a balance to be made here — it might be that the XML is used in lots of different ways, such that in the long run it's worthwhile retrieving a lot of information from the database in one fell swoop rather than having multiple transactions with it.

If the data held in your XML isn't held within a database or you can't make the database give you only the information you need, you could use a SAX filter instead. SAX is the Simple API for XML, an event-based API that's used by the vast majority of XML parsers, especially those written in Java. A SAX filter catches the events generated by a SAX `XMLReader` when it parses an XML document. The `XMLReader` is known as the SAX filter's *parent*. The SAX filter generates its own events based on the ones that it catches. As far as the parent is concerned, it looks like an application; as far as the application is concerned, it looks like a parser.

The Java version of SAX2 holds an interface — `org.xml.sax.XMLFilter` — and a new helper class — `org.xml.sax.XMLFilterImpl` — that you can use to create these filters. If you use `org.xml.sax.XMLFilterImpl` as a basis, all you need to do is add methods for the events that you're interested in, calling the superclass's method with altered arguments or using an empty method to completely filter out the event. Have a look at `http://www.megginson.com/SAX/Java/filters.html` to learn more.

You can plug multiple SAX filters into each other to do multiple filters: each one acts as the parent of another. You *can* use SAX filters to implement multiple filters, each of which is an XSLT transformation. If you are using TrAX, the Transformation API for XML, `javax.xml.transform.sax.SAXTransformerFactory` provides `newXMLFilter` methods to create SAX filters from XSLT stylesheets. Visit `http://xml.apache.org/xalan-j/apidocs/javax/xml/transform/sax/SAXTransformerFactory.html` for more information.

```
<xsl:template match="@*|node()">
   <xsl:apply-templates />
</xsl:template>
```

And then use the identity template to match the parts that you are interested in:

```
<xsl:template match="included-nodes">
  <xsl:copy>
    <xsl:apply-templates select="@*|node()"/>
  </xsl:copy>
</xsl:template>
```

Isolating the included or excluded nodes simply involves writing patterns that match them. For example, to filter out db:id attributes, you could use:

```
<xsl:template match="@db:id" />
```

 There is no point in applying templates to the content of an attribute — attributes only have a value, not content.

Filtering Sections

If you're filtering particular sections in or out, you can use the basic templates outlined previously, and have templates that match the section and all its descendants. For example, to filter out a section with the ID 'details', you could use the general identity template as a default, and then have the following:

```
<xsl:template match="id('details') | id('details')//node()">
  <xsl:apply-templates />
</xsl:template>
```

Actually, this just creates more work for the processor – it has to work through the descendants of the section, applying templates to each of them. Instead, you should just use an empty template to filter out the section as a whole:

```
<xsl:template match="id('details')" />
```

Similarly, while you could ensure that you copied the section with the following recursive template, based on the identity template:

```
<xsl:template match="id('details') | id('details')//node() | id('details')//@*">
  <xsl:copy>
    <xsl:apply-templates select="@*|node()" />
  </xsl:copy>
</xsl:template>
```

you may as well copy the entire section in one go when you find it, using `xsl:copy-of` to create a deep copy rather than recursing down the tree, as follows:

```
<xsl:template match="id('details')">
   <xsl:copy-of select="." />
</xsl:template>
```

Even better is to select a section that you want to filter in as high up the stylesheet as you can. If the only thing that should be copied to the output is that particular section, it would be better to use the following template:

```
<xsl:template match="/*">
   <xsl:copy-of select="id('details')" />
</xsl:template>
```

This would avoid any recursion whatsoever – the processor can just go straight to the section and copy it. This method is a *pull* method, though – the stylesheet drives the process.

The push and pull methods are discussed in Chapter 17.

In general, you should use a push method if you want to make the stylesheet extensible and modular or if you want to maintain ordering information from the original document. For example, if you wanted to be able to easily add other sections that you wanted to keep, in the order that they appear in the original, you should use a template to copy it.

Filtering Namespaces

One property that is frequently used to filter an XML document is the namespace of the elements and attributes being copied. For example, in your bank account application, the XML for the transactions actually includes meta information for the transactions that is only relevant to the bank and shouldn't be seen by the customer:

```
<transactions>
   <bank:rate-change old="1.32" new="1.17" />
   <transaction bank:ref="4325636767" type="DD"
               currency="GBP">13.99</transaction>
   <transaction bank:ref="7854926664" type="CR"
               currency="USD">125.00</transaction>
```

```
<transaction bank:ref="0324638846" type="WD"
             currency="GBP">50.00</transaction>
...
</transactions>
```

The filtering operation needs to filter out anything within the bank's namespace. With a default identity template that copies nodes, you need only an empty template that matches attributes and elements in the bank's namespace and does nothing with them:

```
<xsl:template match="bank:*|@bank:*" />
```

It's not an issue in this example, but in similar situations you may have elements in a namespace that you're *not* interested in containing information that you *are* interested in. An empty template, as in the preceding example, disregards both the element itself and all its content. If instead you want to process the content, you need a template that applies templates to its child nodes, as follows:

```
<xsl:template match="bank:*|@bank:*">
  <xsl:apply-templates />
</xsl:template>
```

This template matches attributes in the bank's namespace. They don't have any content, so effectively they are ignored. If you prefer, you could have a separate empty template for the attributes as follows:

```
<xsl:template match="@bank:*" />
```

Filtering Languages

In multilingual applications, you often need to filter a particular set of information so that it contains only text in a particular language. Usually the language that you want to filter by is passed into the stylesheet as a parameter:

```
<xsl:param name="lang" select="'en'" />
```

As the default is to ignore information, the obvious thing to do is to have a default template matching all nodes, which simply applies templates to its content (in case it contains anything in a different language), and to have an exception template that matches those nodes that are in the desired language (as revealed through the lang() function):

```
<xsl:template match="node()[lang($lang)]|@*[lang($lang)]">
  <xsl:copy>
```

```
      <xsl:apply-templates select="@*|node()" />
   </xsl:copy>
</xsl:template>
```

However, you cannot use parameter or variable references (such as `$lang`) within the `match` attribute of `xsl:template`. Parameter and variable references are banned here to prevent circular references, in which the value of a variable or parameter is determined by applying templates but which templates are applied relies on the value of the variable or parameter. Similarly, they're banned from the `match` and `use` attributes of `xsl:key` to prevent circular references in which the value of the variable or parameter is determined using the key, but the value of the key relies on the value of the variable or parameter.

Instead, then, you need to have a template that matches all nodes but only copies those that are in the required language:

```
<xsl:template match="node()|@*">
   <xsl:choose>
      <xsl:when test="lang($lang)">
         <xsl:copy>
            <xsl:apply-templates select="@*|node()" />
         </xsl:copy>
      </xsl:when>
      <xsl:otherwise>
         <xsl:apply-templates />
      </xsl:otherwise>
   </xsl:choose>
</xsl:template>
```

You may also run into other complications. For example, your source XML may have an implicit default language that isn't declared as a default language using the `xml:lang` attribute. Alternatively, you may be in a situation where nodes that are in no particular language should be always copied. The `lang()` function will return false for nodes whose language is unspecified, just as it would if they were in a different language. In these cases, you need to test whether no ancestor element has an `xml:lang` attribute, as in the following expression:

```
lang($lang) or not(ancestor-or-self::*/@xml:lang)
```

Multiple Filters

Filtering XML is often the first step in a transformation – the result of the filtering process then becomes the input to the next transformation step, which might be another filter or one of the more complex transformations that you will encounter in this part of the book.

You can link filtering transformations together, either by managing the filters through a central stylesheet or by running each stylesheet on the output of a previous transformation. How you do the latter depends on the XSLT processor you're using and whether you are running it from the command line, or through scripting or code.

Multiple Transformations in a Single Stylesheet

Every transformation in XSLT produces a result tree fragment. When you control multiple transformations from a single stylesheet, you need to be able to handle these result tree fragments as if they were node sets, so that they can become the source of the next transformation. You can use a `node-set()` extension function to do this, or you can use a processor that implements the XSLT 1.1 working draft. In either case, however, you create a stylesheet that is tied to the particular processor that you're using, which may limit you in the future.

The various `node-set()` extension functions are detailed in Chapter 18.

To manage the multiple filters within one stylesheet, you need to incorporate the various filtering stylesheets into one XSLT application. Basically you add a distinct mode to the templates in each stylesheet and then import all the stylesheets into the main stylesheet for the transformation.

For more detail about how to do this, see Chapter 13.

For example, you might have two filtering transformations for the bank account application – one that filters out debits to the account, and one that filters out transactions in pounds. If you combine them in sequence, you can get hold of only those transactions that involve debits to foreign companies. In the main stylesheet, import the two filtering stylesheets:

```
<xsl:stylesheet version="1.0"
                 xmlns:xsl="http://www.w3.org/1999/XSL/Transform" />

<xsl:import href="debits.xsl" />
<xsl:import href="foreign.xsl" />
...

</xsl:stylesheet>
```

You can then have a main template that controls the transformation. You want to filter in the debits first – apply templates in debit mode. Then you want to take the result of this transformation (captured in a variable), convert it to a node set, and use it to filter in the foreign transactions – apply templates in foreign mode:

```
<xsl:template match="/">
  <xsl:variable name="debits">
    <xsl:apply-templates select="." mode="debit" />
  </xsl:variable>
  <xsl:apply-templates select="exsl:node-set($debits)"
                       mode="foreign" />
</xsl:template>
```

Doing multiple transformations within a single stylesheet has its downsides. It's a fair amount of work to merge stylesheets into a single application, especially if they override shared utility templates. Also, the memory consumption may be higher because all the transformations are happening within a single process. Sometimes, therefore, you may want to run the separate stylesheets in sequence.

Multiple Transformations Through the Command Line

Some XSLT processors can be run from the command line, and accept input from stdin. With these processors, you can use pipes to direct the output of one transformation as the input to the next. For example, with the command line version of the Microsoft XSLT processor, MSXML, you could run debits.xsl on my account.xml, and then pipe the output of this into a transformation as the input to foreign.xsl to generate the output in foreign-debits.xml with the following:

```
msxsl account.xml debits.xsl | msxsl - foreign.xsl -o foreign-debits.xml
```

Other processors insist that the source XML is held in a file. For these, you have to use an intermediate file:

```
saxon -o debits.xml account.xml debits.xsl
saxon -o foreign-debits.xml debits.xml foreign.xsl
```

Using an intermediate file does have some advantages in that you can examine the intermediate step if you need to debug the process.

Multiple Transformations with Cocoon

Cocoon is a server-side framework that can help you manage XSLT processing. Within Cocoon, you can pipe transformations by adding processing instructions to the output of the first transformation, telling Cocoon to continue processing it.

See Chapter 15 for a detailed discussion of Cocoon.

As mentioned earlier in this chapter, an alternative method of managing sequential server-side transformations is to use SAX Filters built from stylesheets.

In the bank statement example from the last section, for instance, you could add processing instructions to the top-level template in `debits.xsl` that generate two processing instructions: an `xml-stylesheet` processing instruction that links the output to the stylesheet managing the next stage in the transformation (`foreign.xsl`), and a `cocoon-process` processing instruction that indicates that the file should be processed with the Cocoon XSLT processor:

```
<xsl:template match="/">
   <xsl:processing-instruction name="xml-stylesheet">
     <xsl:text>type="text/xsl" href="foreign.xsl"</xsl:text>
   </xsl:processing-instruction>
   <xsl:processing-instruction name="cocoon-process">
     <xsl:text>type="xslt"</xsl:text>
   </xsl:processing-instruction>
   <xsl:apply-templates />
</xsl:template>
```

When Cocoon transforms `account.xml` with `debits.xsl`, the resulting XML holds the processing instructions:

```
<?xml-stylesheet type="text/xsl" href="foreign.xsl"?>
<?cocoon-process type="xslt"?>
```

Cocoon processes this file according to the instructions, running `foreign.xsl` to produce the double filtering that you're after.

The big problem with this approach is that the filters aren't independent — each filter points to the next one explicitly. If you have lots of filters and want each series to use different ones you can get around this by making a controller stylesheet and passing information about each step using processing instructions.

Within the individual filters, have the top-level template create processing instructions that tell Cocoon to process the output with the controller stylesheet, and add a processing instruction indicating the name of the filter. For example, in `debits.xsl` you use:

```
<xsl:template match="/">
   <xsl:processing-instruction name="xml-stylesheet">
      <xsl:text>type="text/xsl" href="controller.xsl"</xsl:text>
   </xsl:processing-instruction>
   <xsl:processing-instruction name="cocoon-process">
      <xsl:text>type="xslt"</xsl:text>
   </xsl:processing-instruction>
   <xsl:processing-instruction name="applied-filter">
      <xsl:text>debits.xsl</xsl:text>
   </xsl:processing-instruction>
   <xsl:apply-templates />
</xsl:template>
```

The source XML is processed by the controller stylesheet. If the controller stylesheet doesn't find an `applied-filter` processing instruction, it means that it is processing the original source XML. The controller stylesheet knows that the first stylesheet to be applied is the first filter (`details.xsl`). If it does find an `applied-filter` processing instruction, it can use the value of the processing instruction to work out which filter should be applied next, if one should be applied at all. The template for this example is as follows:

```
<xsl:template match="/">
   <xsl:choose>
      <!-- foreign.xsl is the last filter -->
      <xsl:when test="processing-instruction('applied-filter') =
                  'foreign.xsl'" />
      <xsl:otherwise>
         <xsl:processing-instruction name="xml-stylesheet">
            <xsl:text>type="text/xsl" href="</xsl:text>
            <xsl:choose>
               <!-- details.xsl adds the applied-filter processing instruction,
                  so foreign.xsl must be next -->
               <xsl:when test="processing-instruction('applied-filter')">
                  <xsl:text>foreign.xsl</xsl:text>
```

```
        </xsl:when>
        <!-- no applied-filter processing instruction, so must be the
             source XML - apply debits.xsl -->
        <xsl:otherwise>debits.xsl</xsl:otherwise>
      </xsl:choose>
      <xsl:text>"</xsl:text>
    </xsl:processing-instruction>
    <xsl:processing-instruction name="cocoon-process">
      <xsl:text>type="xslt"</xsl:text>
    </xsl:processing-instruction>
  </xsl:otherwise>
</xsl:choose>
<xsl:copy-of select="*" />
</xsl:template>
```

TIP   If you were doing this a lot, you might find it helpful to draw out the information about the series of transformations that should be used into an XML structure and use this structure to determine which transformation should occur after which.

Multiple Transformations with MSXML

You can use a script to do multiple transformations using MSXML by storing the output of the first transformation within a DOM that you then use as the input of the next transformation. In this case, the relevant code would be as follows (assuming that `accountDOM`, `debitsXSLTDOM` and `foreignXSLTDOM` hold the `DOMDocument` objects generated from `account.xml`, `debits.xsl` and `foreign.xsl` respectively):

```
try {
   // get a processor to apply debits.xsl to account.xml
   debitsTemplate = new ActiveXObject('Msxml2.XSLTemplate');
   debitsTemplate.stylesheet = debitsXSLTDOM;
   debitsFilter = debitsTemplate.createProcessor();
   debitsFilter.input = accountDOM;
   // create an empty DOM to hold the output of the transformation
   debitsDOM = new ActiveXObject('Msxml2.DOMDocument');
   debitsFilter.output = debitsDOM;
   debitsFilter.transform();
   // create a processor to apply foreign.xsl to the output of the
   // previous transformation
   foreignTemplate = new ActiveXObject('Msxml2.XSLTemplate');
   foreignTemplate.stylesheet = foreignXSLTDOM;
   foreignFilter = foreignTemplate.createProcessor();
```

```
    foreignFilter.input = debitsDOM;
    foreignFilter.transform();
    // write the result to the page
    document.open();
    document.write(foreignFilter.output);
    document.close();
} catch (exception) {
    alert('Error creating processor:\n' + exception.description);
    return;
}
```

 For details about scripting with MSXML, see Chapter 14.

In general, multiple transformations, especially involving filtering, should be avoided if you're using client-side processing. You should avoid sending more information to the client than is absolutely necessary because it takes up bandwidth and slows down the rate at which the end user sees the information you want them to see. Usually it's best to filter XML on the server side, send the client the filtered XML, and let it apply the final transformation to display it.

Summary

In this chapter, I've briefly examined how to do one of the most basic transformations — a filter. In fact, you're usually better off filtering XML at an early stage than using XSLT to do it — if the information is held in a database, you should try to access only the information that you need; otherwise, you should probably use a SAX filter to filter the XML.

Nevertheless, XSLT can be used to filter XML on any property of the XML you like through templates using a push transformation based on the identity transformation. How you arrange the templates depends on whether you are filtering information in or out. Either way, you have to design match patterns for the XML you want to filter in or out. The most common of these are matches by whole sections (which are usually best approached through pull rather than push), matches by namespace, and matches by language (which are complicated by the fact that XSLT doesn't allow variable or parameter references in the `match` attribute of `xsl:template`).

Filters are frequently used in combination. You've seen how to manage these in detail in four ways:

◆ Within a stylesheet built of a number of filtering stylesheets

◆ Through a pipe command line or a series of command lines

◆ Using Cocoon to process the output of previous filters

◆ Scripting MSXML to hold the result of a filter in a DOM, then using it as the source for the next transformation

You can also use a series of SAX filters created from stylesheets, if you're comfortable programming with Java.

Chapter 6

Translating Between Similar Structures

IN THIS CHAPTER

- ◆ Translating element and attribute names
- ◆ Changing element substructures
- ◆ Adding attributes
- ◆ Adding styling information
- ◆ Debugging translations

IN THIS CHAPTER, I look at how to manage transformations between similar kinds of XML structures — I call these *translations*.

XML vocabularies can be roughly categorized into data-oriented XML and document-oriented XML. The goal of data-oriented XML is to store data and it often has a structure similar to (or perhaps even derived from) a database. Data-oriented XML documents tend to contain element-only and text-only content in a regimented structure, with the vocabulary itself depending on the domain of the information it holds. The goal of document-oriented XML is to hold textual information. Document-oriented XML documents tend to contain mixed content in a loose structure, using general vocabularies for document structures such as DocBook or HTML.

Of course there isn't a strict division between the two — data-oriented XML often contains islands of document-oriented XML, giving natural language descriptions for example, and similarly document-oriented XML can contain data. Nevertheless, the distinction can be useful when considering which approach to take in an XSLT stylesheet.

In this chapter, I look at translations from data to data and from document to document. Data-to-data translations typically occur in business-to-business transactions when changing from your internal XML vocabulary into a partner organization's XML vocabulary. Document-to-document translations typically occur when moving some textual information into a presentation vocabulary such as HTML or XSL-FO.

Typically, these translations involve translating element and attribute names, changing element substructures, adding attributes, and adding styling information.

119

In this chapter I examine how to address each of these translations and how to add information that may help debug translations.

Translating Element and Attribute Names

The basic translation between similar structures is a straightforward copy from one to the other. This is a *push* transformation, where the structure of the result is dependent on the structure of the source XML. The default template to use is the identity template, which recursively copies the structure of the source XML to the result:

```
<xsl:template match="@*|node()">
   <xsl:copy>
      <xsl:apply-templates select="@*|node()" />
   </xsl:copy>
</xsl:template>
```

 In Chapter 5, I looked at how to ignore elements and attributes, effectively deleting them, through filtering transformations that were based on this same template.

With translations, the elements and attributes need to be changed. However, remember that XSLT transformations aren't about altering a single node tree; they're about mapping from one node tree (the source) onto another (the result). With translations, the elements and attributes in the result often follow the same pattern as the ones in the source, but they are nevertheless *new* elements and attributes. You need to create them.

Thus, you need to create a new element if you want to "change" the name of an element from the source to the result. You can create elements in three ways:

1. By copying an existing element

2. By creating a new element with a literal result element

3. By creating a new element with the xsl:element instruction

Obviously, you cannot copy an existing element if you want to change its name. If you know the name of the element that you want to create, it is easiest to use a literal result element to do so. For example, to change a para element into a p element, you can use the following template:

```
<xsl:template match="para">
   <p>
      <xsl:apply-templates select="@*|node()" />
   </p>
</xsl:template>
```

 You need to be aware of namespaces when performing this mapping. In the preceding example, the para element must be in the null namespace within the XML source as it does not have a prefix (the default namespace is ignored within XPaths). The p element, on the other hand, is created in the default namespace, which may be something different. You can change the namespaces by changing the prefixes on the match pattern and the literal result element name.

You can create attributes in a similar set of ways:

◆ Copying an existing attribute

◆ Creating a new attribute on a literal result element

◆ Creating a new attribute with the xsl:attribute instruction

In the basic architecture used here (based on recursive applications of the identity template on the attributes and children of an element), you can't create a new attribute on a literal result element because it's being created in a different template. You have to use xsl:attribute instead. For example, to change the lang attribute into an xml:lang attribute, you can use the following:

```
<xsl:template match="@lang">
   <xsl:attribute name="xml:lang">
      <xsl:value-of select="." />
   </xsl:attribute>
</xsl:template>
```

In fact, creating the attribute by applying templates is the best way to change its name because you want to create attributes only if their equivalent attribute exists in the source XML. You could fix the attribute on a literal result element, for example, with the following:

```
<xsl:template match="para">
    <p xml:lang="{@lang}">
        <xsl:apply-templates />
    </p>
</xsl:template>
```

However, if you did so, the `xml:lang` attribute would be created whether the `lang` attribute existed or not. If the `lang` attribute didn't exist, then the `xml:lang` attribute would have an empty string as a value, making the result invalid as `xml:lang` should have a language code as a value.

These techniques for changing the names of elements and attributes work fine if there are a restricted number of elements, but it is tedious to write separate templates for every single element and attribute whose name must be changed. This is especially the case when there is an underlying algorithm for translating one name into another, such as when changing the case of names.

Changing the Case of Names

Parts of XML vocabularies sometimes differ by the smallest amount, simply differing in the case that's used for element and attribute names, for example. Changing from all lowercase to all uppercase involves translating all the lowercase letters in the name into their uppercase equivalent. You can use the `translate()` function to do this:

```
translate(local-name(), $lowercase, $uppercase)
```

 You can change from lowercase into title case, where only the first letter is in uppercase, by translating only the first character in the name and concatenating this with the rest of the name:

```
concat(translate(substring(local-name(), 1, 1),
                 $lowercase, $uppercase),
       substring(local-name(), 2))
```

The definitions of the `$lowercase` and `$uppercase` variables depend on the language that you're translating. For English, the definitions can simply be:

```
<xsl:variable name="lowercase" select="'abcdefghijklmnopqrstuvwxyz'" />
<xsl:variable name="uppercase" select="'ABCDEFGHIJKLMNOPQRSTUVWXYZ'" />
```

In other languages, you need to add other characters to these variables, making sure that the lowercase version of a character is in the same position in the $lowercase variable as the uppercase version of the character is in the $uppercase variable.

In some languages, the uppercase version of a character is in fact two characters long, such as the uppercase version of ß being the two characters SS. In these cases, you need to search and replace within the string using one of the techniques discussed in Chapter 2, assign the result to a variable, and then use this to set the name of the new element.

The names of elements and attributes can be fixed dynamically if you use the xsl:element or xsl:attribute instructions with an attribute value template within the name attribute. For example, you can translate all element and attribute names into uppercase with the following templates:

```
<xsl:template match="*">
   <xsl:element name="{translate(local-name(), $lowercase, $uppercase)}">
      <xsl:apply-templates select="@*|node()" />
   </xsl:element>
</xsl:template>

<xsl:template match="@*">
   <xsl:attribute name="{translate(local-name(), $lowercase, $uppercase)}">
      <xsl:value-of select="." />
   </xsl:attribute>
</xsl:template>
```

Special care is needed with namespaces here. In the preceding templates, the new names consisted of the translated versions of the *local names* of the elements and attributes (that's everything after the colon, if they have a namespace prefix or the whole name if they don't). I haven't specified a namespace prefix in the new name, and I haven't fixed the namespace for the created nodes using the namespace attribute on xsl:element or xsl:attribute.

When elements are created like this, the element names are interpreted according to all the namespace declarations that are in effect at the point of the instruction in the stylesheet, so the elements are created in the default namespace used in the stylesheet. The attribute names, on the other hand, are interpreted according to the namespace declarations *aside from the default namespace*; since no prefix is given, they are created in the null namespace.

Changing a Node's Namespace

If you want to assign the elements (and attributes) that you create to a particular namespace, you can use a prefix within the name attribute of xsl:element (or xsl:attribute). These prefixes are interpreted according to the namespace declarations that are in effect on the XSLT instruction. For example, say you need to tidy up some HTML, making all the names lowercase and placing the new elements in the XHTML namespace. If you define the XHTML namespace on the xsl:stylesheet element, you can use the following:

```
<xsl:template match="*">
  <xsl:element name="html:{translate(local-name(), $uppercase, $lowercase)}">
    <xsl:apply-templates select="@*|node()" />
  </xsl:element>

</xsl:template>
```

The html prefix in the preceding template must be associated with the XHTML namespace within the stylesheet.

You can also use the namespace attribute to fix the namespace for the element or attribute, but this is usually much more verbose; really you only need to use the namespace attribute if you're dynamically computing the namespace of the node you're creating. The equivalent of the preceding template is the following, which will work whether or not the html prefix has been associated with the XHTML namespace:

```
<xsl:template match="*">
  <xsl:element name="html:{translate(local-name(), $uppercase, $lowercase)}"
               namespace="http://www.w3.org/1999/xhtml">
    <xsl:apply-templates select="@*|node()" />
  </xsl:element>

</xsl:template>
```

This difference between the resolution of names for elements and attributes stems from the Namespaces Recommendation, which specifies that attributes that don't have a prefix are not in any namespace.

Defining Translations with XML

Translations that involve simply changing the names of elements and attributes (as opposed to changing their content) can often be defined in a separate XML structure that you then access to perform the mapping. For example, you could define some of the mapping between DocBook and HTML with the following XML:

```
<map docbook="para" html="p" />
<map docbook="itemizedlist" html="ul" />
<map docbook="orderedlist" html="ol" />
<map docbook="item" html="li" />
```

 Chapter 1 discusses how to store XML structures within variables so that you can access them later.

With these `map` elements stored in a `$maps` variable, you can find the HTML equivalent of a current DocBook element with the following expression. This looks for the `map` element whose `docbook` attribute is the same as the local name of the current node, and then takes the `html` attribute of that `map` element to give the name in HTML:

```
$maps[@docbook = local-name(current())]/@html
```

Thus, you can perform these transformations with the following:

```
<xsl:template match="*">
   <xsl:element name="html:{$maps[@docbook = local-name(current())]/@html}">
      <xsl:apply-templates select="@*|node()" />
   </xsl:element>
</xsl:template>
```

You can travel quite a long way down this path, adding syntax to the `map` elements to allow them to encode more and more sophisticated mappings — renaming attributes, renaming elements differently in different contexts and so on. However, the more complex the mappings that you support with the `map` elements, the more complex it gets to parse the expressions that contain the information about the mapping (for example, the values of the `docbook` and `html` attributes). The whole point of XSLT is that it provides a syntax for mapping between nodes in the source and the result that you want to obtain — there's no point in reinventing the syntax for it.

Having said this, using an XML syntax to describe simple mappings has three advantages. It's shorter than the equivalent XSLT, and can be placed in a separate file to ease maintenance. Also, it describes the mappings *in both directions* — in the preceding example, from DocBook to HTML *and* from HTML to DocBook. If you want to translate information in both directions, this can be very useful.

Changing Names Conditionally

I've dealt with the common types of name changes — ones that are predefined and ones involving case changes. Other name changes occur conditionally based on attribute values or other properties of the element.

CHANGING NAMES BASED ON ATTRIBUTE VALUES

As an example, let's use the bank statement vocabulary that you've been working with. Within this vocabulary, the type of a transaction is specified with the type attribute:

```
<transaction type="DD" currency="GBP">13.99</transaction>
<transaction type="CR" currency="USD">125.00</transaction>
<transaction type="WD" currency="GBP">50.00</transaction>
```

To allow this information to be imported into a financial package, you have to create a stylesheet to translate from this vocabulary to one in which elements are named according to the type of the transaction:

```
<DirectDebit currency="GBP">13.99</DirectDebit>
<Credit currency="USD">125.00</Credit>
<Withdrawal currency="GBP">50.00</Withdrawal>
```

You can do this in several ways. You could create separate templates for each of the different types of transaction element, as follows:

```
<xsl:template match="transaction[@type = 'DD']">
   <DirectDebit>
      <xsl:apply-templates select="@*|node()" />
   </DirectDebit>
</xsl:template>

<xsl:template match="transaction[@type = 'CR']">
   <Credit>
      <xsl:apply-templates select="@*|node()" />
   </Credit>
</xsl:template>

<xsl:template match="transaction[@type = 'WD']">
   <Withdrawal>
      <xsl:apply-templates select="@*|node()" />
```

```
    </Withdrawal>
</xsl:template>
```

Or, you could use a variable, set conditionally, to hold the name of the new element within a template that matches any kind of transaction:

```
<xsl:template match="transaction">
   <xsl:variable name="new-name">
      <xsl:choose>
         <xsl:when test="@type = 'DD'">DirectDebit</xsl:when>
         <xsl:when test="@type = 'CR'">Credit</xsl:when>
         <xsl:when test="@type = 'WD'">Withdrawal</xsl:when>
      </xsl:choose>
   </xsl:variable>
   <xsl:element name="{$new-name}">
      <xsl:apply-templates select="@*|node()" />
   </xsl:element>
</xsl:template>
```

The advantage of this second method is that the processing required to get the content of the new element can be centralized rather than being repeated within different templates. This isn't particularly important in this example, in which all that happens is that templates are applied to the attributes and content of the transaction, but in cases where the content is reordered or reformatted it can make a lot of difference.

The third approach is to store the information about the mapping somewhere central and to reference it to find the new names. You can set up a variable ($trans) holding transaction types with a structure such as the following:

```
<trans type="DD">DirectDebit</trans>
<trans type="CR">Credit</trans>
<trans type="WD">Withdrawal</trans>
```

With this variable in place, the template looks like this:

```
<xsl:template match="transaction">
   <xsl:element name="{$trans[@type = current()/@type]}">
      <xsl:apply-templates select="@*|node()" />
   </xsl:element>
</xsl:template>
```

The advantage of this third method is that the mappings are defined separately from the XSLT code — you could even place them in a different document. This makes them easier to edit later on, if another transaction type needs to be added to the list.

CHANGING NAMES BASED ON LEVELS

A common problem in mapping from document-oriented vocabularies to HTML is that HTML uses numbered headings to indicate the depth of a section whereas other document-oriented vocabularies often use nested sections instead (or as well). In DocBook, for example, the `title` subelement of a `section` element holds the heading of a section, and the depth of the `section` element in the hierarchy indicates the level of the heading.

When you translate from a DocBook section into an HTML heading, you need to work out the depth of the `title` element. You can calculate the depth by counting how many `section` elements there are above it:

```
count(ancestor::section)
```

The HTML heading elements consist of an `h` followed by a number indicating the level of the heading. You can create these with the following template:

```
<xsl:template match="title">
   <xsl:element name="h{count(ancestor::section)}">
      <xsl:apply-templates select="@*|node()" />
   </xsl:element>
</xsl:template>
```

There is a danger here, however — there is no limit to the depth that the `section` elements can be nested to in DocBook, but HTML allows only headings down to level 6. You should really make this more stable by testing whether the depth is more than 6 and creating an `h6` element if so. You can accomplish this with a long template that creates the new element name using a variable ($new-name). If the depth of the section is less than 6, the heading with the relevant depth is created. Otherwise, an `h6` element is generated.

```
<xsl:template match="title">
   <xsl:variable name="depth" select="count(ancestor::section)" />
   <xsl:variable name="new-name">
      <xsl:choose>
         <xsl:when test="$depth &lt; 6">
            <xsl:text />h<xsl:value-of select="$depth" />
         </xsl:when>
         <xsl:otherwise>h6</xsl:otherwise>
      </xsl:choose>
   </xsl:variable>
   <xsl:element name="{$new-name}">
      <xsl:apply-templates select="@*|node()" />
   </xsl:element>
</xsl:template>
```

A shorter version of the preceding template uses a path to only select a maximum of six ancestor sections, and count how many were discovered:

```
<xsl:template match="title">
   <xsl:element name="h{count(ancestor::section[position() &lt;= 6}">
      <xsl:apply-templates select="@*|node()" />
   </xsl:element>
</xsl:template>
```

Changing Element Substructures

Markup languages usually differ from each other by more than just the names used for elements and attributes — often the substructures of elements are different as well: elements are placed in different orders, for example.

Where these kinds of changes occur, you have to start using a *pull* method — get the stylesheet to determine what to process rather than letting the source XML lead the transformation. This is simply a matter of applying templates to the children of an element in a specific order. For example, to ensure that the account information is processed before the transactions in the bank statement, you can do the following:

```
<xsl:template match="statement">
   <xsl:apply-templates select="account" />
   <xsl:apply-templates select="transactions" />
</xsl:template>
```

Of course you can use this pull method all the time, but if the same ordering is needed in the result as is already present in the source, there's no reason to.

When you need to process a particular child element before all the other child elements, but want the rest kept in document order, you need to be able to select all the elements that are *not* that particular element. You should do this using the self axis.

See Chapter 17 for more detail about various ways of selecting elements that do not have a particular name.

For example, to make sure that the account information is processed first, followed by whatever other information there is in document order, you can use the following:

```
<xsl:template match="statement">
   <xsl:apply-templates select="account" />
   <xsl:apply-templates select="node()[not(self::account)]" />
</xsl:template>
```

Having this kind of catchall expression means that if you change the source XML, these changes will be reflected in the result. That might be what you want because it enables the XSLT to cope with changes that occur in the source vocabulary, but might not be, in that such changes may invisibly give an invalid result. Which method you choose depends on the maintenance strategy for the application.

Adding Attributes

As well as defining what elements and attributes should be present in a document, and the structure of the content of elements, DTDs (and some schemas) often indicate the default or fixed values for certain attributes. For example, in the bank statement application, the currency used for a transaction defaults to GBP:

```
<!ATTLIST transaction
    type     (CR|WD|DD|SO)  #REQUIRED
    currency (GBP|USD)       'GBP'>
```

When an application, such as an XSLT processor, parses an XML document, it may read the DTD and if an attribute isn't present in the document, add it with the default or fixed value that's defined by the DTD. As far as the XSLT processor is concerned, it's just as if the attribute had been defined in the document itself. For example, with a validating parser and the preceding DTD, the following two transactions are identical:

```
<transaction type="CR">150.00</transaction>
<transaction type="CR" currency="GBP">150.00</transaction>
```

The use of defaulted and fixed values means that a document can have different logical content (a different *infoset*) depending on whether the DTD or schema is accessible or not. If it is, then a number of attributes are defined within the document that aren't present when the DTD isn't accessible. For example, if the DTD isn't accessible for some reason, then the preceding two transaction elements are different.

When you're writing an XSLT application, you should make sure that the presence or absence of a DTD or schema does not make a difference to the stylesheet. If an attribute has a default or fixed value according to the DTD, then the stylesheet should treat a missing attribute in the same way as it would an attribute with the default or fixed value.

A particular problem in some markup languages is that the default namespace declaration is declared as a fixed attribute within the DTD. When the DTD is available, an element is in the markup language's namespace; when the DTD is not available, then the element is in no namespace. This is a more serious problem as namespaces are built in at a low level in XSLT. One solution is to use a two-pass transformation in which the first transformation moves all elements in no namespace into the desired namespace, using one of the techniques described earlier in this chapter.

It's often the case that different XML vocabularies have different default values for attributes, or different requirements for attributes to be present or not. For example, the vocabulary for the financial package to which you're translating the bank statement vocabulary defaults to USD as the currency for the transactions it defines:

```
<!ENTITY currency-att "currency (USD|GBP) 'USD'">
<!ATTLIST Credit %currency-att;>
<!ATTLIST Withdrawal %currency-att;>
<!ATTLIST DirectDebit %currency-att;>
<!ATTLIST StandingOrder %currency-att;>
```

You need to make sure that the translated document has the same semantic meaning as the original. If the currency attribute is ever omitted, then your applications will assume GBP whereas the financial package will assume USD. To avoid this, you need to fix the values of attributes in the result so that you can guarantee that the meaning of the original document is preserved.

This means going through the DTD for your original XML and adding tests to add attributes if they are not present. So, within the template matching the transaction element, you can test for and add the currency attribute:

```
<xsl:template match="transaction">
  <xsl:element name="{$trans[@type = current()/@type]}">
    <xsl:if test="not(@currency)">
```

```
      <xsl:attribute name="currency">GBP</xsl:attribute>
    </xsl:if>
    <xsl:apply-templates select="@*|node()" />
  </xsl:element>
</xsl:template>
```

In fact, within XSLT, attributes are added to elements in the order they're specified in the stylesheet. If an attribute is added with the same name as an attribute that already exists, it is overwritten. So, given that if it exists, the currency attribute is simply going to be copied onto the new element when templates are applied to it, the preceding template could be simplified to:

```
<xsl:template match="transaction">
  <xsl:element name="{$trans[@type = current()/@type]}">
    <xsl:attribute name="currency">GBP</xsl:attribute>
    <xsl:apply-templates select="@*|node()" />
  </xsl:element>
</xsl:template>
```

The currency attribute is added each time, but if it's already specified on the original transaction element, it will be added for a second time, with the value the source XML specifies.

You can also specify default attribute values directly as attributes on literal result elements, or within an attribute set. For example, you can define an attribute set holding all the default values of the attributes on the new transaction elements:

```
<xsl:attribute-set name="transaction-atts">
  <xsl:attribute name="currency">GBP</xsl:attribute>
</xsl:attribute-set>
```

You can then reference this attribute set when creating the new element:

```
<xsl:template match="transaction">
  <xsl:element name="{$trans[@type = current()/@type]}"
               use-attribute-sets="transaction-atts">
    <xsl:apply-templates select="@*|node()" />
  </xsl:element>
</xsl:template>
```

One thing to notice here, though, is that the attribute values that are being specified are the equivalent of the default *values* from the original XML (in this example, the original bank statement vocabulary) on the *attributes* from the target XML (in this example, the financial package vocabulary). In the example so far this hasn't been a problem because the two attributes have had the same name and allowed the same values. But the financial package vocabulary might instead define currency through a `curr` attribute, taking the values $ (for dollars) and £ (for pounds):

```
<!ENTITY currency-att "curr CDATA '$'">
```

If the `currency` attribute in the original document is missing, it needs to be translated into a `curr` attribute with a value of £:

```
<xsl:template match="transaction">
   <xsl:element name="{$trans[@type = current()/@type]}">
      <xsl:attribute name="curr">&#163;</xsl:attribute>
      <xsl:apply-templates select="@*|node()" />
   </xsl:element>
</xsl:template>
```

This is the same mapping of attribute values as occurs within the template that matches the `currency` attribute:

```
<xsl:template match="@currency">
   <xsl:attribute name="curr">
      <xsl:choose>
         <xsl:when test=". = 'USD'">$</xsl:when>
         <xsl:otherwise>&#163;</xsl:otherwise>
      </xsl:choose>
   </xsl:attribute>
</xsl:template>
```

Ideally this mapping should be defined once and once only – really you want to add the defaulted attributes to the original XML before you translate it. This task should be done by the validating processor based on the DTD, but if the DTD is missing or if the required defaults are calculated based on other factors rather than being fixed, then you need to do it yourself.

The best approach, then, is to have a two-stage process. During the first stage, the original XML is expanded to add any default values, essentially changing the infoset of the document in the same way as a DTD or schema would. The second stage involves the actual translation into the target vocabulary. This separation also enables you to use schema information to give the default values of attributes. For example, the XML Schema for the `transaction` elements might look like the following:

```
<xs:element name="transaction">
   <xs:complexType>
      <xs:simpleContent>
         <xs:extension base="xs:decimal">
```

```
            <xs:attribute name="currency" default="GBP">
                <xs:simpleType>
                    <xs:restriction base="xs:NMTOKEN">
                        <xs:enumeration value="GBP" />
                        <xs:enumeration value="USD" />
                    </xs:restriction>
                </xs:simpleType>
            </xs:attribute>
        </xs:extension>
    </xs:simpleContent>
</xs:complexType>
</xs:element>
```

Information about the attribute default is accessible because it is stored in a schema, in XML, rather than in a DTD. If the preceding declaration were held in an `$element-definition` variable, you could create all the relevant default attributes with the following:

```
<xsl:for-each select="$element-definition//xs:attribute[@default]">
    <xsl:attribute name="{@name}">
        <xsl:value-of select="@default" />
    </xsl:attribute>
</xsl:for-each>
```

Accessing information from an XML Schema can be a lot more complicated than demonstrated here unless you use XML Schema in a very regular way. However, as with any other XML-based markup language, you can always transform an XML Schema into a form that makes it easier to identify defaulted attributes, and then use that.

Adding Styling Information

If you're doing a document-to-document conversion, such as from DocBook to HTML or from HTML to XSL-FO (Extensible Stylesheet Language Formatting Objects), you will probably need to add some styling information to get the look that you're after, which may be implicit in the source markup language. How you do this depends on whether you're using HTML or XSL-FO.

Style in HTML

Presentational details can be added to HTML with CSS (Cascading Style Sheets). Global stylesheets can be defined internally or externally, or you can use the style attribute to give styles on particular elements. If you're using XML to separate content from presentation, you may as well continue that separation in the HTML that you produce, rather than using deprecated presentational elements and attributes like font or bgcolor.

The CSS can be situated in a separate file, and referenced by the HTML with a link element within the head element:

```
<link rel="stylesheet" type="text/css" href="style.css" />
```

Alternatively, you can include styles inline, with the style element, again within the head element in the HTML document:

```
<style type="text/css">
  ...
</style>
```

It's often helpful to add styling hooks to the HTML that you produce in the form of class attributes. For example, DocBook declares the elements caution, important, note, tip, and warning that should all be transformed into HTML paragraphs (p elements), but need to be presented slightly differently. You can add the name of the original element to the class attribute to give the CSS stylesheet the opportunity to style these paragraphs in different ways, as follows:

```
<xsl:template match="caution | important | note | tip | warning">
  <p class="{local-name()}">
    <xsl:apply-templates />
  </p>
</xsl:template>
```

Internal and external stylesheets work well for general styles for your document. However, it's likely that the document format that you're translating from will allow some degree of control over the formatting of individual elements. For example, in DocBook, the numbering of items in lists is controlled by the numeration attribute on the orderedlist element. The values that are allowed have CSS equivalents, as shown in Table 6-1:

TABLE 6-1 DOCBOOK AND CSS STYLES FOR LIST ITEMS

DocBook numeration	CSS list-style-type
Arabic	decimal
loweralpha	lower-latin

Continued

Table **6-1 DOCBOOK AND CSS STYLES FOR LIST ITEMS** *(Continued)*

DocBook numeration	CSS list-style-type
lowerroman	lower-roman
upperalpha	upper-latin
upperroman	upper-roman

If the source markup language allows element-specific control over presentation, you need to include style information on specific elements using the `style` attribute. For example, to translate the `orderedlist` element from DocBook into the equivalent `ol` element in HTML, you could use the following:

```
<xsl:template match="orderedlist">
   <ol>
      <xsl:if test="@numeration">
         <xsl:attribute name="style">
            <xsl:text>list-style-type: </xsl:text>
            <xsl:choose>
               <xsl:when test="@numeration = 'loweralpha'">
                  <xsl:text>lower-latin;</xsl:text>
               </xsl:when>
               <xsl:when test="@numeration = 'lowerroman'">
                  <xsl:text>lower-roman;</xsl:text>
               </xsl:when>
               <xsl:when test="@numeration = 'upperalpha'">
                  <xsl:text>upper-latin;</xsl:text>
               </xsl:when>
               <xsl:when test="@numeration = 'upperroman'">
                  <xsl:text>upper-roman;</xsl:text>
               </xsl:when>
               <xsl:otherwise>decimal;</xsl:otherwise>
            </xsl:choose>
         </xsl:attribute>
      </xsl:if>
      <xsl:apply-templates />
   </ol>
</xsl:template>
```

The `style` attribute can be a little irritating to work with because you need to specify it only if there is styling information to be added to it, but the styling information can come from all over the place. A good way of getting around this is to collect together all the nodes that indicate styling information. If there are any of these attributes, then create the `style` attribute and apply templates to the styling nodes to give the value for the attribute.

For example, you could use XSLT to tidy up some transitional XHTML to create strict XHTML, moving the deprecated attributes into the equivalent CSS styles. The template for the `table` element, for example, would look like the following:

```
<xsl:template match="table">
   <xsl:variable name="style-atts"
                 select="@width | @bgcolor | ..." />
   <table>
      <xsl:if test="$style-atts">
         <xsl:attribute name="style">
            <xsl:apply-templates select="$style-atts" mode="style" />
         </xsl:attribute>
      </xsl:if>
      <xsl:apply-templates />
   </table>
</xsl:template>

<xsl:template match="@width" mode="style">
   <xsl:text />width: <xsl:value-of select="." />; <xsl:text />
</xsl:template>

<xsl:template match="@bgcolor" mode="style">
   <xsl:text />background-color: <xsl:value-of select="." />; <xsl:text />
</xsl:template>
```

Style with XSL-FO

Within XSL-FO, all the necessary styling information about a particular formatting object is included as attributes on that formatting object. There is no separation of content from presentation because XSL-FO is *all about* presentation. When an element in, say, DocBook, is transformed into an XSL-FO element, you need to add attributes to specify any formatting that you want for the element. Every `para` element, for example, needs to be translated to a block with the required spacing around it, as follows:

```
<xsl:template match="para">
   <fo:block space-before="6pt" space-after="6pt">
      <xsl:apply-templates />
   </fo:block>
</xsl:template>
```

This makes it very easy to override formatting on a per-element basis — you just have to add the relevant attribute if it's required. For example, to set the width and background color of a table based on the attributes specified in some XHTML, you need the following:

```
<xsl:template match="table">
   <fo:table>
      <xsl:apply-templates select="@*|node()" />
   </fo:table>
</xsl:template>

<xsl:template match="@width">
   <xsl:copy-of select="." />
</xsl:template>

<xsl:template match="@bgcolor">
   <xsl:attribute name="background-color">
      <xsl:value-of select="." />
   </xsl:attribute>
</xsl:template>
```

However, the fact that the style of an element is determined by a number of attributes makes it more difficult to assign default styles to sections of the document, especially if these styles are shared. You can make these easier to handle if you use attribute sets to add a number of attributes to a particular element at the same time.

See Chapter 12 for detailed information on how to use attribute sets.

Debugging Translations

As you're debugging your translation, it's often helpful to know where a particular part of the result that's been generated comes from. With a translation, because of the close association between the source and the result, you can add comments to indicate the source of different parts of the result document, for example to generate the result:

```
<!--transaction type="CR" currency="USD"-->
<Credit curr="$">250.00</Credit>
<!--/transaction-->
```

or:

```
<!--orderedlist numeration="decimal"-->
<ol>
   <!--item-->
   <li>

      ...
   </li>
   <!--/item-->
   ...
</ol>
<!--/orderedlist-->
```

Adding comments such as these is simply a matter of creating comments with `xsl:comment` that hold the relevant information. The following two templates can be used with any element to add such comments:

```
<xsl:template match="*" mode="start-element-comment">
   <xsl:comment>
      <xsl:value-of select="name()" />
      <xsl:for-each select="@*">
         <xsl:text> </xsl:text>
         <xsl:value-of select="name()" />="<xsl:text />
         <xsl:value-of select="." />"<xsl:text />
      </xsl:for-each>
   </xsl:comment>
</xsl:template>

<xsl:template match="*" mode="end-element-comment">
   <xsl:comment>
      <xsl:text />/<xsl:value-of select="name()" />
   </xsl:comment>
</xsl:template>
```

Applying templates in `start-element-comment` and `end-element-comment` mode allows you to add the relevant comments. For example:

```
<xsl:template match="transaction">
   <xsl:apply-templates select="." mode="start-element-comment" />
   ...
   <xsl:apply-templates select="." mode="end-element-comment" />
</xsl:template>
```

Another method of tracing back the original XML for a particular element is to create an XPath that points to that element. You can include this within a comment or as an attribute on the generated element. For example:

```
<Credit src:xpath="/statement/transactions[1]/transaction[4]"
        curr="$">250.00</Credit>
```

The XPath used here can be generated through the following template. This iterates over the ancestors of the current element and the element itself. For each of them, it gives the step separator (/) followed by the name of the element. If the element isn't the document element (if it has an element as a parent, rather than the root node), then a predicate is added giving the index of the element amongst its similarly named siblings, as follows:

```
<xsl:template match="*" mode="xpath-attribute">
   <xsl:attribute name="src:xpath">
      <xsl:for-each select="ancestor-or-self::*">
         <xsl:text />/<xsl:value-of select="name()" />
         <xsl:if test="parent::*">
            <xsl:text />[<xsl:number />]<xsl:text />
         </xsl:if>
      </xsl:for-each>
   </xsl:attribute>
</xsl:template>
```

Summary

Translations are only slightly more complex than filters — they are simple transformations involving the mapping of one element to another, usually converting data to data or documents to documents. In this chapter, you saw how to achieve some of the frequent actions that are needed with translations:

◆ Translating element and attribute names

◆ Changing element substructures

◆ Adding attributes

◆ Adding styling information

You also looked at how to debug translations by adding comments or attributes either giving or pointing to the original XML the result was translated from.

Like filters, a basic translation of some kind often forms part of a more complex transformation. Part of a data-oriented XML structure might be translated into a table for presentation, for example. The techniques that I described in this chapter form the bedrock for the more complex techniques that I'll turn to in the rest of this part of the book.

Chapter 7

Sorting

IN THIS CHAPTER

- ◆ Sorting on calculated values
- ◆ Sorting by date
- ◆ Sorting dynamically
- ◆ Sorting by multiple values

YOU PROBABLY ALREADY KNOW that you can change the order that you process nodes in using the xsl:sort element. You can use the xsl:sort element to change the order in which nodes have templates applied to them, or the order that they're iterated over using the xsl:for-each instruction. In this chapter, you can explore various aspects of using xsl:sort that you might not be aware of, and examine what to do when xsl:sort is just not enough and you need to use something else.

Chapter 9 discusses grouping and those sorts that involve collecting items into different categories.

Sorting on Calculated Values

The select attribute of xsl:sort enables you to sort on anything for which you can construct an expression. For example, bank statement transactions are held in some XML that looks like:

```
<transaction type="CR">235.00</transaction>
<transaction type="DD">16.50</transaction>
<transaction type="WD" currency="USD">50</transaction>
```

These transactions can be sorted by value with:

```
<xsl:for-each select="transaction">
  <xsl:sort select="." data-type="number" />
```

```
    . . .
</xsl:for-each>
```

If you use a select expression that returns a Boolean value, then those nodes with a sort value of false come before those with a sort value of true.

You can sort a set of nodes into reverse document order by sorting on their position in descending order:

```
<xsl:sort select="position()" order="descending"
          data-type="number" />
```

Calculating Sort Values with Expressions

Sometimes these sorts get a little trickier. For example, if you want to sort by value, taking into account that credit transactions are positive whereas other transactions are negative, you must construct a conditional XPath.

For additional details on how to construct a conditional XPath, please refer to Chapter 3.

You can use the following:

```
<xsl:for-each select="transaction">
   <xsl:sort select=". * (2 * (@type = 'CR') - 1)"
           data-type="number" />
   . . .
</xsl:for-each>
```

Here, if the type attribute is equal to the string 'CR', the expression evaluates as the value of the transaction element times 1. If the type attribute is not equal to the string 'CR', the expression evaluates as the value of the transaction element times -1.

An alternative XPath expression to calculate the positive or negative transaction value is:

```
sum(current()[@type = 'CR']) -
sum(current()[@type != 'CR'])
```

Here, if the `type` attribute is equal to the string `'CR'`, the expression is the value of the current transaction minus zero. If the `type` attribute is not equal to the string `'CR'` then the expression is zero minus the value of the current transaction.

An alternative technique for dealing with conditional sort values is to combine a number of sorts. You could sort the transactions in this example by first sorting on the numerical value of the transaction, but only if it is a credit transaction, and then sorting on the numerical value of the transaction in descending order:

```
<xsl:for-each select="transaction">
   <xsl:sort select="current()[@type = 'CR']" data-type="number" />
   <xsl:sort select="." data-type="number" order="descending" />
   ...
</xsl:for-each>
```

This double sort works because when non-credit transactions are encountered during the first sort, they are assigned a sort value of NaN. NaN sorts before other values, so all these transactions form a single group at the start of the sorted list. The second sort then focuses on these non-credit transactions and sorts them in descending order. It has no effect on the order of the credit transactions because each credit transaction has its own sort group from the first sort and later sorts will only change the order within the sort groups from the earlier sorts.

At this point, you also want to ensure that the sort takes into account that the transactions may be in different currencies. The current exchange rate is stored in the `$exchange-rate` parameter, and if the `currency` attribute is equal to the string USD then you want to multiply the value by this parameter value. Adapting the conditional expression involves adding another conditional multiplier once:

```
<xsl:for-each select="transaction">
   <xsl:sort select=". * (1 + (@currency = 'USD') * ($exchange-rate - 1)) *
                     (2 * (@type = 'CR') - 1)"
           data-type="number" />
   ...
</xsl:for-each>
```

Using the double sort, on the other hand, means adding this conditional multiplier in both sorts:

```
<xsl:for-each select="transaction">
   <xsl:sort select="current()[@type = 'CR'] *
                     (1 + (@currency = 'USD') * ($exchange-rate - 1))"
           data-type="number" />
   <xsl:sort select=". * (1 + (@currency = 'USD') * ($exchange-rate - 1))"
           data-type="number" order="descending" />

   ...
</xsl:for-each>
```

These calculations can be made a lot easier if you write your own extension function to carry them out, which you can call from the select expression. Chapter 20 describes the various ways of creating your own extension functions.

Calculating Sort Values with Intermediate XML

As you can see from the conditional expressions in the previous section, the more complex the calculation of the sort value, the more unreadable and unmaintainable the select expression becomes. Instead of using conditional expressions, a more easily understandable and maintainable way is often to construct and use some intermediate XML holding the calculated value.

Using intermediate XML within a single stylesheet (rather than creating an intermediate XML document) makes your stylesheet less portable because it involves using a node-set() extension function or relying on support for the XSLT 1.1 working draft within your processor.

Chapter 5 discusses the various ways of managing sequential transformations.

USING INTERMEDIATE COPIES

For example, the transactions at the moment appear as follows:

```
<transaction type="CR">235.00</transaction>
<transaction type="DD">16.50</transaction>
<transaction type="WD" currency="USD">50</transaction>
```

This XML does not contain an easy way of accessing the calculated value — a `value` attribute, for example — but a `value` attribute could be added in some intermediate XML containing copies of the transactions. Creating the intermediate XML is straightforward because you are not restricted to a single expression to calculate the value of the `value` attribute:

```
<xsl:for-each select="transaction">
   <xsl:copy>
      <xsl:attribute name="value">
         <xsl:variable name="value-in-GBP">
            <xsl:choose>
               <xsl:when test="@currency = 'USD'">
                  <xsl:value-of select=". * $exchange-rate" />
               </xsl:when>
               <xsl:otherwise>
                  <xsl:value-of select="." />
               </xsl:otherwise>
            </xsl:choose>
         </xsl:variable>
         <xsl:choose>
            <xsl:when test="@type = 'CR'">
               <xsl:value-of select="$value-in-GBP" />
            </xsl:when>
            <xsl:otherwise>
               <xsl:value-of select="-$value-in-GBP" />
            </xsl:otherwise>
         </xsl:choose>
      </xsl:attribute>
      <xsl:copy-of select="@*|node()" />
   </xsl:copy>
</xsl:for-each>
```

You can iterate over these copied `transaction` elements in the next step of the transformation, using their new `value` attribute as the sort value:

```
<xsl:for-each select="transaction">
   <xsl:sort select="@value" data-type="number" />
   ...
</xsl:for-each>
```

USING NODES WITH REFERENCES

There is a disadvantage with the previously mentioned technique, which is especially relevant if you use XSLT 1.1 or an extension function to enact it. A subtle problem arises because the nodes that are processed by the `xsl:for-each` in the second step of the preceding example are actually new nodes, distinct from the `transaction` elements in the source XML. You can access information about each transaction's type, currency, and value, as these are all held either on the `transaction` element (as attributes) or within it (as descendants). But you *can't* step up the node tree from the `transaction` element to find information about the account or the customer. The variable that you create to hold the intermediate XML is essentially a new document — the only ancestor any of the `transaction` elements have is the root node of this new document.

 Copied nodes are also different because they have a different base URI and belong to a different "document." This affects things such as how the `document()`, `id()`, and `key()` functions work with them.

Often this isn't a problem — the only information you want about a node is usually held on or in that node, and you don't have to look elsewhere in the document to get it. However, sometimes relevant information is held elsewhere in the document. In these situations, you have two choices. You can copy all the information that you need onto the new nodes as you create them (which can be laborious), or you can create a set of nodes that can be sorted, using these nodes to reference the nodes that you actually want.

Using a `node-set()` extension function with the preceding example, rather than copying the `transaction` elements, you can create a set of `node` elements — each of which has the calculated value that you want to sort on, and has a `ref` attribute that holds the unique ID for the `transaction` element the `node` element is based upon. The values themselves are calculated in the same way as before:

```
<xsl:variable name="nodes">
   <xsl:for-each select="transaction">
      <node ref="{generate-id()}">
         <xsl:variable name="value-in-GBP">
            <xsl:choose>
               <xsl:when test="@currency = 'USD'">
                  <xsl:value-of select=". * $exchange-rate" />
               </xsl:when>
               <xsl:otherwise>
                  <xsl:value-of select="." />
               </xsl:otherwise>
            </xsl:choose>
```

```
        </xsl:variable>
        <xsl:choose>
            <xsl:when test="@type = 'CR'">
                <xsl:value-of select="$value-in-GBP" />
            </xsl:when>
            <xsl:otherwise>
                <xsl:value-of select="-$value-in-GBP" />
            </xsl:otherwise>
        </xsl:choose>
      </node>
   </xsl:for-each>
</xsl:variable>
```

You can iterate over these node elements, sorting them by their value:

```
<xsl:for-each select="exsl:node-set($nodes)/node">
   <xsl:sort select="." data-type="number" />
   ...
</xsl:for-each>
```

Now, given the set of transaction elements from the source XML (which should be held in a variable, say $transactions), you can find the one that a particular node element relates to by finding the transaction element with the generated ID indicated by the ref attribute of the node element:

```
<xsl:variable name="transactions" select="transaction" />
<xsl:for-each select="$nodes">
   <xsl:sort select="." data-type="number" />
   <xsl:variable name="transaction"
                 select="$transactions[generate-id() = current()/@ref]" />
   ...
</xsl:for-each>
```

This can be very laborious for the XSLT processor. Generating IDs is something that can require a great deal of time, as will searching through all the transaction elements for one with a particular unique ID. You may find that it's more efficient to use a key to index the transaction elements by their ID:

```
<xsl:key name="transactions" match="transaction" use="generate-id()" />
```

However, within the xsl:for-each, the current node is a node element, in a completely new "document" – the one that you've created with the content of the xsl:variable. The key has to reference transaction elements in the source XML, and one of the features of keys is that they can only be used to access nodes in the same document as the current node. Therefore, within the xsl:for-each that iterates over the node elements, you can change the current node (with another xsl:for-each) to a single node in the original document, before using the key to access the transaction element:

```
<xsl:variable name="transactions" select="transaction" />
<xsl:for-each select="$nodes">
   <xsl:sort select="." data-type="number" />
   <xsl:variable name="id" select="@ref" />
   <xsl:for-each select="$transactions[1]">
      <xsl:variable name="transaction" select="key('transactions', $id)" />
      ...
   </xsl:for-each>
</xsl:for-each>
```

Sorting by Date

Dates and times are common types of information in XML files, but there's no built-in support for them within XSLT. For example, date is not an allowed data-type for xsl:sort. Instead, you must ensure that the date being sorted is in a format that sorts properly when arranged alphabetically. For example:

```
2001-03-08T10:35:02
```

Sorting Dates with Fixed Formats

Sorting by date involves either constructing a string that matches a format such as the previous example or having a multilevel sort that sorts first by year, then by month, then by day, and so on. So, from a date format of:

```
MM/DD/YY
```

You can sort by date either with the following, which constructs a date in the format *YYMMDD* and sorts on that:

```
<!-- construct date in format YYMMDD to sort on -->
<xsl:sort select="concat(substring(@date, 7, 2),
                         substring(@date, 1, 2),
                         substring(@date, 4, 2))" />
```

Or with the following three separate sorts:

```
<!-- sort by year -->
<xsl:sort select="substring(@date, 7, 2)" />
<!-- sort by month -->
```

Date and Time Data Types

The date/time format *CCYY-MM-DDThh:mm:ss* is the one specified for xs:dateTime in the XML Schema Part 2: Data Types Recommendation, and complies with ISO 8601. It is likely that XSLT 2.0 will use similar data types as those in XML Schema as values for the data-type attribute on xsl:sort. As well as xs:dateTime, these include the following:

- xs:duration — Periods of time in the format P*n*Y*n*M*n*DT*n*H*n*M*n*S
- xs:time — A time in the format *HH:MM:SS*
- xs:date — A date in the format *CCYY-MM-DD*
- xs:gYearMonth — A month in a particular year in the format *CCYY-MM*
- xs:gYear — A year in the format *CCYY*
- xs:gMonth — A month each year in the format *--MM--*
- xs:gMonthDay — A date each year in the format *--MM-DD*
- xs:gDay — A day of the month in the format *---DD*

For example, if your date represents an instant in time, you may be able to sort with:

```
<xsl:sort select="@date" data-type="xs:dateTime" />
```

This gives extra functionality because sorting with a data type of xs:dateTime forces the processor to take into account any time zone information supplied with the date time.

However, taking advantage of this built-in formatting means either using these formats within the source XML that you're transforming, or constructing strings in these formats on the fly.

```
<xsl:sort select="substring(@date, 1, 2)" />
<!-- sort by day -->
<xsl:sort select="substring(@date, 4, 2)" />
```

The dates must all be in the same century to sort properly, but this is due to the format of the date in the source XML. You could use a conditional XPath to add '19' or '20' to the front of the string or as the value of the first sort instruction, such as the following, which places the date in the 21st century if the year is less than or equal to 10:

```
19 + (substring(@date, 7, 2) &lt;= 10)
```

Sorting Dates with Flexible Formats

In the previous examples, the structure of the date string is fixed, and you can use the substring() function to pick the characters from the string that represent the year, month, and day. If the date drops leading zeros (for example, 8th March 2001 becomes 3-8-01) then the year, month, and day have to be retrieved using substring-before() and substring-after() instead. In addition, you can either pad them with leading zeros before concatenating them or sort on them individually, specifying the number data type.

This example shows the padding:

```
<!-- construct date in format YYMMDD to sort on -->
<xsl:sort
    select="concat(substring-after(substring-after(@date, '-'), '-'),
                format-number(
                    substring-before(substring-after(@date, '-'), '-'), '00'),
                format-number(substring-before(@date, '-'), '00'))" />
```

While here, the sorts are done individually:

```
<!-- sort by year -->
<xsl:sort select="substring-after(substring-after(@date, '-'), '-')" />
<!-- sort by month -->
<xsl:sort select="substring-before(substring-after(@date, '-'), '-')"
        data-type="number" />
<!-- sort by day -->
<xsl:sort select="substring-before(@date, '-')" data-type="number" />
```

Sorting with Named or Abbreviated Months

These methods are fine and dandy until you come up against date formats that use month names or abbreviations rather than month numbers. You need to convert the month names into month numbers. This involves specifying a variable ($months) that holds some XML giving the names and abbreviations for the months in order:

```
<month abbr="Jan">January</month>
<month abbr="Feb">February</month>
<month abbr="Mar">March</month>
<month abbr="Apr">April</month>
<month abbr="May">May</month>
<month abbr="Jun">June</month>
<month abbr="Jul">July</month>
<month abbr="Aug">August</month>
<month abbr="Sep">September</month>
<month abbr="Oct">October</month>
<month abbr="Nov">November</month>
<month abbr="Dec">December</month>
```

Various methods for creating variables holding static XML are explained in detail in Chapter 1.

With this variable in place, you can get the month element that corresponds to a particular month name with:

```
$months/month[. = month-name]
```

Then, given this month element, you can get the month number by counting its preceding siblings (the earlier months) and adding one to it:

```
count($months/month[. = month-name]/preceding-sibling::month) + 1
```

So, given dates such as 8 March 2001, you can sort with:

```
<!-- sort by year -->
<xsl:sort select="substring-after(substring-after(@date, ' '), ' ')" />
<!-- sort by month -->
<xsl:sort
   select="count($months/month
                 [. = substring-before(substring-after(@date, ' '), ' ')]
                 /preceding-sibling::month) + 1" data-type="number" />
<!-- sort by day -->
<xsl:sort select="(substring-before(@date, ' ')" data-type="number" />
```

In fact, you don't need to get an accurate month number — you can number them from 0 to 11 instead and they still are sorted in the same order, so there's no need to add one to the count of preceding siblings.

Similarly, with a date such as 8-Mar-01, in which the month name is abbreviated, you could sort by identifying the month element with the appropriate abbreviation in its abbr attribute:

```
<!-- sort by year -->
<xsl:sort select="substring-after(substring-after(@date, '-'), '-')" />
<!-- sort by month -->
<xsl:sort
    select="count($months/month
                    [@abbr = substring-before(substring-after(@date, '-'), '-')]
                    /preceding-sibling::month) + 1" data-type="number" />
<!-- sort by day -->
<xsl:sort select="(substring-before(@date, '-')" data-type="number" />
```

TURNING THE SORT AROUND

Another way of using the $months variable to define the sort order is actually to iterate over the month elements that it defines and then select the data in which the date is in that month. Assuming that the data is held in a $data variable, this resembles the following:

```
<xsl:for-each select="$months/month">
    <xsl:apply-templates select="$data[substring-before(
                                    substring-after(@date, '-'), '-') =
                                    @abbr]" />
</xsl:for-each>
```

This method doesn't sit at all well with sorting by year (although you can sort by day just by adding an appropriate xsl:sort to the xsl:apply-templates in the preceding code). However, it's a good general method when you want to sort in a particular non-computable order and want to avoid the inefficiency of counting preceding siblings to identify that order but don't want to use an intermediate node set.

INCREASING THE EFFICIENCY OF SORTS ON MONTHS

If you're sorting numerous records with dates on them, this technique may be slightly inefficient because the processor must do quite a lot to find the sort value for each record. For instance, it must pull out the month from the date string, find the relevant month element, collect its preceding siblings, and then count them.

You can make it more efficient by first making it easier to get the month number from the month name or abbreviation by adding a `num` attribute to hold it:

```
<month num="1" abbr="Jan">January</month>
<month num="2" abbr="Feb">February</month>
<month num="3" abbr="Mar">March</month>
<month num="4" abbr="Apr">April</month>
<month num="5" abbr="May">May</month>
<month num="6" abbr="Jun">June</month>
<month num="7" abbr="Jul">July</month>
<month num="8" abbr="Aug">August</month>
<month num="9" abbr="Sep">September</month>
<month num="10" abbr="Oct">October</month>
<month num="11" abbr="Nov">November</month>
<month num="12" abbr="Dec">December</month>
```

This simplifies the sort expression to:

```
<xsl:sort select="$months/month
                  [@abbr = substring-before(substring-after(@date, '-'), '-')]
                  /@num" data-type="number" />
```

If the sorting is still slowing things down, it may be worthwhile to change it into a two-step process in which you construct copies of the nodes that you want to sort with the dates converted into the format you want, and then sort this new node set. (I discussed details about how to do this in the last section, along with drawbacks of creating a new node set.)

GETTING MONTH NUMBERS WITH KEYS

In this case, the two-step approach has the added advantage that you can set up and use a key to quickly get at the number of a month from its name or abbreviation, something you cannot do if you use a one-step sort. The keys must match the node holding the information that you want to get (the month number) and use the month name or abbreviation. You could set up two keys:

```
<xsl:key name="months-by-name" match="@num" use=".." />
<xsl:key name="months-by-abbr" match="@num" use="../@abbr" />
```

However, because the names and abbreviations never clash with each other, you may as well use just one key for both:

```
<xsl:key name="months" match="@num" use=".. | ../@abbr" />
```

With this key defined, getting the month number for a particular month name or abbreviation means using the key() function:

```
key('months', month)
```

However, you have to ensure that the current node when the key() function is used is in the same document as the nodes that you want to access. In this case, the month elements are in their own separate document, not part of the source XML, so you have to change the current node to be in this document before calling the key. Thus, getting the number of the month involves using the xsl:for-each instruction to change the current node to one in the $months node set:

```
<xsl:for-each select="$months">
  <xsl:value-of select="key('months', $month)" />
</xsl:for-each>
```

Sorting Dynamically

Most things about a single sort can be defined dynamically based on information in your source XML or passed into the stylesheet through parameters. Aside from the select attribute (which is dynamic by dint of it being an expression), the attributes on xsl:sort are attribute value templates, so you can dynamically choose their values:

◆ order — Sort in ascending or descending order

◆ data-type — Sort different types of values (strings or numbers)

◆ case-order — Choose whether uppercase or lowercase should come first

◆ lang — Pick the language used for alphabetical sorts

One common scenario that requires dynamic sorting is to convert a number of records into an HTML table, and to allow the user to decide which of the columns of the table it should be sorted by. The user chooses a column (often by clicking the column header) and the stylesheet determines which column has been selected and uses that to decide how to sort the records.

For example, in the bank statement application, you want to construct a table of the transactions in the account. The XML for the transactions resembles the following:

```
<transaction date="2001-03-01" type="DD" payee="TV License">8.91</transaction>
<transaction date="2001-03-01" type="DD" payee="British Gas">22.00</transaction>
<transaction date="2001-03-03" type="CR" payee="Client">400.00</transaction>
<transaction date="2001-03-09" type="SO" payee="Rent">633.00</transaction>
<transaction date="2001-03-10" type="WD" payee="Cash">50.00</transaction>
```

```
<transaction date="2001-03-15" type="CR" payee="Interest">0.58</transaction>
```

The table that you want to create shows the date, type, and amount of the transaction (the value of the `transaction` element), as well as the person that made it (the value of the `payee` attribute). The screenshot in Figure 7-1 shows the table that you're aiming for (you can use CSS to make it prettier later).

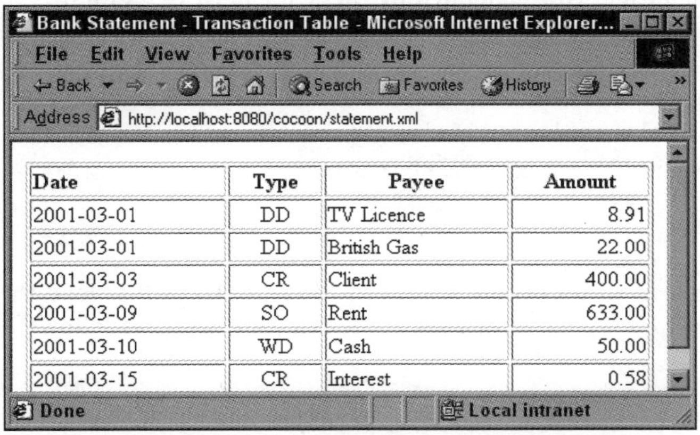

Date	Type	Payee	Amount
2001-03-01	DD	TV Licence	8.91
2001-03-01	DD	British Gas	22.00
2001-03-03	CR	Client	400.00
2001-03-09	SO	Rent	633.00
2001-03-10	WD	Cash	50.00
2001-03-15	CR	Interest	0.58

Figure 7-1: The basic table of transactions in the bank statement application

You can construct the table by applying templates to each of the transactions, each one creating a row of the table. The order in which the XSLT processor processes the `transaction` elements depends on the `xsl:sort` – to sort them by date, you can use the following:

```
<xsl:sort select="@date" />
```

whereas to sort by type, you must use:

```
<xsl:sort select="@type" />
```

These select expressions are fine if the sort is in a fixed order, but you want to determine which of these sorts to do depending on a parameter, `$sort-by`. The `$sort-by` parameter can hold the names of one of the three attributes that give most of the information for the transaction (`date`, `type`, or `payee`) or the keyword `value` to give the value of the `transaction` element. This parameter is defined at the top level of the stylesheet and its default value is set to the string `'date'` so that by default the table is sorted by date:

```
<xsl:parameter name="sort-by" select="'date'" />
```

The value of the $sort-by parameter must be determined by the column header that the user clicks. The method of processing you're using determines how you can do this.

For client-side processing, you must have a JavaScript function that takes one argument — the new value for $sort-by. (I won't go into detail about this function here because you can read all about it in Chapter 14, but for now let's call it sortTable().) When someone clicks a header, you need to call that function with the relevant value. So the header row generated by the XSLT must be as follows:

```
<tr>
   <th><a onclick="sortTable('date')">Date</a></th>
   <th><a onclick="sortTable('type')">Type</a></th>
   <th><a onclick="sortTable('payee')">Payee</a></th>
   <th><a onclick="sortTable('value')">Amount</a></th>
</tr>
```

For server-side processing with Cocoon, you need to create URLs that load the same XML but with the $sort-by parameter set to the relevant value, as follows:

```
<tr>
   <th><a onclick="?sort-by=date">Date</a></th>
   <th><a onclick="?sort-by=type">Type</a></th>
   <th><a onclick="?sort-by=payee">Payee</a></th>
   <th><a onclick="?sort-by=amount">Amount</a></th>
</tr>
```

Chapter 15 contains more details about creating dynamic applications using Cocoon.

Selecting the value to sort by

In pure XSLT, without using extension functions, you can't change the value of the select attribute dynamically. Instead, you must create an expression based on the $sort-by parameter that chooses the relevant attribute or the element (value) itself as appropriate. To get the relevant attribute you need the attribute whose name is equal to the $sort-by parameter:

```
@*[name() = $sort-by]
```

You can use a similar expression to get the value of a child of the element being sorted:

```
*[name() = $sort-by]
```

If the `$sort-by` parameter is equal to the string `'value'`, you want the current node. You can do this with:

```
current()[$sort-by = 'value']
```

The first expression won't return anything if `$sort-by` is equal to `'value'` because an attribute called `value` doesn't exist. So you can safely union the two expressions together — it creates a node set that has only one node in it, and you can sort on the value of that node:

```
<xsl:sort select="@*[name() = $sort-by] |
                  current()[$sort-by = 'value']" />
```

Picking the data type for the sort

Now you have the table being sorted according to the `$sort-by` parameter, but there's another problem in doing dynamic sorts. While most of the sorts work, when you try to sort by value, the transactions are sorted by amount *alphabetically* rather than *numerically*. Thus, you must change the `data-type` attribute dynamically as well.

This is actually fairly easy to do, especially when compared to changing the `select` attribute dynamically. You just need to set up a variable that holds either the string `'text'` or the string `'number'` depending on the value of `$sort-by`, and use this within the attribute value template for the `data-type` attribute:

```
<xsl:variable name="data-type">
   <xsl:choose>
      <xsl:when test="$sort-by = 'value'">number</xsl:when>
      <xsl:otherwise>text</xsl:otherwise>
   </xsl:choose>
</xsl:variable>
<xsl:apply-templates select="transaction">
   <xsl:sort select="@*[name() = $sort-by] | current()[$sort-by = 'value']"
           data-type="{$data-type}" />
</xsl:apply-templates>
```

Complex Sort Specifications

In general, sorts are done according to an attribute value or a child element of the nodes that are being sorted. However, you may want more flexibility than this. For example, my transaction elements could have a more complex structure:

```
<transaction time="2001-03-01T11:32" type="DD">
   <payee>
      <name>TV License</name>
   <payee>
   <amount>8.91</amount>

</transaction>
```

With this structure, the different values for $sort-by mean very different things, as shown in the following table:

$sort-by	Select expression
'date'	substring(@time, 1, 10)
'type'	@type
'payee'	payee/name
'value'	amount

One way of managing this is to set up different xsl:sort elements for each of the $sort-by values. Each xsl:sort should contain the relevant select expression, but any nodes that are chosen within the select expression should only be chosen if the $sort-by parameter has the relevant value. If a node isn't chosen in the select expression of the sort, the value generated by the sort is the same each time — essentially xsl:sort won't sort the elements.

In the previous example, then, the sorts would be:

```
<xsl:sort select="substring(@time[$sort-by = 'date'], 1, 10)" />
<xsl:sort select="@type[$sort-by = 'type']" />
<xsl:sort select="payee[$sort-by = 'payee']/name" />

<xsl:sort select="amount[$sort-by = 'value']" />
```

This can be a bit tedious and is fairly inefficient as the processor *tries* to do each of the searches, even if only one is actually relevant. An alternative solution is to construct a new node set containing copies of the elements that you're sorting, with the relevant sort value in a new attribute. Although you read a discussion about this (and the problems with it) in the first section of this chapter, in this example an alternative solution also involves adding a `sort-value` attribute with the following XSLT code:

```
<xsl:attribute name="sort-value">
   <xsl:choose>
      <xsl:when test="$sort-by = 'date'">
         <xsl:value-of select="substring(@time, 1, 10)" />
      </xsl:when>
      <xsl:when test="$sort-by = 'type'">
         <xsl:value-of select="@type" />
      </xsl:when>
      <xsl:when test="$sort-by = 'payee'">
         <xsl:value-of select="payee/name" />
      </xsl:when>
      <xsl:when test="$sort-by = 'value'">
         <xsl:value-of select="amount" />
      </xsl:when>
   </xsl:choose>
</xsl:attribute>
```

Some XSLT processors, such as Saxon, have extension functions that enable you to evaluate strings as expressions. These processors open other options to you. Rather than have the `$sort-by` parameter hold keywords that specify the search, you can make it hold the select expression that you actually want to use. So, you could set the parameter to one of:

```
"substring(@time, 1, 10)"
"@type"
"payee/name"

"amount"
```

and then use the `saxon:evaluate()` extension function in the `select` attribute of `xsl:sort`:

```
<xsl:sort select="saxon:evaluate($sort-by)" />
```

You can use the same technique to choose the case order, language order, or even sort order of the sort dynamically based on what's being sorted. Normally, you'll want to change the sort order using a separate stylesheet parameter.

To make the previous example more extensible, you could separate the information about the data type to use for each sort in some XML. For example, you could store it in sort elements such as the following:

```
<sort by="date" data-type="text" />
<sort by="type" data-type="text" />
<sort by="payee" data-type="text" />
<sort by="value" data-type="number" />
```

If this XML were stored in a variable called $sorts, then the relevant data type could be retrieved by finding the sort element whose by attribute matches $sort-by, and then by getting its data-type attribute:

```
$sorts/sort[@by = $sort-by]/@data-type
```

With this, the xsl:apply-templates instruction would be as follows:

```
<xsl:apply-templates select="transaction">
  <xsl:sort select="@*[name() = $sort-by] | current()[$sort-by = 'value']"
            data-type="{$sorts/sort[@by = $sort-by]/@data-type}" />
</xsl:apply-templates>
```

Doing Multiple Sorts

Thus far, all of the sorts that you've examined have had a fixed number of sorts. You've either been sorting by one element (such as the type attribute) or by three (such as the year, month, and day of the date) and so on.

Unfortunately, real life is sometimes more complicated than that. You may want your user to be able to define a number of sorts. So they may begin sorting by date, but then they may want to sort by the transaction type with the transaction's date as a secondary sort.

Sorting with Separate Parameters

You could specify four different parameters, each of which can take different values to make up the complete sort:

```
<xsl:param name="sort-by1" />
<xsl:param name="sort-by2" />
<xsl:param name="sort-by3" />
<xsl:param name="sort-by4" />
```

Then you would have four distinct sorts, one using each of the parameters:

```
<xsl:sort select="@*[name() = $sort-by1] | current()[$sort-by1 = 'value']"
          data-type="{$sorts/sort[@by = $sort-by1]/@data-type}" />
<xsl:sort select="@*[name() = $sort-by2] | current()[$sort-by2 = 'value']"
          data-type="{$sorts/sort[@by = $sort-by2]/@data-type}" />
<xsl:sort select="@*[name() = $sort-by3] | current()[$sort-by3 = 'value']"
          data-type="{$sorts/sort[@by = $sort-by3]/@data-type}" />
<xsl:sort select="@*[name() = $sort-by4] | current()[$sort-by4 = 'value']"
          data-type="{$sorts/sort[@by = $sort-by4]/@data-type}" />
```

When you come to the code that fixes the parameter for the next transformation, you must shift the selected column to give the value for $sort-by1, and move each of the current parameter values down one, unless an earlier parameter value was equal to the new value of $sort-by1.

Having to adjust all four parameters makes things a lot more complicated when creating the column headers. For example, the JavaScript function for client-side processing now has to take four arguments (one for each of the parameters), and those values have to be fixed dynamically. The following piece of XSLT code shows the generation of the call to the JavaScript function for the Date column heading alone:

```
<th>
  <a>
    <xsl:attribute name="onclick">
      <xsl:text>sortTable('date', '</xsl:text>
      <xsl:choose>
        <xsl:when test="$sort-by1 = 'date'">
          <xsl:value-of select="$sort-by2" />
        </xsl:when>
        <xsl:otherwise>
          <xsl:value-of select="$sort-by1" />
        </xsl:otherwise>
      </xsl:choose>
      <xsl:text>', '</xsl:text>
      <xsl:choose>
        <xsl:when test="$sort-by1 = 'date' or $sort-by2 = 'date'">
          <xsl:value-of select="$sort-by3" />
        </xsl:when>
        <xsl:otherwise>
          <xsl:value-of select="$sort-by2" />
        </xsl:otherwise>
      </xsl:choose>
      <xsl:text>', '</xsl:text>
      <xsl:choose>
```

```
        <xsl:when test="$sort-by1 = 'date' or $sort-by2 = 'date' or
                        $sort-by3 = 'date'">
          <xsl:value-of select="$sort-by4" />
        </xsl:when>
        <xsl:otherwise>
          <xsl:value-of select="$sort-by3" />
        </xsl:otherwise>
      </xsl:choose>
      <xsl:text>')</xsl:text>
    </xsl:attribute>
    <xsl:text>Date</xsl:text>
  </a>
</th>
```

Sorting with a String

There are two limitations with using separate parameters for each of the sorts. First, it's hard to maintain — you do the same calculations in the `select` and `data-type` attributes of each of the sorts, so the same code is repeated four times. And somewhere in all that testing and changing of the `$sort-byN` parameters something is bound to go wrong.

Second, you can do only a certain number of levels of sorts — between none and four. If you add another column to the table, you have to do quite a few changes to the XSLT to cope with them — add another parameter, add another `xsl:sort`, and add another heading to the table, including all the complex code that goes with it.

You can overcome these limitations by specifying the sort with a single parameter (`$sort-by`) holding a structured string rather than using separate parameters. The string can have a flexible length, so just:

```
:date:
```

means that the processor can generate a table with rows sorted by date alone whereas:

```
:type:date:payee:
```

means that the rows are sorted by type, date, and payee.

DOING THE SORTING WITH FIXED LEVELS

You can continue to fix the number of levels of sorts with separate `xsl:sort` instructions for each level, choosing the relevant part of the string using `substring-before()` and `substring-after()`. Not only is this tedious but each of the bits of the string must be tested a number of times within the `xsl:sort`, so you may as well recreate the various `$sort-byN` variables to do it:

```
<!-- $cropped-sort-by is the same as $sort-by, but without the leading and
     trailing colons -->
<xsl:variable name="cropped-sort-by"
              select="substring($sort-by, 2, string-length($sort-by) - 2)" />
<xsl:variable name="sort-by1"
              select="substring-before($cropped-sort-by, ':')" />
<xsl:variable name="sort-by2"
              select="substring-before(
                          substring-after($cropped-sort-by, ':'), ':')" />
<xsl:variable name="sort-by3"
              select="substring-before(
                          substring-after(
                            substring-after($cropped-sort-by, ':'), ':'),
                          ':')" />
<xsl:variable name="sort-by4"
              select="substring-before(
                          substring-after(
                            substring-after(
                              substring-after($cropped-sort-by, ':'), ':'),
                          ':'), ':')" />
```

With these variables set up, the sorts are exactly the same as they were as separate parameters.

DOING THE SORTING WITH FLEXIBLE LEVELS

Because sort order defaults to document order, specifying that transactions be sorted by type, then date, then payee, gives exactly the same result as sorting transactions by payee, storing the result in an intermediate variable, then sorting that by date, and storing the result in some intermediate XML, and finally sorting by type. In other words, take a look at the following multilevel sort:

```
<xsl:apply-templates select="transaction">
   <xsl:sort select="@type" />
   <xsl:sort select="@date" />
   <xsl:sort select="@payee" />
</xsl:apply-templates>
```

This is exactly the same as the following, which uses variables that are turned into node sets using a node-set() extension function to hold the intermediate XML:

```
<xsl:variable name="transactions-by-payee">
   <xsl:for-each select="transaction">
      <xsl:sort select="@payee" />
      <xsl:copy-of select="." />
```

```
    </xsl:for-each>
  </xsl:variable>
  <xsl:variable name="transactions-by-date-and-payee">
    <xsl:for-each
        select="exsl:node-set($transactions-by-payee)/transaction">
      <xsl:sort select="@date" />
      <xsl:copy-of select="." />
    </xsl:for-each>
  </xsl:variable>
  <xsl:apply-templates
      select="exsl:node-set($transactions-by-date-and-payee)">
    <xsl:sort select="@type" />
  </xsl:apply-templates>
```

Chapter 5 discusses various methods of doing multiple sequential transformations, including using `node-set()` extension functions which are described in more detail in Chapter 18.

Now, using intermediate XML still fixes the number of levels of the sort. But it shows that you can work through the string backwards, one step at a time, to get the sort order that you would get through a variable number of `xsl:sort` elements.

To do this using a `node-set()` extension function, you need a recursive template that takes a string specifying the sort, and a set of `transaction` elements:

```
<xsl:template match="transactions" mode="sort" name="sort">
  <xsl:param name="transactions" select="transaction" />
  <xsl:param name="sort-by" select="$sort-by" />
  ...
</xsl:template>
```

Making this a named and moded template makes it easier to call. See Chapter 13 for more details.

This template needs to sort a set of `transaction` elements. If the `$sort-by` parameter is comprised of more than one item, it needs to call itself to get a set of `transaction` elements sorted according to the rest of the items in the `$sort-by` parameter. Otherwise, it can just sort a copy of the `transaction` elements that it's passed.

```
<xsl:template match="transactions" mode="sort" name="sort">
   <xsl:param name="transactions" select="transaction" />
   <xsl:param name="sort-by" select="$sort-by" />
   <xsl:variable name="cropped-sort-by"
                 select="substring($sort-by, 2, string-length($sort-by) - 2)" />
   <xsl:variable name="sorted-transactions">
      <xsl:choose>
         <xsl:when test="contains($cropped-sort-by, ':')">
            <xsl:call-template name="sort">
               <xsl:with-param name="transactions" select="$transactions" />
               <xsl:with-param name="sort-by"
                  select="concat(':',
                                     substring-after($cropped-sort-by, ':'))" />
            </xsl:call-template>
         </xsl:when>
         <xsl:otherwise>
            <xsl:copy-of select="$transactions" />
         </xsl:otherwise>
      </xsl:choose>
   </xsl:variable>
   ...
</xsl:template>
```

The final action is to generate a copy of the transaction elements from the sorted list, and this time it's sorted according to the first item in the sort specification:

```
<xsl:template match="transactions" mode="sort" name="sort">
   <xsl:param name="transactions" select="transaction" />
   <xsl:param name="sort-by" select="$sort-by" />
   <xsl:variable name="cropped-sort-by"
                 select="substring($sort-by, 2, string-length($sort-by) - 2)" />
   <xsl:variable name="sorted-transactions">
      <xsl:choose>
         <xsl:when test="contains($cropped-sort-by, ':')">
            <xsl:call-template name="sort">
               <xsl:with-param name="transactions" select="$transactions" />
               <xsl:with-param name="sort-by"
                  select="concat(':',
                                     substring-after($cropped-sort-by, ':'))" />
            </xsl:call-template>
         </xsl:when>
         <xsl:otherwise>
            <xsl:copy-of select="$transactions" />
         </xsl:otherwise>
      </xsl:choose>
```

```
    </xsl:variable>
    <xsl:variable name="this-sort"
                  select="substring-before($cropped-sort-by, ':')" />
    <xsl:for-each select="exsl:node-set($sorted-transactions)/transaction">
       <xsl:sort select="@*[name() = $this-sort] |
                          current()[$this-sort = 'value']"
                 data-type="{$sorts/sort[@by = $this-sort]/@data-type}" />
       <xsl:copy-of select="." />
    </xsl:for-each>
</xsl:template>
```

You can apply templates to the transaction elements to actually get rows for them. So you should store the result of the sort in some intermediate XML, here demonstrated using a variable and a node-set() extension function, and then apply templates to them:

```
<xsl:template match="transactions">
   ...
   <xsl:variable name="sorted-transactions">
      <xsl:apply-templates select="." mode="sort" />
   </xsl:variable>
   <xsl:apply-templates
      select="exsl:node-set($sorted-transactions)/transaction" />
   ...
</xsl:template>
```

The fact that the template matches the transactions element means that you can apply templates to the transactions element in sort mode rather than writing out a full call to the template. The alternative would have been to write:

```
<xsl:call-template name="sort">
   <xsl:with-param name="transactions"
                   select="transaction" />
</xsl:call-template>
```

MAKING THE LINKS ON THE COLUMN HEADERS

Changing a string to reflect a new sort is a lot easier than changing the values of separate parameters for each sort. You just give the sort the value that you want to be first, followed by anything that's before it in the existing string, followed by anything that's after it in the existing string. With client-side processing, for example, generating the Date heading now resembles the following:

```
<th>
  <a onclick="sortTable('{concat(':date:',
                                substring-before($sort-by, ':date:'),
                                substring-after($sort-by, ':date:')}')">
    <xsl:text>Date</xsl:text>
  </a>
</th>
```

Sorting with XML

A final way of representing all the different sorts that you want to do is by using XML, which has the advantage that it's fairly easy to manipulate. In addition, you can add extra information about the sort, such as the order it needs to be in. So, you could use the following to represent a sort by type, date, and payee, with date in descending order:

```
<sort order="ascending">type</sort>
<sort order="descending">date</sort>
<sort order="ascending">payee</sort>
```

Sorting based on XML is similar to sorting with strings, except that you can use the position of the node in the XML sort specification to decide what to do rather than messing around with substring(), substring-before(), and substring-after(). The sorting template is basically the same, with the only difference residing in the way that the type of recursion is selected:

```
<xsl:template match="transactions" mode="sort" name="sort">
  <xsl:param name="transactions" select="transaction" />
  <xsl:param name="sort-by" select="$sort-by" />
  <xsl:variable name="sorted-transactions">
    <xsl:choose>
      <xsl:when test="$sort-by/sort[position() > 1]">
        <xsl:call-template name="sort">
          <xsl:with-param name="transactions" select="$transactions" />
          <xsl:with-param name="sort-by"
                          select="$sort-by/sort[position() > 1]" />
        </xsl:call-template>
      </xsl:when>
      <xsl:otherwise>
        <xsl:copy-of select="$transactions" />
      </xsl:otherwise>
    </xsl:choose>
  </xsl:variable>
  <xsl:variable name="this-sort" select="$sort-by/sort[1]" />
  <xsl:for-each select="$sorted-transactions/transaction">
```

```
        <xsl:sort select="@*[name() = $this-sort] |
                           current()[$this-sort = 'value']"
                  data-type="{$sorts/sort[@by = $this-sort]/@data-type}"
                  order="{$this-sort/@order}" />
        <xsl:copy-of select="." />
      </xsl:for-each>
    </xsl:template>
```

USING AN XML SPECIFICATION WITH A STRING PARAMETER

Passing a parameter indicating the XML specification is a little more complicated. To accomplish this, make a string of the parameter that's passed back and forth, but parse it into some XML and use that to do the sorting as in the previous section. For example, if you're using Cocoon, the parameters you pass have to be strings. You can make a string that holds the same information as the XML that you used in the preceding example:

```
Atype:Ddate:Apayee:
```

The first letter in each item in the string represents the order for the sort. Parsing this string into the XML involves a recursive template such as those constructed in Chapter 2. For example, you could use:

```
<xsl:template name="parse-sort-by-string">
  <xsl:param name="sort-by-string" select="$sort-by-string" />
  <sort order="ascending">
    <xsl:if test="substring($sort-by-string, 1, 1) = 'D'">
      <xsl:attribute name="order">descending</xsl:attribute>
    </xsl:if>
    <xsl:value-of
        select="substring(substring-before($sort-by-string, ':'), 2)" />
  </sort>
  <xsl:variable name="rest"
                select="substring-after($sort-by-string, ':')" />
  <xsl:if test="contains($rest, ':')">
    <xsl:call-template name="parse-sort-by-string">
      <xsl:with-param name="sort-by-string"
                      select="substring-after($rest, ':')" />
    </xsl:call-template>
  </xsl:if>
</xsl:template>
```

If the string is passed in as the $sort-by-string parameter, then creating the $sort-by XML variable involves calling the preceding template and converting the result to a node set, which you can do in Xalan, the XSLT processor that ships with

Cocoon, using the `xalan:nodeSet()` extension function. (You don't need to specify the parameter because it's set to the `$sort-by-string` by default.)

```
<xsl:variable name="sort-by">
   <xsl:call-template name="parse-sort-by-string" />
</xsl:variable>
```

In the column headings, you must recreate the string to be passed as the parameter value next time. As you are using extensions to XSLT anyway, it's easiest to do this in two steps: create the new XML for the sort, and then apply templates to that to generate the desired string. This is a more maintainable method than creating the string directly because it keeps the assumptions about the format of the `$sort-by-string` limited to two places in the stylesheet – the place where it's parsed into XML and the templates that turn it into the string.

Creating the new XML involves first creating a `sort` element with a value of date. You can set the `order` attribute on this `sort` element to ascending by default. However, if the first `sort` element in the current `$sort-by` parameter defines a sort by date and the `order` attribute on it is `ascending` (for example, the user clicked the Date heading last time), then you can override it with an `order` attribute with a value of `descending`. The remaining `sort` elements (if any exist) are copied afterwards.

```
<xsl:variable name="new-sort-by">
   <sort order="ascending">
      <xsl:if test="$sort-by/sort[1][@by = 'date' and @order = 'ascending']">
         <xsl:attribute name="order">descending</xsl:attribute>
      </xsl:if>
      <xsl:text>date</xsl:text>
   </sort>
   <xsl:copy-of select="$sort-by/sort[@by != 'date']" />
</xsl:variable>
```

Given this new set of `sort` elements, you need to recreate the string, using a simple template in which you give a letter indicating the sort order based on the order attribute, and then add the value of the `sort` element:

```
<xsl:template match="sort" mode="to-string">
   <xsl:choose>
      <xsl:when test="@order = 'descending'">D</xsl:when>
      <xsl:otherwise>A</xsl:otherwise>
   </xsl:choose>
   <xsl:value-of select="." />
</xsl:template>
```

Because you're using Cocoon here, you must give the new sort string as part of the URL in the links from the column headers. You begin by creating the new sort XML, then converting this to a string, and finally adding the value of the string as part of the link. Putting this together, creating the Date heading resembles the following:

```
<th>
  <xsl:variable name="new-sort-by">
    <sort order="ascending">
        <xsl:if test="$sort-by/sort[1]
                        [@by = 'date' and @order = 'ascending']">
          <xsl:attribute name="order">descending</xsl:attribute>
        </xsl:if>
        <xsl:text>date</xsl:text>
    </sort>
    <xsl:copy-of select="$sort-by/sort[@by != 'date']" />
  </xsl:variable>
  <xsl:variable name="new-sort-by-string">
    <xsl:apply-templates select="$new-sort-by" mode="to-string" />
  </xsl:variable>
  <a href="?sort-by-string={$new-sort-by-string}">Date</a>
</th>
```

MAKING THE LINKS WITH CLIENT-SIDE PROCESSING

Using a string for the parameter that specifies the sort is easier than passing XML back and forth, but it can be a headache to create strings that mirror nested XML structures or ones with lots of attributes. In this instance, you want to actually pass the XML back and forth rather than converting it down to a string each time. You can pass XML structures as parameters client-side but it's not something that you can easily do with Cocoon. Basically, you need to construct a serialization of the XML and pass that, as a string, to the JavaScript function, which can then parse it and pass it (as a DOM) to the processor.

Chapter 14 discusses how to pass XML structures as parameters in more detail.

Again, it's easiest to create this string by creating the XML first, and then serializing it. You can use the same code as previously mentioned to create the new XML for the Date heading. You can serialize this with a set of templates that serialize nodes, such as those developed in Chapter 3. Finally, you must pass the result of that serialization as the argument to the JavaScript sortTable() function. This code is very similar to the one for Cocoon shown at the end of the previous section.

The only changes are to the mode used to apply templates to the new sort XML and the way that the parameter is passed to the next stage:

```
<th>
   <xsl:variable name="new-sort-by">
     <sort order="ascending">
        <xsl:if test="$sort-by/sort[1]
                           [@by = 'date' and @order = 'ascending']">
          <xsl:attribute name="order">descending</xsl:attribute>
        </xsl:if>
        <xsl:text>date</xsl:text>
     </sort>
     <xsl:copy-of select="$sort-by/sort[@by != 'date']" />
   </xsl:variable>
   <xsl:variable name="new-sort-by-string">
      <xsl:apply-templates select="$new-sort-by" mode="serialize" />
   </xsl:variable>
   <a onclick="sortTable('{$new-sort-by-string}')">Date</a>
</th>
```

The serializing templates need to both serialize the XML and then escape it according to JavaScript escaping conventions. A discussion on this topic is found in Chapter 14.

Summary

This chapter examines in detail how to sort things. In the first section, I introduced the two basic methods of sorting values that are calculated – using single XPaths (which can get very complicated very quickly) or using some intermediate XML.

In the second section, I discussed sorting by date, both because it's one of the more common things to sort by and because it shows some of the issues involved with sorting in a predefined and non-computable order (such as month names).

Then I discussed dynamic sorts, focusing on the common problem of getting the rows in a table to sort according to an order specified by the user. I examined ways of choosing the value that should be sorted by when it's specified only with a keyword, and I examined dynamically choosing the type of sort to do, and the order that it should be done in.

The final sections of this chapter cover doing multiple sorts in which the levels of sorting are chosen dynamically, either with separate parameters, or through a string, or XML representation of the different levels. I discussed the pros and cons of each method in terms of both doing the sort itself and creating links to get the sort to run dynamically.

Chapter 8

Numbering

IN THIS CHAPTER

◆ Numbering with `xsl:number`

◆ Numbering without `xsl:number`

◆ Numbering groups and sorted content

NUMBERING IS MOST USEFUL when you're creating some output for presentation, such as numbered items in a list, numbered footnotes or figures across sections, or numbered sections and subsections. It can also be handy for creating stable unique IDs for particular bits of data (unlike those created with the `generate-id()` function, which may change on subsequent transformations, even with the same stylesheet).

You'll learn how to create and use stable unique IDs in Chapter 10.

Many types of numbering can be done with `xsl:number`, and I'll use this instruction a lot in this chapter. The `xsl:number` instruction has a lot of functionality, but it can be hard to comprehend. It also has two big disadvantages. The first is that using it can have a negative impact on the performance of your stylesheet. For that reason, I'll also describe other numbering methods that you can use, even when you can get the same functionality with `xsl:number`. The second disadvantage is that it always reflects the original order of the items you're numbering in the source XML, so if you change that order by sorting or grouping your data, you need another method of numbering. I'll cover numbering in these contexts later in the chapter.

You learned various ways of doing sorts in Chapter 7. Chapter 9 covers creating groups.

Numbering Simple Lists

The simplest type of numbering is just a list of items, such as the transactions in the following XML bank statement. In the most basic situation, all the items are siblings. In the following example, all the `transaction` elements, which are the things to be numbered, are children of the `transactions` element:

```
<transactions>
   <transaction date="2001-03-01" type="DD"
                payee="TV License">8.91</transaction>
   <transaction date="2001-03-01" type="DD"
                payee="British Gas">22.00</transaction>
   <transaction date="2001-03-03" type="CR"
                payee="Client">400.00</transaction>
   <transaction date="2001-03-09" type="SO"
                payee="Rent">633.00</transaction>
   <transaction date="2001-03-10" type="WD"
                payee="Cash">50.00</transaction>
   <transaction date="2001-03-15" type="CR"
                payee="Interest">0.58</transaction>
</transactions>
```

If you're generating HTML, you could just use an ordered list to number the transactions – you don't have to worry about generating the numbers yourself. However, if you're listing the transactions within a table, you do have to generate a number for each (see Figure 8-1). The first column provides the number of each transaction.

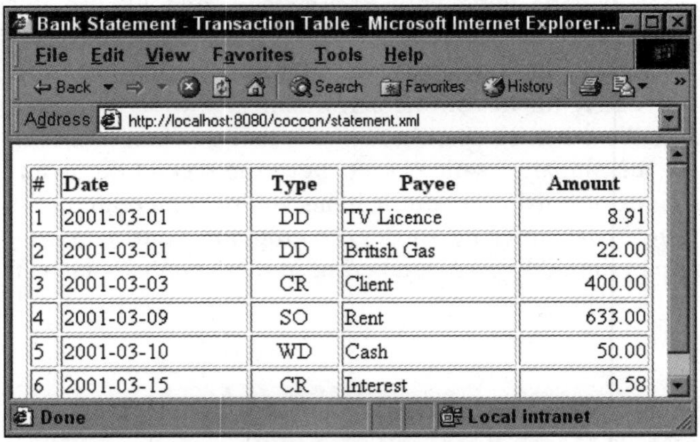

#	Date	Type	Payee	Amount
1	2001-03-01	DD	TV Licence	8.91
2	2001-03-01	DD	British Gas	22.00
3	2001-03-03	CR	Client	400.00
4	2001-03-09	SO	Rent	633.00
5	2001-03-10	WD	Cash	50.00
6	2001-03-15	CR	Interest	0.58

Figure 8-1: A numbered table of transactions in the bank statement application

Numbering Simple Lists with xsl:number

The basic form of xsl:number provides you with numbering of a set of nodes with the same parent. If you use xsl:number when the current node is one of the trans-action elements, they will be numbered within their siblings. Therefore, the XSLT to create the preceding table simply involves adding the following basic form:

```
<xsl:template match="transaction">
   <tr>
      <td><xsl:number /></td>
      <td><xsl:value-of select="@date" /></td>
      <td align="center"><xsl:value-of select="@type" /></td>
      <td><xsl:value-of select="@payee" /></td>
      <td align="right"><xsl:value-of select="." /></td>
   </tr>
</xsl:template>
```

To illustrate the technical details a little, the default values for the attributes of xsl:number that produce this result are shown in Table 8-1:

TABLE 8-1 ATTRIBUTES OF xsl:number

Attribute	Value	Notes
level	single	The number is based on the number of sibling nodes that match the count pattern.
count	transaction	The only nodes that are counted are those that are transaction elements.
format	1	The number string simply consists of an Arabic number.

See Chapter 1 for a description of how to specify the format of numbers using the format attribute of xsl:number.

The count attribute is assigned a value that is based on the node type and name of the current node. It has the default value of transaction in this example because the current node is a transaction element when xsl:number is used. If the current node were an `item` element, it would have the value `item`. If the current node were a text node, it would have the value `text()`.

Changing the Format of the Number

Nested simple lists often use different formats at different levels; for example, a top-level ordered list might use Arabic numerals, whereas lists nested inside it use alphabetical numbering, and the ones listed inside those use roman numbering. If you're using the DocBook markup language for your source XML, for example, you could achieve this different numbering at different nesting levels of the `orderedlist` element with three templates:

```
<xsl:template match="orderedlist/listitem" priority="1">
   <xsl:number format="1. " />
   <xsl:apply-templates />
</xsl:template>

<xsl:template match="orderedlist/listitem//orderedlist/listitem"
            priority="2">
   <xsl:number format="a. " />
   <xsl:apply-templates />
</xsl:template>

<xsl:template
    match="orderedlist/listitem//orderedlist/listitem//orderedlist/listitem"
    priority="3">
   <xsl:number format="i. " />
   <xsl:apply-templates />
</xsl:template>
```

These templates all have the same default priority of 0.5, because they all have some ancestry information included in their match pattern. I've therefore given each of the templates an explicit priority, so that a `listitem` element matches the most specific pattern that it can.

Another method of dealing with nested lists that use different numbering formats at different levels is to use a single template and have a variable hold the relevant format pattern according to the depth of the list. The `format` attribute on `xsl:number` is an attribute value template, so you can use a variable to indicate its value dynamically, rather than fixing it within the stylesheet:

```
<xsl:template match="orderedlist/listitem">
   <xsl:variable name="depth" select="count(ancestor::orderedlist)" />
```

```
<xsl:variable name="format">
  <xsl:choose>
    <xsl:when test="$depth mod 3 = 1">1. </xsl:when>
    <xsl:when test="$depth mod 3 = 2">a. </xsl:when>
    <xsl:otherwise>i. </xsl:otherwise>
  </xsl:choose>
</xsl:variable>
<xsl:number format="{$format}" />
<xsl:apply-templates />
</xsl:template>
```

Note two advantages to this approach. One, it makes it a lot easier to deal with ordered lists nested to any depth. With the preceding template, fourth-level lists will use Arabic numbers, fifth-level lists will use letters, and so on. With the separate templates, any lists below the third level will use roman numbering. Two, the other aspects of formatting the list items are kept in one place, rather than being distributed across three templates.

Starting the Count at a Different Number

With some processors, if you use a number in a format string, the processor will start numbering from that formatting string. However, it's best not to rely on that — other processors will always start from 1. In the bank statement application, I deliver the transactions one page at a time, so the transaction numbering shouldn't always start at 1; instead, I need it to start at a number that I pass into the stylesheet as the `$start-from` parameter.

In these cases, you need to manually perform all the work that `xsl:number` does. The basic `xsl:number` instruction, without any attributes, tells the processor to count the preceding siblings of the current node that are like the current node (that is, are of the same type and have the same name, if they have a name), and add one to get the number. Of course, you can do that yourself with an XPath. In this case, to get the simple numbering given by `xsl:number` by default, you could use the following:

```
count(preceding-sibling::transaction) + 1
```

If you wanted to start from the number given by the `$start-from` parameter, you could add that number to the count instead:

```
count(preceding-sibling::transaction) + $start-from
```

Calculating the number is only half of what `xsl:number` does, however — the other half is formatting that number using a format string. Fortunately, you can still take advantage of this part of the processing because you can pass any numeric value into `xsl:number` and have it format it for you, just by putting it in the `value` attribute. Therefore, you could take advantage of the formatting done by xsl:number with the following:

```
<xsl:number select="count(preceding-sibling::transaction) + $start-from"
             format="1." />
```

Making Numbering more Efficient

The big disadvantage of numbering by counting the preceding siblings of a transaction, whether you do it manually as shown previously or use xsl:number, is that each time the instruction is processed, the processor has to gather up all those siblings into a node set and count them. The more siblings you have to count, the more inefficient this becomes.

There are two solutions to this problem. The first is to write some XSLT that is the equivalent of a loop with an updating variable. Of course, you cannot update a variable using XSLT, so you have to use a recursive solution in which you pass a parameter that keeps track of the current count. In this case, the template steps through the transaction elements one by one, providing the row for each and then moving on to the sibling that immediately follows, passing along the new count each time:

```
<xsl:template match="transaction">
   <xsl:param name="count" select="1" />
   <tr>
      <td><xsl:number value="$count" format="1." /></td>
      <td><xsl:value-of select="@date" /></td>
      <td align="center"><xsl:value-of select="@type" /></td>
      <td><xsl:value-of select="@payee" /></td>
      <td align="right"><xsl:value-of select="." /></td>
   </tr>
   <xsl:apply-templates select="following-sibling::transaction[1]">
      <xsl:with-param name="count" select="$count + 1" />
   </xsl:apply-templates>
</xsl:template>
```

If you use this method, be careful to apply templates to only the first transaction element:

```
<xsl:apply-templates select="transaction[1]" />
```

With this method, you can start numbering at something other than 1 by passing the start number as the $count parameter into the template when you first call it. For example, you could start the counting at 21 with the following:

```
<xsl:apply-templates select="transaction[1]">
    <xsl:with-param name="count" select="21" />
</xsl:apply-templates>
```

The other solution for numbering items more efficiently is to use the position of the node in the current node list. When a processor is told to apply templates to (or iterate over) a set of nodes, this set of nodes becomes the current node list. When one of these nodes is being processed, it becomes the current node, and the position() function can be used to access its index within the current node list. The processor always keeps track of the position of the current node, so it's easy and efficient to access that information.

In this example, you want to make the current node list the set of transaction elements; you can do this by applying templates to all the transaction elements at once:

```
<xsl:apply-templates select="transaction" />
```

If you use this technique, you should always explicitly select the nodes that you want to number. Otherwise, it's easy to get bewildering results due to either the built-in templates or the whitespace-only text nodes, both of which can give you current node lists other than the ones you expect.

Within the template for the transaction elements, you can then access the position of the current node with the position() function:

```
<xsl:template match="transaction">
  <tr>
      <td><xsl:number value="position()" format="1." /></td>
      <td><xsl:value-of select="@date" /></td>
      <td align="center"><xsl:value-of select="@type" /></td>
      <td><xsl:value-of select="@payee" /></td>
      <td align="right"><xsl:value-of select="." /></td>
  </tr>
</xsl:template>
```

With this method, you could start the numbering at 21 by adding 20 to the result of `position()`:

```
<xsl:number value="position() + 20" format="1. " />
```

There's a big distinction between these methods and either `xsl:number` or the equivalent counting XPath. With `xsl:number`, you always get the position of the node in the original source XML. With the `position()` function, the number depends on the order in which these nodes are processed. This is a distinction covered in the section "Numbering Sorted and Grouped Items" later in this chapter.

Using an Ancestor's Number

Often, the elements that contain the information that you're interested in aren't actually siblings. For example, the bank statement XML may use a more generic wrapper element around each transaction:

```
<event>
    <transaction date="2001-03-01" type="DD"
                payee="TV License">8.91</transaction>
</event>
<event>
    <transaction date="2001-03-01" type="DD"
                payee="British Gas">22.00</transaction>
</event>
<event>
    <transaction date="2001-03-03" type="CR"
                payee="Client">400.00</transaction>
</event>
<event>
    <transaction date="2001-03-09" type="SO"
                payee="Rent">633.00</transaction>
</event>
<event>
    <transaction date="2001-03-10" type="WD"
                payee="Cash">50.00</transaction>
</event>
<event>
    <transaction date="2001-03-15" type="CR"
                payee="Interest">0.58</transaction>
</event>
```

The elements that you're interested in are still the transaction elements, but they aren't siblings. If you try to use the basic form of xsl:number, they'll all be numbered 1, as each transaction element is the first transaction element within its parent.

You can still use xsl:number in this situation if you change the count attribute to match the elements that you actually want to number. In this example, the numbers come from the event elements, so you make the xsl:number instruction count event elements, rather than transaction elements:

```
<xsl:number count="event" format="1." />
```

Similarly, you can use an XPath to count the number of preceding siblings the parent event element has:

```
count(../preceding-sibling::event) + 1
```

If you're using the recursive approach, passing parameters into recursive templates, adapting to the new structure just means changing the expressions used to select the initial and subsequent transaction elements that are processed. You still apply templates to the first transaction element:

```
<xsl:apply-templates select="event/transaction[1]" />
```

Within that template, you need to apply templates to the next transaction, which means going up to the parent event element, across to its immediately following sibling, and then down to its child transaction element:

```
../following-sibling::event[1]/transaction
```

If you use the final method, using the position of the transaction in the current node list, you again need to ensure that the current node list consists of the set of transactions. This means applying templates to the transaction elements as a group, rather than relying on the built-in templates to recurse down the node tree:

```
<xsl:apply-templates select="event/transaction" />
```

If you did rely on the built-in templates, the processor would process the children of each event element separately. This means that the current node list would consist of a single transaction element each time, so the position of each transaction element within this list would be 1.

Numbering Figures Across a Document

The second kind of numbering that `xsl:number` handles is the numbering of nodes that are spread across the document. These typically occur in document-oriented XML in which you have figures or footnotes that need to be sequentially numbered.

Setting the `level` attribute of `xsl:number` to `any` gives you this type of numbering. For example, you could number DocBook footnotes with the following:

```
<xsl:template match="footnote">
   <xsl:number level="any" format="[a] " />
   <xsl:apply-templates />
</xsl:template>
```

Numbering at "any level" means that the number is based on all the preceding nodes (and ancestor nodes) in the document. Therefore, the number produced by the preceding example is equivalent to that produced by the following expression:

```
count(preceding::footnote | ancestor-or-self::footnote)
```

The other aspect to this kind of numbering that you need to consider is where the numbered items occur in the result. As discussed in the previous section, with simple lists, you can process all the items in the list at once and use the `position()` function to number them (or step through them one by one for the same result). However, these techniques only work if you want to output a list of items in the same place; they don't work if the items are spread out across the document.

For example, if you were preparing a list of footnotes to be included in the table of contents, you could iterate over all the footnotes in the document and use the position of the `footnote` element in the list you were processing to indicate its number:

```
<xsl:for-each select="//footnote">
   <xsl:number value="position()" format="[a] " />
   <xsl:apply-templates />
</xsl:for-each>
```

However, if you were processing the footnotes as part of the text of the document, they would be spread throughout the document, and their position would never reflect the number you wanted.

In long documents, you'll often want to restart the numbering of footnotes or figures at the beginning of each chapter. In these situations, the number of a footnote is based on the number of footnotes that have occurred since the beginning of the chapter.

With `xsl:number`, you can tell the processor to count only those nodes that occur after a specified node. The node to count from is identified through a pattern provided by the `from` attribute. The processor finds the closest node that matches this pattern, and then starts counting from that node. Therefore, to number footnotes and reset their numbers at each new chapter, you could use the following:

```
<xsl:number from="chapter" format="[a] " />
```

When the processor tries to number a `footnote` element, it will find the footnote's closest `chapter` element, and then count the number of `footnote` elements that occur before the footnote within that `chapter` element.

The node matched by the `from` pattern might not be an ancestor of the node you're numbering — it could be any node that starts before the current node. For example, you could use processing instructions to indicate the point at which the numbering should be restarted.

The processing that is done to restart numbering is complicated. Constructing equivalent XPaths so that you can restart numbering from something other than 1 is not straightforward. You first need to identify the preceding or ancestor node that you're counting from and assign that to a variable:

```
<xsl:variable name="from"

        select="(preceding::chapter | ancestor::chapter)[last()]" />
```

You can usually make this simpler and more efficient if you know whether the node you're counting from is an ancestor or just a preceding node. For example, in this case, you know that the `chapter` element is an ancestor, so you could use the following:

```
<xsl:variable name="from"
            select="ancestor::chapter[1]" />
```

You then need to find the nodes that you want to count, but only those that also have the node you're counting from as a preceding or ancestor node. In this case, you want to find those `footnote` elements that have the same `chapter` element as an ancestor (or preceding node). You can accomplish this with the following expression:

```
count((preceding::footnote | ancestor-or-self::footnote)
        [(preceding::chapter | ancestor::chapter)
          [count(.|$from) = 1]])
```

Again, we could simplify this to reflect the knowledge that we have about the structure of the document; we know that the other footnote elements cannot be ancestors of this one and that they will be descendants of the chapter element, so we can use the following simpler expression:

```
count(preceding::footnote
        [ancestor::chapter[count(.|$from) = 1)]])
```

An alternative design is to use a key to get quick access to all the footnotes within a particular chapter by indexing each footnote by the ID of its immediately preceding or ancestor chapter:

```
<xsl:key name="footnotes-by-chapter"
        match="footnote"
        use="generate-id((preceding::chapter | ancestor::chapter)[last()]" />
```

This key makes it easy to get all the footnotes in the chapter that you're starting the count from. To get the number of the current footnote, though, you need to find those footnotes returned by the key that occur prior to the current footnote as follows:

```
count(key('footnotes-by-chapter', generate-id($from))
        [(following::footnote | descendant::footnote)
          [count(.|current()) = 1]])
```

Whichever method you use, numbering across a document is inefficient because the paths have to use axes like preceding, following and descendant, which are likely to contain a lot of nodes and therefore take a long time to traverse.

Numbering Subsections

The final type of numbering supported by xsl:number is the most complicated — it involves multi-level numbering. In multi-level numbering, each part of the number represents a different level of the document.

Numbering Nested Subsections

Two types of subsections might need numbering. The first, and easiest, are those that include nested subsections, in which the structure of the number is reflected by the structure of the XML. For example, the following XML shows the structure of the first chapter of this book.

```
<section>
    <title>Manipulating Numbers</title>
    <section>
        <title>Formatting numbers as strings</title>
        <section>
            <title>Formatting decimal numbers</title>
            <section><title>Localizing numbers</title></section>
            <section><title>Formatting patterns</title></section>
            <section><title>Interpreting localized numbers</title></section>
        </section>
        <section>
            <title>Formatting integers</title>
            <section><title>Formatting long integers</title></section>
            <section><title>Interpreting alphanumeric strings</title></section>
        </section>
        <section><title>Turning numbers into ordinals</title></section>
        <section><title>Spelling out numbers</title></section>
    </section>
    <section>
        <title>Changing the Base of Numbers</title>
        <section><title>Converting from hexadecimal to decimal</title></section>
        <section><title>Converting from decimal to hexadecimal</title></section>
    </section>
</section>
```

We want to generate a table of contents for the book that numbers each of these sections in a manner such as the following:

```
1 Manipulating Numbers
    1.1 Formatting numbers as strings
        1.1.1 Formatting decimal numbers
            1.1.1.1 Localizing numbers
            1.1.1.2 Formatting patterns
            1.1.1.3 Interpreting localized numbers
        1.1.2 Formatting integers
            1.1.2.1 Formatting long integers
            1.1.2.2 Interpreting alphanumeric strings
        1.1.3 Turning numbers into ordinals
```

NUMBERING SIMPLE NESTED SECTIONS

Here, the numbers are multi-level – 1.2.1 indicates the first subsection of the second section of the first chapter. We can achieve this numbering system by setting the level attribute of xsl:number to multiple:

```
<xsl:template match="section">
   <xsl:number level="multiple" />
   <xsl:apply-templates />
</xsl:template>
```

With this setting, the processor creates a node set made up of all the ancestors of the current node that match the count pattern (which defaults to section in this case), and the current node itself if it matches. Each one of those nodes is then used as the source of one of the numbers within the multi-level number. The first number is calculated by counting the preceding siblings of the first node (in document order) that matches the count pattern and adding one; the second number by counting the preceding siblings of the second node that matches the count pattern and adding one, and so on.

NUMBERING NESTED STRUCTURES WITH DIFFERENT ELEMENTS

In the previous example, all the counted nodes were section elements, but they are often different types of elements. For example, the structure of Chapter 1 could have been represented as follows:

```
<chapter>
  <title>Manipulating Numbers</title>
  <sect1>
    <title>Formatting numbers as strings</title>
    <sect2>
      <title>Formatting decimal numbers</title>
      <sect3><title>Localizing numbers</title></sect3>
      <sect3><title>Formatting patterns</title></sect3>
      <sect3><title>Interpreting localized numbers</title></sect3>
    </sect2>
    <sect2>
      <title>Formatting integers</title>
      <sect3><title>Formatting long integers</title></sect3>
      <sect3><title>Interpreting alphanumeric strings</title></sect3>
    </sect2>
    <sect2><title>Turning numbers into ordinals</title></sect2>
```

```
   <sect2><title>Spelling out numbers</title></sect2>
 </sect1>
 <sect1>
   <title>Changing the Base of Numbers</title>`
   <sect2><title>Converting from hexadecimal to decimal</title></sect2>
   <sect2><title>Converting from decimal to hexadecimal</title></sect2>
 </sect1>
</chapter>
```

Here, the elements are different at different levels — chapter for the chapter level, sect1 for the top-level sections, and so on. To use xsl:number in this situation, the count pattern has to match all the types of elements that need to be counted:

```
<xsl:number level="multiple"
            count="chapter | sect1 | sect2 | sect3" />
```

> The value of the count attribute is a pattern, just like the value of the match attribute on xsl:template. Using a | here is a way of indicating alternative patterns — it doesn't influence the order in which the numbers are inserted in the multi-level number.

This will fix the levels of the numbering to the third-level sections. To proceed further down the hierarchy, we need a more general count pattern:

```
<xsl:number level="multiple"
            count="chapter | *[starts-with(local-name(), 'sect')]" />
```

FORMATTING MULTI-LEVEL NUMBERS

Chapter 1 covered the basics of how xsl:number formats numbers. Multi-level numbers are somewhat special because the processor uses the format string to format a list of numbers, rather than just one number. I'll use the following format string as an example to show how the number is constructed:

```
[1-A.a.i]
```

The format string is split up into a number of *format tokens*, each of which represents a number in a particular format. Within a format string, any letter or number is considered part of a format token. In this string, the format tokens are the numbers and letters in the string, as indicated in bold here:

```
[1-A.a.i]
```

Given a list of numbers, the processor uses the format tokens in turn to format those numbers. In this case, if the list of numbers were 1, 2, 3, the 1 would be used to format the 1 (giving 1), the A would be used to format the 2 (giving B) and the a would be used to format the 3 (giving c). If the list of numbers is longer than the list of format tokens, the processor uses the last format token in the string to format the number. If it's shorter then the extra format tokens are ignored.

For the numbers after the first number, the processor also adds a separator to the resulting string. The separator is made up of any characters between the format token and the preceding one. Therefore, in this example, the separator for the second format token is the character -, whereas the separator for the third format token is the character .. If you don't specify a format token for the second number in the list, the processor will use a . as a separator by default.

Finally, the processor adds any text that occurs before the first format token and after the last format token. In this case, these are the square brackets, indicated in bold:

[1-A.a.i]

These characters will be added to the start and end of every number, no matter what the level. In this case, all the numbers will be bracketed with square brackets.

The Table 8-2 shows the result of using this format string with different lists of numbers.

TABLE 8-2 EXAMPLE MULTI-LEVEL NUMBERS

Numbers	Result
1	[1]
2, 3	[2-C]
4, 5, 6	[4-E.f]
7, 8, 9, 10	[7-G.h.x]
11, 12, 13, 14, 15	[11-L.m.xiv.xv]

USING ALTERNATIVE NUMBERING METHODS FOR NESTED SECTIONS

Just as with other uses of xsl:number, you can create the same kinds of numbers using XPaths to manually count the number of nodes involved. This can be an advantage if you can use information about the structure of the source XML to target the nodes that you want to count. It can also give you more flexibility; for example, enabling you to start the numbering at a different number.

In the simple example shown previously, where every section was represented by a `section` element, you could construct a similar number by iterating over the ancestor `section` elements using `xsl:for-each`, providing the number for each of them and adding a period after all but the last to separate the numbers:

```
<xsl:template match="section">
   <xsl:for-each select="ancestor-or-self::section">
      <xsl:number value="count(preceding-sibling::section) + 1" />
      <xsl:if test="position() != last()">.</xsl:if>
   </xsl:for-each>
   <xsl:apply-templates />
</xsl:template>
```

You can get more flexibility if you use moded templates to generate the numbers for the different levels. If you apply templates to all the ancestors of a section in `number` mode, for example, you can use different types of formatting for different levels of the hierarchy. The following templates use numbers for chapters, capital letters for level 1 sections, lowercase letters for level 2 sections, and roman numerals for level 3 sections. Applying templates to an element at one level calls the numbering pattern of the level above it automatically, so that the numbering is consistent down the tree. The numbers are generated by a basic `xsl:number` instruction, with the `format` attribute providing the desired format pattern for the number, which includes the separator between the number of this section and the number of the higher section.

```
<xsl:template match="*" mode="number">
   <xsl:apply-templates select="ancestor::*[1]" mode="number" />
</xsl:template>

<xsl:template match="chapter" mode="number">
   <xsl:number format="1" />
</xsl:template>

<xsl:template match="sect1" mode="number">
   <xsl:apply-templates select="ancestor::*[1]" mode="number" />
   <xsl:number format="-A" />
</xsl:template>

<xsl:template match="sect2" mode="number">
   <xsl:apply-templates select="ancestor::*[1]" mode="number" />
   <xsl:number format=".a" />
</xsl:template>

<xsl:template match="sect3" mode="number">
   <xsl:apply-templates select="ancestor::*[1]" mode="number" />
```

```
    <xsl:number format=".i" />
</xsl:template>
```

NUMBERING IN DIFFERENT WAYS AT DIFFERENT LEVELS

I like to number tables with a multi-level number in which the first number indicates the chapter in which the table is found, the second indicates the number of the first level header, and the third number indicates the number of the table within that chapter. For example, the third table to appear in Section 5 of Chapter 4 would be numbered 4.5.3, even if it actually occurred in the second subsection of that section.

You can't use a single xsl:number to do this, as the multi-level numbering system used by xsl:number only counts siblings of the relevant nodes — the various tables within a section may very well not be siblings of one another, as they might occur in different subsections. However, you can use two xsl:number instructions to do it. The first provides the number for the section, and the second provides the number for the table, but only within the chapter:

```
<xsl:number level="multiple" count="chapter | chapter/section" format="1.1." />
<xsl:number level="any" count="table" from="chapter/section" format="1" />
```

The first xsl:number counts chapter elements and section elements that are children of a chapter element. This ensures that the lower-level section elements aren't included in the numbering scheme.

An alternative method is to apply templates to the relevant section element in number mode, and let it provide the number itself. This has the advantage that the format used for the section number will be "inherited" within the table number — if you change it within the template, that change will be reflected in the table numbering:

```
<xsl:apply-templates select="ancestor::section[parent::chapter]"
                     mode="number" />
<xsl:number level="any" count="table" from="chapter/section" format="1" />
```

Numbering Un-nested Subsections

Some XML vocabularies, notably XHTML, don't use nesting to identify subsections, but instead use heading levels. In XHTML, for example, the outline of Chapter 1 would look like the following:

```
<h1>Manipulating Numbers</h1>
<h2>Formatting numbers as strings</h2>
<h3>Formatting decimal numbers</h3>
<h4>Localizing numbers</h4>
<h4>Formatting patterns</h4>
<h4>Interpreting localized numbers</h4>
<h3>Formatting integers</h3>
<h4>Formatting long integers</h4>
<h4>Interpreting alphanumeric strings</h4>
<h3>Turning numbers into ordinals</h3>
<h3>Spelling out numbers</h3>
<h2>Changing the Base of Numbers</h2>
<h3>Converting from hexadecimal to decimal</h3>
<h3>Converting from decimal to hexadecimal</h3>
```

Here, you can't use `xsl:number` to automatically give you the multi-level numbering that you want, as the headings at all levels are siblings. However, you can use it to calculate each number for you if you want. The following set of templates identify the number of each level of heading using `xsl:number` to count heading elements at that level that have occurred after the closest heading at a level one higher. Therefore, you can get the number of an h3 element within its h2 element by counting the h3 elements that occur after the closest h2 element.

```
<xsl:template match="h1">
   <xsl:number level="any" format="1. " />
   <xsl:apply-templates />
</xsl:template>

<xsl:template match="h2">
   <xsl:number level="any" count="h1" format="1." />
   <xsl:number level="any" count="h2" from="h1" format="1. " />
   <xsl:apply-templates />
</xsl:template>

<xsl:template match="h3">
   <xsl:number level="any" count="h1" format="1." />
   <xsl:number level="any" count="h2" from="h1" format="1." />
   <xsl:number level="any" count="h3" from="h2" format="1. " />
   <xsl:apply-templates />
</xsl:template>

<xsl:template match="h4">
   <xsl:number level="any" count="h1" format="1." />
   <xsl:number level="any" count="h2" from="h1" format="1." />
   <xsl:number level="any" count="h3" from="h2" format="1." />
```

```
   <xsl:number level="any" count="h4" from="h3" format="1. " />
   <xsl:apply-templates />
</xsl:template>

<xsl:template match="h5">
   <xsl:number level="any" count="h1" format="1." />
   <xsl:number level="any" count="h2" from="h1" format="1." />
   <xsl:number level="any" count="h3" from="h2" format="1." />
   <xsl:number level="any" count="h4" from="h3" format="1. " />
   <xsl:number level="any" count="h5" from="h4" format="1. " />
   <xsl:apply-templates />
</xsl:template>

<xsl:template match="h4">
   <xsl:number level="any" count="h1" format="1." />
   <xsl:number level="any" count="h2" from="h1" format="1." />
   <xsl:number level="any" count="h3" from="h2" format="1." />
   <xsl:number level="any" count="h4" from="h3" format="1. " />
   <xsl:number level="any" count="h5" from="h4" format="1. " />
   <xsl:number level="any" count="h6" from="h5" format="1. " />
   <xsl:apply-templates />
</xsl:template>
```

This is a little difficult to maintain because if you want to change the format of the chapter-level number to use capital letters instead, you have to change it in all the templates. It's better to use moded templates to generate the numbers of the headings at each level. That way, you only have to change the number format in one place:

```
<xsl:template match="h1 | h2 | h3 | h4 | h5 | h6">
   <xsl:apply-templates select="." mode="number" />
   <xsl:apply-templates />
</xsl:template>

<xsl:template match="h1" mode="number">
   <xsl:number level="any" format="1" />
</xsl:template>

<xsl:template match="h2" mode="number">
   <xsl:apply-templates select="preceding-sibling::h1[1]" mode="number" />
   <xsl:number level="any" from="h1" format=".1" />
</xsl:template>

<xsl:template match="h3" mode="number">
   <xsl:apply-templates select="preceding-sibling::h2[1]" mode="number" />
```

```
    <xsl:number level="any" from="h2" format=".1" />
</xsl:template>

<xsl:template match="h4" mode="number">
    <xsl:apply-templates select="preceding-sibling::h3[1]" mode="number" />
    <xsl:number level="any" from="h3" format=".1" />
</xsl:template>

<xsl:template match="h5" mode="number">
    <xsl:apply-templates select="preceding-sibling::h3[1]" mode="number" />
    <xsl:number level="any" from="h4" format=".1" />
</xsl:template>

<xsl:template match="h6" mode="number">
    <xsl:apply-templates select="preceding-sibling::h3[1]" mode="number" />
    <xsl:number level="any" from="h5" format=".1" />
</xsl:template>
```

Numbering Sorted and Grouped Items

As shown in the rest of this chapter, xsl:number is a very powerful tool for calculating the numbers of items in your source XML. However, xsl:number has one big drawback: it always operates on the source node tree. This means it always gives you the numbers of items as they appeared in the original document; if you sort or group these items, you can't use xsl:number to generate the numbers for them.

You can still use xsl:number to *format* numbers in different ways, by specifying the numbers with the value attribute. You just can't use xsl:number to calculate the relevant number for a node.

There are three techniques you can use if the numbers that you want are indicative of the order of the output, rather than the input:

1. Use a two-stage process: do the sorting or grouping, and then number the result of that.

2. Use a recursive process: pass the number of each node as a parameter into a template.

3. Use the position of the node in the current node list.

You learned the latter two methods in the first section of this chapter, as ways of making the numbering process more efficient. However, as well as making numbering more efficient, these two techniques both operate on the order in which nodes are processed, rather than their original order in the XML document.

Which technique you use depends on the type of grouping or sorting that you are doing. If you can, it's usually easier to apply templates to the nodes that you want to number, and use their position within the current node list to indicate the number that you output. However, as you'll see in Chapter 9, some grouping techniques require you to step through the nodes one by one; and in these cases, the number of the node can be passed as a parameter instead.

With complex sorting and grouping, it's often handy to break up the process into two simple parts. Numbering sorted or grouped nodes can be fairly awkward, so being able to concentrate on one step at a time can simplify the stylesheets that you use and make them easier to maintain.

There are two techniques for doing two-stage processing. One is to have a single process, but split it into two phases: the first phase creates a result tree fragment, which you then convert into a node set and process for the second phase. The second technique is to have two separate stylesheets to carry out each phase, with the output for one becoming the input for the next, and control the process with a script, a batch file, or some other method.

Chapter 5 covers techniques for combining transformations in detail.

Summary

In this chapter, you learned four methods for numbering nodes:

◆ Using the `xsl:number` instruction

◆ Counting preceding nodes with an XPath expression

◆ Stepping through nodes, passing a parameter with the current count

◆ Using the position of the current node in the current node list

The `xsl:number` instruction does a lot of work for you in terms of counting nodes, and is especially useful with multi-level numbering. You can still use the formatting side of `xsl:number` if you use one of the other methods, by giving the number in the `value` attribute. This can be handy if you want the numbering to start from a different base, which is impossible with `xsl:number` alone.

The first two methods work on the original document order of nodes within the source tree, whereas the latter two number items in the order that they're actually processed. This means that the latter two techniques are the only ones that can be used with sorted or grouped information, unless you use a two-stage process to first sort or group the information, and then number it. The latter two are also more efficient, as they don't require sets of nodes to be collected and counted at each step.

Chapter 9

Grouping

IN THIS CHAPTER

- ◆ Breaking up records into pages
- ◆ Finding the unique values in a document
- ◆ Grouping records by their values
- ◆ Turning flat structures into hierarchies

GROUPING ITEMS TOGETHER IS a very common goal for a transformation. It's particularly useful with data-oriented XML applications in which the XML vocabulary is fairly flat, similar to a database structure, rather than having a hierarchical structure. Unfortunately, XSLT 1.0 and XPath 1.0 do not explicitly support grouping, so for now you have to learn some cunning tricks to get around their limitations.

One of the requirements for XSLT 2.0 is that it must simplify grouping (see Requirement 4 at http://www.w3.org/TR/xslt20req). See Chapter 19 for a discussion of extension functions and elements that help with grouping, in particular in Saxon.

This chapter describes several different kinds of grouping: grouping by position, such as getting 20 transactions per page; grouping by value, such as splitting up transactions into different types; and grouping into hierarchies, such as adding list elements around groups of item elements.

Tackling each of these grouping tasks requires the same general approach, so you'll be introduced to that first, before looking at the tasks and how to achieve them in detail.

General Grouping Methods

Grouping a set of items together involves performing actions at two levels:

1. Group level, such as giving a header or creating a wrapping element

2. Item level, such as simply copying the items or transforming them in some other way

This chapter, as in previous chapters, uses a bank statement application as an example. In this application, some XML holds details of transactions for a particular bank account:

```
<transaction date="2001-03-01" type="DD" payee="TV License">8.91</transaction>
<transaction date="2001-03-01" type="DD" payee="British Gas">22.00</transaction>
<transaction date="2001-03-03" type="CR" payee="Client">400.00</transaction>
<transaction date="2001-03-09" type="SO" payee="Rent">633.00</transaction>
<transaction date="2001-03-10" type="WD" payee="Cash">50.00</transaction>
<transaction date="2001-03-15" type="CR" payee="Interest">0.58</transaction>
```

These `transaction` elements are contained within a `transactions` element wrapper. When you group these transactions by their type, for example, you might add wrapper elements at the group level and copy the transactions themselves at the item level (omitting the `type` attribute, as that information is now available from the hierarchy). The following XML shows the result — the XML shown in bold is generated at the group level; the rest is generated at the item level:

```
<credit>
    <transaction date="2001-03-15" payee="Interest">0.58</transaction>
    <transaction date="2001-03-03" payee="Client">400.00</transaction>
</credit>
<direct-debit>
    <transaction date="2001-03-01" payee="TV License">8.91</transaction>
    <transaction date="2001-03-01" payee="British Gas">22.00</transaction>
</direct-debit>
<standing-order>
    <transaction date="2001-03-09" payee="Rent">633.00</transaction>
</standing-order>
<withdrawal>
    <transaction date="2001-03-10" payee="Cash">50.00</transaction>
</withdrawal>
```

In addition to grouping the transactions, I am also sorting them by amount.

Alternatively, if you were generating an HTML table, and adding header rows to indicate the groups, the group level would add the heading row, while the item level would add rows holding the details for the transactions. The following HTML shows the result – again, the HTML in bold is generated at the group level, the rest is generated at the item level:

```
<tr><th colspan="3">Credit</th></tr>
<tr><td>2001-03-03</td><td>Client</td><td>400.00</td></tr>
<tr><td>2001-03-15</td><td>Interest</td><td>0.58</td></tr>
<tr><th colspan="3">Direct Debit</th></tr>
<tr><td>2001-03-01</td><td>TV License</td><td>8.91</td></tr>
<tr><td>2001-03-01</td><td>British Gas</td><td>22.00</td></tr>
<tr><th colspan="3">Standing Order</th></tr>
<tr><td>2001-03-09</td><td>Rent</td><td>633.00</td></tr>
<tr><th colspan="3">Withdrawal</th></tr>
<tr><td>2001-03-10</td><td>Cash</td><td>50.00</td></tr>
```

Predictable and Unpredictable Groups

It is very easy to fall into the trap of over-complicating grouping problems and applying a method that's overly complex and inefficient. You should always try to take full advantage of everything you know about the source XML that you're processing and the output that you want to generate.

One of the biggest pitfalls is not taking advantage of knowing in advance what the various groups will be. In the previous examples, if the type attribute can only be one of a set number of values (CR, DD, SO or WD), then rather than use a complicated grouping method, you can generate the group-level output by hand, and populate it by selecting the relevant transactions, as shown in the following template:

```
<xsl:template match="transactions">
   <credit>
      <xsl:apply-templates select="transaction[@type = 'CR']">
         <xsl:sort data-type="number" />
      </xsl:apply-templates>
   </credit>
   <direct-debit>
```

Contnied

Predictable and Unpredictable Groups *(continued)*

```
        <xsl:apply-templates select="transaction[@type = 'DD']">
            <xsl:sort data-type="number" />
        </xsl:apply-templates>
    </direct-debit>
    <standing-order>
        <xsl:apply-templates select="transaction[@type = 'SO']">
            <xsl:sort data-type="number" />
        </xsl:apply-templates>
    </standing-order>
    <withdrawal>
        <xsl:apply-templates select="transaction[@type = 'WD']">
            <xsl:sort data-type="number" />
        </xsl:apply-templates>
    </withdrawal>

</xsl:template>
```

If you want to allow for future expansion, you can use XML to store the information about the possible groups, and process that XML to generate the groups. For example, you could set up the $transaction-types variable to hold a node set of the form:

```
<type code="CR">credit</type>
<type code="DD">direct-debit</type>
<type code="SO">standing-order</type>

<type code="WD">withdrawal</type>
```

You might store this information in a separate file, or even within an XML Schema for the source XML. A template can use this to generate the groups as follows:

```
<xsl:template match="transactions">
    <xsl:variable name="transactions" select="transaction">
    <xsl:for-each select="$transaction-types">
        <xsl:variable name="code" select="@code" />
        <xsl:element name="{.}">
            <xsl:apply-templates
                    select="$transactions[@type = $code]">
                <xsl:sort data-type="number" />
            </xsl:apply-templates>
        </xsl:element>
    </xsl:for-each>

</xsl:template>
```

Adding new transaction types would then just be a matter of changing the XML that lists them. The grouping methods described in this chapter are primarily worthwhile when you *don't* know what the groups are going to be in advance.

The three approaches to grouping are described in the following Table 9-1:

TABLE 9-1 THREE APPROACHES TO GROUPING

Name	Restrictions	Method
Flat	Items are already sorted in groups and the output order you desire; you are only adding headers or footers (not wrapping elements).	Apply templates to all the items; within each template test whether the item is the first in the group, and add the group-level header or footer if it is.
Recursive	Items are already sorted in the output order you desire.	Apply templates to the first item; recurse through subsequent items to get output.
Hierarchical	None.	Apply templates to items that are first in each group; within the template, collect items that are in the group and apply templates to them.

You can always use the hierarchical method with a grouping problem, but it is more complex than the other two methods, and can be overkill for simple grouping. The recursive method is great, as long as you don't want to change the order of the items that you're grouping (although you can always use a two-pass solution and sort the items on the second pass). The flat method is fairly restricted in that it requires everything to be in the right order and cannot generate nested structures, but is the simplest to apply.

If you're getting data from a database, ensuring that the items have the desired order can greatly simplify the grouping in your stylesheet.

The following sections describe each of these approaches in general; the rest of the chapter shows them in action in various circumstances.

Flat Grouping Method

The flat grouping method only works if the items are already in the right order—
that is, they are arranged in the groups that you want them to be in, and the sort
order within those groups is the one that you want. To use this method with the
transactions, they would have to be sorted by type and by amount, to give the order
shown:

```
<transaction date="2001-03-15" type="CR" payee="Interest">0.58</transaction>
<transaction date="2001-03-03" type="CR" payee="Client">400.00</transaction>
<transaction date="2001-03-01" type="DD" payee="TV License">8.91</transaction>
<transaction date="2001-03-01" type="DD" payee="British Gas">22.00</transaction>
<transaction date="2001-03-09" type="SO" payee="Rent">633.00</transaction>
<transaction date="2001-03-10" type="WD" payee="Cash">50.00</transaction>
```

You can always apply a two-pass solution in which you first sort the items,
and then group them. Chapter 5 describes how to link transformations
together to achieve this.

The other restriction of the flat grouping method is that it can only be used to
add group-level headers and footers, not to add wrapping elements. Therefore, of
the two examples outlined previously, we could only use it to create the table
content:

```
<tr><th colspan="3">Credit</th></tr>
<tr><td>2001-03-03</td><td>Client</td><td>400.00</td></tr>
<tr><td>2001-03-15</td><td>Interest</td><td>0.58</td></tr>
<tr><th colspan="3">Direct Debit</th></tr>
<tr><td>2001-03-01</td><td>TV License</td><td>8.91</td></tr>
<tr><td>2001-03-01</td><td>British Gas</td><td>22.00</td></tr>
<tr><th colspan="3">Standing Order</th></tr>
<tr><td>2001-03-09</td><td>Rent</td><td>633.00</td></tr>
<tr><th colspan="3">Withdrawal</th></tr>
<tr><td>2001-03-10</td><td>Cash</td><td>50.00</td></tr>
```

However, this method is very easy to use. You apply templates to everything,
which means you don't have to worry about selecting unique nodes as you do with
the other two techniques. To create the transaction table, for example, the
transactions-matching template has a basic instruction for applying templates:

```
<xsl:template match="transactions">
  <table><xsl:apply-templates /></table>
</xsl:template>
```

Within the template for each of the items, you just need to test whether the item is the first item in the group. If it is the first item, you need to add the relevant header or footer. How you determine whether an item is the first in its particular group depends on the type of grouping that you are doing (by position, by value, or into hierarchies), as described in the last three sections of this chapter.

In this particular example, you can determine whether a transaction element is the first in its group by checking the type attribute of the immediately preceding transaction element – if it's different from this one, you need to start a new group. In the following template, you apply templates to the type attribute to get the relevant header:

```
<xsl:template match="transaction">
   <xsl:if test="preceding-sibling::transaction[1]/@type != @type">
      <xsl:apply-templates select="@type" mode="header" />
   </xsl:if>
   <tr>
      <td><xsl:value-of select="@date" /></td>
      <td><xsl:value-of select="@payee" /></td>
      <td><xsl:value-of select="." /></td>
   </tr>
</xsl:template>
```

In all these methods, you could process the items with xsl:for-each, rather than using templates; I prefer using templates because it divides up the code.

Recursive Grouping Method

The recursive grouping method only works if the items are already sorted in the order that you want the content of the groups to be in, as with the flat grouping method. The items also need to be partially ordered such that the first items in each of the groups are in the order that you want the groups to appear in. To use this method with the bank transactions, they would have to be partially sorted by type and by amount, for example to give the order shown here:

```
<transaction date="2001-03-15" type="CR" payee="Interest">0.58</transaction>
<transaction date="2001-03-01" type="DD" payee="TV License">8.91</transaction>
<transaction date="2001-03-03" type="CR" payee="Client">400.00</transaction>
<transaction date="2001-03-09" type="SO" payee="Rent">633.00</transaction>
<transaction date="2001-03-01" type="DD" payee="British Gas">22.00</transaction>
<transaction date="2001-03-10" type="WD" payee="Cash">50.00</transaction>
```

As with the flat grouping method, you can always apply a two-pass solution in which you first sort the items, and then group them.

The recursive method is also more flexible than the flat method in that you can use it to create wrapping elements around the items. For example, you can use it to create elements indicating the transaction types to group them as follows:

```
<credit>
   <transaction date="2001-03-15" payee="Interest">0.58</transaction>
   <transaction date="2001-03-03" payee="Client">400.00</transaction>
</credit>
<direct-debit>
   <transaction date="2001-03-01" payee="TV License">8.91</transaction>
   <transaction date="2001-03-01" payee="British Gas">22.00</transaction>
</direct-debit>
<standing-order>
   <transaction date="2001-03-09" payee="Rent">633.00</transaction>
</standing-order>
<withdrawal>
   <transaction date="2001-03-10" payee="Cash">50.00</transaction>
</withdrawal>
```

The first step in this method is to simply apply templates to the first item in the list. I usually use a `group` mode to indicate that templates are being applied to generate group-level output. In the example, you can do this from the template matching the `transactions` element. The template looks like the following:

```
<xsl:template match="transactions">
   <xsl:apply-templates select="transaction[1]"
                        mode="group" />
</xsl:template>
```

The `group`-mode template needs to do three things:

1. Generate group-level output for the group

2. Start the recursive process to generate item-level output for the group

3. Move on to the next group

In the recursive method, you generate the item-level output by stepping through the items one by one. Starting this process off involves applying templates to the current item (which is the first in the group), this time in `item` mode. How you identify the first item in the next group depends on the type of grouping that you're doing, so I won't cover that in detail here.

In our present example, the group-level output is a wrapper element (assume that the name of the wrapper element can be accessed by applying templates to the type attribute in wrapper mode). The template for transaction elements in group mode, therefore, looks like the following (this template will only be applied once per group):

```
<xsl:template match="transaction" mode="group">
   <xsl:variable name="wrapper">
      <xsl:apply-templates select="@type" mode="wrapper" />
   </xsl:variable>
   <xsl:element name="{$wrapper}">
      <xsl:apply-templates select="." mode="item" />
   </xsl:element>
   <xsl:variable name="next-group" select="..." />
   <xsl:apply-templates select="$next-group" mode="group" />
</xsl:template>
```

The final stage is to write a template that matches the items in item mode. This template needs to give the item-level output and to move on to the next item recursively. Again, how you determine the identity of the next item depends on the type of grouping that you're doing.

In our example, the item-level output is a copy of the transaction element (without the type attribute). The next transaction element in the group is the next sibling transaction that has the same value for the type attribute as this one does. The item-mode template, therefore, looks like the following:

```
<xsl:template match="transaction" mode="item">
   <xsl:variable name="type" select="@type" />
   <xsl:copy>
      <xsl:copy-of select="@*[local-name() != 'type']" />
   </xsl:copy>
   <xsl:apply-templates mode="item"
         select="following-sibling::transaction[@type = $type][1]" />
</xsl:template>
```

 Depending on the type of grouping that you're doing, the recursion may require passing extra information (such as a count of nodes or the identity of a node at which to stop) from step to step using parameters.

Hierarchical Grouping Method

The hierarchical grouping method is the most general and least restricted method, but it can also be the most technically challenging. The hierarchical grouping method doesn't require the source items to be arranged in any particular order, and it can create nested groups as well as add headers and footers. The following example uses the hierarchical grouping method to generate the nested output:

```
<credit>
   <transaction date="2001-03-15" payee="Interest">0.58</transaction>
   <transaction date="2001-03-03" payee="Client">400.00</transaction>
</credit>
<direct-debit>
   <transaction date="2001-03-01" payee="TV License">8.91</transaction>
   <transaction date="2001-03-01" payee="British Gas">22.00</transaction>
</direct-debit>
<standing-order>
   <transaction date="2001-03-09" payee="Rent">633.00</transaction>
</standing-order>
<withdrawal>
   <transaction date="2001-03-10" payee="Cash">50.00</transaction>
</withdrawal>
```

The first step in this method is to identify representative items for each group (these are usually those that occur first in the group). How you do this depends on the type of grouping that you're doing (by position, by value, and so on). You should usually apply templates to these items from their closest common ancestor; again, I usually use a group mode to indicate that templates are generating group-level output at this stage. The template is as follows:

```
<xsl:template match="transactions">
   <xsl:variable name="unique-transactions" select="..." />
   <xsl:apply-templates select="$unique-transactions"
                        mode="group" />
</xsl:template>
```

Because you're applying templates to a set of nodes here, you can sort those nodes using xsl:sort to get the order of groups that you desire. For example, to group alphabetically by type, you could add the following xsl:sort within the xsl:apply-templates:

```
<xsl:apply-templates select="$unique-transactions"
                     mode="group">
```

```
        <xsl:sort select="@type" />
    </xsl:apply-templates>
```

The `group`-mode template generates the group-level output. Within it, you also need to apply templates to all the remaining items in the group at once, rather than stepping through them one by one. Again, how you select these items depends on the type of grouping that you're doing. Importantly, because you're applying templates to all the items in the group at the same time, you can change the order in which they're processed using `xsl:sort`.

In this example, you need to produce a wrapper element at the group level (assume that the name of the wrapper element can be accessed by applying templates to the `type` attribute in `wrapper` mode). The template for `transaction` elements in `group` mode, therefore, looks like the following (this template will only be applied once per group):

```
<xsl:template match="transaction" mode="group">
    <xsl:variable name="wrapper">
        <xsl:apply-templates select="@type" mode="wrapper" />
    </xsl:variable>
    <xsl:variable name="group-items" select="..." />
    <xsl:element name="{$wrapper}">
        <xsl:apply-templates select="$group-items" mode="item">
            <xsl:sort data-type="number" />
        </xsl:apply-templates>
    </xsl:element>
</xsl:template>
```

 In the preceding template, you're sorting the transactions within the group by their value, something that you couldn't do with the other methods.

The `item`-mode template then simply gives the output required for each item. In this example, this is just a copy of the `transaction` element (without the `type` attribute):

```
<xsl:template match="transaction" mode="item">
    <xsl:copy>
        <xsl:copy-of select="@*[local-name() != 'type']" />
    </xsl:copy>
</xsl:template>
```

Grouping by Position

Grouping by position is typically used in paging applications, where you want to display only a subset of results within a particular page. For example, you might want to split up the transactions appearing in the statement into groups of 10 and enable a user to page through them. It's also common to group by position if you're creating tables with a certain number of columns, with the items wrapping around the columns (the rows are the group-level output and the cells are the item-level output).

You'll learn a bit about dynamic paging first, but you don't really need to do grouping with dynamic paging applications — you just need to focus the output on a particular part of the data. It's really when you're creating a number of pages, or sections in a document, in a batch process, that you need to group by position.

Paging Dynamically

In a dynamic application, you can create pages by defining a stylesheet parameter (for example, $start-index) that indicates the index of the first item that you want to display, and then using that to identify the group of items that you want on the page. You can declare the parameter with an xsl:param element at the top level of the stylesheet, setting it to a default of 1:

```
<xsl:param name="start-index" select="1" />
```

TIP   It's handy to keep the size of the groups that you want in a global variable, such as $group-size, so that you can later change it easily if you want.

Within the stylesheet, you can then select the group of transaction elements starting from this index, and process only them:

```
<xsl:template match="transactions">
  ...
  <xsl:apply-templates
    select="transaction[position() >= $start-index and
                        position() &lt; $start-index + $group-size]" />
  ...
</xsl:template>
```

Alternatively, you could apply templates to the transaction element at that index, and have the template that matches it select the appropriate number of subsequent siblings:

```
<xsl:template match="transactions">
   ...
   <xsl:apply-templates select="transaction[$start-index]" />
   ...
</xsl:template>

<xsl:template match="transaction">
   ...
   <xsl:apply-templates
      select="following-sibling::transaction[position() &lt; $group-size]" />
</xsl:template>
```

Make sure that the `$start-index` value is a number, or explicitly convert it to one using the `number()` function. Otherwise the value of `$start-index` will be converted to a Boolean and you will end up applying templates to all the items (or none of them) rather than the single one that you want.

Be careful not to do more processing that you need to with dynamic paging applications. For example, if you are getting 100 results from a database and then selecting only 10 of those for display, you would save a lot of XML parsing and processing by targeting the database query to retrieve only the 10 desired results in the first place.

How you pass the value for the `$start-index` parameter into the stylesheet in the first place depends on the processor that you're using. Chapter 14 describes how to do it with MSXML in client-side applications, and Chapter 15 describes how to do it with Cocoon in server-side applications.

Creating Batches of Pages

Grouping by position comes into its own when you need to create a number of pages (or sections in a single page) that contain a certain amount of information all at once. You might create all these pages using an extension element that creates a named file, or create a single document that you later divide into separate pages. Either way, you want to output all the data in a single process, but have it divided up based on the position of the items.

By definition, items that are grouped by position are already in the order that you want them in the output. This means that you can use either the flat method for grouping (if you only want to add headers and footers) or the recursive method (if you need to produce nested structures). Of course, you can use the hierarchical method as well, but you may find one of the other two simpler.

ADDING HEADERS TO PAGES

If you are just adding headers (or footers) to the positional groups that you're creating, you can use the flat grouping method. For the flat grouping method, you need to be able to determine which items are the first within the groups. If you're grouping into groups of 10, these are the first, eleventh, twenty-first, thirty-first, and so on, items. If you're grouping into groups of four, these are the first, fifth, ninth, thirteenth, and so on, items. You can identify these items by checking their position divided by the size of the desired group. If the remainder of this division is 1, then the item is the first in the group. In other words, you should check whether the position of the item mod the size of the group is 1:

```
position() mod $group-size = 1
```

Whenever you use the position() function, make sure that the context node list contains the nodes that you're interested in. If you have the test within a predicate, make sure that the location path is selecting the right set of nodes and that you're applying the predicate to the location path as a whole, rather than to the final step within it.

With the flat grouping method, you apply templates to all the items, and then test within the template for each item to determine whether it is the first item in the group. In the bank statement example, this yields the following:

```
<xsl:template match="transactions">
   ...
   <xsl:apply-templates select="transaction" />
   ...
</xsl:template>

<xsl:template match="transaction">
   <xsl:if test="position() mod $group-size = 1">
      <!-- group-level output -->
   </xsl:if>
   <!-- item-level output -->
</xsl:template>
```

Using this method, you must be careful to apply templates only to the nodes that you're interested in, and avoid things such as whitespace-only text nodes that will skew the position of the items within the context node list. I find that using an xsl:for-each instruction helps in these circumstances, as the select expression that determines the context node list (in the select attribute of xsl:for-each) and the call to position(), which relies on the context node list (in the body of the xsl:for-each), are in close proximity to each other. The following templates show the equivalent processing to the previous templates, this time using xsl:for-each instead of xsl:apply-templates to iterate over the transaction elements:

```
<xsl:template match="transactions">
   ...
   <xsl:for-each select="transaction">
      <xsl:if test="position() mod $group-size = 1">
         <!-- group level output -->
      </xsl:if>
      <xsl:apply-templates select="." />
   </xsl:for-each>
   ...
</xsl:template>

<xsl:template match="transaction">
   <!-- item-level output -->
</xsl:template>
```

ADDING WRAPPERS AROUND PAGES

If you're adding wrappers around pages, you need to use either the recursive or the hierarchical grouping approach (recall that you cannot use the flat grouping method to generate wrapping elements).

In the recursive method, you need to apply templates to only the first item in the page – in this case, the first transaction element in the set, in group mode:

```
<xsl:template match="transactions">
   <xsl:apply-templates select="transaction[1]" mode="group" />
</xsl:template>
```

The group-mode template needs to give the group-level result nodes, and needs to apply templates to the first node in the group (which is the current node) in item mode. It also needs to move on to apply templates in group mode to the first item on the next page. You can identify this item by looking at the nth following sibling, where n is the size of the group. The following template shows this in action for this example:

```
<xsl:template match="transaction" mode="group">
   <!-- group level output -->
   <xsl:apply-templates select="." mode="item" />
```

```
<!-- group level output -->
<xsl:apply-templates select="following-sibling::transaction[$group-size]"
                     mode="group" />
</xsl:template>
```

With the full recursive approach, you need to step through the items one by one. In grouping by position, you only want to step from one node to the next a certain number of times. Therefore, you need to keep track of how many steps you've taken, and use that count to decide whether to continue through the items. You can keep track of the number of steps taken (or the number of steps remaining) by passing a parameter each time you apply templates to the next node.

 TIP If you don't want to use full recursion, you could just apply templates to the next *n* items, where *n* is the size of the group minus one. This approach brings the recursive method closer to the hierarchical method described later in this section.

In this example, you could use a $remaining parameter, which starts at the group size minus 1 (for example, 9 with groups of size 10), and decreases by one on each step. You only need to continue on to the next step if there is a $remaining count:

```
<xsl:template match="transaction" mode="item">
   <xsl:param name="remaining" select="$group-size - 1" />
   <!-- item level output -->
   ...
   <xsl:if test="$remaining">
      <xsl:apply-templates mode="item"
          select="following-sibling::transaction[1]">
         <xsl:with-param name="remaining"
                         select="$remaining - 1" />
      </xsl:apply-templates>
   </xsl:if>
</xsl:template>
```

Equally, you could use a $count parameter, which starts at 1 and increases by one at each step. With this approach, you should only continue on to the next node if the count is less than the size of the group that you want to create:

```
<xsl:template match="transaction" mode="item">
   <xsl:param name="count" select="1" />
   <!-- item level output -->
   ...
```

```
    <xsl:if test="$count &lt; $group-size">
      <xsl:apply-templates mode="item"
            select="following-sibling::transaction[1]">
        <xsl:with-param name="count"
                          select="$count + 1" />
      </xsl:apply-templates>
    </xsl:if>
</xsl:template>
```

Both approaches give the same result; the latter is better if you need to number the items sequentially, as you can use the $count parameter as the basis of the numbering.

In the hierarchical approach, the first step involves applying templates to the first items in the groups. You've already learned how to identify the first node in each group using the mod operator; here, this test is placed in a predicate to filter the items. Templates are applied in group mode to get the group-level output:

```
<xsl:template match="transactions">
  ...
  <xsl:apply-templates mode="group"
     select="transaction[position() mod $group-size = 1]" />
  ...
</xsl:template>
```

The group-mode template in the hierarchical approach needs to select and apply templates in item mode to all the items in the group, rather than just the initial node within it. Because the group-mode template is only applied to the first node in each group, you can identify the rest of the group by taking the next *n* siblings of that node, where *n* is the group size minus one (that one being the item that you're looking at, the first in the group). In our example, this looks like the following:

```
<xsl:template match="transaction" mode="group">
  <!-- group level output -->
  <xsl:apply-templates mode="item"
       select=". |
              following-sibling::transaction[position() &lt; $group-size]" />
  <!-- group level output -->

</xsl:template>
```

The item-mode template only needs to give the output for the item — there's no need for parameters (you can use the position() function if you need to number the items):

```
<xsl:template match="transaction" mode="item">
   <!-- item level output -->
</xsl:template>
```

Grouping by Value

Grouping by value is the most common kind of grouping, in which there is some property of the items by which you want to group (often an attribute or subelement value). In the example of bank transactions, you might want to group the transactions by their type (as in the earlier examples), by date, or even by ranges of values.

Any of the three grouping approaches can be appropriate; which ones you can use depends on the ordering of the items in your source XML and the type of output that you want to create.

Adding Headers to Sorted Records

If the records that you're grouping are already in the correct sort order (arranged in groups and in the desired sequence within that group), and you only want to add headers to them, you can use the flat grouping method. The flat grouping method, remember, involves applying templates to everything and then identifying, within the template, whether the particular item is the first in the group.

Identifying the first node in a group in this situation is a matter of looking at the immediately preceding record in the list. The first item in a group will have a different value for its grouping property than the immediately preceding record. You saw this illustrated with the set of transaction elements sorted by their type attribute earlier in this chapter. There, the transaction-matching template was as follows:

```
<xsl:template match="transaction">
   <xsl:if test="preceding-sibling::transaction[1]/@type != @type">
      <!-- group level output -->
   </xsl:if>
   <!-- item level output -->
</xsl:template>
```

Make sure that you select only the immediately preceding record (with a
[1] predicate), rather than all the preceding records.

It's usually the case that the records that you're sorting are siblings, as they are
in this example, so you'll normally use the `preceding-sibling` axis to find the
immediately preceding record. In some cases, you might want to use the `preceding`
axis instead, but avoid this if you can as it can be quite inefficient. Instead, you
should walk up, across, and down the node tree to get to the preceding record.

Chapter 17 provides some tips about improving the efficiency of location
paths.

Adding Wrappers to Sorted Records

If you want to wrap elements around the groups, you cannot use the flat grouping
method, and have to move to the recursive method. With the recursive method, you
initially apply templates to only the first of the records. In the bank statement
example, this would be as follows:

```
<xsl:template match="transactions">
   <xsl:apply-templates mode="group" select="transaction[1]" />
</xsl:template>
```

The `group`-mode template needs to provide the group-level result nodes, and
needs to apply templates to the first node in the group (which is the current node)
in `item` mode within the wrapper that you create. It also needs to move on to the
next item that has a different value for the grouping property, and apply templates
to that in `group` mode. In this example, you must apply templates to the next
`transaction` element that has a different value for the `type` attribute than the one
on the current transaction:

```
<xsl:template match="transaction" mode="group">
   <!-- group level output -->
   <xsl:apply-templates select="." mode="item" />
   <!-- group level output -->
   <xsl:variable name="type" select="@type" />
```

```
    <xsl:apply-templates mode="group"
        select="following-sibling::transaction[@type != $type][1]" />
</xsl:template>
```

With the recursive approach, you also need to step through the members of the group one by one. In grouping by value, the members of the group are those items that have the same value for the property by which you're grouping. You can select the next item in the group by finding the next node that has the same value for the property as the current node does.

In this example, you're grouping by the `type` attribute of the `transaction` element, so within the item-mode template, you need to find the next `transaction` element that has the same value for its `type` attribute as the current node does:

```
<xsl:template match="transaction" mode="item">
    <!-- item level output -->
    <xsl:variable name="type" select="@type" />
    <xsl:apply-templates mode="item"
        select="following-sibling::transaction[@type = $type][1]" />
</xsl:template>
```

> The preceding template groups the next transaction with the same type, even if there is another transaction with a different type first. If you only want to group adjacent transactions of the same type, then you should apply templates to the immediately following transaction, but only if its type attribute is equal to the current transaction's type, swapping the predicates as follows:
>
> ```
> <xsl:apply-templates mode="item"
>         select="following-sibling::transaction
>                                     [1][@type = $type]" />
> ```

Grouping Unsorted Records by Value

When the items that you're grouping are not sorted, you need to use the hierarchical method. The hierarchical method applies templates to the first item in each group in `group` mode; then, within the `group`-mode template, it applies templates to all of the items in the group at once. The following sections describe the different ways of identifying these groups, and introduces the Muenchian Method (named after Steve Muench) as a way of accessing them and identifying the first item in each group.

IDENTIFYING GROUPS OF RECORDS

The first problem is how to determine which items belong to a group, given a value of the property for that group. For example, how do you find every credit transaction (the `transaction` elements with a `type` attribute equal to 'CR')? The obvious way is to use a predicate to filter the `transaction` elements by their `type` attribute:

```
transaction[@type = 'CR']
```

In a grouping situation, you need to do this for each of the possible values for the groups. Each time you do it, you go through the entire set of items and test their property to see if it's equal to the value. In the transactions example, you need to look at all the `transaction` elements and test their `type` attribute for each of the groups – given four groups (`CR`, `DD`, `SO` and `WD`), you sift through all the `transaction` elements four times.

This is not very efficient; it's better to define a key so that you can quickly retrieve every item that has a particular value for the property by which you're grouping. You can define a key with the `xsl:key` element. The name of the key can be anything you like as long as it doesn't conflict with another key. The match pattern has to match the nodes that you want to group. The use expression points from one of these nodes to the property that you want to test.

In this example, you could call the key `transactions`; the match pattern needs to match `transaction` elements, and the use expression needs to access the `type` attribute of the `transaction` element. The key definition looks like the following:

```
<xsl:key name="transactions" match="transaction" use="@type" />
```

With this key defined, getting the credit transactions just involves a quick call with the `key()` function:

```
key('transactions', 'CR')
```

IDENTIFYING UNIQUE RECORDS

The second challenge in grouping by value with unsorted items is to find the unique values for the property by which you're grouping, and hence the first item in each of the groups. These are the items that you need to apply templates to in `group` mode, to get the group-level output.

The basic method of finding the first items in each group is to find those items for which *none* of the preceding items have the same value for the particular property by which you're grouping. In the transactions example, you need to find those `transaction` elements for which no preceding (sibling) `transaction` element has a `type` attribute that's equal to the context transaction. This translates to the following expression:

```
transaction[not(preceding-sibling::transaction/@type = @type)]
```

Focusing Keys on Subtrees

The example shown here is a very simple one designed to illustrate how you can construct a key by which to group items. In reality, the keys that you use may be more complicated. You may have to use more complex match patterns to focus the key on the nodes that you're interested in, or you may have to use more complex expressions to access key values, such as the conditional expressions covered in Chapter 3.

One of the limitations of keys, though, is that they always operate across the entirety of the current document. Sometimes, you'll want to scope the key to a particular branch of the node tree, particularly if you have partially grouped items already. In these cases, you need to define a key that incorporates information about the ancestry of the item into the key value.

For example, the transactions that you're dealing with might already be grouped by month:

```
...
<transactions month="03">
    <transaction ...>...</transaction>
    ...
</transactions>
<transactions month="04">
    <transaction ...>...</transaction>
    ...
</transactions>

...
```

If you want to add wrapper elements within those existing month groups, you need a way to focus the key to return the transaction elements with a particular type *and* from a particular month.

To cope with these situations, you need to make keys whose key values are dependent on a combination of values, rather than on just one. The easiest way to do this is to concatenate the values. If you're lucky, you'll be able to use a property of the ancestor to identify it (such as the month attribute of the transactions element in our example); if not, you have to use generate-id() to provide a unique ID for the ancestor. In this example, you can define your key as follows:

```
<xsl:key name="transactions"
         match="transaction"

         use="concat(../@month, '-', @type)" />
```

Then, with the relevant `transactions` element as the current node, you can select all the credit `transaction` elements within that `transactions` element with the following:

```
key('transactions', concat(@month, '-CR'))
```

The more general key, if there were no identifier on the `transactions` element, would be as follows:

```
<xsl:key name="transactions"
         match="transaction"
         use="concat(generate-id(..), '-', @type)" />
```

As you'll learn later in the section "Multi-level Grouping", you can also use concatenated key values to do multi-level grouping in a similar way.

> You can use the `preceding-sibling` axis here because all the `transaction` elements are siblings of one another; if they weren't, you would have to either use the `preceding` axis or climb up and down the node tree to access all the preceding `transaction` elements.

However, if you think about what the processor is going to do when it evaluates this location path, you'll see that it isn't very efficient. For each of the `transaction` elements, the processor has to go through all its preceding siblings until it finds one whose `type` attribute is equal to the `type` attribute of the `transaction` element it's looking at. That means numerous visits to the various `transaction` elements, and is therefore very inefficient.

This is where the Muenchian Method comes into play. In the last section, you set up a key to quickly get to those `transaction` elements that had a particular type. You want to get the first node returned by that key for each of the possible values of the `type` attribute. Unfortunately, you don't know what these possible values are. However, you can go through each of the `transaction` elements and determine whether it is the first `transaction` element returned by the key for its particular type or not. This method of using a key to identify unique values, and hence group items by those values was thought up by Steve Muench and is therefore known as the Muenchian Method.

You can get the set of `transaction` elements that are the first ones in their particular group, therefore, with the following location path:

```
transaction[count(.|key('transactions', @type)[1]) = 1]
```

Testing Node Identity

There are three ways of testing whether two nodes are the same node. The easiest and most efficient way is to use some unique property of the node, such as an ID attribute. For example, if the transaction elements were given a unique value in a num attribute, you could compare a transaction element with the first node returned by the transactions key for that type with the following:

```
@num = key('transactions', @type)[1]/@num
```

Often, however, the nodes that you're grouping don't have a unique property, so you have to use another method. The most intuitive of these (for me, at least) is to generate a unique ID for the two nodes using generate-id() and compare them:

```
generate-id() = generate-id(key('transactions', @type))
```

There's no need to specify the current node as the argument of generate-id(); calling generate-id() with no arguments returns a unique ID for the current node. In addition, using generate-id() on a node set (such as that returned by the key) returns the generated ID for the first node in that node set, so there's no requirement to put in a [1] predicate to select this first node explicitly, although it doesn't hurt to do so if you find it clearer.

While testing generated IDs is intuitive, it can be somewhat inefficient, particularly with processors that aren't optimized when it comes to generating IDs.

The final option is to use set logic to compare the two nodes. A node set can contain only one copy of a particular node. Therefore, if you union the two node sets (each containing a single node), you will get either a node set consisting of two nodes (in which case they are different nodes) or one containing one node (in which case they are the same node). In this example, you could use the following:

```
count(. | key('transactions', @type)[1]) = 1
```

See Chapter 18 for a discussion of the extension functions that enable you to test whether two nodes are the same.

If you just wanted to find out what values these were, you could access their type attributes to find out.

GENERATING THE GROUPS

You've learned how to identify the first items in each group, and how to quickly retrieve all the items in a group. These are the two basic steps in the hierarchical grouping method. You first need to apply templates to the first items in each group in group mode:

```
<xsl:template match="transactions">
   <xsl:apply-templates mode="group"
      select="transaction[count(.|key('transactions', @type)[1]) = 1]" />
</xsl:template>
```

Within the group-mode template, you need to specify the group-level output and apply templates to all the items in the group in item mode:

```
<xsl:template match="transaction" mode="group">
   <!-- group level output -->
   <xsl:apply-templates select="key('transactions', @type)"
                        mode="item" />
   <!-- group level output -->
</xsl:template>
```

Finally, you need an item-mode template to provide the item-level output:

```
<xsl:template match="transaction" mode="item">
   <!-- item level output -->
</xsl:template>
```

Multi-level Grouping

Multi-level grouping involves doing further grouping on items that you've already grouped. For example, you might want to group your transactions first by type (as already shown) and then by the month in which the transaction took place.

ADDING HEADERS AT MULTIPLE LEVELS WITH SORTED ITEMS

When you are just adding headers with items that are already sorted, you can use the flat grouping method in a similar way to the examples already shown. You can apply templates to all the transaction elements and then test within the template – first, whether they have a different type than the previous transaction; and second, whether they occurred in a different month:

```
<xsl:template match="transaction">
   <xsl:if test="preceding-sibling::transaction[1]/@type != @type">
      <!-- type group level output -->
   </xsl:if>
   <xsl:if test="substring(preceding-sibling::transaction[1]/@date, 4, 2) !=
               substring(@date, 4, 2)">
      <!-- month group level output -->
   </xsl:if>
   <!-- item level output -->
</xsl:template>
```

ADDING WRAPPER ELEMENTS AT MULTIPLE LEVELS WITH SORTED ITEMS

If you need to add wrapper elements and the items are already sorted, you can use the recursive method. Note that you need three levels of templates:

- Type group level, to provide group-level output for the types and direct the processing of the month groups within that

- Month group level, to provide group-level output for the months and apply templates to the first item in the group

- Item level, to provide the item-level output

As usual, you need a high-level template to apply templates to only the first item in the set. In this case, you can apply templates in type-group mode to the first transaction:

```
<xsl:template match="transactions">
   <xsl:apply-templates mode="type-group" select="transaction[1]" />
</xsl:template>
```

The difference occurs at the group level. Rather than apply templates to the current node in item mode, you need to apply it in a mode to provide the second-level group. In this example, that means applying templates to the current node in month-group mode within the group-level output for the type. As with the single-level grouping, you also need to apply templates to the next item that has a different type in type-group mode. This results in the following template:

```
<xsl:template match="transaction" mode="type-group">
   <!-- type group level output -->
   <xsl:apply-templates select="." mode="month-group" />
   <!-- type group level output -->
   <xsl:variable name="type" select="@type" />
   <xsl:apply-templates mode="type-group"
      select="following-sibling::transaction[@type != $type][1]" />
</xsl:template>
```

The month groups are the lowest-level groups in the hierarchy. Therefore, you need to apply templates to the current node (the first node in the month group) in item mode, and step through the rest of the transactions recursively. You also need to access the first item in the next month group. However, because this is a multi-level group, you need to make sure that the transaction chosen for the next step in the recursion shares the same type as the current transaction, as well as having a different month:

```
<xsl:template match="transaction" mode="month-group">
```

```
<!-- month group level output -->
<xsl:apply-templates select="." mode="item" />
<!-- month group level output -->
<xsl:variable name="type" select="@type" />
<xsl:variable name="month" select="substring(@date, 4, 2)" />
<xsl:apply-templates mode="month-group"
      select="following-sibling::transaction
                  [@type = $type and substring(@date, 4, 2) != $month][1]" />
</xsl:template>
```

The recursion through the items in item mode needs to take into account that the next item in the group must have both a matching type and a matching month:

```
<xsl:template match="transaction" mode="item">
   <!-- item level output -->
   <xsl:variable name="type" select="@type" />
   <xsl:variable name="month" select="substring(@date, 4, 2)" />
   <xsl:apply-templates mode="item"
         select="following-sibling::transaction
                     [@type = $type and substring(@date, 4, 2) = $month][1]" />
</xsl:template>
```

GROUPING AT MULTIPLE LEVELS WITH UNSORTED ITEMS

If the items aren't sorted, you again need to use the hierarchical method to build the groups. It's easiest and cleanest to do this using the Muenchian Method. You first need to set up the keys to give you the different levels of groups. In this example, you want to group first by type, so the key for that is just as it was before (except that I've changed the name to reflect the fact that transactions can be grouped in different ways):

```
<xsl:key name="transactions-by-type"
         match="transaction"
         use="@type" />
```

The second level of grouping needs to divide the set of items up both by type and by month. Here, you need a combined key, one in which the key value is dependent on multiple properties of the node. You can create a combined key by concatenating the values of the two properties, using a delimiter that cannot occur in the first property to separate them:

```
<xsl:key name="transactions-by-type-and-month"
         match="transaction"
         use="concat(@type, ':', substring(@date, 4, 2))" />
```

As with the recursive method just discussed, you need templates at several different levels to deal with the different levels of grouping. You want to apply templates in `type-group` mode to the first `transaction` elements in each type group:

```
<xsl:template match="transactions">
  <xsl:apply-templates mode="type-group"
     select="transaction
                [count(.|key('transactions-by-type', @type)[1]) = 1]" />
</xsl:template>
```

Within the `type-group`-mode template, you need to provide the output for the type group and then apply templates in `month-group` mode to those transactions that have the same type as the current node and that have a unique month:

```
<xsl:template match="transaction" mode="type-group">
  <!-- type group level output -->
  <xsl:variable name="type" select="@type" />
  <xsl:apply-templates mode="month-group"
     select="key('transactions-by-type', $type)
                [count(.|key('transactions-by-type-and-month',
                            concat($type, ':', substring(@date, 4, 2)))[1]) =
                1]" />
  <!-- type group level output -->
</xsl:template>
```

Here, you use the `transactions-by-type` key to narrow the search through the `transaction` elements for the first items in each month group to only those that have a matching type in the first place. This is a lot more efficient than going through all the `transaction` elements to get those with a matching type and unique month.

The `month-group`-mode template is applied to those nodes that are first in each item group within a particular type group. To get the rest of that particular group, you can use the `transactions-by-type-and-group` key again:

```
<xsl:template match="transaction" mode="type-group">
  <!-- month group level output -->
  <xsl:apply-templates mode="item"
       select="key('transactions-by-type-and-month',
                   concat(@type, ':', substring(@date, 4, 2)))" />
  <!-- month group level output -->
</xsl:template>
```

As always with the hierarchical method, the item-level template is very simple, providing only the item-level details for each of the nodes:

```
<xsl:template match="transaction" mode="item">
   <!-- item level output -->
</xsl:template>
```

Grouping in Hierarchies

The final type of grouping involves going from a flat structure into a hierarchical one. There are two common examples of this. The first goes from a flat class structure (which might describe object classes or a parent-child hierarchy of another type) to a nested representation of the hierarchy. The second goes from a flat document structure to a more structured one.

Nesting Class Structures

The most obvious type of ownership structure is one in which you have a class structure encoded within XML, with each class pointing with a reference to its parent within the hierarchy. For example, you might have the following XML to encode a taxonomic hierarchy:

```
<class name="animal" />
<class name="canine" parent="animal" />
<class name="dog" parent="canine" />
<instance name="Abby" parent="dog" />
<class name="wolf" parent="canine" />
<class name="feline" parent="animal" />
<class name="tiger" parent="feline" />
<class name="cat" parent="feline" />
<instance name="Ben" parent="cat" />
<instance name="Hedge parent="cat" />
```

This flat structure could be translated into a hierarchical structure as follows:

```
<class name="animal">
   <class name="canine">
      <class name="dog">
         <instance name="Abby" />
      </class>
      <class name="wolf" />
   </class>
   <class name="feline">
```

```
      <class name="tiger" />
      <class name="cat">
         <instance name="Ben" />
         <instance name="Hedge" />
      </class>
   </class>
</class>
```

It's easiest to approach this transformation with the hierarchical grouping method. You can set up a key to access the classes and instances with a particular parent by indexing the classes by their parent attribute:

```
<xsl:key name="children" match="class | instance" use="@parent" />
```

The top of the hierarchy is the class that doesn't have a parent. This class will have an empty string for its key value, as it doesn't have a parent attribute. The first step is to apply templates to this node:

```
<xsl:template match="classes">
   <xsl:apply-templates select="key('children', '')" />
</xsl:template>
```

For each class, you want to generate a class element with the same name. The content of the class element needs to be the result of applying templates to the children of that particular class. These can be retrieved from the children key using the name of the current class. The template, therefore, looks like the following:

```
<xsl:template match="class">
   <xsl:copy>
      <xsl:copy-of select="@name" />
      <xsl:apply-templates select="key('children', @name)" />
   </xsl:copy>
</xsl:template>
```

Finally, of course, the instance elements need to be copied:

```
<xsl:template match="instance">
   <xsl:copy-of select="." />
</xsl:template>
```

Adding Structure to Documents

The method to use when adding structure to documents is less clear-cut because you need to maintain the order of the items within the document. In these cases, you can use a hierarchical grouping method like the one previously shown, or you can use a recursive method whereby you step through the document. The following sections describe two common problems and how they can be solved with both methods.

ADDING A WRAPPER AROUND ITEMS OF THE SAME SORT

The first example transformation demonstrates adding a wrapper element around sets of items of the same sort. For example, you might have paragraphs interspersed with sets of item elements that you want to group into lists, as shown in Figure 9-1.

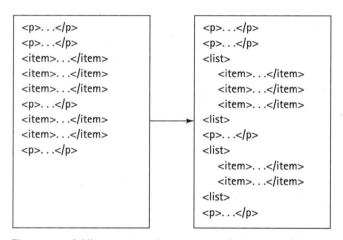

Figure 9-1: Adding wrapper elements around elements of the same type

USING THE RECURSIVE METHOD   The first method of tackling this transformation is to use recursion. As usual, this means applying templates to the first element in the set to be grouped in `group` mode, and stepping through the rest of the elements in the group one by one to determine what to do with them. In this case, for most elements, you just want to copy that element and move on to the next one:

```
<xsl:template match="*" mode="group">
   <xsl:copy-of select="." />
   <xsl:apply-templates select="following-sibling::*[1]"
                        mode="group" />
</xsl:template>
```

The exception is the item element. If you come across an item element, you want to create a wrapper list element, and within that list element apply templates in item mode to the current node (the item element that starts the list). After the list element, you need to move on to the next node that isn't an item element to continue with the rest of the document:

```
<xsl:template match="item" mode="group">
   <list>
      <xsl:apply-templates select="." mode="item" />
   </list>
   <xsl:apply-templates mode="group"
         select="following-sibling::*[not(self::item)][1]" />
</xsl:template>
```

The item-mode template needs to copy the item and move on to the next sibling, but only if it is an item element. The location path here could trip you up — you don't want to get the next item element, because at the end of a list this would be the first item of the next list. Instead, you want the next sibling element, but only if it is an item element:

```
<xsl:template match="item" mode="item">
   <xsl:copy-of select="." />
   <xsl:apply-templates mode="item"
         select="following-sibling::*[1][self::item]" />
</xsl:template>
```

USING THE HIERARCHICAL METHOD With the hierarchical method, the main work is done when selecting the nodes to which to apply templates. In group mode, you want to process nodes that aren't item elements, plus the first item element in each list. You can tell whether an item element is the first item in a list by looking at its immediately preceding sibling — if it's not an item element, the element is the first in the list:

```
<xsl:template match="body">
   <xsl:apply-templates mode="group"
      select="*[not(self::item)] |
            item[not(preceding-sibling::*[1][self::item]]" />
</xsl:template>
```

Here, you just want to copy the elements by default:

```
<xsl:template match="*" mode="group">
   <xsl:copy-of select="." />
</xsl:template>
```

The item-matching template in group mode needs to generate the wrapper element and to add, as its content, the rest of the items in the list. It's easiest to find these item elements by setting up a key so that you can access the items quickly. The one thing that's common to each of the item elements in a particular list, and not to the item elements in other lists, is the identity of the immediately preceding element that is *not* an item element (that is, the element that immediately precedes the start of the list). You can therefore set up the key as follows:

```
<xsl:key name="items" match="item"
        use="generate-id(preceding-sibling::*[not(self::item)][1])" />
```

With this key in place, finding the items in a list is a matter of using the key with the appropriate generated ID. Within a template matching an item element in group mode, this ID is the ID of its immediately preceding sibling (which *cannot* be an item element, because otherwise the template would not have been applied to this item element). The template therefore looks like the following:

```
<xsl:template match="item" mode="group">
   <list>
      <xsl:apply-templates mode="item"
            select="key('items', generate-id(preceding-sibling::*[1]))" />
   </list>
</xsl:template>
```

The item-mode template is then very simple — it just copies the item it matches:

```
<xsl:template match="item" mode="item">
   <xsl:copy-of select="." />
</xsl:template>
```

ADDING SECTIONS TO A FLAT DOCUMENT

The second example transformation involves adding hierarchical sections to a document structure that doesn't make these explicit, such as that used in HTML. This transformation is illustrated in Figure 9-2, where the HTML structure is translated into an equivalent DocBook structure.

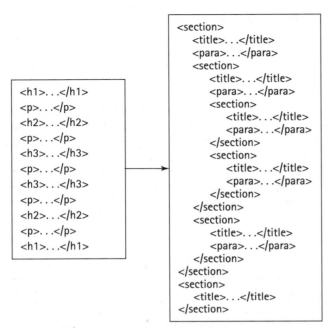

Figure 9-2: Adding sections to a flat document structure

USING THE RECURSIVE METHOD   The recursive method of approaching this transformation is to apply templates to the first element in the document and to step through the elements one by one to determine what to do with them. In this example, you want to translate the elements in element-specific ways, and then move on to the next one. You can approach this by separating these steps into two different templates so that you only have to define how to move on to the next element in the document once. The group mode will define the recursive stepping through the elements, and the item mode will perform the translation of the element into the relevant DocBook element. Thus, for this simple example, you need the following two templates:

```
<xsl:template match="*" mode="group">
   <xsl:apply-templates select="." mode="item" />
   <xsl:apply-templates select="following-sibling::*[1]"
                        mode="group" />
</xsl:template>
```

and:

```
<xsl:template match="p" mode="item">
   <para><xsl:apply-templates /></para>
</xsl:template>
```

The exceptions to this treatment are the heading elements (h1, h2, and so on). When you get to one of these, you want to create a section element. Within this section element, you need to create a title element to hold the value of the heading. You need to perpetuate two types of recursion. The first moves on to the next heading at the same level, to get the next sibling section element in the result; and the second moves on to the next element in the section that you're creating. The basic form of the template is as follows:

```
<xsl:template match="h1 | h2 | h3 | h4 | h5 | h6" mode="group">
   <section>
      <title><xsl:apply-templates /></title>
      <!-- recurse into section -->
   </section>
   <!-- recurse on to next section -->
</xsl:template>
```

To recurse on to the next section, you need to find the next heading element at the same level as or higher than this one. You can determine the depth of this element by looking at the second character in the name:

```
substring(local-name(), 2)
```

Thus, you can find the next heading element to move on to by comparing the depth from its name with the depth of the current heading element:

```
<xsl:template match="h1 | h2 | h3 | h4 | h5 | h6" mode="group">
   <xsl:variable name="depth" select="substring(local-name(), 2)" />
   <xsl:variable name="next-section"
                 select="following-sibling::*
                            [starts-with(local-name(), 'h') and
                             substring(local-name(), 2) &lt;= $depth]" />
   <section>
      <title><xsl:apply-templates /></title>
      <!-- recurse into section -->
   </section>
   <xsl:apply-templates select="$next-section" mode="group" />
</xsl:template>
```

Recursing into the section to generate its content is a matter of choosing the next sibling of the heading element, but you need to make sure that it isn't the heading element that starts the next section. You need to apply templates in group mode again, as you want to continue building the hierarchy. The template is thus as follows:

```
<xsl:template match="h1 | h2 | h3 | h4 | h5 | h6" mode="group">
   <xsl:variable name="depth" select="substring(local-name(), 2)" />
   <xsl:variable name="next-section"
                 select="following-sibling::*
                            [starts-with(local-name(), 'h') and
                             substring(local-name(), 2) &lt;= $depth]" />
   <section>
      <title><xsl:apply-templates /></title>
      <xsl:apply-templates mode="group"
           select="following-sibling::*
                      [count(.|$next-section) != count($next-section)]" />
   </section>
   <xsl:apply-templates select="$next-section" mode="group" />
</xsl:template>
```

USING THE HIERARCHICAL METHOD With the hierarchical method, the first thing to tackle is identifying to which section a particular element belongs. For normal elements, this is easy — it's the immediately preceding heading element of whatever level. The key can thus be as follows:

```
<xsl:key name="items"
         match="*"
         use="generate-id(preceding-sibling::*
                            [self::h1 | self::h2 | self::h3 |
                             self::h4 | self::h5 | self::h6][1]" />
```

For heading elements, it depends on the level of the heading. An h2 element belongs to its closest h1 element; an h3 element belongs to its closest h2 or h1 element (allowing both headings from higher up in the hierarchy means that the headings needn't be strictly nested in order for the sections to work), and so on. Fortunately, if you define two keys with the same name in XSLT, the hash tables that they produce are merged. Therefore, you can build a set of keys with the same name. Each key in the set can match a different heading level and use a different expression dependent on the level of the matched heading, to produce the key value. The keys are as follows:

```
<xsl:key name="items"
         match="h2"
```

```
                    use="generate-id(preceding-sibling::h1[1])" />
<xsl:key name="items"
         match="h3"
         use="generate-id(preceding-sibling::*[self::h1 | self::h2][1])" />
<xsl:key name="items"
         match="h4"
         use="generate-id(preceding-sibling::*
                          [self::h1 | self::h2 | self::h3][1])" />
<xsl:key name="items"
         match="h5"
         use="generate-id(preceding-sibling::*
                          [self::h1 | self::h2 | self::h3 | self::h4][1])" />
<xsl:key name="items"
         match="h6"
         use="generate-id(preceding-sibling::*
                          [self::h1 | self::h2 | self::h3 |
                           self::h4 | self::h5][1])" />
```

Starting from the top of the section hierarchy, then, the first set of nodes that you want to apply templates to are the h1 elements, which appear at the top of the section hierarchy:

```
<xsl:template match="body">
   <xsl:apply-templates select="h1" mode="group" />
</xsl:template>
```

Whenever you process any kind of heading element in group mode, you want to generate a section element, with a title inside it. You then want to move on to the items that are (direct) children of that element, as provided by the items key. The template looks like the following:

```
<xsl:template match="h1 | h2 | h3 | h4 | h5 | h6" mode="group">
   <section>
      <title><xsl:apply-templates /></title>
      <xsl:apply-templates select="key('items', generate-id())"
                           mode="group" />
   </section>
</xsl:template>
```

Now you just need to translate other elements to their appropriate DocBook equivalent, and the work is done:

```
<xsl:template match="p" mode="group">
   <para><xsl:apply-templates /></para>
</xsl:template>
```

Summary

This chapter described a wide variety of types of grouping, and showed you several methods of approaching each of them. The three main types of grouping are as follows:

- Grouping by position; for example, in paging applications or to arrange items in a table

- Grouping by value, using properties of a particular node to identify which group(s) it should be in; you also looked at grouping at multiple levels

- Grouping in hierarchies, producing nested hierarchies from flat information, including class structures; and adding structure to documents

You also learned about three general methods of approaching grouping problems, which are appropriate in different situations, depending on the structure of your source XML and the complexity of the output that you want to produce. These three methods are as follows:

- Flat grouping, which is only worthwhile for simple grouping in which the source is already in the correct order and you just want to add headers or footers to the groups

- Recursive grouping, which is also only useful if the source XML already holds the information in the correct order, but it can be used to add wrapping elements around groups

- Hierarchical grouping, which is the most general but can be relatively complicated; one common technique that assists with the hierarchical grouping method is the Muenchian Method for identifying unique nodes

A secondary result of learning how to group items is learning how to identify the unique values for a particular property on a set of nodes. This can be very handy when you come on to summarizing information, as you'll see in Chapter 10.

Chapter 10

Creating Summaries

IN THIS CHAPTER

◆ Building tables of contents

◆ Constructing unique IDs

◆ Creating indexes

INFORMATION STORED IN XML tends to be stripped to the bare bones—the XML holds as little information as is required to encode the message, no more. When you present this information to users, however, you often want to create summaries, indexes, or tables of contents that enable users to navigate the information quickly. In this chapter, you'll learn how to do that.

The summaries you create might include information such as totals, averages, minima and maxima. You learned how to pull these out of your source XML in Chapter 4.

Processing the Same XML Twice

The secret of creating summaries is to process the same set of source XML more than once in different ways. For example, if you were creating a book, you might include the following summary sections:

◆ A table of contents

◆ A list of figures

◆ A bibliography

◆ An index

235

Each of these sections contains a summary of some aspect of the contents of the book, a summary that needs to be constructed based on information from the DocBook XML:

- A table of contents — the `title` element child of `section` elements
- A list of figures — the `title` element child of `figure` elements
- A bibliography — `citation` elements
- An index — `indexterm` elements

Generally, you want to use the information included in a summary section within the main content of the document as well. For example, you want to use the section titles as titles for the sections in the document, as well as listing them within the table of contents. Therefore, you need to process the same information from the source XML in different ways.

You have two ways of doing this in XSLT. The first is to use modes to direct the processing. The second is to pass parameters in to the template to determine what to do. The former approach is simpler and usually less verbose, but the latter approach makes it easier to set the processing mode dynamically and to share common processing between the modes.

I'll use the table of figures to illustrate the two approaches. Suppose your DocBook document contains the following figure, illustrating a sample node tree:

```
<figure>
   <title>An Example Node Tree</title>
   <graphic fileref="figures/node-tree.gif" />
</figure>
```

You want this figure to be listed as an item within your table of figures, with the HTML:

```
<li>Figure 3-5: An Example Node Tree</li>
```

Within the content of the document, on the other hand, you want the figure to be included with an `img` element:

```
<p>
   <img src="figures/node-tree.gif" alt="An Example Node Tree" />
   <br />
   Figure 3-5: An Example Node Tree
</p>
```

Using Modes

Achieving this dual processing using modes involves applying templates to the same nodes in different modes in different places. For example, you could have a high-level template that organizes the flow of processing in the XSLT stylesheet:

```
<xsl:template match="book">
   ...
   <div class="ToF">
      <h2>Table of Figures</h2>
      <ul>
         <xsl:apply-templates select=".//figure" mode="ToF" />
      </ul>
   </div>
   <div class="content">
      <xsl:apply-templates />
   </div>
   ...
</xsl:template>
```

The figure elements in the XML will have templates applied to them twice — once directly in ToF mode, to create the table of figures, and once during the recursion through the book, during which they need to be included.

You mirror these two different types of processing with two templates. The first gives the table of figures item for a figure:

```
<xsl:template match="figure" mode="ToF">
   <li>
      <xsl:text>Figure </xsl:text>
      <xsl:number count="chapter" />
      <xsl:number level="any" format="-1" />
      <xsl:text>: </xsl:text>
      <xsl:apply-templates select="title" />
   </li>
</xsl:template>
```

See Chapter 8 for a description of how to generate numbers.

The second template generates the HTML for the figure when it is included in the main text:

```
<xsl:template match="figure">
   <p>
      <img src="{graphic/@fileref}" alt="{title}" />
      <br />
      <xsl:text>Figure </xsl:text>
      <xsl:number count="chapter" />
      <xsl:number level="any" format="-1" />
      <xsl:text>: </xsl:text>
      <xsl:apply-templates select="title" />
   </p>
</xsl:template>
```

As you can see, these templates have quite a lot in common — they both add some fixed text, a generated number, and the result of applying templates to the title of the figure. If you wanted to change one of these things in the future — for example, the way the figures were numbered — you would have to make sure you changed it in both places. This makes the templates hard to maintain.

To reduce the amount of repeated code, you can introduce a new template that processes the same figure element in a different mode to generate the common result that's used in both of the templates. You might call this mode caption mode, as you're actually generating the caption within it:

```
<xsl:template match="figure" mode="caption">
   <xsl:text>Figure </xsl:text>
   <xsl:number count="chapter" />
   <xsl:number level="any" format="-1" />
   <xsl:text>: </xsl:text>
   <xsl:apply-templates select="title" />
</xsl:template>
```

Splitting this shared processing into a separate template simplifies the other templates:

```
<xsl:template match="figure" mode="ToF">
   <li>
      <xsl:apply-templates select="." mode="caption" />
   </li>
</xsl:template>

<xsl:template match="figure">
   <p>
      <img src="{graphic/@fileref}" alt="{title}" />
```

```
    <br />
    <xsl:apply-templates select="." mode="caption" />
  </p>
</xsl:template>
```

As you can see, using modes gives you relatively simple, modular templates. However, as with any modular code, it can be hard to trace exactly what processing is going on through all the templates.

Using Parameters

The second way of approaching the problem is to use parameters to instruct a single template to process the same node in different ways. With this technique, the high-level template needs to pass a different value for the parameter for the different sections of the document:

```
<xsl:template match="book">
  ...
  <div class="ToF">
    <h2>Table of Figures</h2>
    <ul>
      <xsl:apply-templates select=".//figure">
        <xsl:with-param name="mode" select="'ToF'" />
      </xsl:apply-templates>
    </ul>
  </div>
  <div class="content">
    <xsl:apply-templates />
  </div>
  ...
</xsl:template>
```

Unlike modes, parameters do not propagate through templates. If you rely on the built-in templates for the processing, the parameter can easily get lost on the way down the node tree. Therefore, you should define a default template that can receive the parameter and pass it through to the next level:

```
<xsl:template match="*">
  <xsl:param name="mode" select="'content'" />
  <xsl:apply-templates>
    <xsl:with-param name="mode" select="$mode" />
  </xsl:apply-templates>
</xsl:template>
```

The `figure` elements in the XML will have templates applied to them twice—once with the $mode parameter equal to 'ToF', to create the table of figures; and once during the recursion through the book (where the $mode parameter defaults to 'content'), during which they need to be included.

A single template deals with both situations, taking the $mode parameter and testing it to see what type of output to create. Because you're using a single template, you can share the code that creates the caption within the template itself, using it for whichever type of output you're generating. The template looks like the following:

```
<xsl:template match="figure">
   <xsl:param name="mode" select="'content'" />
   <xsl:variable name="caption">
      <xsl:text>Figure </xsl:text>
      <xsl:number count="chapter" />
      <xsl:number level="any" format="-1" />
      <xsl:text>: </xsl:text>
      <xsl:apply-templates select="title" />
   </xsl:variable>
   <xsl:choose>
      <xsl:when test="$mode = 'ToF'">
         <li><xsl:copy-of select="$caption" /></li>
      </xsl:when>
      <xsl:otherwise>
         <p>
            <img src="{graphic/@fileref}" alt="{title}" />
            <br />
            <xsl:copy-of select="$caption" />
         </p>
      </xsl:otherwise>
   </xsl:choose>
</xsl:template>
```

As you can see, the template itself is a lot more complicated than the simple templates that you used when using modes. However, all the code that determines how the figure information is constructed in both places is kept within the same template, so you don't have to worry about navigating between templates, trying to reconstruct how the output is generated.

Generating Different Output Dynamically

Using parameters, rather than modes, makes it easier to change the output of a transformation dynamically. For example, you might want to use the same stylesheet to generate either the table of figures or the content of the document (rather than both at once, as shown previously). You still want to process the same nodes in different ways within the same stylesheet, but each run will only generate one part of the output.

You learn about building dynamic client-side and server-side XSLT applications in Chapters 14 and 15.

The only way to change how a stylesheet operates under different conditions is to pass in information about the type of processing it should do using a stylesheet parameter. Stylesheet parameters are declared with the `xsl:param` element at the top level of the stylesheet. The following example declares a stylesheet parameter called `$view`, which will contain a string like `'ToF'` or `'content'` to indicate which section of the output is wanted for viewing:

```
<xsl:param name="view" select="'content'" />
```

Within the stylesheet, you need to test what the value of the `$view` parameter is in order to decide what to do with it. Using modes, you need to check the parameter and then use that check to determine the mode in which to apply templates:

```
<xsl:template match="book">
   ...
   <xsl:choose>
      <xsl:when test="$view = 'ToF'">
         <xsl:apply-templates select=".//figure" mode="ToF" />
      </xsl:when>
      <xsl:otherwise>
         <xsl:apply-templates />
      </xsl:otherwise>
   </xsl:choose>
   ...
</xsl:template>
```

You cannot set modes dynamically without an `xsl:choose` — the mode attribute on `xsl:apply-templates` cannot take an attribute value template as a value.

With parameters, you just need to pass the value of the $view stylesheet parameter as the value of the $mode template parameter:

```
<xsl:template match="book">
  ...
  <xsl:apply-templates>
     <xsl:with-param name="mode" select="$view" />
  </xsl:apply-templates>
  ...
</xsl:template>
```

If you look closer, though, you'll see that there is an advantage to the first approach. You only ever need to perform a test on the $view parameter once, in the controlling stylesheet. If you use template parameters, the parameter will be checked each time the template matches, even though you know by that point which type of processing you should be doing. That will slow down the stylesheet.

Creating Links

When you're creating summaries for online presentation, you often want to create links between the summary and the main part of the text. This can be illustrated with a table of contents, using the section hierarchy that we used before, the outline of the first chapter of this book:

```
<chapter>
   <title>Manipulating Numbers</title>
   <section>
      <title>Formatting numbers as strings</title>
      <section>
         <title>Formatting decimal numbers</title>
         <section><title>Localizing numbers</title></section>
         <section><title>Formatting patterns</title></section>
         <section><title>Interpreting localized numbers</title></section>
      </section>
      <section>
         <title>Formatting integers</title>
         <section><title>Formatting long integers</title></section>
         <section><title>Interpreting alphanumeric strings</title></section>
      </section>
      <section><title>Turning numbers into ordinals</title></section>
      <section><title>Spelling out numbers</title></section>
   </section>
   <section>
      <title>Changing the Base of Numbers</title>
```

```
  <section><title>Converting from hexadecimal to decimal</title></section>
  <section><title>Converting from decimal to hexadecimal</title></section>
  </section>
</chapter>
```

You might want to enable various types of navigation between the table of contents and the content of the chapter. Each of these different types needs slightly different handling.

Creating Local Links

The first type of navigation has the entire chapter, including the table of contents, appear in the same HTML page, with local links between the table of contents and the relevant content on the page. The HTML page would look something like the one shown in Figure 10-1, with the items in the table of contents linking to headings within the same page.

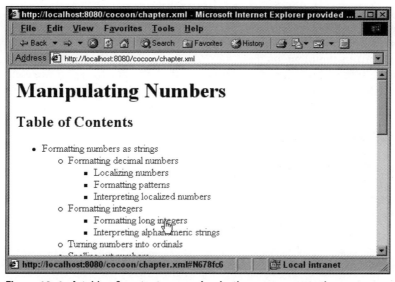

Figure 10-1: A table of contents appearing in the same page as the content

To enable this navigation, you need to create an anchor on the headings that you want to link to, and create a link to that anchor from the entries in the table of contents. The outlines for the templates are as follows (in the normal flow of the section, you want to create a header for the section and add an id attribute to the header, giving it a unique name):

```
<xsl:template match="section">
  <!-- work out the depth of the section -->
```

```
<xsl:variable name="level"
              select="count(ancestor::section) + 2" />
<!-- create a heading element at the appropriate level -->
<xsl:element name="h{$level}">
    <xsl:attribute name="id">
        <xsl:apply-templates select="." mode="id" />
    </xsl:attribute>
    <xsl:value-of select="title" />
</xsl:element>
<xsl:apply-templates select="*[not(self::title)]" />
</xsl:template>
```

If you're catering for older browsers, you should use an a element with a name attribute, as well as use the id attribute of the heading element.

In the table of contents, you want to create a link to this section, with an a element. The href for the a element needs to reference the same section ID you used to create the anchor in the previous template. You create this ID by applying templates to the section in a particular mode, so that you don't have to repeat the code for working out the section ID:

```
<xsl:template match="section" mode="ToC">
    <xsl:variable name="section-id">
        <xsl:apply-templates select="." mode="id" />
    </xsl:variable>
    <li>
        <a href="#{$section-id}"><xsl:value-of select="title" /></a>
        <xsl:if test="section">
            <ul>
                <xsl:apply-templates select="section" mode="ToC" />
            </ul>
        </xsl:if>
    </li>
</xsl:template>
```

If you want to create a printable document using XSL-FO, and want to include page numbers to reference sections, you need to use the same general technique, but rather than using a link to the content, you need to insert the page number on which the content is found. You can do this with a fo:page-number-citation element that refers to the ID of the content.

Therefore, instead of the preceding example, you would use something like the following:

```
<xsl:value-of select="title" />
<fo:leader xsl:use-attribute-sets="ToC-leader-attrs" />
<fo:page-number-citation ref-id="{$section-id}" />
```

USING ID ATTRIBUTES

The best kind of ID that you can get for an element in your result is the ID that was used for the original element in the source XML. These IDs are likely to be meaningful—the ID for a section would likely reflect the contents of the section, or the ID for some customer information might be the customer's number. This makes IDs easy to read and easy to refer to. IDs that are given in the source XML are also easy and efficient to access. Therefore, if you have some identifying information about the items to which you want to link, use it.

 If you are merging several documents, then you cannot guarantee that an element's ID is unique. In these cases, you should disambiguate IDs by concatenating them with the file name of the source document, for example.

For example, if you had id attributes on each of the section elements, you could use those to provide a unique identifying value very simply:

```
<xsl:template match="section" mode="id">
   <xsl:value-of select="@id" />
</xsl:template>
```

USING GENERATE-ID()

Often, however, there is no property that uniquely identifies a particular item to which you want to link. In these cases, you need to make up your own identifier. The obvious way of doing this is to use generate-id(), which is guaranteed to provide a unique ID for each node with which you use it. Using generate-id(), the id-mode template would simply look like the following:

```
<xsl:template match="section" mode="id">
   <xsl:value-of select="generate-id()" />
</xsl:template>
```

In this situation, where you're generating local links, using generate-id() works fine. The only problem with it is that the IDs given to the links are basically random strings of letters and numbers. If you look at the status bar shown in

Figure 10-1, you'll see that the "Formatting long integers" link over which the cursor is hovering corresponds to an ID of `N678fc6`, which is completely meaningless.

However, another feature of `generate-id()` limits its utility dramatically; namely, you cannot rely on it to give the same unique ID for different runs of the same stylesheet. The next time you run the stylesheet, the "Formatting long integers" heading might have an ID of `Nc436b`. Certainly, if you run the stylesheet with a different processor or add new information to the source XML, you'll get different IDs for the nodes in which you're interested.

Some processors might give you the same ID on each run of the stylesheet, but it's best not to rely on this in case you later switch to a processor that doesn't.

With local links like the ones described here, this may not be a problem. If you're creating the pages as a batch process, rather than dynamically, you can guarantee that the local links won't change with each access to the page, which at least means that you can quote the links without worrying about the links breaking. However, if you're creating the page dynamically, the links may change with each access, so you need a different technique for creating the IDs. You'll learn about these other techniques in the next section.

Linking in Frames

If you have a site that uses a frameset to enable navigation through the page, then the content of the navigation frame and the content of the main frame will most likely be created from two runs of different stylesheets over the same XML. One stylesheet creates the summary view (the table of contents), while the other stylesheet creates the main view (the content of the document).

If you were using a batch process, you could create both files at the same time with an extension element that redirected output to a particular file; you can learn more about these extension elements in Chapter 19.

In these situations, you need an ID that is not dependent on the run of the stylesheet, but instead draws all its information from the source node tree itself. The best types of IDs here are those that use information as close to the node as possible. Not only does this make them easy and efficient to process, but it also extends their lifetime, as it limits the effect that changes to the node tree might have on the IDs that you use.

The following sections describe three methods for creating IDs for the section hierarchy that we've been using in our example:

◆ Using the title of the section

◆ Numbering the sections sequentially

◆ Numbering the sections hierarchically

 One thing to remember about all these IDs is that you're creating the ID for a node in the source tree, and then using that ID on an element that you're creating in the result. When you use these IDs within a link, the link goes to the anchor that you've generated elsewhere; it doesn't point to the node in the original XML.

CREATING IDS FROM SECTION TITLES

The closest thing that the `section` elements in this example have to a unique identifier is the value of the `title` element. However, the `title` element values can't be used directly as ID attribute values for four reasons:

◆ They may contain subelements. You need to use the string value of the element to ignore these.

◆ They contain characters that may not be allowed within ID attributes, such as whitespace or ampersands. You can use `normalize-space()` to turn all the whitespace into spaces and then use `translate()` to turn any non-name characters into hyphens or underscores.

◆ They might start with a number. You should add a word such as `'sec-tion'` at the beginning to make sure that they don't.

◆ They might not be unique, particularly in structured documentation where the sections all follow the same format. You could add the titles of the parent sections to disambiguate them.

Thus, you could create a valid ID from one of the section titles with the following instructions:

```
<xsl:text>section-</xsl:text>
<xsl:value-of select="translate(normalize-space(),
                       concat(' &amp;&lt;>!&quot;$%^*(){}[];@#?,/\|',
                              &quot;'&quot;),
                       '-------------------------')" />
```

It's likely that the elements in the XML that you're using have even better properties from which to create unique IDs. You could concatenate a number of attributes and elements to create them. These identifiers require you to look more closely at the XML that you're actually processing, but they are more efficient for the XSLT processor to create than the more general ones described next. They are also more stable, as only changes to the local properties of the node will affect its ID.

CREATING IDS FROM SEQUENTIAL NUMBERS

A more general method of assigning a unique ID to an element is to number it within the document. IDs cannot begin with numbers, so you need to add some text before the number; using the name of the element that you're numbering is a good choice. In our example, this would give the sections identifiers of section-1, section-2, section-3, and so on.

The easiest way to create these numbers is to use the xsl:number element with the level attribute set to any. This will give the number of the element within its own element type across the entire document. For example, the following code generates the identifiers outlined previously:

```
<xsl:value-of select="local-name()">-<xsl:number level="any" />
```

You learned about numbering nodes in Chapter 8; in particular, you may want to use an XPath to create the number, rather than use xsl:number itself.

The permanency of these IDs depends on the type of structural changes that the document author is likely to make to the document. If the changes add more of that particular type of element to the document, then the IDs are relatively unstable; if an element of the same type is added before an existing element, then the existing element's ID will change. If the changes are likely to involve other elements, however, the ID won't change. For example, if you're happy with the section structure, you could use these types of IDs for the section, even if you anticipate adding paragraphs within them. You wouldn't want to use these kinds of IDs for the paragraphs, however, as they change more frequently.

Creating these types of IDs is more involved than generating IDs based on local information about the element. However, it is less processor-intensive than creating hierarchical IDs, which are described next.

CREATING IDS FROM HIERARCHICAL NUMBERS

IDs based on hierarchical numbering are another general type. Again, IDs cannot start with numbers, so you need to add some text before the number; either the name of the element that you're numbering or just a letter. In our example, we might generate IDs of the form N1, N1.1, N1.2, and so on.

The easiest way to create these numbers is to use the `xsl:number` element, this time with the `level` attribute set to `multiple`. You can use the `count` attribute to determine which nodes to take into account in the numbering scheme. The most general numbering uses a `count` attribute of `node()`, to match any nodes. For example, the following code generates the identifiers outlined previously:

```
<xsl:text />N<xsl:number level="multiple" count="node()" />
```

You learned about creating hierarchical numbers in Chapter 8.

Again, how long the IDs will last depends on what kinds of changes are likely to be made later to the structure of the document. These kinds of IDs are sensitive to changes to the preceding siblings of any ancestor nodes, so if new sections are added or taken away, the IDs of the sections would change. However, changes that occur within a preceding section would not cause the ID to change. Hierarchical IDs are also very costly to process, as a lot of nodes are counted to determine the numbering, so avoid them if you can for that reason alone.

Creating Indexes

The final topic that we'll look at in this chapter is how to create an index in which the index terms are arranged in alphabetical groups (and in alphabetical order within those groups).

Creating indexes isn't limited to document-oriented XML. The same principles apply if you're creating an index for a set of records.

Creating indexes usually involves grouping, which is covered in Chapter 9; and sorting, which is covered in Chapter 7.

Creating XPointers

Most of this section has focused on creating IDs for elements. Another type of link that you might want to create is an XPointer that points to the relevant element in the XML that you're processing. Currently, XPointer is still a Working Draft, but once it becomes a Recommendation, there are likely to be browsers that can use an XPointer to focus on a particular section in an XML document. Some browsers may also be able to link to the result of processing a section with a stylesheet. Therefore, it's helpful to know how to create them.

XPointers are based on XPaths, and for simple linking to a particular element, that's all you need to use. Therefore, you need to be able to create an XPath to a particular node. As your experience with XSLT will tell you, you have numerous ways to get to a particular node using XPath. The easiest XPath to create is one that steps from the root node down to the current node, using the name and index of the child node at each step. For example, the "Formatting long integers" section could have the following XPath:

```
/chapter[1]/section[1]/section[2]/section[1]
```

You can create this XPath by iterating over the ancestors of the node and providing their name and index. You can calculate the index of a node within its similarly named siblings (which is what you need here) using a simple `xsl:number`:

```
<xsl:for-each select="ancestor::*">
   <xsl:text />/<xsl:value-of select="name()" />
   <xsl:text />[<xsl:number />]<xsl:text />

</xsl:for-each>
```

The step to the current node is a little more complicated because the current node could be of any type (whereas the ancestors have to be elements). Therefore, you need to check the type of the current node before adding a reference to it:

```
<xsl:text>/</xsl:text>
<xsl:choose>
   <xsl:when test="self::node()">
      <xsl:choose>
         <xsl:when test="self::*">
            <xsl:value-of select="name()" />
         </xsl:when>
         <xsl:when test="self::text()">text()</xsl:when>
         <xsl:when test="self::comment()">comment()</xsl:when>
         <xsl:when test="self::processing-instruction()">
            <xsl:text>processing-instruction(</xsl:text>
            <xsl:value-of select="name()" />)<xsl:text />
         </xsl:when>
```

```
        </xsl:choose>
        <xsl:text />[<xsl:number />]<xsl:text />
    </xsl:when>
    <xsl:otherwise>
        <xsl:text />@<xsl:value-of select="name()" />
    </xsl:otherwise>

</xsl:choose>
```

Of course, if you are only creating XPaths to elements in the first place, you don't have to worry about the extra tests in the preceding example; in that case, it's easier to use the `ancestor-or-self` axis to create the path within a single loop:

```
<xsl:for-each select="ancestor-or-self::*">
    <xsl:text />/<xsl:value-of select="name()" />
    <xsl:text />[<xsl:number />]<xsl:text />

</xsl:for-each>
```

Identifying Index Items

The terms that you want to use as index terms within the document must be marked up in some way. In DocBook, for example, you can indicate an index term using the `indexterm` element, which has a `primary` element child that contains the primary term, as well as (optional) secondary and tertiary terms and `see` and `seealso` elements to refer to other index entries. Because this is a little complicated, for now we'll concentrate on just the primary terms. For example, the DocBook version of this section might include the following:

```
<indexterm>
    <primary>index</primary>
</indexterm>
<indexterm>
    <primary>grouping</primary>
</indexterm>
<indexterm>
    <primary>DocBook</primary>
</indexterm>
```

Merging Keywords with Documents

In some situations, you may know the keywords or index terms by which you want to index the document, but not know which sections in your document contain them. In this situation, you are best served by a two-pass solution:

1. Add information about which keywords are held in which section to the document.

2. Use this information to create the index for the document, as described in this section.

You first need to decide the level at which you want the document to be indexed: sections, individual paragraphs, or even individual words within the document.

If you're indexing elements, rather than linking to words in the text, you need to go through the elements and test whether their string value contains any of the keywords. If you were indexing para elements, for example, and the keywords that you wanted to use were stored in the $keywords variable, you could copy these keywords at the beginning of the paragraph with the following template:

```
<xsl:template match="para">
   <para>
      <xsl:copy-of select="$keywords[contains(current(), .)]" />
      <xsl:copy-of select="node()" />
   </para>

</xsl:template>
```

If you're indexing to words within the text, you need to do a search and replace of the keywords, adding a wrapper to the keywords as they appear. See Chapter 2 for information about searching and replacing.

The index terms in a book may be scattered throughout it. To create an alphabetical index, you need to be able to retrieve these terms according to the letter with which they start. This is a classic situation for which a key can help speed things up enormously — rather than searching through all the index terms for each letter of the alphabet, you can store them in a hash table and retrieve them very quickly.

You can create an index that is based on something other than alphabetical groups by using a key that is based on something other than the first letter of the index term.

The key needs to index a term based on its first letter. You can get the first letter using the `substring()` function. Because a term may start with a lowercase or uppercase letter, you should make them all the same case (which may as well be uppercase). You can make sure that's the case (no pun intended) using the `translate()` function. Unfortunately, the `use` attribute on `xsl:key` doesn't allow variables (to avoid circular key definitions), so you can't define these as variables. You therefore need the following key definition:

```
<xsl:key name="terms"
         match="indexterm"
         select="translate(substring(primary, 1, 1),
                           'abcdefghijklmnopqrstuvwxyz',
                           'ABCDEFGHIJKLMNOPQRSTUVWXYZ')" />
```

 You can define entities for the uppercase and lowercase strings in the DOC-TYPE declaration in the stylesheet:

```
<!ENTITY lowercase "'abcdefghijklmnopqrstuvwxyz'">
<!ENTITY uppercase "'ABCDEFGHIJKLMNOPQRSTUVWXYZ'">
```

This makes the key definition more readable:

```
<xsl:key name="terms" match="indexterm"
         select="translate(substring(primary, 1, 1),
                           &lowercase;,
                           &uppercase;)" />
```

With this key in place, you can, given a letter, collect all the index terms that begin with that letter and apply templates to them in alphabetical order. Here, you may as well make this into a template:

```
<xsl:template name="create-index-section">
  <xsl:param name="letter" />
  <h3><xsl:value-of select="$letter" /></h3>
  <xsl:apply-templates select="key('terms', $letter)">
     <xsl:sort select="primary" />
  </xsl:apply-templates>
</xsl:template>
```

We've assumed here that no terms will be repeated in the document, which is unlikely. If they are repeated, you need to filter the returned set of terms to find only those with unique values. You learned how to do this in Chapter 9.

One problem with this key is handling index terms that don't start with a letter. You want these index terms to go in a special *miscellaneous* section, and to be able to retrieve all of them at once. You could make another key to do this or make the terms key use different key values for the different types of index term. However, because you're only going to access the miscellaneous index terms once, you may as well create a variable in which to hold them.

You can retrieve the first letter of the index term as before, with the substring() function. You can test whether it is a letter by seeing if a string containing all letters (uppercase and lowercase) holds this character using the contains() function; if it doesn't, then its one of the miscellaneous index terms and should be part of the node set held by the variable:

```
<xsl:variable name="other-index-terms"
              select="//indexterm[not(contains(concat(&lowercase;, &uppercase;),
                                   substring(primary, 1, 1)))]" />
```

Working Through the Alphabet

The next stage of creating the index is to work through the alphabet to create the groups. The easiest way to do this is to set up a variable to hold the letters that you want to iterate over, and then use a recursive template to work through these letters one by one.

You need to first organize the output within a high-level template. Provide a title for the index and add a section for the other index terms that you've found. Now kick off the recursive process:

```
<h2>Index</h2>
<xsl:if test="$other-index-terms">
   <h3>Miscellaneous</h3>
   <xsl:apply-templates select="$other-index-terms">
      <xsl:sort />
   </xsl:apply-templates>
</xsl:if>
<xsl:call-template name="create-index" />
```

The create-index template needs to create the index sections by passing letters to the create-index-section template. The advantage that you have when building an index is that you know in advance what the possible groups are. Rather than troll through the document trying to determine which terms are unique, you can step through the alphabet one letter at a time. The following template moves through the alphabet character by character, using the substring() function to break up the string:

```
<xsl:template name="create-index">
   <xsl:param name="letters" select="$uppercase" />
   <xsl:call-template name="create-index-section">
      <xsl:with-param name="letter" select="substring($letters, 1, 1)" />
   </xsl:call-template>
   <xsl:variable name="remainder" select="substring($letters, 2)" />
   <xsl:if test="$remainder">
      <xsl:call-template name="create-index">
         <xsl:with-param name="letters" select="$remainder" />
      </xsl:call-template>
   </xsl:if>
</xsl:template>
```

Because you don't want a heading to appear for letters for which no terms are found, you should add a condition to your create-index-section template such that there's only output if terms are found for a given letter:

```
<xsl:template name="create-index-section">
   <xsl:param name="letter" />
   <xsl:variable name="terms" select="key('terms', $letter)" />
   <xsl:if test="$terms">
      <h3><xsl:value-of select="$letter" /></h3>
      <xsl:apply-templates select="$terms">
         <xsl:sort select="primary" />
      </xsl:apply-templates>
   </xsl:if>
</xsl:template>
```

If you need to create a reference and you don't know in advance what the groups are, you need to use one of the methods for finding unique values, as described in Chapter 9.

The final step for the index is to link from the index entry to the section that uses the particular term. You can generate these links in the template for the `indexterm` elements; they can apply templates to their parent element in `id` mode to retrieve a suitable ID for the link:

```
<xsl:template match="indexterm">
   <xsl:variable name="id">
      <xsl:apply-templates select=".." mode="id" />
   </xsl:variable>
   <a href="{$id}"><xsl:value-of select="primary" /></a><br />
</xsl:template>
```

Again, you will find Chapter 9 useful if you are dealing with documents where multiple sections can involve the same index term.

Summary

In this chapter, you learned how to populate and use different types of summaries, including tables of figures, tables of contents, and indexes. We focused on creating these summaries from document-oriented XML, but the same principles apply when creating any kind of summary information.

Each of these summaries involves processing the same nodes in different ways on different occasions. You learned two ways of doing this: using modes to split the different processing into different templates, and using parameters to pass in information about how the node should be processed. Knowing how to differentiate between different types of processing of the same node is useful in many other situations as well, as you'll see from the discussion about stylesheet modularity in Chapter 12.

You also learned about the generation of IDs for nodes. You saw how to generate IDs in order to link between summary information and the main content. Of course, IDs are useful for a lot more than that; adding IDs to your output makes it easy to reference sections and help people link to the document from outside.

Finally, you learned how to group by an initial letter, and how to use information you already have about the groups you want to create to make the grouping process more efficient, both of which are useful when creating indexes.

Part III

Building Your XSLT Application

Chapter 11

Separating Data from Presentation

IN THIS CHAPTER

◆ Reusing XML snippets

◆ Using page templates

◆ Supporting internationalization and customization

One of the basic aims of XML was to separate data from presentation. In HTML, elements usually indicate, at least in popular use, the kind of formatting that the browser should use for them (for example, p elements mean blocks, and em elements mean italics). XML was intended to be more abstract, to encode the meaning behind the different parts of the document.

Once data is stored in XML, a technology is needed to structure and format the XML for presentation. This was and still is the primary aim of XSL as a whole, although XSLT, to some extent, has taken on a life of its own as a generic transformation language. The idea is that XSLT should be a way of designing pages and deciding the style that should be given to different items within those pages.

In order for a styling language to be used, it has to be approachable and usable by designers, not just programmers. However, XSLT requires that the people who use it have some understanding of XML, namespaces, and XPath, as well as the basic XSLT instructions.

This chapter describes various ways in which designers can specify parts of the output without touching XSLT, and even without knowing anything about XML. These techniques enable designers to concentrate on the design of a page and use the various tools that are at their disposal for creating it, rather than worry about the syntax of XSLT. They also enable you to reuse XML and add customizations, including internationalization, to the output that you're producing.

Reusing XML Snippets

The first way to separate the output that you want to generate from the XSLT code that generates it is to isolate parts of the literal result that can be drawn from elsewhere — well-formed fragments that are static and self-contained. Examples of this include navigation bars, standard disclaimers or copyright notices, and banner ads.

TIP

If you're generating HTML, other examples include embedded scripts and CSS stylesheets. However, in these cases, HTML already has mechanisms for separating the CSS stylesheet or the script into separate files and linking to them — you should use these techniques, rather than embedding them in the HTML in the first place.

These parts of a page can be separated into self-contained XHTML documents and then pulled in to the result that you're creating within the stylesheet. For example, in the HTML pages that you're producing for the bank statements, there are quite a few bits of static information. Currently, the HTML page is generated within a template matching the `statement` element (which is the document element in the source XML) as follows:

```
<xsl:template match="statement">
   <html>
      <head>
         <title>Bank Statement: <xsl:value-of select="$username" /></title>
         <link rel="stylesheet" href="/style/site.css" />
         <link rel="stylesheet" href="/style/statement.css" />
         <script content="text/javascript" src="/script/site.js" />
         <script content="text/javascript" src="/script/statement.js" />
      </head>
      <body>
         <table id="navigation">
            <tr>
               <td><a href="/">Home</a></td>
               <td><a href="/accounts.html">Accounts</a></td>
               <td>Statement</td>
               <td><a href="/options.html">Options</a></td>
               <td><a href="/logout.html">Logout</a></td>
            </tr>
         </table>
         ... statement information ...
      </body>
   </html>
</xsl:template>
```

As you can see from this template, two self-contained sections of the page contain static content that doesn't use any information from the source XML. The first section is the content of the `head` element (aside from the `title` element), highlighted here:

```
<xsl:template match="statement">
   <html>
      <head>
         <title>Bank Statement: <xsl:value-of select="$username" /></title>
         <link rel="stylesheet" href="/style/site.css" />
         <link rel="stylesheet" href="/style/statement.css" />
         <script content="text/javascript" src="/script/site.js" />
         <script content="text/javascript" src="/script/statement.js" />
      </head>
      ...
   </html>
</xsl:template>
```

The second is the navigation table, highlighted in the following:

```
<xsl:template match="statement">
   <html>
      ...
      <body>
        <table id="navigation">
           <tr>
              <td><a href="/">Home</a></td>
              <td><a href="/accounts.html">Accounts</a></td>
              <td>Statement</td>
              <td><a href="/options.html">Options</a></td>
              <td><a href="/logout.html">Logout</a></td>
           </tr>
        </table>
        ... statement information ...
      </body>
   </html>
</xsl:template>
```

Both of these snippets could be separated out and placed in their own files.
Doing this, head.xml contains the following:

```
<link rel="stylesheet" href="/style/site.css" />
<link rel="stylesheet" href="/style/statement.css" />
<script content="text/javascript" src="/script/site.js" />
<script content="text/javascript" src="/script/statement.js" />
```

And navigation.xml contains this:

```
<table id="navigation">
   <tr>
```

```
      <td><a href="/">Home</a></td>
      <td><a href="/accounts.html">Accounts</a></td>
      <td>Statement</td>
      <td><a href="/options.html">Options</a></td>
      <td><a href="/logout.html">Logout</a></td>
   </tr>
</table>
```

 These files are XML files (or XHTML files), rather than HTML files — for example, the `link` and `script` elements use XML syntax for empty elements, rather than HTML syntax. Note one major distinction between these two XML files; namely, that `navigation.xml` is a well-formed XML document in its own right, whereas `head.xml` is not, as it does not have its own document element.

Separating these into their own files enables designers to focus on particular parts of the design, rather than having to edit the stylesheet to alter which CSS stylesheets are used or what the navigation bar looks like.

There are three main ways to include this static content within the page that you're producing:

◆ Use external references within the stylesheet.

◆ Use the `document()` function to retrieve and copy the XML.

◆ Generate external references within the result.

The following sections describe each of these solutions in detail.

Using External References

XSLT stylesheets are XML documents just like any other, which means that all the mechanisms that you can use with normal XML documents for reusing portions of the document can be used here as well. Thus, you can use XML entities or XInclude to include the content of some external XML.

USING ENTITIES

To use entities, you must define them within the DOCTYPE for the stylesheet document, and then refer to them where you want them to be inserted. In the preceding exapmle, you could include the content of `head.xml` and `navigation.xml` into the result by defining `&head;` and `&navigation;` entities. The following code shows the stylesheet, with the bold sections indicating the definition of and references to the two entities:

```
<!DOCTYPE xsl:stylesheet [
<!ENTITY head SYSTEM 'head.xml'>
<!ENTITY navigation SYSTEM 'navigation.xml'>
]>
<xsl:stylesheet version="1.0"
                xmlns:xsl="http://www.w3.org/1999/XSL/Transform">

<xsl:template match="statement">
   <html>
      <head>
         <title>Bank Statement: <xsl:value-of select="$username" /></title>
         &head;
      </head>
      <body>
         &navigation;
         ... statement information ...
      </body>
   </html>
</xsl:template>

...

</xsl:stylesheet>
```

Using this technique, the physical content of the external files is inserted into the stylesheet when it's initially parsed. Therefore, this technique could be used to include sections of the stylesheet that use XSLT instructions — the content would be interpreted as if it were defined within the stylesheet itself.

Extending this idea, Chapter 13 describes how you can use entities to break up a stylesheet into separate documents.

One good thing about this method is that the external documents do not have to be XML *documents* (that is, have a single document element) — you can use it with both `navigation.xml`, which is a well-formed XML document, and `head.xml`, which is not.

The external documents need to be well-formed *external parsed general entities*, which means that they cannot have a DTD of their own; they can, however, consist purely of text, as long as the significant characters in the text (for example, < and &) are escaped.

USING XINCLUDE

The content of this section is based on the XInclude Working Draft dated May 16, 2001; the XPointer Working Draft dated January 8, 2001; and the current capabilities of XSLT processors.

XInclude is designed as a replacement for entities, enabling you to include one set of XML into another using their logical content, rather than their physical form. One limitation of XInclude is that the content it includes must be (part of) an XML *document* — the content must have a single document element. Thus, you have to add a document element to head.xml to use it with XInclude:

```
<head>
    <link rel="stylesheet" href="/style/site.css" />
    <link rel="stylesheet" href="/style/statement.css" />
    <script content="text/javascript" src="/script/site.js" />
    <script content="text/javascript" src="/script/statement.js" />
</head>
```

Given that, including the document using XInclude a matter of defining the XInclude namespace and using xi:include elements in the appropriate places within the template:

```
<xsl:stylesheet version="1.0"
                xmlns:xsl="http://www.w3.org/1999/XSL/Transform"
                xmlns:xi="http://www.w3.org/2001/XInclude">

<xsl:template match="statement">
    <html>
        <head>
            <title>Bank Statement: <xsl:value-of select="$username" /></title>
            <xi:include href="head.xml#xpointer(/head/*)" />
        </head>
        <body>
            <xi:include href="navigation.xml" />
            ... statement information ...
        </body>
    </html>
</xsl:template>
```

```
...

</xsl:stylesheet>
```

 You don't have to explicitly include the `table` element from `navigation.xml` because including a document includes the document element by definition.

Currently, XInclude is not a Recommendation, and support for it is in its infancy. In particular, XSLT processors won't automatically process `xi:include` elements. Instead, the inclusion process may occur at two possible points in the overall process. First, the `xi:include` elements could be processed as the stylesheet node tree is being built, in which case the external documents are included in the same way as entities are, and could therefore contain XSLT instructions. Second, the `xi:include` elements in the result of the transformation could be processed, in which case the external documents shouldn't contain XSLT instructions (unless you're creating a document that contains XSLT instructions, naturally).

Copying Documents

The second method for including information from another file into your document is to use the `document()` function to access the external document, and copy the content that it holds. As with XInclude, the `document()` function can only be used to access XML documents – the content must have a single document element, so you need to add a document element to `head.xml`:

```
<head>
    <link rel="stylesheet" href="/style/site.css" />
    <link rel="stylesheet" href="/style/statement.css" />
    <script content="text/javascript" src="/script/site.js" />
    <script content="text/javascript" src="/script/statement.js" />
</head>
```

With this amended definition, you can copy the contents of the two files with **xsl:copy-of** by accessing them with the `document()` function and using a path to retrieve the content that we want to copy:

```
<xsl:template match="statement">
    <html>
        <head>
            <title>Bank Statement: <xsl:value-of select="$username" /></title>
            <xsl:copy-of select="document('head.xml')/head/*" />
```

```
      </head>
      <body>
        <xsl:copy-of select="document('navigation.xml')" />
        ... statement information ...
      </body>
    </html>
  </xsl:template>
```

 You don't have to explicitly copy the `table` element from `navigation.xml` because copying a root node copies the document element (and any other children of the root node) by definition.

With this approach, the two external documents are parsed and node trees are created for them; the relevant nodes are copied into the result tree in the same way they would be if they were defined in the source. Unlike when using entities, if you were to include XSLT instructions in the files, they wouldn't be interpreted; they would just be added to the result tree.

Because the external documents are being accessed as a node tree, you could actually merge the two documents, rather than keep them separate. You could place both sets of XML into a single file, `resources.xml`, which holds snippets of static XML for inclusion in the page you're creating:

```
<resources>
  <head>
    <link rel="stylesheet" href="/style/site.css" />
    <link rel="stylesheet" href="/style/statement.css" />
    <script content="text/javascript" src="/script/site.js" />
    <script content="text/javascript" src="/script/statement.js" />
  </head>
  <navigation>
    <table id="navigation">
      <tr>
        <td><a href="/">Home</a></td>
        <td><a href="/accounts.html">Accounts</a></td>
        <td>Statement</td>
        <td><a href="/options.html">Options</a></td>
        <td><a href="/logout.html">Logout</a></td>
      </tr>
    </table>
  </navigation>
  <icons>
    ...
  </icons>
```

```
   ...
</resources>
```

This resource document can be stored in a global variable and accessed in a number of places throughout the stylesheet:

```
<xsl:variable name="resources" select="document('resources.xml')/resources" />

<xsl:template match="statement">
   <html>
      <head>
         <title>Bank Statement: <xsl:value-of select="$username" /></title>
         <xsl:copy-of select="$resources/head/*" />
      </head>
      <body>
         <xsl:copy-of select="$resources/navigation/*" />
         ... statement information ...
      </body>
   </html>
</xsl:template>
```

TIP If you have a number of resources, such as icons, that should be accessed by name, you could use a key to make that access quicker. However, make sure that the current node is one within the resource document at the point you use the key (using xsl:for-each to change the current node if necessary).

Having a single resource file has the advantage of putting all the resources that are used within the page into one file, which makes it easy to edit them all at once. Moreover, the document is accessed only once. On the down side, the document, and hence its node tree, is larger, which will take up more memory and be more processor-intensive. It also means that you may sometimes access more information than is absolutely necessary.

Generating External References

The final way to incorporate external information within the result that you create is to create the constructs that will be processed to include them, such as entity definitions and references or xi:include elements, within the result itself. This approach is advantageous if you have server-side or batch transformations in which numerous result pages hold the same information. Keeping this information in separate files means that the browser can cache and reuse relevant parts of the pages.

If you're using server-side transformations with these inclusion methods, the document you include into your result can itself be the result of the transformation of an XML document.

If you're creating XML, some markup languages enable you to specify inclusions with vocabulary-specific elements (xsl:include in XSLT is one of them). If you're creating HTML, you may be able to use either the object element or the iframe element to include an entire document from elsewhere.

The object and iframe elements are relatively late additions to HTML and may not be supported by all browsers. In addition, they can only be used to reference external HTML documents, and only to include them into the body of the HTML. For example, if you made navigation.xml into a full HTML document, you could include that, but you couldn't include head.xml into the document in that way.

GENERATING XINCLUDE REFERENCES

At a more generic level, you can use XInclude to reference and include documents from elsewhere. However, remember that XSLT processors might interpret xi:include elements when they load the XSLT stylesheet. You want to create the xi:include element within the XML that you're generating, not interpreted when the stylesheet is parsed. Thus you have to be careful to distinguish between xi:include elements that you use to include information into the stylesheet (such as those you used previously) and xi:include elements that you want to generate in the result.

Using XInclude in your XHTML document means that you need to create a document that looks like the following:

```
<html xmlns="http://www.w3.org/1999/xhtml"
          xmlns:xi="http://www.w3.org/2001/XInclude">
   <head>
     <title>Bank Statement: Bill Beacham</title>
     <xi:include href="head.xml#xpointer(/head/*)" />
   </head>
   <body>
     <xi:include href="navigation.xml" />
     ... statement information ...
   </body>
</html>
```

Browsers will ignore the xi:include elements in this XHTML; you need to post-process this result with an XInclude processor to get the final XHTML that you're aiming for.

If you created the xi:include elements using literal result elements, a XInclude processor would not be able to distinguish between them and the xi:include elements that should be processed to include content into the stylesheet. Therefore, you should create them using xsl:element instead, so that there can be no confusion:

```
<xsl:stylesheet version="1.0"
                xmlns:xsl="http://www.w3.org/1999/XSL/Transform"
                xmlns:xi="http://www.w3.org/2001/XInclude">

<xsl:template match="statement">
   <html>
      <head>
         <title>Bank Statement: <xsl:value-of select="$username" /></title>
         <xsl:element name="xi:include">
            <xsl:attribute name="href">
               <xsl:text>head.xml#xpointer(/head/*)</xsl:text>
            </xsl:attribute>
         </xsl:element>
      </head>
      <body>
         <xsl:element name="xi:include">
            <xsl:attribute name="href">navigation.xml</xsl:attribute>
         </xsl:element>
         ... statement information ...
      </body>
   </html>
</xsl:template>

...

</xsl:stylesheet>
```

Alternatively, you could use the namespace aliasing technique that's more commonly used when generating XSLT from a stylesheet. To use this method, you need to set up two namespaces: the XInclude namespace and a dummy namespace that is used as an alias for the XInclude namespace. For example, in the following stylesheet the alias namespace uses a namespace URI similar to the one for XInclude, but with Alias appended:

```
<xsl:stylesheet version="1.0"
                 xmlns:xsl="http://www.w3.org/1999/XSL/Transform"
                 xmlns:xinclude="http://www.w3.org/2001/XInclude"
                 xmlns:xi="http://www.w3.org/2001/XIncludeAlias">
...
</xsl:stylesheet>
```

TIP   You should assign the alias namespace the prefix that you want the elements to be given in the result.

You can then use the prefix for the XInclude namespace for the elements that you want to be interpreted during the interpretation of the stylesheet, and the alias namespace for the elements that you want to be generated in the result. You then need to use an `xsl:namespace-alias` element to map the alias namespace onto the XInclude namespace. The following stylesheet shows how to create the `xi:include` elements using a namespace alias:

```
<xsl:stylesheet version="1.0"
                 xmlns:xsl="http://www.w3.org/1999/XSL/Transform"
                 xmlns:xinclude="http://www.w3.org/2001/XInclude"
                 xmlns:xi="http://www.w3.org/2001/XIncludeAlias">

<xsl:namespace-alias stylesheet-prefix="xinclude" result-prefix="xi" />

<xsl:template match="statement">
   <html>
     <head>
        <title>Bank Statement: <xsl:value-of select="$username" /></title>
        <xi:include href="head.xml#xpointer(/head/*)" />
     </head>
     <body>
        <xi:include href="navigation.xml" />
        ... statement information ...
     </body>
   </html>
</xsl:template>

...

</xsl:stylesheet>
```

GENERATING EXTERNAL ENTITY REFERENCES

If you're creating XML, a final way to include information from external files is to create entity definitions and entity references. XSLT has no support for creating either, so the only way to do so is to build them by hand, by disabling output escaping.

Some XSLT processors, notably Saxon, have extension elements that enable you to create entity definitions and references. These are covered in Chapter 19.

In this case, the output that you want to generate is as follows:

```
<!DOCTYPE html [
<!ENTITY head SYSTEM 'head.xml'>
<!ENTITY navigation SYSTEM 'navigation.xml'>
]>
<html xmlns="http://www.w3.org/1999/xhtml">
   <head>
      <title>Bank Statement: Bill Beacham</title>
      &head;
   </head>
   <body>
      &navigation;
      ... statement information ...
   </body>
</html>
```

As with XInclude, most HTML browsers will balk at the preceding XHTML, as they do not support entities. Only browsers that understand XHTML will process it correctly. However, if you're producing XML for parsing by XML parsers, this technique will work fine.

The first task, then, is to create the DOCTYPE declaration. Because this involves using less-than signs as something other than the start of a tag, these need to be created using disabling output escaping: the text of the DOCTYPE declaration itself needs to be written to the result:

```
<xsl:template match="statement">
   <xsl:text disable-output-escaping="yes"><![CDATA[
      <!DOCTYPE html [
```

```
    <!ENTITY head SYSTEM 'head.xml'>
    <!ENTITY navigation SYSTEM 'navigation.xml'>
    ]>
]]></xsl:text>
<html>
    ...
</html>
</xsl:template>
```

> You can use CDATA sections here to avoid having to escape all the less-than signs that are used in the DOCTYPE declaration.

Similarly, you need to create the entity references by disabling output escaping, to stop them from being interpreted by the stylesheet parser:

```
<xsl:template match="statement">
    <xsl:text disable-output-escaping="yes"><![CDATA[
    <!DOCTYPE html [
    <!ENTITY head SYSTEM 'head.xml'>
    <!ENTITY navigation SYSTEM 'navigation.xml'>
    ]>
]]></xsl:text>
<html>
    <head>
        <title>Bank Statement: <xsl:value-of select="$username" /></title>
        <xsl:text disable-output-escaping="yes">&amp;head;</xsl:text>
    </head>
    <body>
        <xsl:text disable-output-escaping="yes">&amp;navigation;</xsl:text>
        ... statement information ...
    </body>
</html>
</xsl:template>
```

> XSLT processors are not obliged to support the disabling of output escaping, so you need to check whether yours does before using these constructs.

TIP If the entity definitions are static, as they are in this example, then it is better to use an external DTD. You can set the location of this external DTD using the `doctype-system` attribute on the `xsl:output` element as follows:

```
<xsl:output doctype-system="statement.dtd" />
```

Using Page Templates

The last section described how to separate out parts of a page so that snippets of static XML can be reused and so that the XML snippets are easier to maintain, especially by people without any knowledge of XSLT. Using these techniques is very handy if you have a library of components that you use to build a page. In this section, you'll look at a different technique — taking the outline of a page as a static template, and then inserting the generated content as desired.

Looking again at the same initial template that we've been working with, you can see that only two parts of the page actually change due to the source XML. These are highlighted in the following:

```
<xsl:template match="statement">
   <html>
      <head>
         <title>Bank Statement: <xsl:value-of select="$username" /></title>
         <link rel="stylesheet" href="/style/site.css" />
         <link rel="stylesheet" href="/style/statement.css" />
         <script content="text/javascript" src="/script/site.js" />
         <script content="text/javascript" src="/script/statement.js" />
      </head>
      <body>
        <table id="navigation">
          <tr>
             <td><a href="/">Home</a></td>
             <td><a href="/accounts.html">Accounts</a></td>
             <td>Statement</td>
             <td><a href="/options.html">Options</a></td>
             <td><a href="/logout.html">Logout</a></td>
          </tr>
        </table>
        ... statement information ...
      </body>
   </html>
</xsl:template>
```

What you need is a method of allowing designers to define the page layout as a separate template, and then insert in the information you need when you need it. There are three methods of doing this:

◆ Simplified stylesheets

◆ External references in a template page

◆ Insertion instructions in a template page

Creating Simplified Stylesheets

Simplified stylesheets are stylesheets in which the document element of the stylesheet is a literal result element, rather than an `xsl:stylesheet` or `xsl:transform` element. These stylesheets are designed to enable users to quickly and easily construct pages based on a designer's template, just inserting the necessary information from the source XML as desired.

The simplified stylesheet for the HTML page that you've been working on in this chapter would look much like the content of the template, standing on its own except that the document element (the `html` element, in this example) has to define the XSLT namespace and specify an `xsl:version` attribute to indicate the version of XSLT being used within it:

```
<html xsl:version="1.0"
      xmlns:xsl="http://www.w3.org/1999/XSL/Transform">
  <head>
    <title>Bank Statement: <xsl:value-of select="/*/info/username" /></title>
    <link rel="stylesheet" href="/style/site.css" />
    <link rel="stylesheet" href="/style/statement.css" />
    <script content="text/javascript" src="/script/site.js" />
    <script content="text/javascript" src="/script/statement.js" />
  </head>
  <body>
    <table id="navigation">
      <tr>
        <td><a href="/">Home</a></td>
        <td><a href="/accounts.html">Accounts</a></td>
        <td>Statement</td>
        <td><a href="/options.html">Options</a></td>
        <td><a href="/logout.html">Logout</a></td>
      </tr>
    </table>
    ... statement information ...
  </body>
</html>
```

Simplified stylesheets are severely limited, however. As they essentially consist of the body of a single template, they cannot use any top-level elements, such as other templates, attribute sets, keys, imports or includes, and so on. Simplified stylesheets, therefore, can only be used for simple processing.

Nor are they precisely attuned to the requirements of designers, who must still learn XSLT syntax and XPath in order to construct the pages that they want to design. Again, for pages that use information that is easily accessible from the source XML, this isn't an insurmountable hurdle, but for anything more than that it can easily become too complicated for practical use.

Using External References in a Template Page

A second way to use template pages is to use references that point to the result of transforming some source XML. You can see this arrangement illustrated in Figure 11-1. The references can be included with two methods: external parsed entities and XInclude elements, both of which were covered earlier in this chapter.

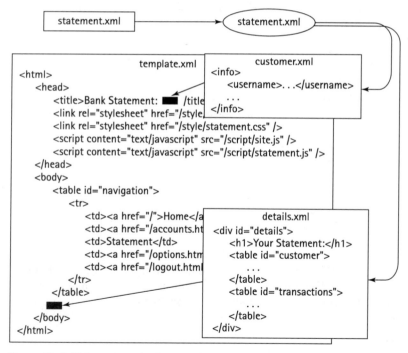

Figure 11-1: Using external references in a template page

The result of the transformation might be generated dynamically, particularly if you have a server-side application framework like Cocoon or XSQL.

Which of external parsed entities or XInclude elements you use will probably depend on the type of information that you want to include, as well as the support for the technology the technique requires. For small amounts of information, using an XInclude with an XPointer into a larger set of information would be better than creating documents that only hold, for example, the name of the user. For larger amounts of information, or if you're not using a framework that supports XInclude, external general entities are more practical.

The next example includes the user name using XInclude. The user name is accessible as part of a set of XML about the customer, which is available through the URL customer.xml. For that, you need to declare the XInclude namespace and insert an xi:include element where you want the customer details to be included. The href attribute of the xi:include element points to the relevant node within the file:

```
<html xmlns:xi="http://www.w3.org/2001/XInclude">
  <head>
    <title>
      <xsl:text>Bank Statement: </xsl:text>
      <xi:include href="customer.xml#xpointer(/info/username/text())" />
    </title>
    <link rel="stylesheet" href="/style/site.css" />
    <link rel="stylesheet" href="/style/statement.css" />
    <script content="text/javascript" src="/script/site.js" />
    <script content="text/javascript" src="/script/statement.js" />
  </head>
  ...
</html>
```

The bulk of the page, though, you can make available through a general entity referencing details.xml. This file contains the result of the transformation of the statement source XML into some XHTML for presentation. Here, you need to declare the entity and reference it. The relevant part of the file looks like the following:

```
<!DOCTYPE html [
<!ENTITY details SYSTEM 'details.xml'>
]>
<html xmlns:xi="http://www.w3.org/2001/XInclude">
  ...
```

```
<body>
  <table id="navigation">
    <tr>
      <td><a href="/">Home</a></td>
      <td><a href="/accounts.html">Accounts</a></td>
      <td>Statement</td>
      <td><a href="/options.html">Options</a></td>
      <td><a href="/logout.html">Logout</a></td>
    </tr>
  </table>
  &details;
</body>
</html>
```

 Some XML parsers treat the presence of a DTD as an indication that the XML document should be validated. If you use one of these parsers, you may run into problems with DTDs like the previous one because it doesn't declare all the elements used in the document, and therefore the document isn't valid. If you do, you usually need to set a flag to stop the parser from validating the document.

As indicated previously, current browsers don't understand XInclude and don't use general entities, so shipping this HTML template page to the browser as it is won't do any good. However, you can run it through a very simple transform to produce the desired result (this is in addition to the transforms you're doing in order to get the content that you're including into the template).

INCLUDING INFORMATION WITH ENTITIES

When you run an XSLT processor on an XML document, part of the XML parsing process involves de-referencing the general parsed entities that you've used. Therefore, if you pass the preceding page template, containing an entity that references `details.xml`, as the source of a stylesheet, the XSLT processor will get a source node tree that contains the content of `details.xml`. If you're only using entities to include information, you can use an identity transform to create the HTML page that you want to ship to the browser. The simplest of these is the following, which copies the entire document directly:

```
<xsl:template match="/">
  <xsl:copy-of select="." />
</xsl:template>
```

INCLUDING WHOLE FILES WITH XINCLUDE

If you've used XInclude to include whole files, you can use the same process to de-reference those inclusions. Here, you need to use a recursive identity template so that you can override the default behavior (copying the node) when it comes to the xi:include elements. Following is a recursive identity template that you could use:

```
<xsl:template match="@*|node()">
   <xsl:copy>
      <xsl:apply-templates select="@*|node()" />
   </xsl:copy>
</xsl:template>
```

You need to override this template for the xi:include element. To do so, access the file referenced by the href attribute and apply templates – using the document() function – to its content, copying it using the default identity template. When you use the value of the href attribute to access the included document, make sure it's interpreted relative to the base URI of the xi:include element (i.e., the URL of the document that it's in), rather than the stylesheet. Thus, you need a second argument to the document() function, which needs to be a node in the source XML (and may as well be the xi:include element itself):

```
<xsl:template match="xi:include">
   <xsl:apply-templates select="document(@href, .)" />
</xsl:template>
```

Applying templates to, rather than directly copying, the nodes referenced by the xi:include element enables you to use xi:include elements in the documents that you're including, and they will also be interpreted correctly.

INCLUDING PARTS OF FILES WITH XINCLUDE

Until XSLT processors deal with XPointers themselves, the previous template will only work if the xi:include elements reference entire documents. If you want to use XInclude to reference parts of a particular document, you need some way of interpreting the XPointer to give you the nodes in which you're interested. Fortunately, most XPointers are XPaths, which means that you can use two methods: you can interpret the XPointer within the stylesheet, or you can use the stylesheet to create another stylesheet that includes the path.

INTERPRETING XPOINTERS WITHIN A STYLESHEET   To use the XPointers within the stylesheet, you first need to retrieve the path, using string functions to get the parts of the string holding the document name and the fragment identifier. With XInclude, the path is held within the `href` attribute of the `include` element, and can be split up as shown in the following template:

```
<xsl:template match="x:include">
   <xsl:variable name="doc" select="substring-before(@href, '#')" />
   <xsl:variable name="path"
                 select="substring-after(
                             substring(@href, 1, string-length(@href) - 1),
                             '#xpointer(')" />
   ...
</xsl:template>
```

If there is no fragment identifier, you can apply templates to the document using the `document()` function. If there is a fragment, you have two options. You can use a recursive template to step through the path and retrieve the relevant node; or you can use an extension function to evaluate the path (which is held as a string); collect the nodes; and apply templates to them. The advantage of the latter option is that it will be able to deal with anything in the path, including predicates, and so on. The former, on the other hand, is only worthwhile if you're dealing with simple paths that don't use predicates or axes.

Chapter 18 describes extension functions for evaluating XPaths in detail.

If you're using a recursive template, you need to pass the path into the template as a parameter. As this recursive template journeys from node to node, you should make it a matching template, rather than a named one; and make it a moded template, to distinguish between this type of traversal and the recursive copying that's being done in the default mode. At each node, the first step in the path indicates which node to move to next. If there's no path left, the node should have templates applied to it with no mode (and hence copied, since the default template is the identity template). The template looks as follows:

```
<xsl:template match="node()|@*" mode="path">
   <xsl:param name="path" />
   <xsl:choose>
      <xsl:when test="not($path)">
         <xsl:apply-templates select="." />
      </xsl:when>
      <xsl:otherwise>
         <xsl:variable name="step">
```

```
<xsl:choose>
    <xsl:when test="contains($path, '/')">
        <xsl:value-of select="substring-before($path, '/')" />
    </xsl:when>
    <xsl:otherwise><xsl:value-of select="$path" /></xsl:otherwise>
</xsl:choose>
</xsl:variable>
<xsl:variable name="rest" select="substring-after($path, '/')" />
<xsl:choose>
    <xsl:when test="starts-with($step, 'id(')">
        <xsl:apply-templates mode="path"
            select="id(substring-before(
                        substring-after($step, 'id('), ')'))">
            <xsl:with-param name="path" select="$rest" />
        </xsl:apply-templates>
    </xsl:when>
    <xsl:when test="starts-with($step, '@')">
        <xsl:apply-templates select="@*[name() = substring($step, 2)]"
                             mode="path">
            <xsl:with-param name="path" select="$rest" />
        </xsl:apply-templates>
    </xsl:when>
    <xsl:when test="$step = 'text()'">
        <xsl:apply-templates select="text()" mode="path">
            <xsl:with-param name="path" select="$rest" />
        </xsl:apply-templates>
    </xsl:when>
    <xsl:otherwise>
        <xsl:apply-templates select="*[name() = $step]" mode="path">
            <xsl:with-param name="path" select="$rest" />
        </xsl:apply-templates>
    </xsl:otherwise>
</xsl:choose>
    </xsl:otherwise>
</xsl:choose>
</xsl:template>
```

This template is by no means a full implementation. It only supports the child axis, and it will not work to access comments or processing instructions. However, it will work for most paths; and if you need something more complicated, you're better off using an extension function or including the XPath in a created stylesheet, as described in the next section.

INTERPRETING XINCLUDES BY CREATING A STYLESHEET FROM ANOTHER
STYLESHEET   The other option for including portions of files that are referenced
by XPointers is to use the stylesheet to create a stylesheet that selects the nodes
pointed to by the XPointers. Just to remind you, in this case, the XPointer is used
within an XInclude element in the header of an XHTML document that's acting as
a page template:

```
<html xmlns:xi="http://www.w3.org/2001/XInclude">
   <head>
      <title>
         <xsl:text>Bank Statement: </xsl:text>
         <xi:include href="customer.xml#xpointer(/info/username/text())" />
      </title>
      <link rel="stylesheet" href="/style/site.css" />
      <link rel="stylesheet" href="/style/statement.css" />
      <script content="text/javascript" src="/script/site.js" />
      <script content="text/javascript" src="/script/statement.js" />
   </head>
   ...
</html>
```

As described earlier in this chapter, a simplified stylesheet can consist of a literal
result element with XSLT instructions embedded within it. Following is the simplified stylesheet that's equivalent to the preceding page template:

```
<html xsl:version="1.0"
      xmlns:xsl="http://www.w3.org/1999/XSL/Transform">
   <head>
      <title>
         <xsl:text>Bank Statement: </xsl:text>
         <xsl:copy-of href="document('customer.xml')/info/username/text()" />
      </title>
      <link rel="stylesheet" href="/style/site.css" />
      <link rel="stylesheet" href="/style/statement.css" />
      <script content="text/javascript" src="/script/site.js" />
      <script content="text/javascript" src="/script/statement.js" />
   </head>
   ...
</html>
```

Unlike the recursive style of the templates in the previous section, where
`xi:include` elements in included documents were also transformed, this
version would generate a direct copy of the relevant information from the
file, without transforming it.

The mapping between the page template and the simplified stylesheet is relatively straightforward. Mostly, everything is just copied; you can use the recursive identity template for that:

```
<xsl:template match="@*|node()">
   <xsl:copy>
      <xsl:apply-templates select="@*|node()" />
   </xsl:copy>
</xsl:template>
```

The first exception to this is the document element (the html element, in this case), to which you have to add an xsl:version attribute:

```
<xsl:template match="/*">
   <xsl:copy>
      <xsl:attribute name="xsl:version">1.0</xsl:attribute>
      <xsl:apply-templates select="@*|node()" />
   </xsl:copy>
</xsl:template>
```

This template will add an xsl:version attribute to any document element, so you can use it even if you're not creating HTML. Note that the XSLT namespace declaration is added automatically because the xsl:version attribute needs it.

The second exception is that the xi:include elements need to be replaced by xsl:copy-of elements. As before, you need to determine the document and the path fragment in order to include these in the select attribute of the xsl:copy-of element that you're creating:

```
<xsl:template match="xi:include">
   <xsl:variable name="doc" select="substring-before(@href, '#')" />
   <xsl:variable name="path"
             select="substring-after(
                        substring(@href, 1, string-length(@href) - 1),
                        '#xpointer(')" />
   ...
</xsl:template>
```

You cannot create the xsl:copy-of element as a literal result element because it would be interpreted as an XSLT instruction, rather than an element to be added to the result. Therefore, you need to either create it using xsl:element or use `xsl:namespace-alias` to set up a namespace alias that you can use to create it literally.

 You learn how to use `xsl:namespace-alias` in the section on `xsl:element` in Chapter 17.

In this case, because the `xsl:copy-of` element is the only XSLT element that you're going to be producing with the stylesheet, you will just use an `xsl:element` instruction to create it. You therefore need to add the `select` attribute using an `xsl:attribute` instruction, which is necessary anyway because of the conditional text that's involved in its value:

```
<xsl:template match="xi:include">
   <xsl:variable name="doc" select="substring-before(@href, '#')" />
   <xsl:variable name="path"
               select="substring-after(
                         substring(@href, 1, string-length(@href) - 1),
                         '#xpointer(')" />
   <xsl:element name="xsl:copy-of">
      <xsl:attribute name="select">
         <xsl:text />document('<xsl:value-of select="$doc" />')<xsl:text />
         <xsl:if test="$path">
            <xsl:if test="not(starts-with($path, '/'))">/</xsl:if>
            <xsl:value-of select="$path" />
         </xsl:if>
      </xsl:attribute>
   </xsl:element>
</xsl:template>
```

Using these templates in a stylesheet will produce a simplified stylesheet that you can then run (even on itself) to create the HTML page that you want to ship to the browser.

Using Insertion Instructions in a Template Page

Thus far, you've only looked at using XSLT instructions and XInclude elements to include information from elsewhere within a page. These elements belong to standardized vocabularies; the XSLT elements are particularly good to use because XSLT processors understand them natively; and in the future, you can expect that they will similarly be able to use and interpret XInclude elements.

However, both of these element types require using an XPath syntax with which you or, more importantly, the designers who are creating the page templates, might not be comfortable. A final option, therefore, is to create your own vocabulary, your own set of elements that the designers can use to indicate where specific information should be inserted within a page. For example, you could use a username element to indicate where the user's name should be inserted on a page.

> You don't have to use elements to indicate where data should be inserted into the document — you could use processing instructions instead. However, elements are easy to process within XSLT, so you might as well use them. Be careful about using comments to represent this kind of information, as they might not be passed through to the XSLT processor.

The design of the vocabulary depends on the amount of control the designers you're working with want and the amount of complexity that they can deal with. Generally, the simpler you make your vocabulary the better; it's a balancing act between the complexity and power of full XPaths and the ease of use of plain names.

> If you do choose a vocabulary that uses XPaths or something like them, you can handle your insertion elements in the same kinds of ways described in the previous section for handling XInclude elements.

For this example, you can just use a simple vocabulary: the username element indicates where the user's name should be put, and the details element indicates where the statement details should be inserted. Ideally, these elements should go in a specific namespace, so that they're easy to identify later:

```
<html xmlns:ins="http://www.example.com/bank/templates">
  <head>
    <title>Bank Statement: <ins:username /></title>
    <link rel="stylesheet" href="/style/site.css" />
    <link rel="stylesheet" href="/style/statement.css" />
    <script content="text/javascript" src="/script/site.js" />
    <script content="text/javascript" src="/script/statement.js" />
  </head>
  <body>
    <table id="navigation">
      <tr>
        <td><a href="/">Home</a></td>
        <td><a href="/accounts.html">Accounts</a></td>
        <td>Statement</td>
```

```
        <td><a href="/options.html">Options</a></td>
        <td><a href="/logout.html">Logout</a></td>
      </tr>
    </table>
    <ins:details />
  </body>
</html>
```

The stylesheet that you're using, `statement.xsl`, operates over `statement.xml`, an XML document holding all the statement information that should be inserted into the page. You need to access the file shown previously, `template.xml`, so that you can work over *its* contents to create the output, copying most of it, but inserting information from `statement.xml` as required by the insertion instructions. When working with multiple documents, it's helpful to have global variables holding the root nodes of each of them in a stylesheet:

```
<xsl:variable name="data" select="/" />
<xsl:variable name="template" select="document('template.xml')" />
```

The focus at the start of the stylesheet is on the root node of the source XML, `statement.xml`. You need to shift this focus to `template.xml` so that you can iterate over it. I usually put this kind of control information into a template matching the root node of the document:

```
<xsl:template match="/">
   <xsl:apply-templates select="$template/*" />
</xsl:template>
```

> Be careful to apply templates to the document element of the template document, rather than its root node; if you applied templates to its root node, the processor would match the same template again, and enter an infinite loop.

Because the stylesheet works over the template document, you mainly need to copy the nodes, using the recursive identity template:

```
<xsl:template match="@*|node()">
   <xsl:copy>
      <xsl:apply-templates select="@*|node()" />
   </xsl:copy>
</xsl:template>
```

The exceptions are the insertion elements from your vocabulary. You need to process these in a special way: the username comes from the user attribute on the statement document element in statement.xml; the HTML holding the details is the result of applying templates to the statement element in details mode; and so on. The actions that are required on encountering these elements are defined within their individual templates:

```
<xsl:template match="ins:username">
   <xsl:value-of select="$data/statement/@user" />
</xsl:template>

<xsl:template match="ins:details">
   <xsl:apply-templates select="$data/statement" mode="details" />
</xsl:template>
```

There are several advantages to using your own vocabulary within a page template: designers don't have to learn complex XSLT, XInclude, or XPath syntax; you can attune the instructions you need to the domain that you're dealing with; and you can choose exactly how to interpret different instruction elements yourself.

Supporting Customization and Internationalization

Supporting customization and internationalization (which is really a form of customization that revolves around the locale of the end-user, rather than their personal preferences) is a matter of focusing the techniques outlined earlier in this chapter on the aspects of a page that need to be customized. This section describes some of the details that are particular to customization and internationalization:

◆ Changing the style of documents

◆ Changing the structure of documents

◆ Inserting localized text

You learned about localizing numerical formats in Chapter 1.

Encoding Customization

If you're creating a customizable application, the particular options associated with a user need to be stored somewhere. The easiest way of storing these such that they remain accessible to the stylesheet is to store them within an XML document, or within a database whose content is accessible via XML.

In the bank statement application, the user's options are available within an options.xml document, which looks like the following:

```
<options>
   <style>default</style>
   <structure navigation="top">
      <header />
      <transactions />
   </structure>
   <language>en</language>
</options>
```

For this particular user, this set of options indicates that the page should be given the default set of styles; that it should be structured with the navigation bar at the top, with the statement details listed first with a header and then with transactions; and that the language used within the statement should be English.

 The options that you want to allow the user should be decided as early as possible, as they can have a big impact on the design of the stylesheet to support them. You should create your own XML vocabulary to encode the particular options that are relevant to your application.

In your statement.xsl stylesheet, these options are made available through a global variable called $options, which is defined as follows:

```
<xsl:variable name="options"
             select="document('options.xml')/options" />
```

Customizing Document Style

The style of a document — the fonts and colors used within it, for example — can be set in two main ways. The first way is at a global level, through a stylesheet — a collection of formats that are applied across the entire document. The second way is through local styles, which are only applied to specific parts of the document.

Generally, user customization of a page occurs at a global level, so customizing the look and feel of a page involves changing the styles associated with it. I'll touch on two main ways of doing this here: first, by changing the CSS stylesheet associated with the stylesheet; and second, by changing the formatting object properties used when creating an XSL-FO document (which is used to create a printed statement via PDF).

CHANGING STYLES IN HTML DOCUMENTS

Changing the CSS stylesheet used with an HTML document is a matter of altering the link element that refers to it. The bank statement application uses two CSS stylesheets – one that holds site-specific styles and one that holds page-specific styles; it is the former that needs to change according to the style desired by the user.

Any of the techniques described earlier in the chapter can be used to insert this information, but we will examine using a page template and inserting the relevant information into that template. Adapting the page template to include style information just means adding another element, in the template namespace, to indicate the location where the link element should be added:

```
<html xmlns:ins="http://www.example.com/bank/templates">
   <head>
      <title>Bank Statement: <ins:username /></title>
      <ins:style />
      <link rel="stylesheet" href="/style/statement.css" />
      <script content="text/javascript" src="/script/site.js" />
      <script content="text/javascript" src="/script/statement.js" />
   </head>
   ...
</html>
```

Inserting the relevant style information is a matter of having a template that matches the ins:style element and inserts the appropriate link element, using the information from the user options to determine to what it should point:

```
<xsl:template match="ins:style">
   <link rel="stylesheet" href="/style/{$options/style}-site.css" />
</xsl:template>
```

With this template and the options that the user's chosen in options.xml, the resulting HTML will point to default-site.css and be styled accordingly.

CHANGING STYLES WITH XSL-FO

XSL-FO works a little differently in that the style of a formatting object isn't defined globally. Instead, attributes are added to the specific formatting objects to give them individual style. Thus, altering the style globally involves changing the attributes that are added to particular elements as they're created.

One way to define an XSL design is to have several attribute sets, defined with `xsl:attribute-set`, with each pertaining to a particular section or inline element within the page. For example, you might have one attribute set for the headings in your table and another for its contents. Each user style would involve a different set of attribute sets, defining different values for the attributes (or not defining them at all). The definitions for the default style might look like the following:

```
<xsl:attribute-set name="table-header"
                   xsl:use-attribute-sets="basic">
  <xsl:attribute name="font-weight">bold</xsl:attribute>
  <xsl:attribute name="text-align">center</xsl:attribute>
</xsl:attribute-set>

<xsl:attribute-set name="table-cells"
                   xsl:use-attribute-sets="basic">
  <xsl:attribute name="font-size">83%</xsl:attribute>
</xsl:attribute-set>
```

Ideally, you want to be able to refer to these attribute sets from within the stylesheet when you run the stylesheet. Unfortunately, because the attribute sets that you want to use depend on something that changes with each run of the stylesheet (i.e., the user preference), they cannot be included dynamically.

 It's also hard work to include all the attribute sets for all the different styles, and choose between them dynamically, in particular because the `xsl:use-attribute-sets` attribute cannot include an attribute value template.

You therefore have two options — you can access the styles programmatically, interpreting the `xsl:attribute-set` and `xsl:attribute` elements within the stylesheet, or you can split the process into two stages, first creating a stylesheet that includes the relevant attribute sets for use in the second stage.

USING ATTRIBUTE DEFINITIONS FROM A FILE The first option, interpreting the `xsl:attribute-set` and `xsl:attribute` elements from within the stylesheet, involves accessing the stylesheet containing the attribute sets and pulling in the attributes from it whenever you want to use it. In this example, the attribute sets are contained in stylesheets named `X-style.xsl`, where X is the style specified by the user in their options (for example, `default-style.xsl`). You can access the relevant file using the `document()` function, with the first argument constructed using `concat()` as follows:

```
<xsl:variable name="style"
              select="document(concat($options/style, '-style.xsl'))
                      /*/xsl:attribute-set" />
```

 If you're using this technique, you don't have to adhere to XSLT syntax for defining the attributes; you might find it handier to use elements such as `<table-header font-weight="bold" text-align="center" />` which would enable you to simply copy the relevant attributes into your result.

The `$style` variable holds a node set consisting of the various `xsl:attribute-set` elements in the relevant stylesheet. Whenever you create a formatting object that you want to style using the attributes defined within that stylesheet, you can add attributes based on those defined in the relevant attribute set. You can do this by applying templates to the attribute set, accessing them by their `name` attribute. For example, when creating a cell in the table header, you apply templates to the `xsl:attribute-set` whose `name` attribute is equal to `table-header`:

```
<fo:table-header>
   <fo:table-row>
      <fo:table-cell>
         <fo:block>
            <xsl:apply-templates select="$style[@name = 'table-header']" />
            ...
         </fo:block>
      </fo:table-cell>
      ...
   </fo:table-row>
</fo:table-header>
```

The template for the `xsl:attribute-set` elements has to process the `xsl:attribute` elements inside it. Attribute sets can include attributes that are specified in other attribute sets, to form hierarchies. If you want to retain this capability, you should use the `use-attribute-sets` attribute on `xsl:attribute-set` to list the attribute sets that an attribute set inherits from. In this case, the template for `xsl:attribute-set` also needs to process these parent attribute sets first, to include the attributes defined in those attribute sets. The templates to do this look like the following:

```
<xsl:template match="xsl:attribute-set">
   <xsl:call-template name="use-attribute-sets" />
   <xsl:apply-templates select="xsl:attribute" />
```

```
</xsl:template>

<xsl:template name="use-attribute-sets">
   <xsl:param name="use-attribute-sets"
              select="normalize-space(@use-attribute-sets)" />
   <xsl:choose>
      <xsl:when test="not(contains($use-attribute-sets, ' '))">
         <xsl:apply-templates
            select="$options/style[@name = $use-attribute-sets]" />
      </xsl:when>
      <xsl:otherwise>
         <xsl:apply-templates
            select="$options/style
                       [@name = substring-before($use-attribute-sets, ' ')]" />
         <xsl:call-template name="use-attribute-sets">
            <xsl:with-param name="substring-after($use-attribute-sets, ' ')" />
         </xsl:call-template>
      </xsl:otherwise>
   </xsl:choose>
</xsl:template>
```

The template for the `xsl:attribute` elements that are being processed needs to create the attributes with an `xsl:attribute` instruction that has the same name and gives the value of the `xsl:attribute` as its content:

```
<xsl:template match="xsl:attribute">
   <xsl:attribute name="{@name}">
      <xsl:value-of select="." />
   </xsl:attribute>
</xsl:template>
```

This approach is fine as long as the values of the attributes are not calculated dynamically. It also requires a lot of coding within the stylesheet.

CREATING A STYLESHEET THAT DYNAMICALLY IMPORTS A STYLESHEET   Using a two-step process in which your stylesheet creates a stylesheet that's later used is more flexible, in particular because you can use it to include attribute values that are calculated dynamically. In this case, the eventual stylesheet that you want to create imports both the `statement.xsl` stylesheet and the stylesheet containing the attribute sets for the particular style (for example, `default-style.xsl`):

```
<xsl:stylesheet version="1.0"
                xmlns:xsl="http://www.w3.org/1999/XSL/Transform">

<xsl:import href="default-style.xsl" />
```

```
<xsl:import href="statement.xsl" />

</xsl:stylesheet>
```

The stylesheet that creates this stylesheet needs to have access to the user options so that it can determine which stylesheet to import; the user options may as well act as the input to the stylesheet. It then needs to create the stylesheet as a whole. Here, because you're creating many XSLT elements, you should use a namespace alias so that you can use literal result elements, rather than xsl:element all the time. Following is the complete stylesheet:

```
<xsl:stylesheet version="1.0"
                xmlns:xsl="http://www.w3.org/1999/XSL/Transform"
                xmlns:oxsl="http://www.w3.org/1999/XSL/TransformAlias">

<xsl:namespace-alias stylesheet-prefix="oxsl" result-prefix="xsl" />

<xsl:template match="options">
   <oxsl:stylesheet version="1.0">
      <oxsl:import href="{style}-style.xsl" />
      <oxsl:import href="statement.xsl" />
   </oxsl:stylesheet>
</xsl:template>


</xsl:stylesheet>
```

Chapter 17 explains the effect of xsl:namespace-alias.

Given that statement.xsl will be imported into the same stylesheet as the attribute set definitions in default-style.xsl, to use them you add xsl:use-attribute-sets attributes to the literal result elements that you're creating. Now, you can add the relevant style to the content of table header cells as follows:

```
<fo:table-header>
   <fo:table-row>
      <fo:table-cell>
         <fo:block xsl:use-attribute-sets="table-header">
            ...
         </fo:block>
```

```
        </fo:table-cell>
        ...
    </fo:table-row>
</fo:table-header>
```

Customizing Document Structure

You can customize a document's structure in two main ways: through global flags that indicate the type of structure that's desired, or through a miniature template of the required structure. The example that we're using shows both. The part of the options that controls structure is as follows:

```
<structure navigation="top">
    <header />
    <transactions />
</structure>
```

The `navigation` attribute acts as a flag, indicating the positions that the navigation bar should take in the document. It can take the values `top` or `left`. Using this information is a matter of having an `xsl:choose` to determine what structure the body of the document should have:

```
<xsl:choose>
    <xsl:when test="$options/structure/@navigation='top'">
        <table id="navigation">
            ...
        </table>
        ...
    </xsl:when>
    <xsl:otherwise>
        <table>
            <tr>
                <td id="navigation">
                    ...
                </td>
                <td id="content">
                    ...
                </td>
            </tr>
        </table>
    </xsl:otherwise>
</xsl:choose>
```

The content of the `structure` element, on the other hand, acts as a template for the body of the statement, indicating that it should contain header information followed by a list of transactions, rather than the other way around. You can use this information in the same way you used insertion instructions in full-page templates, as described earlier in this chapter. For example, you could use the following templates to apply templates to the content of the structure element, and process the header and transactions elements, applying templates to the relevant part of the data node tree to create the output:

```
<xsl:template name="statement-content">
   <xsl:apply-templates select="$options/structure"
                        mode="template" />
</xsl:template>

<xsl:template match="header" mode="template">
   <xsl:apply-templates select="$data/statement/header" />
</xsl:template>

<xsl:template match="transactions" mode="template">
   <xsl:apply-templates select="$data/statement/transactions" />
</xsl:template>
```

You should use modes here to distinguish between applying templates to the template structure and applying templates to the data itself. This is important because the elements used in the template are named the same as those in the data. You could use namespaces to distinguish between the different vocabularies instead.

Localizing Text

The final type of customization that you'll examine in this chapter is localizing the text within the result that you're creating. The text in a document that you create is of two types: dynamic text that comes from the XML that you're processing, and static text that is created by the stylesheet. Localizing your output involves choosing the right text from the source XML and creating appropriate static text within the stylesheet. This section focuses on the latter.

You can choose which text to process from the source XML you're using by selecting it just as you would any other piece of information. The lang() function is particularly useful within a predicate to identify content that is defined as being in a particular language using the xml:lang attribute.

This example has several pieces of localized text: the title for the page you're creating, the labels in the navigation table, and so on. Currently, these are defined statically within the stylesheet, inserted just as text within it. The language in which you want the text is specified within the options XML document, and you can place this in a global variable:

```
<xsl:variable name="lang" select="$options/language" />
```

TESTING LANGUAGES

One approach is simply to query this variable to determine which text to insert in each location that static text is added:

```
<title>
   <xsl:choose>
      <xsl:when test="$lang = 'fr'">...</xsl:when>
      <xsl:when test="$lang = 'de'">...</xsl:when>
      <xsl:when test="$lang = 'nl'">...</xsl:when>
      <xsl:otherwise>Bank Statement</xsl:otherwise>
   </xsl:choose>
   <xsl:text>: </xsl:text>
   <xsl:value-of select="$username" />
</title>
```

There are two problems with this approach. One, it's hard to identify where localized text needs to be added; in particular, adding a new language to the set would involve picking through the stylesheet to find the places where localized text is added. Two, the processor needs to carry out the same test on $lang each time a new piece of static text needs to be added, which is processor-intensive.

CREATING A DICTIONARY

A better approach, then, is to have the various translations of the pieces of static text held within a separate XML document — a dictionary for translating between the different terms. You can organize this dictionary in two ways: by term or by language. For example, if you were organizing it by term, it would look like the following:

```
<dictionary>
   <term id="bank-statement">
      <translation xml:lang="fr">...</translation>
      <translation xml:lang="de">...</translation>
      <translation xml:lang="nl">...</translation>
      <translation xml:lang="en">Bank Statement</translation>
   </term>
   ...
```

```
</dictionary>
```

Organized by language, the same information would look as follows:

```
<dictionary>
   <translations xml:lang="fr">
      <term id="bank-statement">...</term>
      ...
   </translations>
   <translations xml:lang="de">
      <term id="bank-statement">...</term>
      ...
   </translations>
   <translations xml:lang="nl">
      <term id="bank-statement">...</term>
      ...
   </translations>
   <translations xml:lang="en">
      <term id="bank-statement">Bank Statement</term>
      ...
   </translations>
</dictionary>
```

Either form of organization works. The latter is more natural if you have different translators for different languages; the former is more natural if you have a single translator. Moreover, the first method has the advantage of only specifying each term ID once, which makes it less liable to error.

 TIP If you're splitting the dictionary into separate documents, you should organize the documents by language, so that you can retrieve all the text that you need by accessing a single document.

In either case, the most efficient way to access the translation of a term is using a key. Organized by term, the key would look like the following:

```
<xsl:key name="translations" select="translation"
         use="concat(../@id, ':', @xml:lang)" />
```

For organization by language, the key would look as follows:

```
<xsl:key name="translations" select="term"
         use="concat(@id, ':', ../@xml:lang)" />
```

Both these keys give access to the translation of a term in the same way. For example, you could get the relevant translation of "Bank Statement" with the following, as long as you were in the context of the dictionary document:

```
key('translations', concat('bank-statement:', $lang))
```

If you don't use a key, you may be tempted to use the `lang()` function to test the language of a particular translation. Be careful if you do so; the `lang()` function returns true if the language specified by `xml:lang` is a sublanguage of the language you pass as the argument. For example, if `xml:lang` was `en-UK` then `lang('en')` would return true. Unless you're careful, you'll therefore retrieve all the English-language translations rather than just one.

Because it's tedious retrieving keyed nodes from a different document, it's a good idea to set up a template to do it for you. The following template, for example, takes the term required as a parameter and uses `xsl:for-each` to change the context to `dictionary.xml` before using the key:

```
<xsl:variable name="dictionary" select="document('dictionary.xml')" />

<xsl:template name="get-text">
   <xsl:param name="term" />
   <xsl:for-each select="$dictionary">
      <xsl:copy-of select="key('translations', concat($term, ':', $lang)" />
   </xsl:for-each>
</xsl:template>
```

Using `xsl:copy-of` rather than `xsl:value-of` within this template enables you to add elements within the different translations and have those elements copied to the output. You could use this with long pieces of text with internal markup, for example, or to provide locale-specific icons or images.

You could improve this template by making it check for alternative languages, such as ones with less specific codes, or a global default language if the key doesn't return a translation for the specific language.

If the structure of the document is being organized within the stylesheet itself, you can call this template directly:

```
<title>
   <xsl:call-template name="get-text">
      <xsl:with-param name="term" select="'bank-statement'" />
   </xsl:call-template>
   <xsl:text>: </xsl:text>
   <xsl:value-of select="$username" />
</title>
```

On the other hand, if you have designers creating page templates, you need them to insert elements that indicate where the terms should be added, and then interpret these elements within your stylesheet as you work through the template. In this case, the page template might look like the following:

```
<title>
   <ins:term ref="bank-statement" />: <ins:username />
</title>
```

The template to handle the ins:term elements from the template would look like this:

```
<xsl:template match="ins:term">
   <xsl:call-template name="get-text">
      <xsl:with-param name="term" select="@ref" />
   </xsl:call-template>
</xsl:template>
```

CREATING LANGUAGE-SPECIFIC TEMPLATES

One problem with translating everything using a dictionary as shown previously is that certain aspects of the *structure* of localized text might change depending on the language that's being used. For example, in one language you might want to have the term for "Bank Statement" appear before the user's name, whereas you may want it to appear after the user's name in another language.

In these cases, you need to define miniature templates to handle those specific parts of the text, used in the same way as the page templates discussed in the section "Using Insertion Instructions in a Template Page" earlier in this chapter, and the structure templates discussed earlier in this section. Which of the language-specific templates to process can be determined by language and accessed in the same way as the terms as I've outlined above.

The further you go down the customization road, the closer you get to inventing a template language yourself. Be very careful not to reinvent XSLT. Keep the vocabulary that you use in the templates closely tied to the application in which you're using it. If you want a generic template language, use XSLT, and merge the stylesheets that define the customized look and feel of the result together in a two-step process, as outlined in the discussion in the section "Changing Styles with XSL-FO," earlier in this chapter.

Summary

This chapter described various ways of separating the design of the output that you're generating from the logic of incorporating data into it, both to ease the maintenance of your system and to make it easier for designers to concentrate on the design of pages, without having to learn XSLT or XPath.

You first examined various ways of reusing snippets of XML: by using external references such as entities and XInclude within the stylesheet, by copying documents accessed through the document() function, or by generating external references within the result. These techniques are particularly helpful in reusing standard bits of XSLT in various places across a number of documents.

You next looked at creating and using page templates, which make designers' lives easier by enabling them to indicate where the result of processing the data should be inserted. You learned three ways of approaching page templates: using simplified stylesheets, which use XSLT and XPath instructions within them; using external references, either with entities or XInclude; and using application-specific insertion instructions that you interpret within your stylesheet.

Finally, you learned how the techniques described earlier could be applied to problems involving customization and localization; specifically, customizing the style of a document, changing its structure based on use preferences, and changing the static text included in a document based on the user's locale or language.

Chapter 12

Creating Functional Modules

In this chapter, you can discover how to modularize your XSLT stylesheet to make it easier to manage and to maintain. This chapter concentrates on the *logical* structure of an XSLT application, whereas Chapter 13 examines its *physical* structure. Creating functional modules within a stylesheet is useful in several ways. It cuts down on repetition, it highlights generalities between different parts of your stylesheet, and it makes your stylesheet easier to maintain.

The three features of XSLT that can assist in creating functional modules are modes, named templates, and attribute sets. You've used all of these techniques before in previous chapters, but here I focus on identifying situations in which they can be most effective.

Distinguishing Between Threads

I've already discussed using template modes to enable various templates to do different things to the same node in different situations in Chapter 10. As a reminder, the classic example is processing a set of headings once for the table of contents and once when outputting the body of a document.

For example, you could use one template in ToC mode. This template would output one division per section (the div being in the ToCSection class) giving just the number and the title of the section before moving to its subsections in the same, ToC, mode.

```
<xsl:template match="section" mode="ToC">
  <div class="ToCSection">
    <p>
      <xsl:number level="multiple" format="1." />
```

```
      <xsl:text> </xsl:text>
      <xsl:value-of select="title" />
   </p>
   <xsl:apply-templates select="section" mode="ToC" />
  </div>
</xsl:template>
```

A separate template in default mode can handle the sections in the body of the document. This template simply wraps a div in the section class around each section.

```
<xsl:template match="section">
  <div class="section">
    <xsl:apply-templates />
  </div>
</xsl:template>
```

In this situation, you can use a higher-level template to determine which mode was used at any one time. For example, assuming that a single chapter is shown on a single page, and that a table of contents is shown for each chapter, the following template goes through the chapters sections twice: first to build the table of contents and then to show the chapter content.

```
<xsl:template match="chapter">
   ...
   <div class="ToC">
     <h2>Table of Contents</h2>
     <xsl:apply-templates select="section" mode="ToC" />
   </div>
   <div class="body">
     <xsl:apply-templates select="section" />
   </div>
   ...
</xsl:template>
```

Modes aren't only useful in distinguishing between two templates that match on the same kind of node. In large XSLT applications, situations often arise in which you have two threads of processing that deal with different sets of nodes, each involving many different templates. In these applications, modes are a way of labeling the different sections of your stylesheet.

For example, you have to create a Web page for a customer's bank account statement. The Web page has two important parts: the first part contains the general information about the bank account and the customer, and the second part contains a table showing the transactions on the account. The source XML is similarly divided:

```
<statement>
   <custInfo>
      ...
   </custInfo>
   <accountInfo>
      ...
   </accountInfo>
   <transactions>
      <transaction>...</transaction>
      <transaction>...</transaction>
      ...
   </transactions>
</statement>
```

Within the stylesheet, you only visit each node once: the transactions do not need to be summarized. For example, when you match a transaction element you *always* want to create a row for the table.

However, using two different modes for the general information and the transaction table breaks up the stylesheet into two main parts. The stylesheet takes the form shown in the following, with a top-level template controlling the flow from part to part, a set of templates in header mode, and a set of templates in table mode:

```
<xsl:stylesheet version="1.0"
                xmlns:xsl="http://www.w3.org/1999/XSL/Transform">

<!-- controlling template -->
<xsl:template match="statement">
   ...
   <xsl:apply-templates select="custInfo | accountInfo"
                        mode="header" />
   ...
   <xsl:apply-templates select="transactions"
                        mode="table" />
   ...
</xsl:template>

<!-- templates in header mode -->
<xsl:template match="address" mode="header">
   ...
</xsl:template>
...

<!-- templates in table mode -->
<xsl:template match="transaction" mode="table">
```

```
    ...
</xsl:template>
...

</xsl:stylesheet>
```

Mode Names

Mode names are technically qualified names: they have a prefix and a local part, separated by a colon. The prefix is actually interpreted according to the namespace declarations in place at the point where the mode name is used. This means that if you use qualified mode names, and someone imports your stylesheet, they can define a prefix on their stylesheet that differs from the prefix you've used.

For example, in the `header.xsl` stylesheet, which is being used to hold templates in `header` mode, generating account and customer information, you can declare a statement namespace and place all templates that deal with header information in this namespace.

```
<xsl:stylesheet
    version="1.0"
    xmlns:xsl="http://www.w3.org/1999/XSL/Transform"
    xmlns:stmt="http://www.example.com/bank/statement"
    exclude-result-prefixes="stmt">

<xsl:template match="address" mode="stmt:header">
    ...
</xsl:template>
...

</xsl:stylesheet>
```

When someone else imports this `header.xsl` stylesheet, they can use whatever prefix they prefer as long as they use the same namespace URI. For example, if the local rail company wants to include their bank information in their annual report, they may already have a `header` mode and possibly a prefix that's the same as the one you've used (they shorten 'station management' to `stmt`, the prefix you've used in this stylesheet). However, this doesn't matter. They can import the stylesheet knowing that there can't be any conflicts because you've used a unique namespace, and they can use whatever prefix they prefer for this namespace, without even knowing what prefix you used in your stylesheet.

```
<xsl:stylesheet
    version="1.0"
```

```
    xmlns:xsl="http://www.w3.org/1999/XSL/Transform"
    xmlns:stmt="http://www.example.com/station/management"
    xmlns:acnt="http://www.example.com/bank/statement"
    exclude-result-prefixes="stmt acnt">

<xsl:import href="header.xml" />

<xsl:template match="report">
    ...
    <xsl:apply-templates mode="stmt:header" />
    ...
    <xsl:apply-templates select="account"
                         mode="acnt:header" />
    ...
</xsl:template>
...


</xsl:stylesheet>
```

Of course, you can also introduce your own structure into mode names. For example, you can use dots to give a kind of hierarchical structure to the names that you use. You can break down the header information into account information and customer information:

```
<xsl:template match="bank/address" mode="header.account">
    ...
</xsl:template>

<xsl:template match="custInfo/address" mode="header.customer">
    ...
</xsl:template>
```

This is handy in that the template may be sorted in a type of hierarchy in an XSLT stylesheet viewer or editor, but XSLT has no built-in method of prioritizing or selecting alternative templates based on this kind of naming structure, so don't expect miracles.

This approach has its advantages and disadvantages. On the plus side, when you view this stylesheet in an XSLT stylesheet browser or editor, you can sort and possibly filter the templates according to their mode. As a result, you can easily distinguish which templates are used to create which bit of the page. Also, when you come back to this stylesheet in a year's time or even when someone else takes over its maintenance, it's apparent just by looking at a template roughly where the

HTML that it generates will appear in the page. In this way, modes provide a crude form of documentation for a template.

A more important advantage is the fact that using modes makes it harder for you to inadvertently override an existing template with a new one. For example, if you decided that the transaction table should have a header containing the account details, then you need to add a new template matching the relevant element from within the accountInfo element. Without modes, this template could override the template used to give account information in the header portion of the page, so you have to be careful (and add modes on a case-by-case basis). With modes, you do not have to worry about overriding existing templates.

Probably the biggest *disadvantage* of using modes such as this is that you always have to remember to apply templates in whichever mode is relevant and to declare the mode of the templates that you author. Of course, specifying modes in which to apply templates and declaring a mode for a template both add extra characters to the stylesheet, making it slightly larger.

Identifying the different *functional* parts of the stylesheet and distinguishing between them using moded templates prepares the stylesheet for division into separate *physical* stylesheets. Now that your statement stylesheet has been divided into these two functional parts — one for the general information, and one for the transaction table — you can easily dump all the templates in header mode into a separate header.xsl stylesheet. This stylesheet can be included or imported into your stylesheet, or any other stylesheet that uses similar information to create the same kind of HTML.

Using a particular mode for this set of templates has the advantage of ensuring that these templates are unlikely to clash with others in stylesheets that import or include them. However, authors of other stylesheets have to remember to apply templates in header mode as well.

Isolating Reusable Code

As a fully fledged programming language, XSLT has the equivalent of functions, *named templates*. Named templates are pieces of XSLT code that you can call by name and pass arguments to, except that XSLT arguments are called *parameters*.

 Just as with mode names, the names used for named templates are actually qualified names. Thus, you can declare a particular namespace for your named templates and use whatever prefix you want to refer to them within the stylesheet. If you're creating named templates to be used as utilities, it's probably prudent to give them a namespace to help avoid naming conflicts (two templates with the same name causes an error).

The first four chapters of this book used named templates extensively.

Take as an example the following `substring-after-last` template, which returns the string after the *last* occurrence of a search string in a string (as opposed to the `substring-after()` function, which returns the string after the *first* occurrence of a character in a string). The template works through the string by recursion and only returns the string when it has no occurrences of the character in it:

```
<xsl:template name="substring-after-last">
   <xsl:param name="string" />
   <xsl:param name="search" />
   <xsl:choose>
      <xsl:when test="contains($string, $search)">
         <xsl:call-template name="substring-after-last">
            <xsl:with-param name="string"
               select="substring-after($string, $search)" />
            <xsl:with-param name="search" select="$search" />
         </xsl:call-template>
      </xsl:when>
      <xsl:otherwise>
         <xsl:value-of select="$string" />
      </xsl:otherwise>
   </xsl:choose>
</xsl:template>
```

This template demonstrates a problem — recursing through a string — that named templates can easily solve. Named templates are great for recursing through other data types as well, such as node sets and numbers, as you've seen in previous chapters.

To determine other situations in which named templates might be useful, requires the same exercise as used in any programming language: you need to find commonalities between several different sections of code and draw those together into a named template.

Named Templates versus Moded Templates

Named templates and moded templates are actually very similar. They both associate a name with a subset of processing, they can both use parameters, and they both return result tree fragments. Any call to a named template can be substituted with an instruction to apply templates in a particular mode, where the mode is the same as the name, and the selected node is the current node.

For example, a call to the preceding template resembles this:

```
<xsl:call-template name="substring-after-last">
  <xsl:with-param name="string" select="$file" />
  <xsl:with-param name="search" select="'/'" />
</xsl:call-template>
```

In this case, you're trying to find the name of a file (held in the $file variable), without any directory information by getting the substring after the last /. Rather than defining the preceding named template, you could define a moded template that does the same thing, by replacing the template's name attribute with match and mode attributes and changing the recursive call to a recursive application of templates:

```
<xsl:template match="node()" mode="substring-after-last">
  <xsl:param name="string" />
  <xsl:param name="search" />
  <xsl:choose>
    <xsl:when test="contains($string, $search)">
      <xsl:apply-templates select="."
                           mode="substring-after-last">
        <xsl:with-param name="string"
            select="substring-after($string, $search)" />
        <xsl:with-param name="search" select="$search" />
      </xsl:apply-templates>
    </xsl:when>
    <xsl:otherwise>
      <xsl:value-of select="$string" />
    </xsl:otherwise>
  </xsl:choose>
</xsl:template>
```

The "call" to this moded template now consists of applying templates to the current node in the substring-after-last mode:

```
<xsl:apply-templates select="." mode="substring-after-last">
  <xsl:with-param name="string" select="$file" />
  <xsl:with-param name="search" select="'/'" />
</xsl:apply-templates>
```

In this example, moving into a moded template is hardly worthwhile: It adds characters to the XSLT stylesheet and nodes to its tree representation in memory (its DOM). In addition, the XSLT processor must work harder to find the relevant piece of code to apply — looking through all the templates to find the one that matches, rather than going straight to the named template. And in this situation, the identity of the current node does not make any difference to the result of the template.

However, using a moded template rather than a named template is advantageous in situations in which you *do* care about the type of the current node. For example, in the banking application, you often have to format an address, so you could create a named template to output it in the way you want:

```
<xsl:template name="insert-address">
   <address>
      <xsl:for-each select="address/line">
         <xsl:value-of select="." />,<br />
      </xsl:for-each>
      <xsl:value-of select="address/city" /><br />
      <xsl:value-of select="address/postcode" />
   </address>
</xsl:template>
```

You can call this template in various places, with:

```
<xsl:call-template name="insert-address" />
```

If you examine the select expressions in the preceding template, you see that they're all relative, and that the current node has to have an address child for any of them to find any nodes. However, there's absolutely nothing stopping you from calling this template in a totally inappropriate place – the template will always be processed, and you just end up with empty address elements all over the place.

If you use a matching, moded template instead, such as the following one, then you can guarantee that it never activates in inappropriate circumstances. The template can never be processed if there isn't an address element for it to process.

```
<xsl:template match="address" mode="insert">
   <address>
      <xsl:for-each select="line">
         <xsl:value-of select="." />,<br />
      </xsl:for-each>
      <xsl:value-of select="city" /><br />
      <xsl:value-of select="postcode" />
   </address>
</xsl:template>
```

You can call this template with the following instruction:

```
<xsl:apply-templates select="address" mode="insert" />
```

As well as protecting you from variabilities in the source XML, using a moded template enables you to keep track of what the current node is. The type of the current node is completely invisible within a named template: you never know what the context is, what template is calling this one. Using a moded template adds that little bit of extra information that can make a stylesheet easier to maintain in the long run.

TIP Any template can have a name (a template can be both a moded template and a named template). The match pattern and the mode are ignored if the template's called by name, and the name is ignored if the application of templates causes it to be processed. Thus, if you only have one template in a particular mode and you're trying to squeeze the last drop of efficiency out of your stylesheet, you can add a name to that template. Then you can call it in situations where you *know* it's going to be appropriate, and apply templates in the mode when you're not sure (perhaps because an element is optional in that context).

A further advantage of using a moded template in this situation is that you can easily add all-embracing conditions on how a particular address is formatted by adding templates with different match patterns and the same mode to the stylesheet. With a named template, if you wanted to output a warning paragraph when the content of the address is missing, you would have to use a big `xsl:choose` to do so:

```
<xsl:template name="format-address">
   <xsl:choose>
      <xsl:when test="not(address/*)">
         <p class="warning">No address given.</p>
      </xsl:when>
      <xsl:otherwise>
         <address>
            <xsl:for-each select="address/line">
               <xsl:value-of select="." />,<br />
            </xsl:for-each>
            <xsl:value-of select="address/city" /><br />
            <xsl:value-of select="address/postcode" />
         </address>
      </xsl:otherwise>
   </xsl:choose>
</xsl:template>
```

With a moded template, it's just a matter of adding another template for the extra condition:

```
<xsl:template match="address[not(*)]" mode="insert">
   <p class="warning">No address given.</p>
</xsl:template>
```

 If you're used to object-oriented programming, then you might find it useful to think of the difference between named templates and moded templates in terms of the difference between global functions and object methods. As with global functions, named templates are useful in a range of circumstances but they shouldn't really use information about a particular object unless that object is passed as an argument. Object methods, on the other hand, use information about an object and are "inherited" by related objects. You can think of the nodes in the source tree as objects, with moded templates providing methods on those objects.

Limitations of Templates

Two weaknesses of calling named templates or applying templates can make them fairly cumbersome. The first is that calling or applying them, particularly when passing parameters, requires a lot of XSLT code. The substring-after-last template used in the preceding example calls itself recursively with the instruction:

```
<xsl:call-template name="substring-after-last">
   <xsl:with-param name="string"
                   select="substring-after($string, $search)" />
   <xsl:with-param name="search" select="$search" />
</xsl:call-template>
```

As you can see, the call takes up a great deal of space because each of the parameters is passed by a long XSLT element of its own.

The second weakness of named templates is that they always return a result tree fragment. You can't use a named template to directly give you a Boolean, a string, or a number. The closest that you can get is a result tree fragment whose string value is that string or number, or, to mimic a Boolean value, that only has a non-empty string value (which will be converted to true) in certain circumstances.

TIP If you want to create a template that returns a Boolean value, the actual text that you return is ignored by the XSLT processor — you just use the test:

```
string($returned-value)
```

(You have to turn the result tree fragment into a string before testing it because result tree fragments are always evaluated as Boolean true.) I've often found it helpful to return an explanatory string as the "true" value because I can use the returned value while I'm debugging to isolate what's going wrong.

These limitations are indicative of the fact that you're dealing with XSLT elements here, and not XPath functions. In many situations, you can avoid these limitations by storing the returned value from a template in a variable and using that within an expression. For example, if you have a named template that creates a hexadecimal color from an RGB value, you can store the returned value in a variable and test that to determine what to do:

```
<xsl:variable name="color">
   <xsl:call-template name="hex-color">
      <xsl:with-param name="red" select="$red" />
      <xsl:with-param name="green" select="$green" />
      <xsl:with-param name="blue" select="$blue" />
   </xsl:call-template>
</xsl:variable>
<xsl:choose>
   <xsl:when test="$color = 'FFFFFF'">white</xsl:when>
   <xsl:when test="$color = '000000'">black</xsl:when>
   <xsl:otherwise>#<xsl:value-of select="$color" /></xsl:otherwise>
</xsl:choose>
```

There are situations, though, in which calling a template using an XSLT element makes it very difficult to do what you want to do, specifically when you want to use the value returned by a template to filter nodes in a node set.

For example, even if you came up with a really funky template for doing regular expression matches, you couldn't use it within a predicate. Thus, you wouldn't be able to do things such as selecting all the elements in the document whose value matches a particular regular expression. Ideally, you should simply use the following:

```
//*[not(*)][matches(., $regexp)]
```

This path would select all the elements in the document that don't have element children (for example, the leaf elements), and filter that list for those that match (using your matches template) the regular expression held in the $regexp variable.

The closest you can get when using XSLT templates is to create some intermediate XML holding copies of the matching nodes by iterating over the nodes, and then use convert this to a node set:

```
<xsl:variable name="matched-nodes">
   <xsl:for-each select="//*[not(*)]">
      <xsl:variable name="matches">
         <xsl:call-template name="regexp-match">
            <xsl:with-param name="string" select="." />
            <xsl:with-param name="regexp" select="$regexp" />
         </xsl:call-template>
      </xsl:variable>
      <xsl:if test="string($matches)">
         <xsl:copy-of select="." />
      </xsl:if>
   </xsl:for-each>
</xsl:variable>
<xsl:apply-templates select="exsl:node-set($matched-nodes)" />
```

The preceding example uses the exsl:node-set() extension function to convert the result tree fragment that the template returns into a node set. See Chapter 18 for details of this and other extension functions.

The trouble with this intermediate XML is that it does not contain any of the context of the original nodes. The elements within this intermediate XML won't have their original parents or siblings, and the base URI for the nodes will be different, which makes it tricky to resolve any URLs that they refer to. In general, this isn't a problem because you never *just* want to create a node set: you want to *use* the node set by applying templates to it or iterating over it with xsl:for-each. Rather than creating a copy of the node and later doing things to it, you can *do* these things immediately when you find a match:

```
<xsl:for-each select="//*[not(*)]">
   <xsl:variable name="matches">
      <xsl:call-template name="regexp-match">
         <xsl:with-param name="string" select="." />
         <xsl:with-param name="regexp" select="$regexp" />
      </xsl:call-template>
   </xsl:variable>
   <xsl:if test="string($matches)">
      <xsl:apply-templates select="." />
   </xsl:if>
</xsl:for-each>
```

Again, however, you lose information that may be important to you. In particular, consider the position of the node when templates are applied to it. If you apply templates directly to the desired node set (where the node set is constructed within a single path as in the first example), the first matching node has a position of one, the second of two, and so on. They also have these positions if you iterate over them with an xsl:for-each.

However, in the preceding code, the matching elements have a position within the xsl:for-each dependent on their original position within the source document. For example, if the second, sixth, and ninth leaf elements match the regular expression, their positions are two, six, and nine, rather than one, two, and three. Indeed, because the xsl:apply-templates instruction only selects one element each time, then the position of the current element when evaluated in the templates matching those elements is always one.

So how can you avoid this? Well, instead of creating a copy of the node you need to create a list of *references* to the nodes in the source XML, and then use a path to find the nodes whose generated ID is in that list:

```
<xsl:variable name="leaf-elements" select="//*[not(*)]" />
<xsl:variable name="matched-nodes">
   <xsl:for-each select="$leaf-elements">
      <xsl:variable name="matches">
         <xsl:call-template name="regexp-match">
            <xsl:with-param name="string" select="." />
            <xsl:with-param name="regexp" select="$regexp" />
         </xsl:call-template>
      </xsl:variable>
      <xsl:if test="string($matches)">
         <element ref="{generate-id()}" />
      </xsl:if>
   </xsl:for-each>
</xsl:variable>
<xsl:apply-templates
   select="exsl:node-set($leaf-elements)
           [generate-id() = $matched-nodes/element/@ref]" />
```

Again, the preceding example uses an extension function to convert the result tree fragment into a node set.

As you can see, this is just a tad long and tedious. If you really want to define a function that returns something other than a result tree fragment, then it's often a lot easier to create a user-defined function. I'll go into how to do this in Chapter 20.

Designing Templates for Reuse

The preceding material demonstrates how templates can be created to hold snippets of XSLT that you want to use in multiple different situations. In this section, I discuss how to design templates that can be reused, focusing on three particular issues: defining the parameters the template uses, dealing with the indeterminable nature of XSLT value types, and creating templates that are as flexible as possible.

DECIDING WHAT PARAMETERS TO SPECIFY

Possibly the most important issue in designing a reusable template is deciding what parameters to declare. Going back to the earlier example of formatting an address, let's say you are designing a stand-alone named template. One possible design would be to accept an address element as a parameter and use that as the basis of the formatting:

```
<xsl:template name="insert-address">
   <xsl:param name="address" select="/.." />
   <address>
      <xsl:for-each select="$address/line">
         <xsl:value-of select="." />,<br />
      </xsl:for-each>
      <xsl:value-of select="$address/city" /><br />
      <xsl:value-of select="$address/postcode" />
   </address>
</xsl:template>
```

The $address parameter in the preceding template has a default value that's specified by the expression /... This expression selects the parent of the root node; since the root node never has a parent, it therefore selects an empty node set. I use this expression as a default value to indicate that I expect a parameter to be a node set rather than another value type.

This design assumes that the node passed as the value of the $address parameter is an element with (at least) three subelements named line, city, and postcode. An alternative design would specify these three parts of the address separately:

```
<xsl:template name="insert-address">
   <xsl:param name="lines" select="/.." />
   <xsl:param name="city" select="''" />
   <xsl:param name="postcode" select="''" />
   <address>
      <xsl:for-each select="$lines">
         <xsl:value-of select="." />,<br />
      </xsl:for-each>
      <xsl:value-of select="$city" /><br />
      <xsl:value-of select="$postcode" />
   </address>
</xsl:template>
```

In pure XSLT 1.0, the advantage of the second approach is that the template is more reusable with other XML vocabularies: stylesheet authors don't need to have elements with line, city, and postcode subelements defined within them to use the template. If you are happy to force users to use extension functions or a processor that supports the XSLT 1.1 Working Draft, however, it's not as advantageous. Other stylesheet authors can always create the requisite structure within a result tree fragment variable that can be converted to a node set within your template:

```
<xsl:variable name="address">
   <line><xsl:value-of select="Line1" /></line>
   <line><xsl:value-of select="Line2" /></line>
   <city><xsl:value-of select="City" /></city>
   <postcode><xsl:value-of select="Zip" /></postcode>
</xsl:variable>
<xsl:call-template name="insert-address">
   <xsl:with-param name="address"
                   select="exsl:node-set($address)" />
</xsl:call-template>
```

A problem with using this method is that a user of your template must know what XML vocabulary you're expecting. And they already must remember the name of your template, what parameters they can pass to it and the effect of passing different values for those parameters. Having them create a node tree using a particular XML vocabulary is another barrier for them.

Having said that, if you can provide a snippet of the template's XML that they can use for their result tree fragment, and if the vocabulary is fairly straightfoward, then it's really no harder than passing separate parameters.

If you are using node set parameters within your template, you should make as few assumptions as possible about their structure when indexing into them. The fewer assumptions you make, the more flexible your template is for others to use.

DEFINING PARAMETER VALUE TYPES

Parameters can take any type of value: a Boolean, a string, a number, a node set, or a result tree fragment. You can't declare what kind of value a parameter *should* take in the way that you can with argument in many other programming languages, but you may make assumptions about their value types within the template. This can lead to difficulties, especially because of the way that result tree fragments are dealt with.

As an illustrative example, imagine that you have a template that uses a numerical parameter to give the position of a node to be looked at:

```
<xsl:template name="step-backwards-through">
   <xsl:param name="nodes" />
   <xsl:param name="position" />
   <xsl:if test="$position">
      <xsl:apply-templates select="$nodes[$position]" />
      <xsl:call-template name="step-backwards-through">
         <xsl:with-param name="nodes" select="$nodes" />
         <xsl:with-param name="position" select="$position - 1" />
      </xsl:call-template>
   </xsl:if>
</xsl:template>
```

This is a recursive template: assuming that the value of the $position variable is a number. If its value is not zero, templates will be applied to the node from the node set held in the $nodes variable whose position is equal to $position. Then the template calls itself to apply templates to the previous node and so on, in effect working through the nodes in reverse order.

This is just an illustration: it's much easier to achieve this using xsl:for-each or xsl:apply-templates and a descending sort based on position.

I've implicitly assumed that the $position variable is a number in two places in the preceding template: in the xsl:if test and within the predicate on the $nodes variable in the select expression of the xsl:apply-templates instruction. In the first, I'm implicitly using the fact that a number evaluated in a Boolean context (such as a test) evaluates as false if it's equal to zero. In the second, I'm implicitly relying on the fact that a number within a predicate selects the node with a position equal to that number.

Because the position is a parameter in this template (rather than a variable), others can use this template and pass in a value for the position the template first uses.

For example, if they call the template with the position equal to three, it steps backwards through the node set from the third node:

```
<xsl:call-template name="step-backwards-through">
   <xsl:with-param name="nodes" select="li" />
   <xsl:with-param name="position" select="3" />
</xsl:call-template>
```

In the preceding template call, the position is set using the `select` attribute, which means that within the template the `$position` parameter *will* be a number. However, if someone used the *content* of the `xsl:with-param` element instead, the template would actually be passed a *result tree fragment*.

```
<xsl:call-template name="step-backwards-through">
   <xsl:with-param name="nodes" select="li" />
   <xsl:with-param name="position">3</xsl:with-param>
</xsl:call-template>
```

You can't prevent other stylesheet authors from doing this, and unless you program something yourself within the template, they won't be warned that they're passing the wrong value type. Plenty of valid reasons exists for why it may be convenient for them to pass something other than a number as a parameter value. For instance, the number may be determined with an `xsl:choose` element in the content and hence be a result tree fragment; or it may come from an attribute or element value from the XML source, such that the passed value is actually a node set; or it may be derived as a substring of something, making it a string.

Because they're passing something other than a number, the assumptions are broken the first time the template is called (the recursive calls are okay because you're using the `select` attribute to set the value of the `$position` parameter – the + operator ensures that it's set to a number). Testing a result tree fragment in a Boolean context always returns `true` (because a node is always in a result tree fragment). Thus, the content of the `xsl:if` element is always processed the first time. What's more, because the predicate always evaluates as true, templates will be applied to *all* the nodes the first time the template is called.

For this reason, you should avoid making these kinds of implicit assumptions about parameter value types within a template and instead explicitly coerce parameter values into the type that you're expecting:

```
<xsl:template name="step-backwards-through">
   <xsl:param name="nodes" />
   <xsl:param name="position" />
   <xsl:variable name="p" select="number($position)" />
   <xsl:if test="$p">
      <xsl:apply-templates select="$nodes[$p]" />
      <xsl:call-template name="step-backwards-through">
```

```
      <xsl:with-param name="nodes" select="$nodes" />
      <xsl:with-param name="position" select="$p - 1" />
    </xsl:call-template>
  </xsl:if>
</xsl:template>
```

RETRIEVING NODE VALUES IN TEMPLATES

A final aspect of reusable templates that's worth considering is how you retrieve the values of nodes within them. Take the address-formatting template as an example: in that, you get the values of the line, city, and postcode elements using the xsl:value-of element:

```
<xsl:template name="insert-address">
  <xsl:param name="address" select="/.." />
  <address>
    <xsl:for-each select="$address/line">
      <xsl:value-of select="." />,<br />
    </xsl:for-each>
    <xsl:value-of select="$address/city" /><br />
    <xsl:value-of select="$address/postcode" />
  </address>
</xsl:template>
```

Default Values for Parameters

Even where it doesn't actually matter, it is useful to assign default values to template parameters (even if passing values for them is obligatory) according to the value type that you're expecting for them:

```
<xsl:param name="boolean" select="false()" />
<xsl:param name="string" select="''" />
<xsl:param name="number" select="0" />
<xsl:param name="node-set" select="/.." />
<xsl:param name="RTF">
    <xsl:copy-of select="/.." />

</xsl:param>
```

This not only reminds you what value types they are, but it ensures that relevant operations still work on them. For example, even if a value isn't passed for the $node-set variable, you can still safely use it as the beginning of the path without the processor complaining that strings cannot be converted node sets. (Remember, a parameter is set to an empty string if the content and select attribute is not specified).

Now imagine that someone wants to format the city name in bold uppercase. Suddenly the original template is worthless: they have to create a copy of it and add the extra formatting:

```
<xsl:template name="format-insert-address">
   <xsl:param name="address" select="/.." />
   <address>
      <xsl:for-each select="$address/line">
         <xsl:value-of select="." />,<br />
      </xsl:for-each>
      <span style="font-weight: bold;
                   text-transform: uppercase;">
         <xsl:value-of select="$address/city" />
      </span><br />
      <xsl:value-of select="$address/postcode" />
   </address>
</xsl:template>
```

If you use `xsl:apply-templates` rather than `xsl:value-of`, then they have a much easier time. The template is as follows:

```
<xsl:template name="insert-address">
   <xsl:param name="address" select="/.." />
   <address>
      <xsl:for-each select="$address/line">
         <xsl:apply-templates select="." />,<br />
      </xsl:for-each>
      <xsl:apply-templates select="$address/city" /><br />
      <xsl:apply-templates select="$address/postcode" />
   </address>
</xsl:template>
```

And all they have to do is create a template matching the `city` element in which they can include their formatting information:

```
<xsl:template match="city">
   <span style="font-weight: bold;
                text-transform: uppercase;">
      <xsl:value-of select="." />
   </span>
</xsl:template>
```

To improve this even further, you should actually apply templates in a particular mode to prevent conflicts with existing templates:

```
<xsl:template name="insert-address">
    <xsl:param name="address" select="/.." />
    <address>
        <xsl:for-each select="$address/line">
            <xsl:apply-templates select="."
                                 mode="address" />,<br />
        </xsl:for-each>
        <xsl:apply-templates select="$address/city"
                             mode="address" /><br />
        <xsl:apply-templates select="$address/postcode"
                             mode="address" />
    </address>
</xsl:template>
```

Reusing Attribute Definitions

You've seen how you can use named and moded templates to give reusable snippets of XSLT code. If you're creating formatted XML, such as XSL formatting objects or HTML with lots of styling information, one of the more common XSLT snippets is code that adds groups of attributes to elements. This occurs most often with XSL formatting objects, in which a particular style may be comprised of a combination of several different styling attributes.

For example, you might use a warning class in your HTML source indicating warnings in the document. To include warnings in your XSL-FO document that appear in red, with bold text, and a red border, you must add three attributes to the formatting objects for the warnings:

```
<fo:block color="red" font-weight="bold"
        border="thin solid red">
   ...
</fo:block>
```

The content using this style can appear anywhere in the source XML, and it's dealt with in different places in the stylesheet. Two of the templates are shown in the following: one for paragraphs classed as warnings, and one for list items within ordered lists classed as warnings.

```
<xsl:template match="p[@class = 'warning']">
   <fo:block color="red" font-weight="bold"
           border="thin solid red">
```

```
      <xsl:apply-templates />
    </fo:block>
</xsl:template>

<xsl:template match="ol/li[@class = 'warning']">
   <fo:list-item>
      <fo:list-item-label end-indent="label-end()">
         <fo:block><xsl:number /></fo:block>
      </fo:list-item-label>
      <fo:list-item-body start-indent="body-start()"
                         color="red" font-weight="bold"
                         border="thin solid red">
         <fo:block>
            <xsl:apply-templates />
         </fo:block>
      </fo:list-item-body>
   </fo:list-item>
</xsl:template>
```

In the preceding, the attributes are added to literal result elements directly. They could also have been declared using the xsl:attribute element, as shown in the following:

```
<xsl:template match="p[@class = 'warning']">
   <fo:block>
      <xsl:attribute name="color">red</xsl:attribute>
      <xsl:attribute name="font-weight">bold</xsl:attribute>
      <xsl:attribute name="border">thin solid red</xsl:attribute>
      <xsl:apply-templates />
   </fo:block>
</xsl:template>
```

As was described in the previous section, whenever you have a group of XSLT instructions that are repeated several times, it's good to pull these into a separate template — a moded template if the instructions use information about the current node, or a named template if not. However, if the instructions involve adding attributes, *attribute sets* perform the same function as named templates.

To creating an attribute set for the preceding attributes, pull out the xsl:attribute instructions and place them within an xsl:attribute-set element, for example:

```
<xsl:attribute-set name="warning">
   <xsl:attribute name="color">red</xsl:attribute>
   <xsl:attribute name="font-weight">bold</xsl:attribute>
   <xsl:attribute name="border">thin solid red</xsl:attribute>
</xsl:attribute-set>
```

These attributes can then be added to a particular literal result element using the
xsl:use-attribute-sets attribute:

```
<xsl:template match="p[@class = 'warning']">
   <fo:block xsl:use-attribute-sets="warning">
      <xsl:apply-templates />
   </fo:block>
</xsl:template>

<xsl:template match="ol/li[@class = 'warning']">
   <fo:list-item>
      <fo:list-item-label end-indent="label-end()">
         <fo:block><xsl:number /></fo:block>
      </fo:list-item-label>
      <fo:list-item-body start-indent="body-start()"
                        xsl:use-attribute-sets="warning">
         <fo:block>
            <xsl:apply-templates />
         </fo:block>
      </fo:list-item-body>
   </fo:list-item>
</xsl:template>
```

As you'll see in Chapter 13, the names that you use for attribute sets can be
qualified in the same way as mode names and template names.

You can also use attribute sets on elements that you create with the
xsl:element element or with xsl:copy. Both these instructions can take
a use-attribute-sets attribute that functions in the same way as
xsl:use-attribute-sets on literal result elements.

Using Attribute Sets in Context

Attribute sets are very similar to named templates. Although they are called by
name, they can use information about the current node at the point at which
they're included on an element. The great thing about this is that you can use information about the current node to determine the value of an attribute.

For example, if you want your warning list items to be colored blue rather than red, then you could test the identity of the current node within the relevant `xsl:attribute`:

```
<xsl:attribute-set name="warning">
   <xsl:attribute name="color">
      <xsl:choose>
         <xsl:when test="self::li">blue</xsl:when>
         <xsl:otherwise>red</xsl:otherwise>
      </xsl:choose>
   </xsl:attribute>
   <xsl:attribute name="font-weight">bold</xsl:attribute>
   <xsl:attribute name="border">thin solid red</xsl:attribute>
</xsl:attribute-set>
```

For the same reasons that you have to be careful when using named templates, you also have to be careful when doing this. The nature of the current node is implicit, which may make attribute sets hard to maintain unless you add extra documentation about the context in which you use them.

Alternating Styles for Table Rows

You can also use information about the current node list to determine attribute values. For example, you can define an attribute set for a row style that uses the position of the current node to determine the color of the row: red for even rows, blue for odd ones, and green for the first and last:

```
<xsl:attribute-set name="row-style">
   <xsl:attribute name="background-color">
      <xsl:choose>
         <xsl:when test="position() = 1 or
                         position() = last()">green</xsl:when>
         <xsl:when test="position() mod 2">blue</xsl:when>
         <xsl:otherwise>red</xsl:otherwise>
      </xsl:choose>
   </xsl:attribute>
   ...
</xsl:attribute-set>
```

Determining Attribute Names

The xsl:attribute instructions that are held within the xsl:attribute-set are just the same as those used elsewhere. You can determine the name of an attribute using an attribute value template within the name attribute, and its namespace using an attribute value template within the namespace attribute. The only difficulty within an attribute set is that you can't use variables to work out the name or namespace using XSLT code: all the computation has to be done within an XPath expression in the relevant attribute.

For example, let's say that you want your warning paragraphs to be indicated by a border on the *left* of the paragraph, whereas you want your warning list items to be indicated by a border on the *right*. To achieve this, you must determine the name of the attribute, setting the border properties based on the identity of the current node. When the current node is a paragraph, you want to create a border-left attribute, and when the current node is a list item you want to create a border-right attribute.

If this attribute were being created elsewhere – in a named template or a moded one – you could set a variable to either 'border-left' or 'border-right', dependent on the identity of the current node, and use that variable within the attribute value template for the name:

```
<xsl:variable name="border-side">
   <xsl:choose>
      <xsl:when test="self::li">right</xsl:when>
      <xsl:otherwise>left</xsl:otherwise>
   </xsl:choose>
</xsl:variable>
<xsl:attribute name="border-{$border-side}">
   <xsl:text>thin solid red</xsl:text>
</xsl:attribute>
```

However, you're defining this attribute within an attribute set, which can't hold any variable declarations. You also can't define this variable at the point the attribute set is used, and then use it within the attribute set – only *global* variable and parameters definitions are within the scope of attribute sets.

```
<xsl:template match="p[@class = 'warning']">
   <xsl:variable name="border-side">
      <xsl:choose>
         <xsl:when test="self::li">right</xsl:when>
         <xsl:otherwise>left</xsl:otherwise>
      </xsl:choose>
   </xsl:variable>
   <fo:block xsl:use-attribute-sets="warning">
      <xsl:apply-templates />
```

```
      </fo:block>
</xsl:template>

<xsl:attribute-set name="warning">
   ...
   <!-- ERROR: $border-side is out of scope -->
   <xsl:attribute name="border-{$border-side}">
      <xsl:text>thin solid red</xsl:text>
   </xsl:attribute>
</xsl:attribute-set>
```

So what can you do? Well, do you remember the explanation about various methods of generating conditional strings based on source XML in Chapter 3? This is one situation where they come into play. You can use the following expression to create the string `right` or `left` dependent on the identity of the current node:

```
substring('right left', not(self::li) * 6 + 1, 5)
```

If the current node is a list item (and `not(self::li)` returns `false`), the first five characters of the string are used (for example, `right`); if it isn't a list item, then up to five characters are selected starting from the seventh character (for example, `left`). Putting this together, you get the **xsl:attribute** element:

```
<xsl:attribute name="border-{substring('right left',
                             not(self::li) * 6 + 1, 5)}">
   <xsl:text>thin solid red</xsl:text>
</xsl:attribute>
```

Of course, you can approach this problem in other ways. You can define two separate attribute sets: one to be used for the paragraph and one to be used for the list item:

```
<xsl:attribute-set name="list-item-warning-border">
   <xsl:attribute name="border-left">thin solid red</xsl:attribute>
</xsl:attribute-set>

<xsl:attribute-set name="other-warning-border">
   <xsl:attribute name="border-right">thin solid red</xsl:attribute>
</xsl:attribute-set>
```

And then use the appropriate one in the paragraph and list item templates:

```
<xsl:template match="p[@class = 'warning']">
   <fo:block xsl:use-attribute-sets="warning other-warning-border">
      <xsl:apply-templates />
   </fo:block>
</xsl:template>
```

```
<xsl:template match="ol/li[@class = 'warning']">
   <fo:list-item>
      ...
      <fo:list-item-body start-indent="body-start()"
            xsl:use-attribute-sets="warning
                                  list-item-warning-border">
         ...
      </fo:list-item-body>
   </fo:list-item>
</xsl:template>
```

Or you could create two attribute sets, both of which build on the warning attribute set: one for list items, and one for other elements:

```
<xsl:attribute-set name="list-item-warning"
                   use-attribute-sets="warning">
   <xsl:attribute name="border-left">thin solid red</xsl:attribute>
</xsl:attribute-set>

<xsl:attribute-set name="other-warning"
                   use-attribute-sets="warning">
   <xsl:attribute name="border-right">thin solid red</xsl:attribute>
</xsl:attribute-set>
```

And then use the relevant one when creating the paragraph or list item:

```
<xsl:template match="p[@class = 'warning']">
   <fo:block xsl:use-attribute-sets="other-warning">
      <xsl:apply-templates />
   </fo:block>
</xsl:template>

<xsl:template match="ol/li[@class = 'warning']">
   <fo:list-item>
      ...
      <fo:list-item-body start-indent="body-start()"
            xsl:use-attribute-sets="list-item-warning">
         ...
      </fo:list-item-body>
   </fo:list-item>
</xsl:template>
```

One difficulty with this solution is that the border definition — that it should be a thin, solid, red line — is spread over two attribute sets. If you want to make the border blue instead, you have to update both of them. To avoid this, you can define a global variable for the border definition, and use this within both attribute definitions:

```
<xsl:variable name="warning-border"
              select="'thin solid red'" />

<xsl:attribute-set name="list-item-warning"
                   use-attribute-sets="warning">
   <xsl:attribute name="border-left">
      <xsl:value-of select="$warning-border" />
   </xsl:attribute>
</xsl:attribute-set>

<xsl:attribute-set name="other-warning"
                   use-attribute-sets="warning">
   <xsl:attribute name="border-right">
      <xsl:value-of select="$warning-border" />
   </xsl:attribute>
</xsl:attribute-set>
```

Even with these petty details addressed, these solutions only work well with a limited number of possible attribute names. If the attribute name must be constructed in a way that generates a vast number of possibilities and it cannot be generated through a suitable XPath, then your only alternative is to use a named or moded template instead of an attribute set. This enables you to set variables in any way, and to use them to fix the attribute name:

```
<xsl:template match="*" mode="border-attribute">
   <xsl:variable name="border-side">
      <xsl:choose>
         <xsl:when test="self::li">right</xsl:when>
         <xsl:otherwise>left</xsl:otherwise>
      </xsl:choose>
   </xsl:variable>
   <xsl:attribute name="border-{$border-side}">
      <xsl:text>thin solid red</xsl:text>
   </xsl:attribute>
</xsl:template>
```

Applying a moded template requires a lot more room than using an extra or alternative attribute set:

```
<xsl:template match="p[@class = 'warning']">
   <fo:block xsl:use-attribute-sets="warning">
      <xsl:apply-templates select="." mode="border-attribute" />
      <xsl:apply-templates />
   </fo:block>
</xsl:template>
```

But this method can *always* be used, even if the choice of attribute names is unlimited, or if calculating the attribute name simply cannot be done in XPath alone.

Adding Attributes Conditionally

You've looked at conditional attribute values and conditional attribute names: what about conditionally adding attributes as a whole? Well, one big limitation is that the child elements of an `xsl:attribute-set` element must all be `xsl:attribute` elements. For example, if you want to avoid adding a `border` attribute to the `fo:block` for the list items, the following will not work:

```
<xsl:attribute-set name="warning">
   <xsl:attribute name="color">red</xsl:attribute>
   <xsl:attribute name="font-weight">bold</xsl:attribute>
   <!-- ERROR: xsl:if is not allowed here -->
   <xsl:if test="not(self::li)">
      <xsl:attribute name="border">thin solid red</xsl:attribute>
   </xsl:if>
</xsl:attribute-set>
```

In fact, this problem can be solved with exactly the same techniques you used to solve the problem of creating conditional attribute names. Within an attribute set, later attribute definitions override previous attribute definitions that use the same name. Thus, a conditional attribute definition can be treated in the same way as an attribute definition that has two alternative names: the name of the conditional attribute, and the name of an attribute that is defined later in the attribute set.

So, you can move the definition for the `border` attribute above the definition for the `color` attribute. Then you can create an attribute whose name is `border` if the current node isn't a list item and whose name is `color` if it is. If the current node isn't a list item, the `border` attribute is added; if it is, a `color` attribute is added, but this is overridden by the later definition. In effect, the `border` attribute isn't added, and everything else stays the same:

```
<xsl:attribute-set name="warning">
   <xsl:attribute name="{substring('border color',
                                   boolean(self::li) * 7 + 1, 6)}">
      <xsl:text>thin solid red</xsl:text>
   </xsl:attribute>
   <xsl:attribute name="color">red</xsl:attribute>
   <xsl:attribute name="font-weight">bold</xsl:attribute>
</xsl:attribute-set>
```

Adding Alternative Attributes

If you have two attributes where one should be present under a certain condition, and the other should be present otherwise, then you can combine the techniques for defining conditional attribute names with those for defining conditional attribute values. For example, if the color attribute should only be present on list items (whereas the border attribute should only be present on elements that *aren't* list items), you could use the following:

```
<xsl:attribute-set name="warning">
   <xsl:attribute
       name="{substring('border color',
                        boolean(self::li) * 7 + 1,
                        6)}">
      <xsl:choose>
         <xsl:when test="self::li">red</xsl:when>
         <xsl:otherwise>thin solid red</xsl:otherwise>
      </xsl:choose>
   </xsl:attribute>
   ...

</xsl:attribute-set>
```

You can also use other methods for specifying conditional attribute names. For instance, you can define separate attribute sets, and only use the one containing the conditional attribute when it should be applied; or you can create a named or moded template that only adds the attribute when you want it to be added.

Overriding Attributes from Attribute Sets

The attributes defined in attribute sets can be overridden by attributes on literal result elements or by xsl:attribute elements. You can use this to your advantage by creating attribute sets that hold default values for attributes that you want to define, adding them, and overriding them when necessary.

For example, if you have a generic paragraph style that defines the font-family attribute as serif, but you want this particular paragraph to be sans-serif, you can simply do the following:

```
<fo:block xsl:use-attribute-sets="paragraph-style"
          font-family="sans-serif">
   ...
</fo:block>
```

Or, with exactly the same effect:

```
<fo:block xsl:use-attribute-sets="paragraph-style">
  <xsl:attribute name="font-family">sans-serif</xsl:attribute>
  ...
</fo:block>
```

 TIP   In general, it's better to use an attribute to define an attribute on literal result elements rather than use an `xsl:attribute` element. Not only does it mean smaller XSLT stylesheets, but smaller DOMs because fewer elements and text nodes are used.

If *two* styles (that is, attribute sets) apply to a particular paragraph, then both can use the `xsl:use-attribute-sets` attribute. For example, both the paragraph style and a warning style are applicable in a warning paragraph:

```
<xsl:template match="p[@class = 'warning']">
  <fo:block xsl:use-attribute-sets="paragraph-style warning">
    <xsl:apply-templates />
  </fo:block>
</xsl:template>
```

You should, however, be careful when you do this. The order in which you name the useable attribute sets determines which definition should be used in the event that a conflict arises among the attribute names. The attribute set that is listed last has the highest priority. Thus, in this case, if both the paragraph style and the warning style define a `color` attribute, then the `color` attribute from the warning style is used.

Using Attribute Sets Programmatically

You cannot conditionally use an attribute set on a particular element: either you use it or you don't. If you only want to include a set of attributes when a particular condition is satisfied, then you can use an `xsl:choose` to create an element using that attribute set when the condition is satisfied.

For example, you have a template that matches any paragraph and you always want to create an `fo:block` with the `paragraph-style` attribute set. However, you only want to add the attributes from the `warning` attribute set when the paragraph's `class` attribute has a value of warning. Then you can use the following big `xsl:choose`:

```
<xsl:template match="p">
  <xsl:choose>
    <xsl:when test="@class = 'warning'">
      <fo:block xsl:use-attribute-sets="paragraph-style warning">
```

```
            <xsl:apply-templates />
          </fo:block>
        </xsl:when>
        <xsl:otherwise>
          <fo:block xsl:use-attribute-sets="paragraph-style">
            <xsl:apply-templates />
          </fo:block>
        </xsl:otherwise>
      </xsl:choose>
</xsl:template>
```

This approach, however, requires a great deal of code for a fairly simple thing, and it causes maintenance problems because you have to ensure that the two fo:block elements are created in the same way and have the same content. Naturally, it's possible to move the attribute definitions from the warning attribute set into a moded template that only matches warning paragraphs, and then apply templates in that mode:

```
<xsl:template match="p">
   <fo:block xsl:use-attribute-sets="paragraph-style">
      <xsl:apply-templates select="." mode="other-attrs" />
      <xsl:apply-templates />
   </fo:block>
</xsl:template>

<xsl:template match="p[@class = 'warning']" mode="other-attrs">
   <!-- attributes from the warning attribute set -->
</xsl:template>
```

But if you're using the warning attribute set elsewhere as well (on all warning elements, for example), the maintenance issues are even worse. You have to ensure this new template is current with the warning attribute set.

In some circumstances, there is a cunning way around this. If *all* the values and names of the attributes in an attribute set are *plain strings* (they aren't calculated in any way), you can access the stylesheet as a node tree, locate the attribute set, and use the attribute definitions to create the relevant attributes. Here's a stand-alone template that does it for you:

```
<xsl:template name="add-attributes">
   <xsl:param name="attribute-set" />
   <xsl:for-each
       select="document('')/*
                  /xsl:attribute-set[@name = $attribute-set]
                  /xsl:attribute">
      <xsl:attribute name="{@name}">
```

```
            <xsl:value-of select="." />
        </xsl:attribute>
    </xsl:for-each>
</xsl:template>
```

This template takes a single parameter — the name of an attribute set — and accesses the definition of the attribute set within the stylesheet. It works through the attribute definitions one by one, creating attributes using the names specified by the name attribute and the content of the definition. In the preceding example, you could use it as follows:

```
<xsl:template match="p[@class = 'warning']" mode="other-attrs">
    <xsl:call-template name="add-attributes">
        <xsl:with-param name="attribute-set" select="'warning'" />
    </xsl:call-template>
</xsl:template>
```

This technique is also useful if you want to choose what attribute set to add based on some feature of the current node, such as its name. For example, if you've defined numerous attribute sets, each relating to a different kind of source element (a p-style attribute set for p elements, a li-style attribute set for li elements, and so on), then you can determine the value of the $attribute-set parameter passed into the add-attributes template based upon the name of the current element:

```
<xsl:template match="*" mode="add-style">
    <xsl:call-template name="add-attributes">
        <xsl:with-param name="attribute-set"
                        select="concat(local-name(), '-style')" />
    </xsl:call-template>
</xsl:template>
```

Summary

In this chapter, I introduced some of the main issues that are involved in using functional modules within your XSLT application. I discussed various ways of using moded templates, named templates, and attribute sets. When you're thinking about using these techniques, it's worth bearing in mind *why* you're making the changes you're making. You might want to make your code:

◆ Shorter

◆ More readable

- ◆ More maintainable

- ◆ More reusable

But these aims don't always coincide with each other: it's quite easy to make code incomprehensible by making it shorter, or you can triple its length by making it more maintainable and reusable. And if your goal is maintainability and reusability, then focus on assisting the kinds of changes that you may make in the future and the ways in which other people might reuse your code.

In the next chapter, you see how to build XSLT applications involving multiple stylesheets. Some of those methods, especially importing stylesheets, affect how an XSLT processor uses the various functional modules that have been discussed here. But it's the functional modules that lie at the heart of an XSLT application, regardless of how many separate stylesheets you use.

Chapter 13

Using Multiple Stylesheets

IN THIS CHAPTER

◆ Dividing up stylesheets

◆ Writing utility stylesheets

◆ Combining stylesheets

IN CHAPTER 12, I discussed how to modularize your stylesheet with *logical* structures. In this chapter, I look at how to split up large stylesheets, design and use utility stylesheets, and combine several similar stylesheets into one XSLT application. These *physical* divisions should help you to manage, maintain, and reuse parts of your stylesheet.

In this chapter, I look at the XSLT elements `xsl:include`, `xsl:import`, and `xsl:apply-imports`.

Splitting Up a Stylesheet into Multiple Files

In Chapter 12, I talked about how to identify different sections of the stylesheet and label them using modes. Different modes can be used to distinguish between different processing for the same nodes, or between templates that are generating output for different parts of the result tree. The result of introducing modes is a stylesheet divided into groups of templates sharing the same mode. These groups can be physically separated from the main stylesheet by placing them in a separate file and *including* them in the main stylesheet.

As an example, let's use a bank statement, as in Chapter 12. Previously, you divided the stylesheet dealing with the statement into two separate parts: a header, holding customer and account information; and a table, summarizing the transactions on the account:

```
<xsl:stylesheet version="1.0"
            xmlns:xsl="http://www.w3.org/1999/XSL/Transform">

<!-- controlling template -->
<xsl:template match="statement">
```

```
    ...
    <xsl:apply-templates select="custInfo | accountInfo"
                         mode="header" />
    ...
    <xsl:apply-templates select="transactions"
                         mode="table" />
    ...
</xsl:template>

<!-- templates in header mode -->
<xsl:template match="address" mode="header">
    ...
</xsl:template>
...

<!-- templates in table mode -->
<xsl:template match="transaction" mode="table">
    ...
</xsl:template>
...


</xsl:stylesheet>
```

Now that the logical divisions have been indicated through modes, it's easy to create physical divisions in the XSLT application. You create two supplementary stylesheets: header.xsl to hold the templates in header mode, and table.xsl to hold the table mode templates:

```
--- header.xsl ---
<xsl:stylesheet version="1.0"
               xmlns:xsl="http://www.w3.org/1999/XSL/Transform">

<!-- templates in header mode -->
<xsl:template match="address" mode="header">
    ...
</xsl:template>
...

</xsl:stylesheet>
---


--- table.xsl ---
<xsl:stylesheet version="1.0"
               xmlns:xsl="http://www.w3.org/1999/XSL/Transform">
```

```
<!-- templates in table mode -->
<xsl:template match="transaction" mode="table">
   ...
</xsl:template>
...


</xsl:stylesheet>
---
```

The main stylesheet no longer needs to hold these templates itself; instead it can include these two supplementary stylesheets:

```
<xsl:stylesheet version="1.0"
                xmlns:xsl="http://www.w3.org/1999/XSL/Transform">

<!-- controlling template -->
<xsl:template match="statement">
   ...
   <xsl:apply-templates select="custInfo | accountInfo"
                        mode="header" />
   ...
   <xsl:apply-templates select="transactions"
                        mode="table" />
   ...
</xsl:template>

<!-- include templates in header mode -->
<xsl:include href="header.xsl" />

<!-- include templates in table mode -->
<xsl:include href="table.xsl" />

</xsl:stylesheet>
```

Polishing Included Stylesheets

You can, of course, just create stylesheets for inclusion of any set of instructions from the original stylesheet. However, you have to ensure that the included stylesheet is a well-formed XSLT stylesheet, in terms of XML, and that any qualified names (of elements or extension functions, for example) will be interpreted in same way as they were in the original stylesheet. You must do three things to the included stylesheet:

1. Put relevant namespace declarations on the xsl:stylesheet or
   xsl:transform element

2. Identify any namespaces that you use for extension elements or functions with the `extension-element-prefixes` attribute on the `xsl:stylesheet` or `xsl:transform` element

3. Identify any namespaces that shouldn't be included in the output with the `exclude-result-prefixes` attribute on the `xsl:stylesheet` or `xsl:transform` element

TIP

Limiting the namespaces that you use within a particular stylesheet is another motivation for splitting up a stylesheet. You can isolate the places where you use extension elements and functions from a particular namespace by putting them into a separate stylesheet. If you do this, you'll find it easier to update the XSLT application if you need to change to a different XSLT processor in the future.

Adding the required namespaces and the `extension-element-prefixes` and `exclude-result-prefixes` attributes to the `xsl:stylesheet` or `xsl:transform` element of the included stylesheet — essentially making the context for the transplanted instructions the same as it was originally — is all you *need* to do to make the stylesheet run smoothly. However, it helps you maintain the included stylesheet if it can stand alone, at least to some extent. When you're breaking up a stylesheet, you should check the following constructs to see where they're used:

◆ Global variables and parameters

◆ Named and moded utility templates

◆ Attribute sets

◆ Keys

◆ Decimal formats

◆ CDATA section elements as identified by `xsl:output`

If any of the preceding constructs are used exclusively by an included stylesheet, it's worthwhile to move them into the included stylesheet so that you can quickly see the construct's definition when you return to the included stylesheet later.

Positioning xsl:includes in the Main Stylesheet

The positioning of the `xsl:include` instructions is important: the stylesheet is processed as if the instructions from the included stylesheets were inserted at the position of the `xsl:include` instruction. Where the position of an instruction in XSLT has an effect, that effect is always that later instructions override earlier ones. Thus, if you place the instructions at the beginning of the main stylesheet, the instructions in the main stylesheet override those in the included stylesheets. On the other hand, if you place the instructions at the end of the main stylesheet, the instructions in the included stylesheets override those in the main stylesheet.

Of course, the constructs that you put in your included stylesheets may have been scattered throughout the original stylesheet. Generally, you should try to avoid using the position of an instruction to give it priority, but the error recovery of XSLT processors means that it's often difficult to work out where you've done so unwittingly. There are several situations in which XSLT processors resolve conflicts by opting for the last instruction in the stylesheet:

- When two or more templates match the same node and have the same priority

- When two or more attributes with the same name are specified in separate attribute sets with the same name

- When two or more `xsl:output` elements specify values for the same attribute (aside from `cdata-section-elements`)

- When two or more name tests with the same default priority in `xsl:strip-space` and `xsl:preserve-space` elements match the same element in the source tree

- When two or more namespace aliases have the same stylesheet prefix

When you're splitting up a stylesheet, it's worth going through it to check for the preceding situations. If you find one, you should correct it so that you're not depending on the XSLT processor's error recovery mechanisms, which vary from processor to processor. (Correcting recoverable errors will increase the portability of your stylesheet, which I talk about in more detail in the section "Designing Utility Stylesheets," later in this chapter.) Once your stylesheet no longer relies on the position of instructions, you can place the `xsl:include` instructions wherever you like in the main stylesheet without worrying about possible side effects.

 Your processor may be able to assist you in correcting recoverable errors by giving warnings if your stylesheet contains such an error.

Building Inclusion Hierarchies

You may also find it helpful to build a hierarchy of included stylesheets, but you need to be a little careful as you do so to make sure that you don't include the same stylesheet twice. For example, if both `header.xsl` and `table.xsl` use the same named template, `format-money`, you might be tempted to place that in a separate stylesheet, `format-money.xsl`, which you then include in both stylesheets, as shown in Figure 13-1. However, this will lead to the named template being included twice (once in header.xsl and once from table.xsl). To the processor, it's exactly as if the named template was repeated; and having two templates with the same name is an unrecoverable error.

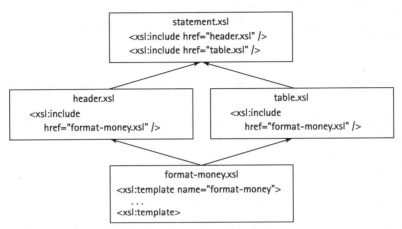

Figure 13-1: Including the same named template twice

Instead then, shared constructs need to be placed "above," where they're used in an include hierarchy. If anything, format-money.xsl, containing the shared named template, should include header.xsl and table.xsl rather than the other way round. In a slightly more elegant design, the main stylesheet should include all three, as shown in Figure 13-2.

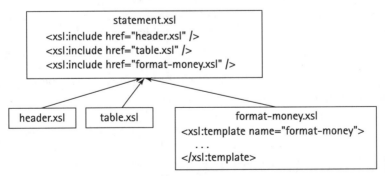

Figure 13-2: Avoiding including the same named template twice

This limitation on stylesheet inclusion can make it quite difficult to design included stylesheets for reuse. If you want to have a stand-alone, reusable stylesheet then you should really be importing it. I discuss using and designing utility stylesheets later in this chapter.

Using XML Entities

Using `xsl:include` as described previously is very similar to using XML entities within your stylesheet. You could instead create `header.ent` to hold the templates in `header` mode, and `table.ent` to hold the templates in `table` mode:

```
--- header.ent ---
<!-- templates in header mode -->
<xsl:template match="address" mode="header">
    ...
</xsl:template>
...
---


--- table.ent ---
<!-- templates in table mode -->
<xsl:template match="transaction" mode="table">
    ...
</xsl:template>
...
---
```

These could then be inserted into the main stylesheet using general entities:

```
<!DOCTYPE xsl:stylesheet [
<!ENTITY header SYSTEM 'header.ent'>
<!ENTITY table SYSTEM 'table.ent'>
]>
<xsl:stylesheet version="1.0"
                xmlns:xsl="http://www.w3.org/1999/XSL/Transform">

<!-- controlling template -->
<xsl:template match="statement">
    ...
    <xsl:apply-templates select="custInfo | accountInfo"
                         mode="header" />
    ...
    <xsl:apply-templates select="transactions"
                         mode="table" />
    ...
</xsl:template>

<!-- include templates in header mode -->
&header.ent;
```

```
<!-- include templates in table mode -->
&table.ent;

</xsl:stylesheet>
```

The primary difference between using general entities and xsl:include instructions is that general entities are inserted into the main stylesheet at an almost physical level — the XML of the general entity is inserted into the XML of the main stylesheet — whereas the content of stylesheets included with xsl:include is included at a logical level.

This has two implications. Whereas you can safely include xsl:import instructions in an included stylesheet, having one in an entity may make the stylesheet invalid (xsl:import elements can only occur as the initial children of the xsl:stylesheet element). In addition, the relevant namespace declarations must be given on the xsl:stylesheet element of the main stylesheet, as must an indication of any extension element prefixes and prefixes that should be excluded from the result tree.

Entities have one useful feature that xsl:include lacks: they can be placed anywhere within the stylesheet, including within a template. See Chapter 11 for information on how this can be used to add headers and footers to pages.

Using XInclude

You can also use XInclude to include bits from one stylesheet in another. The following stylesheet includes the same relevant instructions from header.xsl and table.xsl as in the preceding example.

The content of this section is based on the *XInclude Working Draft* dated May 16, 2001, the *XPointer Working Draft* dated January 8, 2001, and the capabilities of XSLT processors at the time of writing.

```
<xsl:stylesheet version="1.0"
          xmlns:xsl="http://www.w3.org/1999/XSL/Transform"
          xmlns:xi="http://www.w3.org/2001/XInclude">

<!-- controlling template -->
<xsl:template match="statement">
```

```
    . . .
    <xsl:apply-templates select="custInfo | accountInfo"
                        mode="header" />
    . . .
    <xsl:apply-templates select="transactions"
                        mode="table" />
    . . .
</xsl:template>

<!-- include templates in header mode -->
<xi:include href="header.xsl#xpointer(/xsl:stylesheet/*)" />

<!-- include templates in table mode -->
<xi:include href="table.xsl#xpointer(/xsl:stylesheet/*)" />

</xsl:stylesheet>
```

The preceding `xi:include` elements use an XPointer fragment to identify the content of the `xsl:stylesheet` element rather than including the `xsl:stylesheet` element itself.

As with general entities, you can use XInclude to include XML (or indeed text) at any point in a stylesheet — unlike `xsl:include`, it isn't limited to the top level. Also like general entities, XInclude doesn't treat `xsl:import` elements in any special way, so you have to take care that you don't create invalid stylesheets when you use it. XInclude processors are also ignorant of the special XSLT inheritance rules whereby namespace prefixes that indicate extension elements or namespaces that should be excluded from the result tree are inherited from the containing `xsl:stylesheet` or `xsl:transform` element. You don't, though, have to worry about namespace declarations as XInclude automatically includes necessary namespace nodes when it includes an element.

Unlike `xsl:include` or general entities, an XSLT processor may not automatically process XInclude elements. Processing XInclude elements is a separate process from either the initial parse or the processing of the XSLT stylesheet. XSLT processors that support XInclude will often give you the option of either processing the XInclude elements in the stylesheet before it is processed, or processing those in the result afterwards. Obviously, if you're using an `xi:include` element to include XSLT instructions, you want it to be processed before the stylesheet is processed.

The primary advantage that XInclude has over `xsl:include` elements is that you can point precisely at the XSLT constructs that you want to include rather than including all the constructs from a particular stylesheet. For example, if you wanted to include only the `format-money` template in a stylesheet (`format.xsl`) that included a whole bunch of formatting utilities, you could use the following:

```
<x:include href="format.xsl#xpointer(
                  /*/xsl:template[@name = 'format-money'])" />
```

If the XInclude processor was fairly efficient in identifying the selected template, this could prove more efficient overall than including all of `format.xsl`.

Using Utility Stylesheets

In the previous section, you looked at combining stylesheets by inclusion as a means of breaking up a large stylesheet and making it easier to maintain. In this section, I discuss combining stylesheets using `xsl:import`.

Importing stylesheets is a lot like including them: the XSLT constructs in the imported stylesheet are made available to the importing stylesheet. However, stylesheet import brings with it the idea of *import precedence*. When including stylesheets, all the XSLT constructs have the same precedence, which is why you can run into problems if you include the same stylesheet twice or if you put the `xsl:include` elements in the wrong place. When importing stylesheets, on the other hand, the XSLT constructs from any imported stylesheets are overridden by those in their importing stylesheet. The imported XSLT constructs have *lower import precedence* than those in the stylesheet doing the importing.

Import precedence is closely linked to the import tree. You can imagine the import tree as a tree of `xsl:stylesheet` elements, one from each of the stylesheets used in the XSLT application, and each containing the `xsl:stylesheet` elements from its imported stylesheets followed by the XSLT constructs that it declares. For example, if the `statement.xsl` stylesheet imports `header.xsl` and `table.xsl`, both of which import `format.xsl`, then the import tree looks like Figure 13-3.

The XSLT constructs that appear later in the import tree have a *higher* priority. The constructs in `statement.xsl` have higher import precedence than those in `table.xsl`, which have higher import precedence than those in `format.xsl`, and which in turn have a higher import precedence than those in `header.xsl`.

The advantage of this is that you don't have to worry about conflicts as much as you do with `xsl:include`. You can place all the XSLT constructs that you need within as many imported stylesheets as you like. The XSLT constructs will have different import precedence and generally the one with the highest import precedence will be chosen: it's harder to unwittingly have two templates that conflict because they have the same name. Thus, an imported stylesheet can be made into a self-contained module that doesn't rely on anything being defined in the stylesheet that imports it.

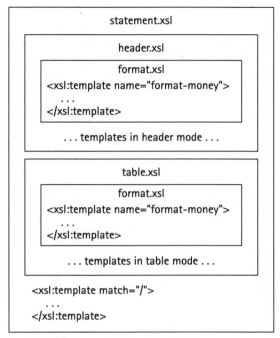

Figure 13-3: A sample import hierarchy

Overriding Constructs from Utility Stylesheets

Probably the biggest advantage of using importing to combine stylesheets is that you can override XSLT constructs in the imported stylesheet with constructs in the stylesheet doing the importing. For example, the format-money template in format.xsl looks like the following:

```
<xsl:template name="format-money">
   <xsl:param name="amount" select="0" />
   <xsl:param name="currency" select="'&#163;'" />
   <xsl:value-of select="$currency" />
   <xsl:value-of select="format-number($amount, '#,##0.00')" />
</xsl:template>
```

To ensure reusability, format.xsl also defines the following default decimal format (I discuss why later on, in the section "Designing Utility Stylesheets"):

```
<xsl:decimal-format decimal-separator="."
                    grouping-separator="," />
```

Now, the table.xsl stylesheet is actually for a European bank, and thus the currencies are all in Euros ( ). However, most European countries format numbers differently from the usual American or British style; a comma indicates the decimal point and groups of digits are separated by periods, rather than vice versa. The European bank wants the numbers formatted in this European style. You therefore need to override the `format-money` template in the `table.xsl` stylesheet to give the correct European formatting:

```
<xsl:template name="format-money">
   <xsl:param name="amount" select="0" />
   <xsl:param name="currency" select="'&#8364;'" />
   <xsl:value-of select="$currency" />
   <xsl:value-of
      select="format-number($amount, '#.##0,00', 'euro')" />
</xsl:template>
```

You also need to specify the decimal format for the European number:

```
<xsl:decimal-format name="euro"
                    decimal-separator=","
                    grouping-separator="." />
```

It wouldn't be sufficient here to try to override the default decimal format given in `format.xsl`. If you could define a new default decimal format giving the European style of numbering:

```
<xsl:decimal-format decimal-separator=","
                    grouping-separator="." />
```

then the format pattern string (the second argument in the call to `format-number()`) would be interpreted differently and therefore give very strange results: `37.9` would be formatted as `37,900.`. Because of this potential for confusion, it's an unrecoverable error to declare the default decimal format or any named decimal format twice unless they share the same attribute values.

This new template in `table.xsl` overrides the template in `format.xsl`. You can call the `format-money` template in `table.xsl` with the following:

```
<xsl:call-template name="format-money">
   <xsl:with-param name="amount" select="@amount" />
</xsl:call-template>
```

and the template defined in `table.xsl` will be processed. What's more, this template will be used *wherever* the template is called from: from `format.xsl`, from `table.xsl` or even, when it's integrated into the larger application, from `stylesheet.xsl` and from `header.xsl`.

Named templates aren't the only constructs that you can override when you import a stylesheet. You can also override:

♦ Matching templates, moded or not

It's also possible to override templates using the `priority` attribute on `xsl:template`; in fact it's safer to do it that way if you can because of the dangers involved with overrides, which I go into later, in the section "Avoiding Dangerous Overrides."

♦ Global variables and parameters
♦ Output instructions, with the exception of the specification of which elements should have their text node children output as CDATA sections (`cdata-section-elements`)
♦ Namespace aliases
♦ Attributes within attribute sets

You can't override whole attribute sets — an importing stylesheet cannot *reduce* the number of attributes in an attribute set defined in an imported stylesheet — but you can override individual attributes or add new ones.

Applying Imported Templates

There are times when you don't want to simply override an existing template; instead you want to extend it in some way — take the result that it generates and manipulate it. If you are using matching (rather than named) templates, you can do this with `xsl:apply-imports`.

The `xsl:apply-imports` instruction is not allowed within an `xsl:for-each`; it has to be used in a context in which the current node is the node that the current template is matching.

The `xsl:apply-imports` instruction takes the current node and tries to find a template in an imported stylesheet to match it. If the processor finds one, it applies it and returns the result. For example, `format.xsl` contains a template in transaction-type mode that matches a transaction element and returns an expansion of its abbreviated type (whether it's a standing order, credit, and so on):

```
<xsl:template match="transaction" mode="transaction-type">
   <xsl:choose>
      <xsl:when test="@type = 'SO'">standing order</xsl:when>
      <xsl:when test="@type = 'CR'">credit</xsl:when>
      <xsl:when test="@type = 'DD'">direct debit</xsl:when>
      <xsl:otherwise>other transaction</xsl:otherwise>
   </xsl:choose>
</xsl:template>
```

In the bank statement application, you might want these transaction types to be colored red if they're a debit (a negative amount), using a span element with an appropriate style attribute in the generated HTML. You could repeat the preceding xsl:choose, but this would cause maintenance headaches if a new transaction type were added in the future. Instead, you can wrap the result from the imported stylesheet in the span element:

```
<xsl:template match="transaction[@amount &lt; 0]"
             mode="transaction-type">
   <span style="color: red;">
      <xsl:apply-imports />
   </span>
</xsl:template>
```

This also demonstrates one of the side effects of xsl:apply-imports — it's a very elegant way of adding conditional parent elements. If the transaction-type template weren't already written for you in function.xsl, your other alternative would have been as follows:

```
<xsl:template match="transaction" mode="transaction-type">
   <xsl:choose>
      <xsl:when test="@amount &lt; 0">
         <span style="color: red;">
            <xsl:apply-templates select="."
                                 mode="transaction-type-code" />
         </span>
      </xsl:when>
      <xsl:otherwise>
         <xsl:apply-templates select="."
                              mode="transaction-type-code" />
      </xsl:otherwise>
   </xsl:choose>
</xsl:template>
```

```
<xsl:template match="transaction" mode="transaction-type-code">
  <xsl:choose>
    <xsl:when test="@type = 'SO'">standing order</xsl:when>
    <xsl:when test="@type = 'CR'">credit</xsl:when>
    <xsl:when test="@type = 'DD'">direct debit</xsl:when>
    <xsl:otherwise>other transaction</xsl:otherwise>
  </xsl:choose>
</xsl:template>
```

As you can see, this is a lot longer and less elegant than the solution using `xsl:apply-imports` because of the unwieldy `xsl:choose`.

It's important to remember that `xsl:apply-imports` works on the *import tree* rather than the *import precedence list* or *template priority* — it looks for templates that are imported into the current stylesheet, not those that have a lower import precedence or that have match patterns with lower priorities. For example, consider the import tree shown previously in Figure 13-3.

This provides an import precedence list of (from highest to lowest):

1. `stylesheet.xsl`

2. `table.xsl`

3. `format.xsl`

4. `header.xsl`

5. `format.xsl`

In general, the first templates to be matched will be those in `stylesheet.xsl`, then those in `table.xsl`, and so on down the list. If `xsl:apply-imports` is used in `table.xsl`, however, the processor will only look for templates in `format.xsl` as that's the only stylesheet imported into `table.xsl`. It won't go on and look in `header.xsl`. This is useful because the result of applying imports will only change if the imported stylesheets themselves change — it doesn't matter what context the stylesheet is used in.

Parameters are not automatically passed when you apply imports and you cannot pass them with `xsl:with-param` elements within `xsl:apply-imports` in XSLT 1.0 (although this feature is introduced in the XSLT 1.1 Working Draft and is therefore likely to be present in XSLT 2.0).

Avoiding Dangerous Overrides

Danger lurks when importing stylesheets. In `header.xsl`, you are interested in displaying a total in the viewer's own currency, with the relevant localized decimal format. The locale and an exchange rate with the Euro are passed in as parameters to the stylesheet, so `header.xsl` has its own `format-money` template that looks like the following:

```
<xsl:template name="format-money">
   <xsl:param name="amount" select="0" />
   <xsl:param name="currency" select="$locale/@currency" />
   <xsl:value-of select="$currency" />
   <xsl:value-of select="format-number($amount * $exchange-rate,
                                        $locale/@format-string,
                                        $locale/@decimal-format)" />
</xsl:template>
```

But take a look at the import precedence of the stylesheets. The import precedence (from highest to lowest) is as follows:

1. `stylesheet.xsl`

2. `table.xsl`

3. `format.xsl`

4. `header.xsl`

5. `format.xsl`

As you can see, the constructs in `header.xsl` have lower import precedence than those in `stylesheet.xsl`, `table.xsl`, or even `format.xsl` (which is imported by a higher-priority stylesheet). When `header.xsl` is incorporated into the application, any constructs that it used to override the constructs in `format.xsl` will be ignored; if `table.xsl` overrides one (as it does with the `format-money` template), then that will be used instead.

So, how do you get around these problems?

Well, if you're lucky, you'll be able to rearrange your `xsl:import` elements so that the imported stylesheet that needs the highest import precedence is imported last. If `table.xsl` didn't override anything in `format.xsl`, you could swap around the `xsl:import` instructions so that `header.xsl` would be imported last and therefore have a higher priority than either of the imports of `format.xsl`.

If you're slightly less lucky, the two imported stylesheets will override different constructs within the utility stylesheet that they both import. So `header.xsl` might override the `format-money` template, whereas `table.xsl` overrides the `format-date` template, both from `format.xsl`. No matter which order you use for the `xsl:import` instructions, one of the overrides won't work. In this case, you need to change the imported stylesheets so that they no longer import the utility stylesheet. But if you want to continue using them as stand-alone stylesheets, it's not enough to simply remove the `xsl:import` element — instead, you have to split the stylesheet in two. Consider `header.xsl` as an example:

```
<xsl:stylesheet version="1.0"
               xmlns:xsl="http://www.w3.org/1999/XSL/Transform">

<xsl:import href="utilities.xsl" />

<!-- templates in header mode -->
<xsl:template match="address" mode="header">
   ...
</xsl:template>
...

</xsl:stylesheet>
```

You must create two stylesheets: one containing the core functionality of `header.xsl`, and the other being a stand-alone version. The core functionality goes into `header-core.xsl`:

```
<xsl:stylesheet version="1.0"
               xmlns:xsl="http://www.w3.org/1999/XSL/Transform">

<!-- templates in header mode -->
<xsl:template match="address" mode="header">
   ...
</xsl:template>
...

</xsl:stylesheet>
```

The stand-alone version (`header-standalone.xsl`) includes this core functionality and imports the utilities from `utilities.xsl` as before:

```
<xsl:stylesheet version="1.0"
               xmlns:xsl="http://www.w3.org/1999/XSL/Transform">

<xsl:import href="utilities.xsl" />
<xsl:include href="header-core.xsl" />

</xsl:stylesheet>
```

If you do the same with `table.xsl`, your main stylesheet (`statement.xsl`) can import the utility stylesheet itself along with the core functionality of the other stylesheets:

```
<xsl:stylesheet version="1.0"
               xmlns:xsl="http://www.w3.org/1999/XSL/Transform">
```

```
<xsl:import href="utilities.xsl" />
<xsl:import href="header-core.xsl" />
<xsl:import href="header-table.xsl" />

...

</xsl:stylesheet>
```

If you're *really* unlucky, both the imported stylesheets will override the *same* constructs from the utility stylesheet. So in the preceding example, both `header.xsl` and `table.xsl` override the `format-money` template in `utilities.xsl`, and conflict with each other. If you're in this kind of situation, your only option is to change the name of the relevant template in one of the stylesheets and change the calls to it as required.

Designing Utility Stylesheets

When you write utility stylesheets, you must author XSLT that can be used and reused in lots of different contexts. Utility stylesheets don't stand alone — you'll never want to just use them on their own on some XML — instead, they should be self-sufficient so that you can just import them into other stylesheets and use them without any problems.

Making Self-Sufficient Stylesheets

Utility stylesheets usually include named or moded templates, possibly attribute sets, and any supporting variables, parameters, keys, namespace aliases, decimal formats, and output instructions. When you first put together a utility stylesheet, you should copy over whatever constructs you want to be made available from a place where you're currently using them and then go through to make sure that it is self-sufficient. This section contains a set of steps that should help you do this.

DECLARING AND USING NAMESPACES

You should do four things to ensure that the namespaces you use in your utility stylesheet are interpreted in the same way as they were in their original location:

- ◆ **Add namespace declarations.** Copy over whatever namespace declarations you need to resolve any prefixes used within the utility.

- ◆ **Declare the prefixes of any extension elements or functions that you use.** Add the prefixes of extension element and functions to the list given in the `extension-element-prefixes` attribute on the `xsl:stylesheet` or `xsl:transform` element.

- ◆ **Declare the prefixes of any other namespaces that you don't use in the result tree.** Add prefixes of other namespaces that aren't result namespaces to the list given in the `exclude-result-prefixes` attribute on the `xsl:stylesheet` or `xsl:transform` element.

◆ **Copy any namespace aliases for namespaces you use in your utility.** Copy over any `xsl:namespace-alias` instructions that have a `stylesheet-prefix` that you use in your utility. Make sure that the namespace for the `result-prefix` is declared in your utility stylesheet as well.

DEFINING GLOBAL VARIABLES AND PARAMETERS

You may have global variables and parameters in the original stylesheet that have values specific to that application. It might be that the value of a variable or the default value of a parameter should *always* be set by the application — overridden within the importing stylesheet. However, if you can come up with a sensible default, you'll save the person importing your utility stylesheet some work in identifying and setting the variable.

If there is no sensible default, you have two choices: declaring the variable or parameter with a null value, or not declaring it at all. The advantage of not declaring the variable or parameter is that the stylesheet will automatically complain if the author of the importing stylesheet forgets to set the value of the variable or parameter. It prevents the utility stylesheet from producing spurious output that the person using it will probably blame you for — instead it bails out with an error.

The advantage of declaring the variable or parameter is that the application will always run, whether or not the author of the importing stylesheet remembers to set the variable or parameter. If you use a null value (such as an empty node set [/..], an empty string [''], or zero [0]) or a horrendously obscure (and hence unique) value (such as `'a-string-that's-very-unlikely-to-be-repeated'`) then you can test the value and output a (possibly terminating) message that tells the user of your utility stylesheet exactly what he or she needs to do to solve the problem. I discuss creating these messages later on in this section.

DEFINING KEYS

If you use a specific key in your utility, that key has to be declared or the utility will exit with an error. As with variables and parameters, this might be the behavior that you want — at least people using your utility will be warned if they forget to declare the key. Unlike with variables, there's really no way to declare a null value that you can test with a key — it's impossible to tell whether it holds any nodes or not. However, if you do want to use an empty key, you can always use the following:

```
<xsl:key name="key-name" match="/@*" use="." />
```

No nodes will belong to this key as there cannot be any attributes on the root node.

DEFINING ATTRIBUTE SETS

Copy over into your utility any attribute sets that you've named with an `xsl:use-attribute-sets` attribute. Go through each of them to weed out any attributes that are application-specific — it's easy to add attributes for a specific application, but it's hard (or rather, impossible) to take them away. If you're unsure, or if you want to let the person using your utility have complete control, you can create a completely empty attribute set:

```
<xsl:attribute-set name="attribute-set-name" />
```

Of course, it might be that the entire purpose of your utility stylesheet is to provide a set of "styles" using attribute sets, in which case don't empty them! Also remember that it's easy for the person using your utility to override the values of the attribute, so there's no harm in declaring it with a default value as long as it's possible to specify a value for the attribute (even an empty string) that gives the equivalent behavior as when the attribute is not specified at all.

For example, if you are generating XSL-FO, you can safely include a background-color attribute for formatting object elements:

```
<xsl:attribute-set name="code">
   <xsl:attribute name="background-color">
      <xsl:text>#CCC</xsl:text>
   </xsl:attribute>
</xsl:attribute-set>
```

Someone using this attribute set can always set the background color back to the default value (transparent) if he or she wants to. However, no value for the color attribute gives the same behavior as if the color attribute wasn't specified. If you defined the following attribute set:

```
<xsl:attribute-set name="code">
   <xsl:attribute name="color">black</xsl:attribute>
</xsl:attribute-set>
```

Anyone using your utility could only override this value with other specific colors or with the inherit keyword, none of which give the same behavior as if the color attribute had not been defined at all.

DEFINING DECIMAL FORMATS

You should copy any decimal formats that you use with format-number() across to your utility stylesheet. If you use the built-in default decimal format, you should also create a new decimal format that reflects the features that you use from the built-in default. Making the default values explicit prevents someone from accidentally creating a new default decimal format that uses different characters from the built-in default, and therefore different characters than the ones you've used in the format pattern strings you used in format-number(). You'll usually want to at least specify the following:

```
<xsl:decimal-format decimal-separator="."
                    grouping-separator="," />
```

GIVING OUTPUT INSTRUCTIONS

Most things about the way the result tree is output are application-dependent so it's rare to have a utility stylesheet that includes an `xsl:output` element. One thing you might want to specify, though, are the elements that are created by your utility that should have the text nodes in their content output in CDATA sections, with the `cdata-section-elements` attribute. For example, if your utility serializes an XML node tree and creates an HTML `pre` element, you probably want to make the output a little more readable by using a CDATA section rather than having a lot of escaped less-than signs:

```
<xsl:output cdata-section-elements="pre" />
```

This will be merged with any similar instructions in the importing stylesheet.

Adding a Namespace for the Utility

One important feature of a utility stylesheet is that the constructs that it contains should not have the same name as those in the importing stylesheet unless the author of the importing stylesheet specifically wants to override them. To ensure this, you can use long and obscure names for the templates, modes, variables, and so on that you use. However, not only does this make the utility stylesheet unwieldy for you when writing it, but it also makes it difficult for the user to remember the names of the constructs that he or she wants to use.

Instead, then, you should use a *namespace* to identify the constructs within your utility stylesheet. Everything that you want to name within an XSLT stylesheet accepts a qualified name: a name associated with a namespace using a prefix. You can use qualified names for the following:

- Template names
- Template modes
- Variables and parameters
- Keys
- Attribute sets
- Decimal formats

You can therefore keep the names of these constructs short and sweet and use a namespace for the utility to prevent conflicts with any importing stylesheets. To do so, do the following:

1. Declare a namespace for the utility on the `xsl:stylesheet` or `xsl:transform` element so that it has the entire utility in its scope. It's handy if this namespace is unique for the utility rather than your organization — this prevents conflicts between your utility and other utilities

produced by your organization. The namespace must have a prefix (the default namespace doesn't apply to qualified names for the preceding constructs) – choose a short one to make your life easier.

2. Add the prefix that you've chosen to the prefixes in the `exclude-result-prefixes` attribute on the `xsl:stylesheet` or `xsl:transform` element. That prevents the namespace from being added to the result tree.

You don't *have* to declare that your namespace shouldn't be used in the result tree if you don't create any element or attribute nodes with your utility, but it doesn't hurt to do so and it saves you from having to remember if you change the stylesheet the future.

3. Add the prefix to the names of any templates, modes, variables, parameters, keys, attribute sets and decimal formats that you use in your utility. Don't forget to also add the prefix as appropriate in the following:

- name attributes on `xsl:call-template` elements
- mode attributes on `xsl:apply-templates` elements
- References to variable and parameter names
- Names of keys used in calls to the `key()` function
- `use-attribute-sets` attributes on `xsl:element` and `xsl:copy` elements
- `xsl:use-attribute-sets` attributes on literal result elements
- Names of decimal formats used in calls to the `format-number()` function

Testing User-Supplied Values

Your stylesheet will be useful as a utility if it catches errors that are made by the person using it. The people who use your utility won't know it inside-out and they won't necessarily take the time to read your lovingly prepared documentation. They may well work by trial and error to get it to do what they want it to do. If you can reflect back to them the impact of the parameters that they pass to your templates, especially if the parameters have strange values and are therefore unlikely to be what they intended, then it will make their lives a little easier.

You can send messages to the users of your stylesheet using the `xsl:message` element. This element can contain practically anything, and can even emit XML. For example, in the following version of the `format-money` template, the values of the parameters are reflected back to the person using it:

```
<xsl:template name="st:format-money">
   <xsl:param name="amount" select="0" />
   <xsl:param name="currency" select="'&#163;'" />
   <xsl:message>
      Calling format-money template:
         $amount   = <xsl:value-of select="$amount" />
         $currency = <xsl:value-of select="$currency" />
   </xsl:message>
   <xsl:value-of select="$currency" />
   <xsl:value-of select="format-number($amount, '#,##0.00')" />
</xsl:template>
```

Of course, all those messages can be little wearing on a user, so it's a kindness to have some kind of debug facility so that the user can at least turn them on and off. You could do this, say, with a global debug variable in the namespace that you're using for your utility:

```
<xsl:variable name="st:debug" select="false()" />
<xsl:template name="st:format-money">
   <xsl:param name="amount" select="0" />
   <xsl:param name="currency" select="'&#163;'" />
   <xsl:if test="$st:debug">
      <xsl:message>
         Called format-money template:
            $amount   = <xsl:value-of select="$amount" />
            $currency = <xsl:value-of select="$currency" />
      </xsl:message>
   </xsl:if>
   <xsl:value-of select="$currency" />
   <xsl:value-of select="format-number($amount, '#,##0.00')" />
</xsl:template>
```

When users want to use your utility in debug mode, they can override the variable declaration in their stylesheet so that it's set to true():

```
<xsl:variable name="st:debug" select="true()" />
```

As well as reflecting back the way in which they're using your utility, you can check that users are not passing any strange values into the utility. For example, you should really prevent users from passing anything but a number as the amount to the preceding template. For these kinds of situations, you can set the terminate attribute on xsl:message to yes so that the processor terminates with the message that you specify:

```
<xsl:template name="st:format-money">
   <xsl:param name="amount" select="0" />
```

```
<xsl:param name="currency" select="'&#163;'" />
<xsl:if test="string(number($amount)) = 'NaN'">
   <xsl:message terminate="yes">
      Error in call to format-money template:
         Invalid $amount: <xsl:value-of select="$amount" />
   </xsl:message>
</xsl:if>
<xsl:if test="$st:debug">
   <xsl:message>
      Called format-money template:
         $amount   = <xsl:value-of select="$amount" />
         $currency = <xsl:value-of select="$currency" />
   </xsl:message>
</xsl:if>
<xsl:value-of select="$currency" />
<xsl:value-of select="format-number($amount, '#,##0.00')" />
</xsl:template>
```

Of course, you could also recover silently from such an error or provide an error-recovery mode to enable the user to decide whether the utility should terminate or recover.

Testing Value Types

XPath doesn't come with any functions that enable you to test the type of values that are passed into a template as a parameter. In most cases, whatever value type is passed will be converted to the value type that is required, and you will end up with a usable value. The processor will terminate anyway if a string, number, or Boolean is passed and used as a node set.

However, if you need to, you can also use the following expressions to test value types of various sorts before you use them:

is not a number	`string(number($value)) = 'NaN'`
is not a number or is 0	`not(number($value))`
is an empty string	`not(string($value))`
is an empty node set	`not(count($value))`
is not passed as a Boolean	not(string($value) = 'true' or string($value) = 'false') or string(number($value)) = 'NaN'

The final type of mistake that the users of your utility template might make is not passing a value for a required parameter. For example, the `format-money` template should always be passed a value for the `$amount` parameter; if `$amount` isn't given a value, it's likely that the user has misspelled "amount" in the template call. The first way of handling this type of error is to set the default value of required parameters to an invalid value for that parameter, and test to see if the parameter has this value in the body of the template. For example, you could set the default value for `$amount` to `'invalid value'`:

```
<xsl:template name="st:format-money">
   <xsl:param name="amount" select="'invalid value'" />
   <xsl:param name="currency" select="'&#163;'" />
   <xsl:if test="$amount = 'invalid value'">
      <xsl:message terminate="yes">
         Error in call to format-money template:
            $amount is a required parameter
      </xsl:message>
   </xsl:if>
   <xsl:if test="string(number($amount)) = 'NaN'">
      <xsl:message terminate="yes">
         Error in call to format-money template:
            Invalid $amount: <xsl:value-of select="$amount" />
      </xsl:message>
   </xsl:if>
   <xsl:if test="$st:debug">
      <xsl:message>
         Called format-money template:
            $amount   = <xsl:value-of select="$amount" />
            $currency = <xsl:value-of select="$currency" />
      </xsl:message>
   </xsl:if>
   <xsl:value-of select="$currency" />
   <xsl:value-of select="format-number($amount, '#,##0.00')" />
</xsl:template>
```

A second method is to use an `xsl:message` element within the `xsl:param` element for the required parameter. In many processors, the body of the `xsl:param` will only be processed if the parameter is not passed a value, so the message will only be emitted (and the process terminated) if the parameter is not passed a value. The following template illustrates this in action:

```
<xsl:template name="st:format-money">
   <xsl:param name="amount">
      <xsl:message terminate="yes">
         Error in call to format-money template:
            $amount is a required parameter
```

```
        </xsl:message>
    </xsl:param>
    <xsl:param name="currency" select="'&#163;'" />
    <xsl:if test="string(number($amount)) = 'NaN'">
        <xsl:message terminate="yes">
            Error in call to format-money template:
                Invalid $amount: <xsl:value-of select="$amount" />
        </xsl:message>
    </xsl:if>
    <xsl:if test="$st:debug">
        <xsl:message>
            Called format-money template:
                $amount   = <xsl:value-of select="$amount" />
                $currency = <xsl:value-of select="$currency" />
        </xsl:message>
    </xsl:if>
    <xsl:value-of select="$currency" />
    <xsl:value-of select="format-number($amount, '#,##0.00')" />
</xsl:template>
```

However, this method is a little dangerous because the XSLT Recommendation does not explicitly state that the body of an xsl:param will not be processed unless the parameter is not passed a value. A conformant processor could feasibly process the content and therefore terminate the application despite the fact that the user does pass a value for the parameter to the template.

Improving Portability Across Processors

When you're authoring a utility stylesheet, you cannot predict what processors will be used with it in the future.

The most obvious implication of this is that you should avoid processor-specific extension functions and elements. If you have to use them, you should provide alternative instructions for different processors to fall back on where possible and warn the user or terminate the process if the wrong processor is used.

 In Part V, I examine the use of extension elements and functions.

FORWARDS AND BACKWARDS COMPATIBILITY

Some elements and functions are not so much processor-specific as XSLT version-specific. At the moment, there are just two versions of XSLT: the 1.0 Recommendation and the 1.1 Working Draft. XSLT 1.1 is backwards-compatible with 1.0 — a stylesheet written for XSLT 1.0 will give exactly the same result with a processor that implements the XSLT 1.1 Working Draft as it does with an XSLT 1.0 processor.

 XSLT 2.0 will introduce several features that are similar to those described in the XSLT 1.1 Working Draft. The discussion in this section also applies to the precautions that you should take to make XSLT 2.0 stylesheets usable by XSLT 1.0 processors, when XSLT 2.0 becomes available.

However, several new features are introduced in the XSLT 1.1 Working Draft, which may cause problems if you test a stylesheet with a processor that implements XSLT 1.1 but others use it with processor that does not. The features introduced in the XSLT 1.1 Working Draft are:

♦ The `xsl:script` top-level element supports user-defined extension functions.

♦ The `xsl:document` element allows you to create multiple result documents.

♦ Result tree fragments can be used as node sets.

♦ The `xsl:output` attributes are now interpreted as attribute value templates.

♦ The `xsl:apply-imports` element can now have `xsl:with-param` children.

XSLT is designed to be forwards-compatible so that unless you use one of these features, the processor will not complain. If a utility in your stylesheet relies on any of these features, you should test the version that the processor supports by querying the `xsl:version` system property. For example, the following utility template makes a deep copy of a node by language and then applies templates to that language-specific copy:

```
<xsl:template match="node()" mode="i18n:apply-templates">
   <xsl:param name="lang" select="'en'" />
   <xsl:variable name="copy">
      <xsl:apply-templates select="." mode="i18n:copy-of">
         <xsl:with-param name="lang" select="$lang" />
      </xsl:apply-templates>
   </xsl:variable>
   <xsl:apply-templates select="$copy" />
</xsl:template>
```

Within this template, the `$copy` variable is implicitly converted into a node set so that templates can be applied to it — an XSLT 1.1 feature. To make this backwards-compatible, you should check whether XSLT 1.1 is supported by the processor being used, and terminate the stylesheet if not:

```
<xsl:template match="node()" mode="i18n:apply-templates">
   <xsl:param name="lang" select="'en'" />
   <xsl:variable name="copy">
      <xsl:apply-templates select="." mode="i18n:copy-of">
         <xsl:with-param name="lang" select="$lang" />
      </xsl:apply-templates>
   </xsl:variable>
   <xsl:choose>
      <xsl:when test="system-property('xsl:version') &gt;= 1.1">
         <xsl:apply-templates select="$copy" />
      </xsl:when>
      <xsl:otherwise>
         <xsl:message terminate="yes">
            i18n:apply-templates requires a processor that
            implements XSLT 1.1.
         </xsl:message>
      </xsl:otherwise>
   </xsl:choose>
</xsl:template>
```

Even better, you should try to use the extension functions that gave similar functionality in XSLT 1.0 processors, if they are available:

```
<xsl:template match="node()" mode="i18n:apply-templates">
   <xsl:param name="lang" select="'en'" />
   <xsl:variable name="copy">
      <xsl:apply-templates select="." mode="i18n:copy-of">
         <xsl:with-param name="lang" select="$lang" />
      </xsl:apply-templates>
   </xsl:variable>
   <xsl:choose>
      <xsl:when test="system-property('xsl:version') &gt;= 1.1">
         <xsl:apply-templates select="$copy" />
      </xsl:when>
      <xsl:when test="function-available('exsl:node-set')">
         <xsl:apply-templates select="exsl:node-set($copy)" />
      </xsl:when>
      <xsl:when test="function-available('saxon:node-set')">
         <xsl:apply-templates select="saxon:node-set($copy)" />
      </xsl:when>
      <xsl:when test="function-available('msxsl:node-set')">
         <xsl:apply-templates select="msxsl:node-set($copy)" />
      </xsl:when>
      <xsl:when test="function-available('xalan:nodeset')">
         <xsl:apply-templates select="xalan:nodeset($copy)" />
      </xsl:when>
```

```
      ...
      <xsl:otherwise>
         <xsl:message terminate="yes">
            i18n:apply-templates requires processor support for
            conversion from result tree fragments to node sets.
         </xsl:message>
      </xsl:otherwise>
   </xsl:choose>
</xsl:template>
```

A similar technique can be used if you rely on the XSLT 1.1 feature that enables you to pass parameters within xsl:apply-imports.

If you use xsl:script, the xsl:script element itself will be ignored but the functions that you've defined with it will not be available: you should check their availability with function-available() before you try to call them.

See Chapter 20 for more details on user-defined extension functions.

Finally, while you can use the preceding technique (checking the xsl:version system property), if you use xsl:document, you may find the xsl:fallback element a neater way to terminate the application. For example, the following utility template adds messages to an error log using xsl:document:

```
<xsl:template name="log:transform-log">
   <xsl:param name="message" />
   <xsl:param name="log-file" select="'transform.log'" />
   <xsl:document href="{$log-file}">
      <transform>
         <log><xsl:copy-of select="$message" /></log>
         <xsl:copy-of select="document($log-file)/transform/log" />
      </transform>
   </xsl:document>
</xsl:template>
```

Rather than testing the xsl:version system property, you can use xsl:fallback for cases in which the xsl:document element is not available:

```
<xsl:template name="log:transform-log">
   <xsl:param name="message" />
   <xsl:param name="log-file" select="'transform.log'" />
   <xsl:document href="{$log-file}">
```

```
<transform>
   <log><xsl:copy-of select="$message" /></log>
   <xsl:copy-of select="document($log-file)/transform/log" />
</transform>
<xsl:fallback>
   <xsl:message terminate="yes">
      transform-log requires a processor that implements
      XSLT 1.1.
   </xsl:message>
</xsl:fallback>
     </xsl:document>
  </xsl:template>
```

PORTABILITY ACROSS PROCESSORS

The XSLT Recommendation leaves how to deal with certain instructions and errors up to the processor, which means that even processors that are fully conformant with the Recommendation can behave differently in the same circumstances. There is no substitute for testing your utility stylesheet on all the major XSLT processors to determine whether it's portable. However, an awareness of some of the areas where the XSLT Recommendation permits processors to behave differently will help you avoid unpleasant surprises.

The most dangerous group of behaviors are those where the processor is permitted to recover from an error in your stylesheet. This can mean that a stylesheet runs perfectly well in one processor but refuses to run at all with another. Many of these situations are also dependent on the source XML – it's worth bearing that in mind when you construct your test cases. The following steps should help improve the portability of your stylesheet:

1. **Check your templates for conflicting match patterns.** You should not have two or more templates in the same mode, with the same import precedence, and with the same priority that could match the same node in the source XML. If you do, add priorities to them to indicate which should be applied in preference, delete the earlier one, combine them, or otherwise alter them to remove the conflict.

2. **Check the** `name` **attribute of your** `xsl:element` **instructions.** Make sure that it's impossible for the attribute value template giving the name of the element to evaluate to an invalid element name.

3. **Check your** `xsl:attribute` **instructions.** Make sure that it's impossible for the attribute value template giving the name of the attribute to evaluate to an invalid attribute name. Check that the only nodes that are generated in the content of the `xsl:attribute` (including those created by templates that are called or applied within it) are text nodes. Make sure that no text nodes are generated with output escaping disabled.

4. **Check that the attribute is being added to an element.** Make sure that it's not being generated as direct content of a variable or parameter. In

particular, if the attribute is being created at the top level of a template, make sure that the template isn't called or applied in the content of an instruction generating something other than an element, or in a variable or a parameter.

Make sure that the attribute is not being generated after any content for the element. In particular, make sure that any `xsl:call-template`, `xsl:apply-templates`, or `xsl:apply-imports` instructions that come before it don't involve creating anything but attributes and namespace nodes.

5. **Check your `xsl:processing-instruction` instructions.** Make sure that it's impossible for the attribute value template giving the name of the processing instruction to evaluate to an invalid processing instruction target or to contain a colon. Check that the only nodes that are generated in the content of the `xsl:processing-instruction` (including those created by templates that are called or applied within it) are text nodes. Make sure that none of the text nodes are generated with output escaping disabled. Check that none of them can include the string '`?>`'.

6. **Check your `xsl:comment` instructions.** Make sure that the only nodes that are generated in the content of the `xsl:comment` (including those created by templates that are called or applied within it) are text nodes. Check that none of them have their output escaping disabled. Make sure that none of them can include the string '`--`' and that the last one cannot end with a '`-`'.

7. **Check the places where you're creating a namespace node by copying an existing one.** Check that the namespace node is being added to an element. Make sure that it's not being generated as direct content of a variable or parameter. In particular, if the namespace node is being copied at the top level of a template, make sure the template isn't called or applied in the content of an instruction generating something other than an element, or in a variable or a parameter.

Make sure that the namespace node is not being copied after any attributes or content for the element. In particular, make sure that any `xsl:call-template`, `xsl:apply-templates`, or `xsl:apply-imports` instructions that come before it don't involve creating anything but namespace nodes.

8. **Check your `xsl:output` instructions.** You should not have two or more `xsl:output` elements with the same import precedence that specify values for the same attribute, unless that attribute is `cdata-section-elements`. If you do, delete the specification of the attribute that comes first in your stylesheet.

Check that the output encoding that you've specified is either `UTF-8` or `UTF-16`. If you need to use another encoding, make sure that you never create a character that can't be represented in that encoding, aside from in places where that character can be escaped. It can always be escaped in attribute values; it can never be escaped if you've given it within a text node whose output escaping is disabled. It also can't be escaped in element or attribute names or processing instruction targets, or in `script` or `style` elements if the output method is `html`.

9. **Don't use `disable-output-escaping`.** XSLT processors aren't required to support the disabling of output escaping. You should avoid using it if you can.

   If you do use it, identify any variables or parameters whose values are set by content (that are given result tree fragment values). Of these, identify those that generate text nodes with output escaping disabled. If there are any, make sure that none of them are converted (implicitly or explicitly) into strings or numbers through an XPath expression. If you want to get their values, for example, you should use `xsl:copy-of` rather than `xsl:value-of`.

10. **Check your attribute sets for conflicting attributes.** You should not have two or more attribute sets with the same name and the same import precedence define the same attribute unless the attribute set is overridden higher up the import tree.

11. **Check your `xsl:strip-space` and `xsl:preserve-space` elements for conflicting match patterns.** You should not have two or more node tests with the same default priority in `xsl:strip-space` and `xsl:preserve-space` instructions with the same import precedence that match the same element in the source XML. If you do, combine them or otherwise disambiguate them.

12. **Check your `xsl:namespace-alias` elements for conflicting stylesheet prefixes.** You should not have two or more `xsl:namespace-alias` elements with the same import precedence that specify the same stylesheet prefix. If you do, delete the first one.

13. **Check the `value` attribute of the `xsl:number` instruction.** Make sure that the expression given in the `value` attribute of the `xsl:number` element cannot evaluate to NaN, infinity, or a number less than 0.5.

14. **Check your calls to the `document()` function.** Check that the stylesheet never uses the `document()` function to access a file that doesn't exist. This can be quite difficult as there's no way of checking whether a file exists within XSLT. In general, if you're creating a utility stylesheet, you should ship all the documents you need with it, even if they are basically empty.

   Avoid specifying fragment identifiers as part of the URI to be retrieved by the `document()` function. XSLT processors may not support the fragment identifier.

   If you use two arguments to the `document()` function, make sure that the second never evaluates to an empty node set, or that the first argument is an absolute URI if it does.

There are other areas in the XSLT Recommendation that leave some flexibility in processor behavior, and therefore where the result of one processor may be different from another. If you've gone through the preceding steps, you shouldn't have problems with other processors reporting errors for your stylesheet, but you may find other processors generate slightly different results.

The most significant difference that may occur between processors is that different XSLT processors may support different languages. This can affect the numbering schemes generated by `xsl:number` and the sort orders given by `xsl:sort`. You can therefore improve the portability of your stylesheet by not relying on a particular sort order or numbering scheme.

Combining Stylesheets

So far in this chapter I've talked about building XSLT applications with a top-down approach: taking a working stylesheet and breaking it up into separate stylesheets. You may also have to work with multiple stylesheets when starting with a number of stand-alone stylesheets and combining them into a single XSLT application.

For example, you may have existing stylesheets for converting some data into HTML and WML, and now want to merge those into an application that takes a parameter ($method, say) and gives either HTML or WML on the basis of that parameter. The starting point, then, is something like the following:

```
<?xml version="1.0"?>
<xsl:stylesheet version="1.0"
                xmlns:xsl="http://www.w3.org/1999/XSL/Transform">

<xsl:import href="html-version.xsl" />
<xsl:import href="wml-version.xsl" />

<xsl:param name="method" select="'html'" />

<xsl:template match="/">
   <xsl:choose>
      <xsl:when test="$method = 'wml'">
         ...
      </xsl:when>
      <xsl:otherwise>
         ...
      </xsl:otherwise>
   </xsl:choose>
</xsl:template>

</xsl:stylesheet>
```

The stylesheets that you're combining—`html-version.xsl` and `wml-version.xsl`—are both imported into the main stylesheet. The `$method` parameter is declared, and a controlling stylesheet is generated that tests the value of this parameter and does something based on it.

 The two stylesheets may generate results that need to be serialized in different ways, with different methods, media-types, document types, and so on. Unfortunately, you cannot do anything about this in XSLT 1.0, but extension elements and attributes, and the XSLT 1.1 Working Draft give you this functionality in some processors. Chapter 19 describes these extensions in detail.

Identifying Common Code

The first step in combining the two stylesheets is to identify the common code between them. You may have already done this—they may both import or include the same set of utility templates. If they *are* using the same utility stylesheets, you should make sure that you avoid the conflicts in template names and the problems involved with overridden constructs, both of which I've discussed at length in previous sections of this chapter.

You can import any common code into the main stylesheet rather than having it imported separately into the HTML and WML stylesheets to avoid the majority of conflicts, but if you want the two versions to stand alone as well as together, then the common code needs to be imported into each separately.

You can make it easier to combine your two stylesheets if the common code does not contain any matching templates aside from those using specific modes. To combine stylesheets, you use modes to distinguish between the templates from the two stylesheets, and it is very difficult to share code between templates that use different modes. If there are shared matching templates, you should recast them as named templates and place matching templates that call them in the separate stylesheets.

Eliminating Conflicts

The second step is to prevent any conflicts between the stylesheets. The most obvious place for conflicts occurs with the templates—it's likely that the stylesheets have different templates matching the same source nodes. Assign each stylesheet a different mode name, for example you might assign `html-version.xsl` the mode `html` and `wml-version.xsl` the mode `wml`. All the matching templates within that stylesheet should be assigned that mode, and any `xsl:apply-templates` instructions within it should use that mode.

Within the main stylesheet, you can then apply templates in that mode and guarantee that the only templates that will be used are the ones in the stylesheet to which you assigned that mode. The main stylesheet for managing the transformation into either HTML or WML contains a template matching the root node of the source and applies templates in an appropriate mode based on the value of the $method parameter:

```
<?xml version="1.0"?>
<xsl:stylesheet version="1.0"
                xmlns:xsl="http://www.w3.org/1999/XSL/Transform">

<xsl:import href="html-version.xsl" />
<xsl:import href="wml-version.xsl" />

<xsl:param name="method" select="'html'" />

<xsl:template match="/">
   <xsl:choose>
      <xsl:when test="$method = 'wml'">
         <xsl:apply-templates select="." mode="wml" />
      </xsl:when>
      <xsl:otherwise>
         <xsl:apply-templates select="." mode="html" />
      </xsl:otherwise>
   </xsl:choose>
</xsl:template>

</xsl:stylesheet>
```

You should watch out for other conflicts, too, and rename templates, variables, parameters, keys, attribute sets, and decimal formats if they are defined differently in the two stylesheets. You can use namespaces to distinguish between the two stylesheets if you want.

Again, be careful that the common code doesn't call or refer to the different constructs; if it does, make copies in both the stylesheets to address the method-specific parts.

Creating High-Level Templates

You now need to create high-level templates in the two stylesheets so that the stylesheets can be used stand-alone as well as part of the larger application. You should have two high-level templates in each. One should match the document element in the stylesheet's mode and should generate the content of the page. For example, the one in html-version.xsl might look like the following:

```
<xsl:template match="/*" mode="html">
   <html>
      <head>
         ...
      </head>
      <body>
         <xsl:apply-templates mode="html" />
      </body>
   </html>
</xsl:template>
```

The second high-level template should match the root node in the default mode. This template is overridden within the main stylesheet, and is therefore only applied when the stylesheet is used on its own. It simply applies templates in the stylesheet's mode:

```
<xsl:template match="/">
   <xsl:apply-templates mode="html" />
</xsl:template>
```

Summary

In this chapter, the discussion surrounds a number of ways to work with XSLT applications using multiple stylesheets.

The most basic methods are to *include* stylesheets with xsl:include, general entities, or XInclude. While general entities and XInclude elements offer you flexibility and can be used to include XML *within* templates as well as at the top level, they are not XSLT-aware, unlike xsl:include, so you should use them with caution.

If you are involved in writing XSLT often, it's likely that you'll start writing utility stylesheets to address common problems. Utility stylesheets can provide a default behavior that you can override in the stylesheets that use them, but even importing stylesheets can be a little unpredictable because of the way import precedence is handled.

When designing utility stylesheets, define all the constructs that they need to function to make them self-sufficient. Providing a utility-specific namespace makes conflicts with templates less likely when importing stylesheets. You can assist the importing-stylesheet author by giving them messages about the values that they're passing to your utility, especially if you test whether those values are valid. Finally, utility stylesheets need to be portable: they should be forwards and backwards compatible. And you should try to make them as processor-independent as possible by avoiding errors, even if your favorite processor can recover from them.

Combining stylesheets requires assigning modes to the different stylesheets while pulling out and reusing as much common code as possible. With high-level templates, you can ensure that stylesheets continue to be used as stand-alone stylesheets as well as combined together.

Chapter 14

Client–Side Processing with MSXML

IN THIS CHAPTER

- ◆ Running client-side transformations
- ◆ Changing stylesheet parameters
- ◆ Changing the data displayed with the stylesheet
- ◆ Changing the stylesheet used with the data
- ◆ Creating frames with client-side XSLT
- ◆ Displaying vector graphics using SVG and client-side XSLT

IN THIS CHAPTER, you learn how to do client-side processing of XSLT using Microsoft's XSLT processor, MSXML. MSXML isn't the only client-side processor available – there's also the Transformiix module for Netscape, for example – but it is the most common and well developed, and it is the nearest conformance to the XSLT 1.0 Recommendation. Thus, MSXML is worth a more in-depth look. However, MSXML is just being used as the basis for illustrations of client-side functionality in this chapter – everything discussed here also can be achieved using the Transformiix module and similar scripting.

The first section of this chapter outlines the features of the MSXML implementation, providing a step-by-step guide for creating general scripts for dynamic client-side transformation. The remainder of the chapter examines specific tasks that you might want to do in a dynamic client-side application and demonstrates ways of doing them.

This chapter assumes that you have downloaded and installed the release version of MSXML 3.0 in replace mode with Internet Explorer 5.0 or 5.5, or are using Internet Explorer version 6. If you are a new MSXML user, you may find the FAQ at http://www.netcrucible.com/xslt/msxml-faq.htm useful. I also recommend downloading the full MSXML Software Development Kit, so you have a copy of the documentation. JavaScript is the scripting language used throughout this chapter.

Scripting XSLT Processing

When you open an XML page in Internet Explorer, MSXML looks for an `xml-stylesheet` processing instruction. If it finds one, it automatically attempts to transform the XML using the indicated stylesheet. For example, if you place the following at the top of the XML source for a bank statement, the statement is automatically formatted into HTML:

```
<?xml-stylesheet type="text/xsl" href="statement.xsl"?>
```

This default processing enables you to apply a stylesheet to XML, but if you want to do more than that — to pass parameters to the stylesheet, to dynamically choose which data or stylesheet to use, or to create frames or Scalable Vector Graphics (SVG) — you must use scripting.

Figure 14-1 illustrates the overall process involved in scripting the transformation. You must load the XML file that is to be transformed and the XSLT stylesheet to do the transformation into separate `DOMDocument` objects. Then, create an `XSLTemplate`, set the `stylesheet` property to the `DOMDocument` for the XSLT stylesheet, and create an `XSLProcessor` from it. Set the `input` of the `XSLProcessor` to be the `DOMDocument` from the XML file, add any parameters, and transform the XML. Once the XML has been transformed, the `output` property of the `XSLProcessor` object is the resultant HTML (or whatever you have transformed the XML into). Each of these steps is discussed in detail in the rest of this section.

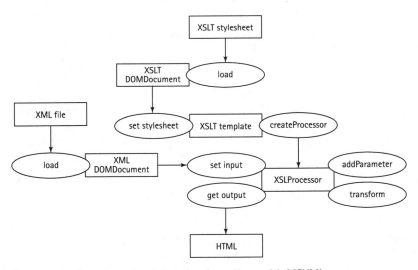

Figure 14–1: Overview of scripted transformations with MSXML

Shipping Single Files

MSXML doesn't support embedded stylesheets, so you can't add an `xsl:stylesheet` element in your source XML and get MSXML to use that. You can, however, embed the data in the stylesheet if you want to only ship one file.

First, create a stylesheet that refers to itself within an `xml-stylesheet` processing instruction:

```
<?xml version="1.0"?>
<?xml-stylesheet type="text/xsl" href="statement.xsl"?>
<xsl:stylesheet version="1.0"
                xmlns:xsl="http://www.w3.org/1999/XSL/Transform">
...

</xsl:stylesheet>
```

Then add the data at the top level of the stylesheet. Because the data is at the top level of the stylesheet, it must be placed in a separate namespace, so you need to define that namespace as well:

```
<?xml version="1.0"?>
<?xml-stylesheet type="text/xsl" href="statement.xsl"?>
<xsl:stylesheet version="1.0"
                xmlns:xsl="http://www.w3.org/1999/XSL/Transform"
                xmlns:st="http://www.example.com/bank/statement">

<st:statement>
  ...
</st:statement>
...

</xsl:stylesheet>
```

Now, you want the stylesheet to process only the data. To accomplish this you must add a template that matches the `xsl:stylesheet` document element and applies the template to the data:

```
<?xml version="1.0"?>
<?xml-stylesheet type="text/xsl" href="statement.xsl"?>
<xsl:stylesheet version="1.0"
                xmlns:xsl="http://www.w3.org/1999/XSL/Transform"
                xmlns:st="http://www.example.com/bank/statement">
```

Continued

Shipping Single Files *(Continued)*

```
<st:statement>
  ...
</st:statement>

<xsl:template match="xsl:stylesheet">
   <xsl:apply-templates select="st:statement" />
</xsl:template>

...

</xsl:stylesheet>
```

You can now add any other templates that you want to; they will be used to transform the data that you've embedded in the stylesheet.

Creating DOMs

The first step in scripting stylesheet transforms with MSXML is to create DOMs (document object models) for both the source XML and that stylesheet. To create a DOM, MSXML reads in the specific XML and builds a DOM from it.

MSXML holds DOMs within a `DOMDocument`. To build the DOM, you must create a `DOMDocument` to hold it, and then load the relevant XML into that `DOMDocument`. There are two kinds of `DOMDocument` objects in MSXML — free-threaded `DOMDocument`s and rental-threaded `DOMDocument`s. It doesn't matter which one you use for the XML source DOM, but the stylesheet DOM has to be free threaded. So, to create the `DOMDocument` intended for the XML source, for example, you can use either of:

```
XMLDOM = new ActiveXObject('Msxml2.DOMDocument');
XMLDOM = new ActiveXObject('Msxml2.FreeThreadedDOMDocument');
```

To create the `DOMDocument` for the XSLT stylesheet, you must use:

```
XSLTDOM = new ActiveXObject('Msxml2.FreeThreadedDOMDocument');
```

After you create the `DOMDocument`, you can set flags to control how the XML is read into it. The `async` property controls whether or not control returns to the script immediately (if it's true — the default) or only after the entire XML document has been read (if it's false). In the vast majority of cases, you want the `async` property to be set to false for both the DOM for the XML source and the DOM for the stylesheet:

```
XMLDOM.async = false;
XSLTDOM.async = false;
```

The only time you want `async` to be true is if you want to have event-driven processing of your XML document.

Another useful flag is the `validateOnParse` property. If set to true, MSXML validates the XML file when it's loaded into the `DOMDocument` according to any DTD or schema it finds to be associated with the XML; if false, it won't. The default is true. You don't need to validate the source XML and you almost never want to validate the stylesheet, so you usually want to set `validateOnParse` to false for both:

```
XMLDOM.validateOnParse = false;
XSLTDOM.validateOnParse = false;
```

The final flag that you should set is the `preserveWhiteSpace` flag. By default, `preserveWhiteSpace` is set to false and MSXML ignores any text that is purely comprised of whitespace characters when it loads XML into the DOM. This bypasses the rules in XSLT that govern how whitespace is handled, which prevents `xsl:strip-space`, `xsl:preserve-space` and `xsl:text` from having the advertised effect. Sometimes this doesn't matter because you're generating HTML, which normalizes whitespace anyway. However, to get conformant behavior from MSXML, you need to set the `preserveWhiteSpace` property to true for both DOMs, as follows:

```
XMLDOM.preserveWhiteSpace = true;
XSLTDOM.preserveWhiteSpace = true;
```

Chapter 16 goes into detail about how to control whitespace in your document.

After these flags have been set, you can load the XML into the `DOMDocument`. The two ways to accomplish this are to load an XML file with the `load` method or to load a string of well-formed XML with the `loadXML` method. (In general, you want to do the former. You may, however, do the latter on occasion; you would do the latter, for example, if you need to have a dynamic XSLT application that takes a node set as a parameter value.) This adds the following lines:

```
XMLDOM.load('statement.xml')
XSLTDOM.load('statement.xsl')
```

Of course, parse problems may arise with either the source XML or the stylesheet itself, so it's worth checking problems before moving to the next stage. You can check whether errors occurred by looking at the errorCode of the DOMDocument's parseError property. If the errorCode is 0, everything is okay — if not, problems exist and any further processing isn't going to get you anywhere:

```
if (XMLDOM.parseError.errorCode != 0) {
   ...
   return;
}
```

The parseError property on DOMDocument holds an XMLDOMParseError object that gives more details.

To put this all together, use the following functions as utilities in the client-side XSLT scripts:

```
function explainParseError(error) {
   return error.reason + '[' + error.url + ': line ' +
          error.line + ', col ' + error.linepos + ']';
}

function getEmptyDOM() {
   DOM = new ActiveXObject('Msxml2.FreeThreadedDOMDocument');
   DOM.async = false;
   DOM.validateOnParse = false;
   DOM.preserveWhiteSpace = true;
}

function getDOMFromFile(File) {
   DOM = getEmptyDOM();
   DOM.load(File);
   if (DOM.parseError.errorCode != 0) {
      alert('Error parsing file:\n' +
            explainParseError(DOM.parseError));
      return;
   }
   return DOM;
}

function getDOMFromXML(XML) {
   DOM = getEmptyDOM();
   DOM.loadXML(XML);
   if (DOM.parseError.errorCode != 0) {
      alert('Error parsing XML:\n' +
            explainParseError(DOM.parseError));
      return;
   }
   return DOM;
}
```

Manipulating DOMs

Once you have an in-memory representation of your XML information, you can change it as much as you want using DOM-based manipulation. You shouldn't use DOM-based manipulation on either your source XML or your stylesheet unless it's absolutely necessary because most of the manipulation you might need to do can be better handled within the XSLT stylesheet. If you need to dynamically change either your source XML or your stylesheet, you should add parameters to the stylesheet to determine the behavior dynamically that way, rather than reaching in and changing them.

Certain aspects of stylesheets can't be controlled through parameters, such as the stylesheets that it includes or imports. But if you want to change them, use a two-pass solution in which you actually generate the stylesheet that you want to use dynamically.

However, there are operations in which DOM manipulation (coupled with JavaScript or your language of choice) is a lot more efficient than an XSLT solution: using regular expressions is one of them. It's also really inefficient to generate stylesheets when you can quickly adjust one that you already have. So, sometimes it may be useful to adapt either or both DOMs.

If you're used to dealing with XPaths (which you should be if you're using XSLT), the easiest way to change the DOM is to select the node or nodes that you want to manipulate using an XPath and the `selectNodes` or `selectSingleNode` methods, and then add to, change, or delete them using DOM methods. Both methods can select nodes based on an XPath; the `selectSingleNode` method selects the first in the tree, whereas the `selectNodes` method selects all of them. However, be careful that you set the `SelectionLanguage` for the DOM to `'XPath'`; otherwise MSXML will try to interpret the path that you provide in terms of its own XPath-like syntax. For example, you could select the `href` attribute of the second `xsl:import` element in the stylesheet with:

```
XSLTDOM.setProperty('SelectionLanguage', 'XPath');
importHref = XSLTDOM.selectSingleNode('/*/xsl:import[2]/@href');
```

 If you use qualified names within your XPath, you may need to set the `SelectionNamespaces` property on the DOM to indicate which prefixes you're associating with which namespaces. For example, the following would allow you to use the prefix `st:` in XPaths to select elements and attributes in the `http://www.example.com/bank/statement` namespace:

```
XMLDOM.setProperty('SelectionNamespaces',
    'xmlns:st="http://www.example.com/bank/statement"');
```

You can change the value of an attribute selected in this way by setting the value property for the attribute. For example, you can change the selected href attribute using:

```
importHref.value = 'utilities2.xsl';
```

It's a little more complicated to change the values of elements. You can use the text property to set the string value of the element in the same way as you can with attributes; doing so creates a single text node as the content of the element node. For lower-level control, or to add subelements, you need to start using DOM methods such as appendChild.

To discuss everything that you can do to a DOM representation of a document requires more space than can be devoted here. If you want to learn more about manipulating the DOM, look at the MSXML SDK documentation and at the DOM standards from W3C at http://www.w3.org/TR/DOM-Level-2-Core.

Creating XSLT Processors

At the most basic level, when you have a DOM for your source XML and your stylesheet, you can transform the XML using the transformNode or transformNodeToObject methods on one of the nodes in the DOM for the source, with the argument being the stylesheet DOM:

```
result = XMLDOM.transformNode(XSLTDOM);
```

The transformNode and transformNodeToObject methods can be very useful because you can focus the transform on a particular node, perhaps to filter what XML is displayed or to update only part of the dynamic page.

However, using the transformNode or transformNodeToObject method doesn't enable you to pass parameters into the stylesheet, which can be very limiting. It also doesn't enable you to cache the result of parsing the stylesheet, which you might want to do if you are using the same stylesheet numerous times. To pass parameters into a stylesheet, you need to create an XSLProcessor object, which holds information about a particular stylesheet being used on a particular input document. To create an XSLProcessor, you need to first create an XSLTemplate object that holds the parsed stylesheet.

To set up an XSLTemplate, you must create it and set its stylesheet property to the DOM of the stylesheet that you want to use:

```
template = new ActiveXObject('Msxml2.XSLTemplate');
template.stylesheet = XSLTDOM;
```

After you do this, you can create an XSLProcessor from the XSLTemplate by calling the createProcessor method on the XSLTemplate and setting the input for the processor to be the DOM for the XML source:

```
processor = template.createProcessor();
processor.input = XMLDOM;
```

When MSXML creates an XSLProcessor, it checks the stylesheet DOM to ensure that the DOM its been given is a valid stylesheet. Any errors in the stylesheet are automatically flagged with an alert, but you may want to have control over this. You can use the following functions to create an XSLProcessor:

```
function getProcessorFromDOMs(XMLDOM, XSLTDOM) {
   try {
      template = new ActiveXObject('Msxml2.XSLTemplate');
      template.stylesheet = XSLTDOM;
      processor = template.createProcessor();
      processor.input = XMLDOM;
      return processor;
   } catch (exception) {
      alert('Error creating processor:\n' + exception.description);
      return;
   }
}


function getProcessorFromFiles(XMLFile, XSLFile) {
   XMLDOM = getDOMFromFile(XMLFile);
   if (XMLDOM) {
      XSLTDOM = getDOMFromFile(XSLFile);
      if (XSLTDOM) {
         return getProcessorFromDOMs(XMLDOM, XSLTDOM);
      }
   }
}
```

Passing Parameters

After the XSLProcessor has been created, you can pass parameters using the addParameter method. For example, to pass the locale-specific version of the current date into the stylesheet, you can use:

```
today = new Date();
processor.addParameter('today', today.toLocaleString());
```

If you are using parameters in a particular namespace, you should use the local name as the first argument to addParameter and the namespace URI as the third argument. For example, if the parameter $today was in the statement namespace, you can use:

```
today = new Date();
processor.addParameter('today', today.toLocaleString(),
                       'http://www.example.com/bank/statement');
```

You can pass strings, numbers, or Booleans into the stylesheet to have parameters with those values. You can also pass node lists or single nodes into the stylesheet to give node-set parameters. In the following example, the $trans parameter is passed a node list of the transaction elements within the statement:

```
transactions = XMLDOM.selectNodes('/statement/transactions/transaction');
processor.addParameter('trans', transactions,
                       'http://www.example.com/bank/statement');
```

The parameter value actually holds that node list rather than a new node set — the generated IDs of the transaction elements passed as a parameter are the same as the generated IDs of the transaction elements as accessed within the stylesheet. As a result, the preceding example is exactly the same as having the following in the stylesheet itself:

```
<xsl:param name="st:trans" select="/statement/transactions/transaction" />
```

The advantage of passing in nodes or node lists as parameters is that you can construct the paths that select them. You can also pass in new or generated nodes; this enables you to use really sophisticated parameters with internal (XML) structure rather than being restricted to strings as you are from the command line. This is demonstrated in the section "Changing Parameters," later in the chapter.

Transforming XML

Now that the XSLT processor is all set up, you're ready to transform the XML. This is as simple as the following:

```
processor.transform();
```

However, the transformation process may not be error free — aspects of the stylesheet cannot be validated until run time. Therefore it's necessary to have something that can catch any errors. You can place the above line in a try-catch statement:

```
try {
    processor.transform();
} catch (exception) {
    alert('Error transforming XML:\n' + exception.description);
}
```

The same kind of construction should be used with the transformNode and transformNodeToObject methods if you use them.

Using the Output

The output of the transform can be accessed either as an object or as a string. If you just want to display the output, it can be a string. For example, you can display it within the browser with:

```
document.open();
document.write(processor.output);
document.close();
```

Also, you can place the result in the content of an existing element in the page (the element can be accessed by its id, for example):

```
body.innerHTML = processor.output;
```

If you have a process that's using more than one pass, the output of the transform must be an object — a DOMDocument. It's easy to do this if you are using the transformNodeToObject method: create a new DOMDocument to hold the output and use this new DOM as a second argument to the method (the first being the DOM of the stylesheet you're using):

```
outputDOM = new ActiveXObject('Msxml2.DOMDocument');
XMLDOM.transformNodeToObject(XSLTDOM, outputDOM);
```

On the other hand, if you're passing parameters to the stylesheet and want to use XSLProcessor, you need to set the output of the XSLProcessor to be the new output DOM *before* you set any parameters or transform the XML:

```
outputDOM = new ActiveXObject('Msxml2.DOMDocument');
processor.output = outputDOM;
processor.addParameter(...);
processor.transform();
```

When the output is a DOMDocument, you can manipulate it in any way, use it as the source XML for another transformation, or even use it as the stylesheet for another transformation — whatever you want.

Dynamic Applications

The previous section examined the basic workings of the MSXML XSLT processing model. In this section, you look at how to combine these with XSLT to create dynamic XSLT applications.

Changing Parameters

A typical dynamic client-side application enables the user of the application to view some XML in many different ways. The end-user should be able to click a particular link or fill in a particular field in a form, with the view changing accordingly.

Often, the different views are similar enough that they can use the same basic stylesheet, with parameters determining the details of the view. For example, the bank statement application contains much the same information, especially concerning the layout and the customer details, but the table showing the various transactions can change from view to view – it can be sorted by date, by amount, by transaction type, and so on.

Your first step is to create a stylesheet that gives the required output based on this parameter. In the application, you declare a parameter called sort-by, which by default is set to the string date:

```
<xsl:param name="sort-by" select="'date'" />
```

Now each transaction element has a number of attributes with date, type, and amount being the important ones. The value of the $sort-by parameter is the name of a single attribute. So, to iterate over the transactions and create a row for each, you can do:

```
<xsl:for-each select="transaction">
   <xsl:sort select="@*[name() = $sort-by]" />
   <tr>
      <td><xsl:value-of select="@date" /></td>
      <td><xsl:value-of select="@type" /></td>
      <td><xsl:value-of select="@amount" /></td>
   </tr>
</xsl:for-each>
```

You can test whether this is working by setting the parameter to different default values by hand within the stylesheet and viewing the statement XML.

Chapter 7 gives more details about how to use parameter values to dynamically control the order of a set of information.

To make this application dynamic, you must have a JavaScript function that changes the view that's displayed by transforming the source XML using the same stylesheet but with different parameter values. The JavaScript function resides in (or is referenced from) the HTML page that's created by the stylesheet. It's often easiest to create a separate file for the JavaScript functions to eliminate putting them inline within the stylesheet. For example, use the following function to load and display the result of a transformation:

```
function transformXML(XMLFile, XSLTFile, params, frame) {
   processor = getProcessorFromFiles(XMLFile, XSLTFile);
   if (processor) {
      frame = frame || top;
      if (params) {
         for (var i = 0; i < params.length; i += 2) {
            processor.addParameter(params[i], params[i + 1]);
         }
      }
      try {
         processor.transform();
         frame.document.open();
         frame.document.write(processor.output);
         frame.document.close();
      } catch (exception) {
         alert('Error transforming XML:\n' + exception.description);
      }
   }
}
```

Here, `getProcessorFromFiles()` is a function that creates a processor for a stylesheet specified in an XSLT file with an input of the DOM from an XML file; the code for this function was given in the section "Creating XSLT Processors" earlier in this chapter.

You can put this in an `XSLTutilities.js` file and get the functions loaded into the HTML that results from a transformation by creating a `script` element in the result:

```
<script type="text/javascript" src="XSLTutilities.js" />
```

For this specific application, you want to be able to change the `$sort-by` parameter that's used by the transformation. Both the source data and the stylesheet that's used are fixed, so your function has to take only one parameter: the new value for the `$sort-by` parameter. Again, this has to be defined in the HTML that you're producing, so you need another `script` element to hold the function:

```
<script type="text/javascript">
   function reSort(sortBy) {
      params = new Array('sort-by', sortBy);
      transformXML('statement.xml', 'statement.xsl', params);
   }
</script>
```

Now reloading the page with the result of the transformation with this changed parameter is as simple as calling the reSort() function with an argument being the name of the attribute on the transaction element that you want to sort by. You want the end-user to click the headers of each column in the table to sort by that column, so create a header for the table:

```
<thead>
   <tr>
      <th onclick="reSort('date');">Date</th>
      <th onclick="reSort('type');">Type</th>
      <th onclick="reSort('amount');">Amount</th>
   </tr>
```

Caching and Reusing DOMs

When you create a dynamic application that uses an XSLT transformation to write an entire page, the XML and XSLT is parsed and DOMs, XSLTemplates and XSLProcessors are created every time the page is loaded. This is necessary because the variables that hold these objects are local to the page; when it is rewritten, the references to the objects are lost. Obviously this is wasteful if you are using the same XML or the same stylesheet in each transformation.

There are two ways to make the objects available after the transformation so that you can reuse them. The first is to change the transformation so that it only generates part of the page, and then write the result of the transformation to the page by setting the innerHTML of an element in the page. For example, if you rewrite the transformation to only generate the body of the page, then you could use the following static HTML page to manage the transformation:

```
<html>
   <head>
      <title>Bank Statement</title>
      <script type="text/javascript" src="XSLTutilities.js">
      </script>
      <script type="text/javascript">
         processor = getProcessorFromFiles('statement.xml',
                                           'statement.xsl');

         function reSort(sortBy) {
            processor.reset();
            processor.addParameter('sort-by', sortBy);
            processor.transform();
            content.innerHTML = processor.output;
         }
```

```
        </script>
    </head>
    <body id="content" onload="reSort('date');">
    </body>
</html>
```

The second way to reuse the objects used in the transformation is to create a dummy frameset, which holds only a single frame that holds the result of the transformation. The script that manages the transformation can go in the frameset document, as follows:

```
<html>
    <head>
        <title>Bank Statement</title>
        <script type="text/javascript" src="XSLTutilities.js">
        </script>
        <script type="text/javascript">
            processor = getProcessorFromFiles('statement.xml',
                                              'statement.xsl');

            function reSort(sortBy) {
                processor.reset();
                processor.addParameter('sort-by', sortBy);
                processor.transform();
                content.document.open();
                content.document.write(processor.output);
                content.document.close();
            }
        </script>
    </head>
    <frameset rows="*" onload="reSort('date');">
        <frame name="content" />
    </frameset>
</html>
```

If you use this latter technique, then you must slightly alter the function calls that you generate within the HTML content, to refer to the functions defined at the top of the frameset, as follows:

```
<thead>
    <tr>
        <th onclick="top.reSort('date');">Date</th>
        <th onclick="top.reSort('type');">Type</th>
        <th onclick="top.reSort('amount');">Amount</th>
    </tr>
</thead>
```

Continued

Caching and Reusing DOMs *(Continued)*

Both the techniques introduced in this sidebar give faster applications with less processing, but they also mean that you no longer generate the information stored in the head of the HTML page, and therefore have to set the title displayed for the page using JavaScript.

You should hang on to only the objects that you want to reuse. If the application uses the same source document and stylesheet, just with different parameters, then you can cache the XSLProcessor object. If you use the same stylesheet again and again, but use different source XML documents, then you should cache the XSLTemplate and generate XSLProcessor objects for the different inputs. If you are using multiple stylesheets with the same data, then you should cache the DOM for the data.

Creating dynamic applications such as these can be a bit confusing because you write JavaScript code within an XSLT stylesheet. Just remember that you're generating the definition and calls to a function using the stylesheet, but that this function isn't called from the stylesheet, it's called from the HTML page that's generated by the stylesheet.

This simple technique for generating calls to JavaScript functions is all well and good if you are passing simple values as parameters. But if you want to pass in node sets for your stylesheet to use, you have to create some serialized XML. The XML can then be parsed to create a DOM, which can be passed as a parameter value.

For example, if you want to pass further information about the sort, such as the data type of the attribute, you can express it as XML:

```
<sort by="..." order="..." data-type="..." />
```

The default for the $sort-by parameter changes to reflect this XML structure. For example, you could use an extension function to set the parameter from a variable that generates the XML as a result tree fragment, as follows:

```
<xsl:variable name="sort-by-rtf">
   <sort by="date" order="ascending" data-type="text" />
</xsl:variable>
<xsl:param name="sort-by" select="exsl:node-set($sort-by-rtf)" />
```

Chapter 1 outlines various ways of assigning XML structures to variables.

Escaping JavaScript

Be careful when you're generating JavaScript code dynamically using an XSLT stylesheet because JavaScript strings need to be escaped — they can't contain new lines, quotes, or backslashes (\), or the JavaScript parser gets confused.

Therefore, you must escape these characters when creating strings that are used in the JavaScript, whether in function definitions or in function calls within attribute values.

As outlined in Chapter 2, the following XSLT does this for you:

```
<js:escapes>
   <replace><from xml:space="preserve">&#xA;</from><to>\n</to></replace>
   <replace><from>&apos;</from><to>\&apos;</to></replace>
   <replace><from>&quot;</from><to>\&quot;</to></replace>
   <replace><from>\</from><to>\\</to></replace>
</js:escapes>

<xsl:template name="js:escape">
   <xsl:param name="string" />
   <xsl:apply-templates select="document('')/js:escapes/replace[1]"
                        mode="js:escape">
     <xsl:with-param name="string" select="$string" />
   </xsl:apply-templates>
</xsl:template>

<xsl:template match="js:escapes/replace" mode="js:escape">
   <xsl:param name="string" />
   <xsl:variable name="next"
        select="following-sibling::replace[contains($string, from)][1]" />
   <xsl:choose>
     <xsl:when test="$next">
        <xsl:apply-templates select="$next" mode="js:escape">
           <xsl:with-param name="substring-before($string, from)" />
        </xsl:apply-templates>
     </xsl:when>
     <xsl:otherwise>
        <xsl:value-of select="substring-before($string, from)" />
     </xsl:otherwise>
   </xsl:choose>
   <xsl:copy-of select="to" />
   <xsl:apply-templates select="." mode="js:escape">
     <xsl:with-param name="substring-after($string, to)" />
   </xsl:apply-templates>

</xsl:template>
```

The code that uses the `$sort-by` parameter is also adjusted:

```
<xsl:for-each select="transaction">
   <xsl:sort select="@*[name() = $sort-by/sort/@by]"
             order="{$sort-by/sort/@order}"
             data-type="{$sort-by/sort/@data-type}" />
   <tr>
      <td><xsl:value-of select="@date" /></td>
      <td><xsl:value-of select="@type" /></td>
      <td><xsl:value-of select="@amount" /></td>
   </tr>
</xsl:for-each>
```

Remember that if you set a variable through its content and convert it to a node set, the node set will consist of a root node with its children being the elements defined as the content of the parameter. On the other hand, when you pass a node set as a parameter, the node set could be anything — a set of elements or attributes. If you're using a default value for the parameter, it's best to stick to passing in whole DOMDocument nodes (which are equivalent to root nodes) rather than anything more specific.

The function that you use to reload the transformed XML has to be adjusted to take this new parameter. It needs to take a string of XML, turn that into a DOMDocument, and pass that as the parameter value:

```
<script type="text/javascript">
   function reSort(sortXML) {
      sortDOM = new ActiveXObject('Msxml2.DOMDocument');
      sortDOM.loadXML(sortXML);
      params = new Array('sort-by', sortDOM);
      transformXML('statement.xml', 'statement.xsl', params);
   }
</script>
```

And finally, you must provide the XML string to the function by constructing XML strings from within the stylesheet. This requires at least two, and sometimes three, sets of escaping — escaping the characters that are significant to the XML (for example, < and &) and escaping the characters that are significant to JavaScript (for example, ', ", and \). If the JavaScript is in an attribute, you also need to worry about escaping the apostrophes and quotes with XML syntax.

For example, the element that you want to pass to the stylesheet is:

```
<sort by="amount" order="ascending" data-type="number" />
```

The JavaScript code for the function call needs to be escaped so that the JavaScript processor doesn't think that the double quotes in the above string are ending the JavaScript string:

```
reSort('<sort by=\"amount\" order=\"ascending\" data-type=\"number\" />');
```

This appears as the value of an `onclick` attribute. You can add the attribute with an `xsl:attribute` element, with the above function call as its content, but any less-than signs need to be escaped within it:

```
<th>
   <xsl:attribute name="onclick">
      <xsl:text>reSort('&lt;sort by=\"amount\" order=\"ascending\" </xsl:text>
      <xsl:text>data-type=\"number\" />');</xsl:text>
   </xsl:attribute>
   <xsl:text>Amount</xsl:text>
</th>
```

If you were to put it directly into an attribute instead, you must escape the quotes used for the attribute as well, so the preceding becomes:

```
<th onclick="reSort('&lt;sort by=\&quot;amount\&quot;
                     order=\&quot;ascending\&quot;
                     data-type=\&quot;number\&quot; />');">
   <xsl:text>Date</xsl:text>
</th>
```

You can avoid doing all this escaping by instead generating XML "data islands" within the HTML, and accessing those data islands to give the XML to be passed as a parameter. For example, you could generate the XML that defined the sort within an HTML `div` that you hide by setting its `display` CSS property to `none`, as follows:

```
<div id="sortAmount" style="display: none;">
   <sort by="amount" order="ascending" data-type="number" />
</div>
```

Accessing the `innerHTML` property of this `div` element will give you a string version of the XML that it contains, which you can pass to the `reSort()` function defined previously. The link to perform the transformation is therefore as follows:

```
<th onclick="reSort(sortAmount.innerHTML);">Amount</th>
```

However, there is a drawback to this approach, namely that MSXML will convert the names of the elements you use within the `div` into uppercase when it accesses the contents as a string using the `innerHTML` property. Therefore, you should use uppercase element names when you use this technique.

Serializing XML

It's often easiest to dynamically generate serialized XML if you first create a node tree with the desired information and apply templates to it to create the serialization. A detailed discussion on how to serialize XML is found in Chapter 3. In this case, XML is being written as a JavaScript string in an HTML file, so it's not possible to cheat by wrapping it within a CDATA section.

Instead, you must use recursive templates, such as those in Chapter 3 or, since you're using MSXML anyway, use the msxsl:script element to write your own extension function to serialize the XML. The extension function can use the xml property of a DOMNode to get a serialized XML representation. The function definition would look as follows:

```
<msxsl:script language="JavaScript" implements-prefix="st">
    function serialize(nodeSet) {
        return nodeSet.item(0).xml;
    }
</msxsl:script>
```

With the preceding function definition, you could generate the XML that you wanted to pass directly, using XSLT constructs or literal result elements:

```
<xsl:variable name="sort-amount">
    <sort by="amount" order="ascending" data-type="number" />
</xsl:variable>
```

Then you can convert it to a node set and pass it as the argument to the st:serialize() function to create a serialized string:

```
<xsl:variable name="amount-sort-amount"
              select="st:serialize(msxsl:node-set($sort-amount))" />
```

And finally, call a JavaScript-escaping template to escape this string:

```
<xsl:variable name="js-escaped-sort-amount">
    <xsl:call-template name="escape:js">
        <xsl:with-param name="string"
                        select="string($amount-sort-amount)" />
    </xsl:call-template>
</xsl:variable>
```

You can put this string value in the attribute value with an attribute value template. You don't have to worry about doing any escaping of the quotes because that's done automatically when the XSLT processor creates the attribute value:

```
<th onclick="reSort('{$js-escaped-sort-amount}')">Amount</th>
```

Choosing the Data to View

You may want to change the source XML that your XSLT application uses on user demand. For example, you may have several statements that all use the same XSLT stylesheet to transform them into HTML. The three main ways to do this are as follows:

◆ Have `xml-stylesheet` processing instructions in each XML file, with each pointing to the same stylesheet. To move among the different XML source files, simply open the relevant one. This method means you don't have to worry about scripts at all.

◆ Use the URL of the XML file that you want to use as the location of the file to be loaded into the XML DOM, and transform it by using a script. This is a good method if you're using parameters anyway, and especially if you want to keep the current view settings rather than resetting the parameters to their default when the XML document changes (as would happen with the above option). It also means that you can create an `XSLTemplate` that can be used to generate `XSLProcessor`s for all the transformations, saving you from reparsing and recompiling the stylesheet each time you use it.

◆ Pass the URL of the XML file that you want to use, or even a `DOMDocument` for the XML file, as a parameter to the XSLT stylesheet, using the techniques discussed in the previous section. If you pass just the file name, the XSLT stylesheet can open this file and apply templates to it using the `document()` function. This has the same advantages as the second method of being able to keep current view settings and cache the `XSLTemplate`. However, it also means that you can create an `XSLProcessor` that can be used for each process by simply resetting it using the `reset` method each time you want to change parameters.

If you're using the third option, where you pass in the location of the source XML as a parameter, it doesn't matter what source XML the stylesheet is applied to. It makes sense to use the stylesheet itself as the source XML — you have to turn the stylesheet into a DOM anyway in order to create the `XSLProcessor`, so you might as well use it.

Choosing the Stylesheet to Use

The basic way to indicate which stylesheet should be used with an XML document is to use the `xml-stylesheet` processing instruction, for example:

```
<?xml-stylesheet type="text/xsl" href="statement.xsl"?>
```

According to the W3C Recommendation *"Associating Style Sheets with XML Documents"* (`http://www.w3.org/TR/xml-stylesheet`), you can put several of these processing instructions in your XML document. Stylesheets that are intended for different media (for example, screen, print, or handheld) can be indicated through the `media` pseudo-attribute in the content of the processing instruction:

```
<?xml-stylesheet title="Screen Version" href="screen-statement.xsl"
                 type="text/xsl" media="screen" ?>
<?xml-stylesheet title="Printed Version" href="print-statement.xsl"
                 type="text/xsl" media="print" ?>
```

You can also provide alternative stylesheets for a single medium with the `alternate` pseudo-attribute:

```
<?xml-stylesheet title="Normal" href="normal-statement.xsl"
                 type="text/xsl" ?>
<?xml-stylesheet title="Summary" href="summary-statement.xsl"
                 type="text/xsl" alternate="yes" ?>
<?xml-stylesheet title="Detailed" href="detailed-statement.xsl"
                 type="text/xsl" alternate="yes" ?>
```

These different processing instructions enable the browser to choose the correct stylesheet according to the type of browser and whether it's displaying or printing the XML. Providing alternative stylesheets means that the browser offers the end-user a choice among the different available stylesheets.

However, this facility isn't supported in many current browsers, and certainly isn't supported in Internet Explorer 5.0 or 5.5, which you'll probably be using with MSXML ; you therefore need to provide different stylesheets for different situations in another way.

One option for using different stylesheets is to actually merge the different stylesheets into a single application, using a parameter to determine which one is actually used. With client-side processing, the downside of this option is that you may use more bandwidth and have less efficient processing because the stylesheets for all the views, not just the one that the end-user wants, is provided. However, once the stylesheet is downloaded, parsed, and compiled, it can be cached as an `XSLProcessor`, and you can use a script to add the relevant parameters to it.

A detailed discussion on how to combine several stylesheets and choose between them using a parameter is found in Chapter 13.

Another option, which can be simpler if you have to combine more than two stylesheets or there's a lot of overlap between the two you need to merge, is to use a script to determine which stylesheet should be used. For example, you could adapt the reSort function to take a second argument – the stylesheet that should be used, and pass this through to the transformXML function:

```
<script type="text/javascript">
    function reSort(sortBy, view) {
        params = new Array('sort-by', sortBy);
        transformXML('statement.xml', view, params);
    }
</script>
```

Creating Frames

Creating an XSLT application that uses independent frames is exactly the same as creating one without frames: Simply create a frameset in which each frame holds a separate XML document, and use xml-stylesheet processing instructions (or other techniques as discussed earlier) to determine what each frame contains.

Using frames becomes slightly more difficult when you want the frames to be linked to each other. HTML frame elements don't hold any content, so you can't put the text that you want to be displayed in each frame within the frame elements. Instead, you have to use a function to write HTML to the document held within the frame and call this function after the frameset loads. For example, if you have a menuFrame and a mainFrame you might have the following HTML:

```
<frameset onload="loadFrames()" cols="10%,*">
    <frame name="menuFrame" />
    <frame name="mainFrame" />
</frameset>
```

You can't write XML to the frame and hope it's transformed — MSXML only automatically transforms XML that is loaded from a file, it doesn't interpret content that is written to a document via a script.

The loadFrames function must generate HTML strings that can be written to the frames. Generating the HTML string to be written to the frame can be done in two ways. First, you can generate the string for each of the frames independently, using a controlling script in the frameset document. Using this method, the two frames are still pretty independent – separate processes and separate (perhaps different) stylesheet runs generate the HTML for each frame. For example, to fill the two frames, you could have a script that resembles the following:

```
function loadFrames() {
    transformXML('statement.xml', 'menu.xsl', false, menuFrame);
    transformXML('statement.xml', 'main.xsl', false, mainFrame);
}
```

The transformXML function is the same as the one defined earlier in the chapter. This method works successfully if you're happy having two separate processes to generate the HTML. However, situations may arise in which you want to generate both frames from the same process, especially if you want to have links between the two that use IDs generated using generate-id() to identify the anchors.

 Chapter 10 describes some alternatives to generating IDs with generate-id(), which enable you to create interdependent HTML pages from the same XML with different processes.

In this instance, you can use a two-step process: generate both sets of XHTML within the same XML document, and then use either DOM manipulation or further transformations to extract the relevant HTML for a particular frame. Whichever technique you use for the second transformation, the first transformation should produce something such as this:

```
<frames>
    <frame id="menuFrame">
        ... HTML for menuFrame ...
    </frame>
    <frame id="mainFrame">
        ... HTML for mainFrame ...
    </frame>
</frames>
```

This result needs to be captured within a DOMDocument that can be used as the source for further manipulation or transformation. The following snippet of JavaScript places the output of the transformation of statement.xml by statement.xsl in outputDOM.

```
processor = getProcessorFromFiles('statement.xml', 'statement.xsl');
if (processor) {
    outputDOM = new ActiveXObject('Msxml2.DOMDocument');
    processor.output = outputDOM;
    try {
        processor.transform();
        ...
    } catch (exception) {
```

```
        alert('Error transforming XML:\n' + exception.description);
    }
}
```

Then you can use the DOM to identify and extract the XML content for the frames that you want:

```
outputDOM.setProperty('SelectionLanguage', 'XPath');
menuFrame.document.open();
menuFrame.document.write(
    outputDOM.selectSingleNode('/frames/frame[@id = 'menuFrame']/html').xml);
menuFrame.document.close();
mainFrame.document.open();
mainFrame.document.write(
    outputDOM.selectSingleNode('/frames/frame[@id = 'mainFrame']/html').xml);
mainFrame.document.close();
```

 Getting the XML of a node, as in the preceding, means that the HTML is generated as XML: empty elements such as img and br are serialized as XML empty element tags (<br />) rather than simply as start tags as they are in HTML (<br>). Because all of the preceding uses Internet Explorer, this doesn't matter — IE can handle most XML-compliant HTML correctly.

Alternatively, you could use a separate stylesheet to extract the relevant content. The following simple stylesheet (get-frame-html.xsl) works on the preceding XML structure. It takes a parameter — the name of a frame — and gives the HTML for it:

```
<?xml version="1.0"?>
<xsl:stylesheet version="1.0"
             xmlns:xsl="http://www.w3.org/1999/XSL/Transform">

<xsl:output indent="yes" method="html" />
<xsl:param name="frame" />

<xsl:template match="frames">
    <xsl:copy-of select="frame[@id = $frame]/html" />
</xsl:template>

</xsl:stylesheet>
```

Using this technique, the following JavaScript code creates an XSLProcessor (frameProcessor) whose stylesheet is the preceding stylesheet and whose input is the output from the main transformation (held in outputDOM). If frameProcessor is generated without problems, it's first used to transform outputDOM with the $frame parameter set to the string 'menuFrame'. The output from this transformation is written to menuFrame. The frameProcessor is reset, and another transformation carried out, this time for the mainFrame.

```
frameXSLTDOM = getDOMFromFile('get-frame-html.xsl');
frameProcessor = getProcessorFromDOMs(outputDOM, frameXSLTDOM);
if (frameProcessor) {
    try {
        frameProcessor.addParameter('frame', 'menuFrame');
        frameProcessor.transform();
        menuFrame.document.open();
        menuFrame.document.write(frameProcessor.output);
        menuFrame.document.close();
        frameProcessor.reset();
        frameProcessor.addParameter('frame', 'mainFrame');
        frameProcessor.transform();
        mainFrame.document.open();
        mainFrame.document.write(frameProcessor.output);
        mainFrame.document.close();
    } catch (exception) {
        alert('Error transforming XML:\n' + exception.description);
    }
}
```

Creating Graphics with SVG

Much of this book concentrates on producing HTML and formatting objects from XML. But you may be also interested in other types of output such as in creating graphics, charts, and diagrams. Of course, most image formats are outside the reach of XML and XSLT because they are binary formats. However, Scalable Vector Graphics (SVG) is an XML vocabulary that enables you to define vector graphics in XML vocabulary. All you need is a stylesheet to take you from the XML you have to the SVG that you want.

This section is based on the SVG Candidate Recommendation dated 2nd November 2000. See http://www.w3.org/TR/SVG/ for the latest version. The code is based on that available with the Adobe SVG Viewer version 2.0. See http://www.adobe.com/svg/viewer/install/ for the latest version.

By now, you should find converting from XML to SVG fairly straightforward. Some things about SVG take a little processing — in particular there's lots of math involved to get all the numbers that you need to define the positions of lines and so on — but other than that it's just another XML format.

Difficulties arise, though, when you start doing client-side transformation of XML into SVG and you want the SVG to be displayed within your page. SVG is included within a page using the embed element in HTML; its usual format is as follows:

```
<embed name="svgDiagram" src="svgDiagram.svg" type="image/svg+xml"
       pluginspage="http://www.adobe.com/svg/viewer/install/" />
```

As you can see, the SVG is identified with the src attribute, which points to a separate file containing the SVG. The embed element has the same problems as the frame element: you can't just put the SVG that you want to display in its content — it has to be a separate file. Again, you need a script to load the SVG you want into the embed element.

Changing the SVG displayed by an embed element requires accessing the SVGDocument that it contains, which you can do with the getSVGDocument method:

```
svg = document.embeds['svgDiagram'].getSVGDocument();
```

The SVGDocument is a DOMDocument, but it's a different implementation from the DOMDocument in MSXML, which means that the two can't really interact with each other. It's not possible to simply copy the document element of the SVG DOMDocument that you've produced in a transformation into the SVGDocument of the embed element — trying to do so results in a type mismatch.

You can, however, work through the nodes in the SVG DOMDocument that you've created one by one, creating matching nodes within the SVGDocument of the embed element. Chris Bayes has made this easier for you with domtodom.js, a script that does exactly that, available from his website at http://www.bayes.co.uk/xml. This script includes the function domtodom, which takes two arguments: the SVG DOMDocument that you've produced from the transformation and the name of the embed element that you want to show it in. In the example, you can use it as follows:

```
domtodom(SVGDOM, 'svgDiagram');
```

This is all well and good, but there is a final obstacle to overcome: how to initiate the loading of the SVG into the embed elements. The problem is that the embed elements are replaced by the Adobe SVG Viewer plugin, which only loads well after the page is loaded. Therefore, you can't use the onload attribute as a trigger to load SVG into the embed elements in the same way as you can use it as a trigger to load HTML into frames.

Luckily, SVG provides a way around this because it includes scripting support, so it's possible to call functions that you define in your document from a piece of SVG that's loaded into the SVG Viewer. The following simple SVG document, for example, calls the `triggerSVGLoading` function when it is loaded:

```
<?xml version="1.0"?>
<svg onload="triggerSVGLoading();" />
```

The `triggerSVGLoading` function is called only when the SVG Viewer has been fully loaded; at that point, it is possible to copy any `SVGDOM` that you've created into the `embed` using the `domtodom` function:

```
function triggerSVGLoading() {
    domtodom(SVGDOM, 'svgDiagram');
}
```

Summary

In this chapter, I covered the basics of how to create dynamic client-side XSLT applications. You've also read a discussion about the way MSXML implementation works and how to use it to script the transformation of your XML, including how to pass parameters, change the XML that's viewed, and change the XSLT that's used to transform the XML. You've also examined two particular areas in more detail — creating framesets and creating SVG graphics within your pages.

Chapter 15

Server-Side Processing with Cocoon

IN THIS CHAPTER

- ◆ Running server-side transformations
- ◆ Changing stylesheet parameters
- ◆ Changing the data displayed with the stylesheet
- ◆ Changing the stylesheet used with the data
- ◆ Creating frames with server-side XSLT
- ◆ Creating SVG with server-side XSLT

IN CHAPTER 14, you learned how to use MSXML and JavaScript to create dynamic XML and XSLT-based applications on the client. This chapter addresses the same goals, but describes how to approach them if you're using server-side transformations. For this, we'll focus on Cocoon.

You can download and learn more about Cocoon from `http://xml.apache.org/cocoon`.

Cocoon is a server-side XML publishing framework that offers good support for XSLT transformations. Other server-side frameworks are available, most notably XSQL from Oracle. We're going to focus on Cocoon here because it's fairly popular and because it's based around files, rather than databases, making it easier to experiment with. Cocoon is a Java servlet that you run in conjunction with a servlet engine such as Apache Tomcat. This chapter does not describe how to install Cocoon; nor does it discuss some of its more sophisticated features. The following sections focus on how to use Cocoon with XSLT to create dynamic applications.

You can configure Cocoon to run with any Java-based XSLT processor by editing the `cocoon.properties` file, but it comes packaged with Xalan and runs with Xalan by default.

Processing XML with Cocoon

When Cocoon receives a request for an XML page, it inspects that page to see if it contains any processing instructions targeted at Cocoon. If it does, it uses these processing instructions to transform and format the page accordingly. For XSLT applications that use Cocoon, the most important processing instruction is as follows:

```
<?cocoon-process type="xslt"?>
```

Placing this processing instruction within an XML page instructs Cocoon to inspect the page for an `xml-stylesheet` processing instruction. If it finds one, Cocoon uses the stylesheet that it points to in order to transform the XML. For example, if you place the following code at the top of the XML source for a bank statement, the statement will be automatically transformed into HTML:

```
<?cocoon-process type="xslt"?>
<?xml-stylesheet type="text/xsl" href="statement.xsl"?>
```

Cocoon doesn't stop there, however. If you generate processing instructions in the result of the transformation, it uses those instructions to process that output and so on. This makes it very easy to chain transformations together.

Chapter 5 describes how to use Cocoon to chain multiple transformations together.

Formatting Output

The other type of processing instruction that Cocoon uses is the `cocoon-format` processing instruction, which specifies the type of serialization that Cocoon should use on the output.

Cocoon ignores the serialization instructions that you put on `xsl:output` — you have to use a `cocoon-format` processing instruction instead, and set things such as the DOCTYPE for that format within the `cocoon.properties` configuration file.

For example, if you want to produce XHTML with your stylesheet, you need to create a `cocoon-format` processing instruction indicating that the page is an XHTML page. You can create this process instruction with the `xsl:processing-instruction` element:

```
<xsl:processing-instruction name="cocoon-format">
   <xsl:text>type="text/xhtml"</xsl:text>
</xsl:processing-instruction>
```

This generates the following processing instruction in the output:

```
<?cocoon-format type="text/xhtml"?>
```

Cocoon interprets this processing instruction and uses the output formatter described in the `cocoon.properties` file to determine how to format the result of the transformation. The formatter controls things such as the DOCTYPE; whether the result is indented or not, and by how much if it is; and the media type used with it.

Generating PDF

One of the formatters available for Cocoon is an XSL-FO to PDF formatter; Cocoon uses FOP for this by default, but you can add any other Java-based formatter if you want.

You can find out more about FOP at `http://xml.apache.org/fop`.

If you are generating XSL-FO with your stylesheet, you should generate a processing instruction that tells Cocoon to format the result using PDF with the following XSLT:

```
<xsl:processing-instruction name="cocoon-format">
   <xsl:text>type="text/xslfo"</xsl:text>
</xsl:processing-instruction>
```

Internet Explorer uses the extension at the end of a URL to work out the content type of the data that it receives, rather than the content type indicated by the HTTP headers. To get around this, you can add a dummy parameter to the end of the URL you use to get the data:

```
statement.xml?format=.pdf
```

This has no impact on the way that Cocoon generates or formats the result (unless you declare and use a $format parameter within your stylesheet), only on the way that the browser interprets it.

Passing Parameters

Passing parameters into the stylesheets you use with Cocoon is simple: You add the name/value pairs to the end of the URL that you use to get the page (using the normal form-submission syntax). You first need to declare the parameter within your stylesheet using xsl:param. For example, to declare the $date parameter, you can use the following:

```
<xsl:param name="date" select="'today'" />
```

After that's set up, you can pass in the value '2001-05-21' by adding the name/value pair to the end of a URL that we use in a link:

```
<a href="statement.xml?date=2001-05-21">2001-05-21</a>
```

Alternatively, you can use a form to let the end user view particular dates. If you use a form, you need to make sure that the names of the fields in the form match the names of the parameters you use in your stylesheet (and, similarly, that the values of the field are the values that you expect for the parameter). For example, you could create a drop-down list of dates that looked like the following:

```
<form action="statement.xml">
   <select name="date">
      <option value="2001-05-21">21 May 2001</option>
      <option value="2001-05-22">22 May 2001</option>
      <option value="2001-05-23">23 May 2001</option>
      ...
   </select>
   ...
</form>
```

Here, the name attribute on the select element indicates the name of the parameter, and the value attribute of the option elements indicates the value that's actually submitted. When the end user selects the value 21 May 2001 from the drop-down list, the browser submits the desired URL:

```
statement.xml?date=2001-05-21
```

When you need to pass more than one parameter, the name/value pairs in the submitting URL need to be separated with ampersand (&) signs. For example, to pass in both a $date parameter with the value '2001-05-21' and a $type parameter with the value 'DD', you need the following URL:

```
statement.xml?date=2001-05-21&type=DD
```

If you're using a form to submit the different values, this will be done automatically. If you write the URL by hand in some HTML (including the HTML that you generate using your stylesheet), you will need to escape the ampersand, as usual:

```
<a href="statement.xml?date=2001-05-21&amp;type=DD">...</a>
```

Dynamic Applications

The last section described how Cocoon operates at a basic level. This section explains how to take advantage of it to create dynamic applications. These applications are the same as those covered in Chapter 14, but here we'll use server-side transformation, rather than client-side transformation, to get the effect that we're after.

Changing Parameters

In Chapter 14, you sorted by different columns within a table to experiment with client-side transformations. You used an example that displayed a table of transactions that could be sorted by date, by amount, by transaction type, and so on.

As before, you need to equip the stylesheet with the capability to accept and use a parameter to determine by which column to sort. You do that by declaring a $sort-by parameter, which by default is set to the string 'date':

```
<xsl:param name="sort-by" select="'date'" />
```

You can sort by this parameter by identifying the attribute that has the same name as the $sort-by parameter. You select this attribute within the select attribute of an xsl:for-each instruction that generates the rows:

```
<xsl:for-each select="transaction">
   <xsl:sort select="@*[name() = $sort-by]" />
   <tr>
      <td><xsl:value-of select="@date" /></td>
      <td><xsl:value-of select="@type" /></td>
      <td><xsl:value-of select="@amount" /></td>
   </tr>
</xsl:for-each>
```

This part of the stylesheet is exactly the same as the XSLT that you wrote for the client-side application. The server-side application differs in the work that you have to do in passing a new parameter to the stylesheet. Whereas with MSXML you need to use a (relatively complicated) script, with Cocoon you can just create links that set the parameter value via the URL that's used to get the next view on the XML.

You want to enable the end user to click on the headers of each column in the table to sort by that column, so you create a header for the table that contains links to the same page, but with different parameters:

```
<thead>
   <tr>
      <th><a href="?sort-by=date">Date</a></th>
      <th><a href="?sort-by=type">Type</a></th>
      <th><a href="?sort-by=amount">Amount</a></th>
   </tr>
</thead>
```

If you don't specify the page to which you link, the browser uses the same basic URL as before, but with different parameters. Similarly, if you leave the `action` attribute of the `form` element blank, it submits the form to the same basic URL. This means that the HTML and, more important, the stylesheet, don't have the URL of the XML source document hard-coded, which makes it more flexible for use with other documents. You should avoid using filenames in your stylesheet if possible.

One big drawback of this server-side model is that the only kind of value that a parameter can have is a string. In the last chapter, you learned how to add more complicated information about a sort, such as allowing sorts on several columns, or in different (ascending or descending) orders using node set parameters, rather than string parameters. This isn't possible with Cocoon, as there is no way to pass a node set value in as a parameter. Instead, you have to use strings for everything, and parse them to get the values that you want, or pass in a URL that you can use with the `document()` function to access the XML that you're after.

You could create XML documents that you access later, when passed their filename through a parameter, with the extension elements available for creating multiple output documents, which are discussed in Chapter 19.

Choosing the Data to View

A second type of common dynamic application uses the same stylesheet on different documents, changing the XML source document that's being used with the XSLT stylesheet. For example, you might have separate statement documents and want to use the same XSLT stylesheet to transform them into HTML. You have two ways of doing this with server-side transformation in Cocoon:

◆ Have `xml-stylesheet` processing instructions in each of the XML files that you want to access, each of which points to the same stylesheet; to move between the different XML source files, simply open the relevant one.

◆ Pass the URL of the XML file that you want to use as a parameter to the XSLT stylesheet, using the techniques discussed in the previous section; the XSLT stylesheet can open this file and apply templates to it using the `document()` function.

Which option you choose depends on how willing you are to fix the stylesheet that's used with a particular document. The advantage of the latter option is that it enables you to use several stylesheets with the same XML document.

TIP If you're using the second option, it doesn't matter to which source XML the stylesheet is applied. You could start with any of the documents, or start with a dummy document that references the stylesheet. What you can't do using Cocoon is use the stylesheet on itself; Cocoon doesn't recognize stylesheets as XML files in this way.

Indicating Which Stylesheet to Use

The basic way to indicate which stylesheet should be used with an XML document is to use an `xml-stylesheet` processing instruction such as the following:

```
<?xml-stylesheet type="text/xsl" href="statement.xsl"?>
```

The W3C Recommendation *"Associating Style Sheets with XML Documents"* (`http://www.w3.org/TR/xml-stylesheet`) indicates that you can put several of these processing instructions in your XML document. The `media` pseudo-attribute indicates the kind of medium for which you're generating information with the transformation.

According to the Recommendation, the intended values for the `media` pseudo-attribute are things such as `screen`, `handheld`, and `print` — the same values recognized in the `media` attribute of the `link` element in HTML. However, Cocoon goes further than that by specifying more specific media, which enables you to specify different stylesheets for different types of browser:

```
<?xml-stylesheet title="MSIE version" href="statement.msie.xsl"
                 type="text/xsl" media="explorer" ?>
<?xml-stylesheet title="Netscape version" href="statement.ns.xsl"
                 type="text/xsl" media="netscape" ?>
<?xml-stylesheet title="WAP version" href="statement.wap.xsl"
                 type="text/xsl" media="wap" ?>
```

Being able to do this is very helpful. The type of user agent that's used enables you to distinguish between different devices (for example, WAP or handheld MSIE). In addition, given the different capabilities of different browsers, it helps you to tailor the output so that it is displayed properly and uses the latest functionality available for whichever browser a visitor uses to access your pages. You can add to the list of user agents that Cocoon recognizes by editing the cocoon.properties file.

Note, however, that Cocoon doesn't support users choosing between alternative stylesheets for a single user agent. According to the Recommendation, you can provide alternative stylesheets for a single medium with the alternate pseudo-attribute:

```
<?xml-stylesheet title="Normal" href="normal-statement.xsl"
                 type="text/xsl" ?>
<?xml-stylesheet title="Summary" href="summary-statement.xsl"
                 type="text/xsl" alternate="yes" ?>
<?xml-stylesheet title="Detailed" href="detailed-statement.xsl"
                 type="text/xsl" alternate="yes" ?>
```

Cocoon uses the last xml-stylesheet processing instruction that it encounters, no matter what the alternate pseudo-attribute is set to.

If you want to allow users to choose which view to use for a particular document, you can merge the different stylesheets into a single application and use a parameter to determine which one is actually used. This is a reasonable option with server-side processing because the publishing framework that you use (whether it's Cocoon or another framework) will generally cache both stylesheets and the result of their transformation to reduce the overall processing that the framework carries out.

Chapter 13 describes how to combine several stylesheets and choose between them using a parameter.

Cocoon uses processing instructions to determine which stylesheet to use. These processing instructions are hard-wired into the XML documents, so a single document can be processed only by a single stylesheet. However, you can use a controlling stylesheet to manage which stylesheet is used by creating a copy of the source XML that contains the desired processing instructions.

The controlling stylesheet needs to accept a single parameter to indicate which stylesheet should be used. This could be the name of the stylesheet file, or a keyword that indicates it (the latter being particularly useful if you have multiple stylesheets for different user agents):

```
<xsl:param name="view" select="'default.xsl'" />
```

The stylesheet needs to create an XML file that holds the same data as the XML source document that's being transformed with the controller stylesheet. This XML file should contain an `xml-stylesheet` processing instruction that points to the stylesheet indicated by the parameter, and one that tells Cocoon to process the result of the transformation by the controller using XSLT. The template matching the document element should therefore look like the following:

```
<xsl:template match="/*">
   <!-- add processing instructions -->
   <xsl:processing-instruction name="cocoon-process">
      <xsl:text>type="xslt"</xsl:text>
   </xsl:processing-instruction>
   <xsl:processing-instruction name="xml-stylesheet">
      <xsl:text>type="text/xsl" href="</xsl:text>
      <xsl:value-of select="$view" />"<xsl:text />
   </xsl:processing-instruction>
   <!-- copy data -->
   <xsl:copy-of select="." />
</xsl:template>
```

 This template discards any existing comments or processing instructions outside the document element.

The XML pages themselves need to point to this controlling template, rather than any individual stylesheet. To change the stylesheet used to view the page, change the value of the parameter passed to the controller stylesheet. For example, you could use the following URL to use `summary.xsl` on the `statement.xml` file:

```
statement.xml?view=default.xsl
```

Any additional parameters that you pass using the URL will be available to all the stylesheets that you use during the transformation, so you can use this method even if the individual stylesheets have their own parameters, as long as they're not called $view.

Creating Frames

If the frames in a frameset that you generate with XSLT are independent of one another, each one can be generated through a separate process. Create the frameset (either dynamically or using a static version), and within it point to the XML document that holds the data to be displayed within the frame. Cocoon will use the xml-stylesheet processing instructions within each XML document to generate the HTML to be displayed in each frame.

The difficulty with using frames is apparent when the content of the various frames are based on the same source XML. HTML frame elements access the HTML to be displayed by referencing a separate document, rather than holding it as content. Therefore, you cannot use a single process to generate the content of the separate frames all at once.

With client-side processing, you have to write a script to manage this, but with server-side processing you can again use parameters and a controlling stylesheet to determine which frame should be created as a result of the request. The controlling stylesheet should generate different HTML according to the frame that's being created. For this, you need a parameter to hold the identity of the frame:

```
<xsl:param name="frame" select="'top'" />
```

The default ('top') indicates that the frameset should be generated. The frames within the frameset should reference the same source XML document, but pass different values for the $frame parameter into Cocoon:

```
<xsl:template match="/*">
   <xsl:choose>
      <xsl:when test="$frame = 'top'">
         <frameset cols="10%,*">
            <frame name="menuFrame" src="?frame=menu" />
            <frame name="mainFrame" src="?frame=main" />
         </frameset>
      </xsl:when>
      <xsl:otherwise>
         ...
      </xsl:otherwise>
   </xsl:choose>
</xsl:template>
```

When the frame is something other than 'top', the controller stylesheet needs to reroute the processing to a different stylesheet as described in the last section, by creating the relevant processing instructions and copying the content of the XML source document:

```
<xsl:template match="/*">
   <xsl:choose>
      <xsl:when test="$frame = 'top'">
         ...
      </xsl:when>
      <xsl:otherwise>
         <!-- add processing instructions -->
         <xsl:processing-instruction name="cocoon-process">
            <xsl:text>type="xslt"</xsl:text>
         </xsl:processing-instruction>
         <xsl:processing-instruction name="xml-stylesheet">
            <xsl:text>type="text/xsl" href="</xsl:text>
            <xsl:value-of select="$frame" />.xsl"<xsl:text />
         </xsl:processing-instruction>
         <!-- copy data -->
         <xsl:copy-of select="." />
      </xsl:otherwise>
   </xsl:choose>
</xsl:template>
```

Tackling frames in this way results in several separate transformations of the same source XML to get the content. There are pitfalls to this approach; in particular, you cannot use generate-id() to create links between content in different frames because the IDs generated by different runs over the source XML may be different. Unfortunately, there's no way to avoid this with Cocoon, unless you use extension elements to create physical files.

Chapter 20 describes these extension elements and how to use them.

Creating Graphics with SVG

You were introduced to Scalable Vector Graphics (SVG) in Chapter 14 as a way of creating graphics such as charts and diagrams. Client-side transformations have trouble with SVG because of the way in which SVG is embedded into HTML documents using embed elements. HTML embed elements indicate the SVG source by referring to it as a separate document; the SVG itself is not embedded within the HTML document.

With server-side transformation, on the other hand, you can use techniques similar to those just described to deal with frames in order to embed SVG. You can use the parameters passed to a single stylesheet to determine whether to generate SVG or not, or redirect the request to a different stylesheet to generate the SVG.

As before, the stylesheet needs to be passed a parameter that indicates what kind of content to generate:

```
<xsl:param name="output" select="'.html'" />
```

A controlling stylesheet then needs to direct processing based on this parameter. The following example uses templates with different modes within the same stylesheet to generate the HTML and the SVG output, rather than redirect Cocoon to use separate stylesheets:

```
<xsl:template match="/">
   <xsl:choose>
      <xsl:when test="$output = '.html'">
         <xsl:apply-templates mode="html" />
      </xsl:when>
      <xsl:when test="$output = '.svg'">
         <xsl:apply-templates mode="svg" />
      </xsl:when>
   </xsl:choose>
</xsl:template>
```

The html-mode template needs to generate the HTML for the page, including the embed element that points to the same data, this time transformed with the $output parameter set to 'svg':

```
<xsl:template match="/*" mode="html">
   <html>
     <head>...</head>
     <body>
        ...
        <embed name="svgDiagram" src="?output=.svg" type="image/svg+xml"
               pluginspage="http://www.adobe.com/svg/viewer/install/" />
        ...
     </body>
   </html>
</xsl:template>
```

A slight trick is used in the preceding example to ensure that Internet Explorer displays the embedded SVG properly; namely, it uses '.svg' as the value of the $output parameter for generating SVG. Internet Explorer has problems using the media type of auto-generated SVG, just as it does with auto-generated PDF. Adding .svg at the end of the URL ensures that it interprets it as SVG.

The svg-mode template needs to generate the SVG for the page. This is relatively straightforward (well, as long as generating the SVG from your XML is straightforward). However, there is one thing to watch out for — remember that you need to use a cocoon-format processing instruction to tell Cocoon to output the result as SVG; otherwise, Cocoon assumes that it's HTML (or whatever you've set as the default formatter) and adds an HTML DOCTYPE to the result. The template should therefore look something like the following:

```
<xsl:template match="/*" mode="svg">
   <xsl:processing-instruction name="cocoon-format">
      <xsl:text>type="image/svg+xml"</xsl:text>
   </xsl:processing-instruction>
   <svg ...>
      ...
   </svg>
</xsl:template>
```

You may need to check the cocoon.properties file to make sure that the image/svg+xml formatter is associated with the correct public and system DOCTYPE for SVG.

Summary

This chapter described how to approach building dynamic server-side XSLT applications with Cocoon. You learned three processing instructions that Cocoon uses to determine how to transform and output a page:

- xml-stylesheet
- cocoon-process
- cocoon-format

You also learned how to pass parameters within a URL, both within links and using forms, and how you can use these to change the look of a page. Finally, you examined several examples of using a controlling stylesheet to redirect the processing of a page to a different stylesheet, or to generate frames or SVG dynamically.

Part IV

Finalizing Your Stylesheet

Chapter 16

Controlling Output

IN THIS CHAPTER

◆ Associating DTDs with output

◆ Controlling whitespace and indentation

◆ Using entities and CDATA sections

◆ Limiting namespace declarations

THEORETICALLY, XSLT WORKS on the abstract structure of documents: It operates over a source tree and produces a result tree. In practice, the majority of transformations generate a file from the result tree — outputting it in a serialization that can be read by the next step in the process.

Usually, the next step in the process is another XML application. As long as the serialization accurately reflects the result tree, you shouldn't really care what it looks like. However, there are several contexts in which you might care:

◆ The next step in the process is someone viewing the result

◆ You want the output to be readable to help you to debug it

◆ You need to limit the size of the output

◆ You're using a non-conformant browser that needs to receive HTML in a certain way

This chapter examines the degree of control that XSLT gives you over various aspects of your output. There are other ways of controlling the way the result tree is output; in particular, you may be able to write your own serializers that plug into the XSLT processor that you use, but I'm not going to go into those in any detail here. You should consult the documentation for your XSLT processor to discover how to use their output formatters.

This chapter focuses on four goals in particular: adding DTD information, managing whitespace, controlling escaping with entities and CDATA sections, and limiting the namespace declarations that are used in your output.

Adding DTD Information

Generally, DTDs are useful for five reasons:

- ◆ To identify the type of your document
- ◆ To validate the elements and attributes that it contains
- ◆ To assign default attribute values
- ◆ To designate a particular attribute as an ID attribute
- ◆ To define entities that you use in the rest of the document

Associating a DTD to the output doesn't mean that the XSLT processor automatically checks the XML you create to make sure that it's valid. You have to manage that yourself.

Referring to External DTDs

If the DTD that you want to associate your output with already exists, you can use a couple of attributes on `xsl:output` to add a DOCTYPE declaration to your output: `doctype-system` to specify the location of the DTD, and `doctype-public` to specify the public identifier for the DTD. For example, to add the following DOCTYPE declaration to your output (here creating SVG):

```
<!DOCTYPE svg PUBLIC "-//W3C//DTD SVG 20001102//EN"
                     "DTD/svg-20001102.dtd">
```

you would use the following `xsl:output` element in your stylesheet:

```
<xsl:output doctype-system="DTD/svg-20001102.dtd"
        doctype-public="-//W3C/DTD SVG 20001102//EN" />
```

The XSLT processor automatically uses the name of the document element in your result tree as the name used in the DOCTYPE declaration.

Technically, it's possible to use XSLT to create non-well-formed XML documents, by generating two elements that are children of the root node in the result tree. If you use a `doctype-system` attribute, XSLT processors may generate an error or output a DOCTYPE declaration that uses the first of the top-level elements in the document, but you should avoid adding DTD information in these cases as the result will be neither a well-formed XML document (which has only one top-level element) nor a well-formed external parsed entity (which cannot have a DOCTYPE declaration).

Similarly, if you only specify the `doctype-system` attribute:

```
<xsl:output doctype-system="DTD/svg-20001102.dtd" />
```

the processor will produce a system DOCTYPE declaration:

```
<!DOCTYPE svg SYSTEM "DTD/svg-20001102.dtd">
```

If you only specify a `public-system` attribute, it will be ignored — DOCTYPE declarations in XML have to specify both.

Building Internal DTDs

On rare occasions, you may want to build an internal DTD. The most common reason for doing this is to generate entity declarations so that you can use external XML entities or general entities within your input. Generating an entity declaration enables you to use them within the generated document; you'll learn how you do that in the section "Using Entities and CDATA Sections" later in this chapter.

XSLT has no built-in way of creating an internal DTD, but some XSLT processors have extension elements that support the creation of DTDs, which are described in Chapter 19.

DTDs use a different syntax from the normal XML syntax of elements and attributes, but less-than signs, ampersands, and so on, are still significant characters. The only way to output an unescaped less-than sign using XSLT is by disabling output escaping.

Normally, an XSLT processor will escape the contents of a text node to ensure that the output it generates is well-formed XML. This involves escaping less-than signs and ampersands wherever they are, and escaping greater-than signs if they occur in the sequence]]>. When you disable output escaping, the processor outputs the text exactly as it is, which makes it very easy to create non-well-formed XML. Normally, generating non-well-formed XML is something that you want to avoid, but here it's precisely what you want to do.

XSLT processors are not obliged to support disabling of output escaping, so using it can limit the portability of your stylesheets.

Because entities only work in XML, we'll use an XML example, rather than HTML — declaring entities with HTML, even with XHTML, won't work, because browsers usually don't implement that part of HTML. The sample *output* that you're aiming for looks like the following, with external entities referring to the separate XML documents that make up the book:

```
<?xml version="1.0"?>
<!DOCTYPE book PUBLIC '-//OASIS//DTD DocBook V3.1//EN'
                      'DTD/DocBook.dtd' [
<!ENTITY partI SYSTEM 'partI.xml'>
...
]>
<book>
   <title>Adventures with Lego</title>
   ...
   &partI;
   ...
</book>
```

You can create the book element and its content using the usual facilities in XSLT. However, before you do that, you need to generate the internal DTD as a text node with output escaping disabled. You can do this by using an xsl:text element, setting the value of its disable-output-escaping attribute to yes:

```
<xsl:text disable-output-escaping="yes">
&lt;!DOCTYPE book PUBLIC '-//OASIS//DTD DocBook V3.1//EN'
                      'DTD/DocBook.dtd' [
&lt;!ENTITY partI SYSTEM 'partI.xml'>
...
]>
</xsl:text>
```

The less-than signs that are used in the internal DTD need to be escaped in the stylesheet, either with entities (as shown in the preceding example) or by using a CDATA section:

```
<xsl:text disable-output-escaping="yes">
<![CDATA[
<!DOCTYPE book PUBLIC '-//OASIS//DTD DocBook V3.1//EN'
                      'DTD/DocBook.dtd' [
<!ENTITY partI SYSTEM 'partI.xml'>
...
]>
]]>
</xsl:text>
```

Make sure that you don't use `xsl:output` to create a DOCTYPE declaration if you are generating a DTD using the preceding technique, or you'll end up with two DOCTYPE declarations.

Managing Whitespace

When you first use XSLT, it often seems as though whitespace is added almost at random to the output that you're generating. This section explains where whitespace can come from and where it can't, and how to remove and add it as desired.

Managing Source Whitespace

The first source of whitespace in your document is from the source XML that you're processing. As an example, look at the following XML:

```
<statement>
   <custInfo>
      <name><title>Mr</title> <surname>Anderson</surname></name>
      <address>
         303 Heart of the City Hotel
         ...
      </address>
   </custInfo>
   ...
</statement>
```

When the XSLT processor parses this XML, it creates a source node tree for the document. Any whitespace that you use in the document is included in this node tree. Figure 16-1 shows what the node tree looks like, with this whitespace included.

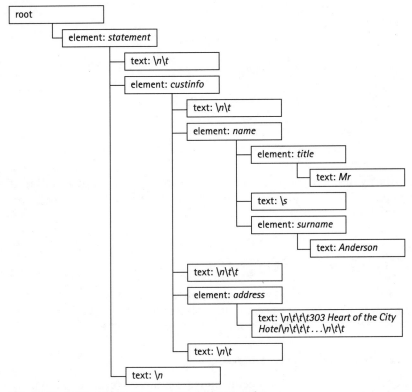

Figure 16-1: Example node tree, showing text nodes

 MSXML3 strips all whitespace from the source node tree by default, so parsing the preceding XML with MSXML would result in the node tree shown in Figure 16-2 instead. You can force MSXML not to do this by setting the `preserveWhiteSpace` property on the source DOM to true before loading the XML file as follows:

```
DOM = new
        ActiveXObject('Msxml2.FreeThreadedDOMDocument');
DOM.preserveWhiteSpace = true;
DOM.load(File);
```

STRIPPING WHITESPACE-ONLY TEXT NODES

As you can see in Figure 16-1, there are text nodes for *all* the text included in the document, not just text that specifies data within the XML. Most of the text nodes are simply indentation and formatting for the XML. These nodes contain whitespace and nothing but whitespace; they're known as *whitespace-only text nodes*.

Whitespace in XML and XSLT includes spaces, tabs, line feeds and carriage returns — it doesn't include nonbreaking spaces.

Processing XSLT using the push method, in which you apply templates to everything, results in these whitespace-only text nodes getting processed. Usually they're processed by the built-in template for text nodes, which adds the value of the text node to the result, and which gives you unexpected whitespace in your output. In addition, they are taken into account when you look at the position of a node, which means that numbering based on the `position()` function can sometimes generate non-adjacent numbers.

You can get around this by stripping these whitespace-only text nodes from the tree using the `xsl:strip-space` element. The `xsl:strip-space` element is declared at the top level of the stylesheet and tells the processor to ignore any whitespace-only text within certain elements, which omits them from the node tree. Whitespace is stripped from elements that are matched by one of the name tests given within the `elements` attribute. You can use it to strip whitespace-only text nodes throughout the document:

```
<xsl:strip-space elements="*" />
```

With this declaration in place, parsing the same XML document will create a node tree that looks like the one shown in Figure 16-2.

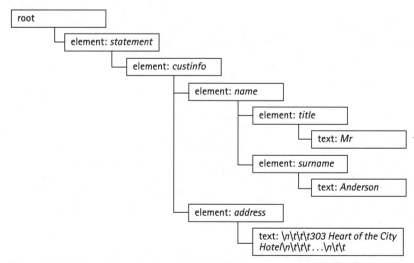

Figure 16-2: Example node tree, with all whitespace-only text nodes stripped

TIP Even if you use a pull method and never process whitespace-only text nodes, it's still worthwhile to strip them from the document. It reduces the size of the source node tree and thus the memory that it uses.

PRESERVING WHITESPACE

You may notice one problem with the node tree shown in Figure 16-2; namely, the space that separates the `title` and `surname` elements within the `name` element has been stripped. That space was included in the first place so that you could use the value of the `name` element to generate a formatted name. With

```
<name><title>Mr</title> <surname>Anderson</surname></name>
```

you can simply get the value of the `name` element to generate the text `'Mr Anderson'`, but with whitespace stripped, the value is `'MrAnderson'`. There are three ways around this. The first is to indicate the exception within the stylesheet using `xsl:preserve-space`:

```
<xsl:preserve-space elements="name" />
```

With this method, you have to specify each of the elements within which you want to preserve whitespace. If the portions of the input for which you want to preserve whitespace can be better defined as everything-under-this-element, then you should use `xml:space` instead. `xml:space` is an XML attribute that defines the way in which spaces should be interpreted — if you give it the value 'preserve', then any whitespace-only text nodes within that entire section of the document will be preserved, unless there is an overriding `xml:space` equal to 'default' lower down. For example, you could keep whitespace-only text nodes within the entire customer information section of the bank statement XML with the following:

```
<custInfo xml:space="preserve">
   ...
</custInfo>
```

A final method, if you only want particular bits of whitespace to be preserved, is to use a character other than those that are interpreted as whitespace. Again, this involves changing the source XML. In this example, you could use a nonbreaking space character to indicate the significant space, which would allow you to format the `name` element as follows:

```
<name>
   <title>Mr</title> <surname>Anderson</surname>
</name>
```

STRIPPING WHITESPACE IN VALUES

The second type of whitespace that you might want to get rid of is whitespace within the values of attributes or elements. In this example, there is a lot of whitespace within the value of the `address` element, but it's mixed in with non-whitespace characters, so this whitespace can't be stripped using `xsl:strip-space`. With `\n` meaning a new line, and `\t` a tab, the `address` element value is as follows:

```
\n\t\t\t303 Heart of the City Hotel\n\t\t\t...\n\t\t
```

You can use the `normalize-space()` function to get rid of this whitespace. The `normalize-space()` function changes all new lines and tabs into spaces, strips any leading or trailing whitespace, and converts contiguous sequences of whitespace into a single space. If you normalized space within the `address` element value, you would get the following:

```
303 Heart of the City Hotel ...
```

Take care not to eliminate whitespace that is actually significant when you do this. The following example eliminates the new lines that indicate the lines of the address along with the indentation. If you needed those new lines, you might be better off just getting rid of tabs using the `translate()` function:

```
translate(address, '&#x9;', '')
```

Managing Stylesheet Whitespace

Technically, whitespace-only text nodes in the stylesheet are stripped in a similar way to those in the source XML, except that the `xsl:strip-space` and `xsl:preserve-space` elements don't apply — instead, the only element within which whitespace-only text nodes are preserved is `xsl:text`.

What this means in practice is that you can put whitespace wherever you want in your stylesheet, and you can indent your XSLT instructions to your heart's content without worrying about the whitespace being added to the output. Whitespace will only be output into the result tree if it's part of some text that includes non-whitespace characters. If you specifically want to include a bit of whitespace in your output, such as a space or a new-line character, you need to put it within an `xsl:text` element.

Chapter 17 gives some tips about when you do and don't need to use `xsl:text` elements.

Because whitespace in the stylesheet is mostly ignored, you need a way of getting indentation in the output so that the output is readable. The best way of controlling this is to add an `xsl:output` element with an indent attribute equal to 'yes':

```
<xsl:output indent="yes" />
```

If you're outputting HTML (this is, using the HTML output method), the processor will indent it automatically. You can turn this indentation off using the `indent` attribute set to no instead.

Telling the processor to indent your output means that it is free to add whitespace-only text nodes between tags. Essentially, this means that if you were to read in the output again, with `xsl:strip-space` stripping all whitespace-only text nodes, you'd get the same source tree you had as a result tree. The XSLT processor won't add whitespace to text nodes that you create.

Some processors have extension attributes that give you extra control over the indentation that they use in the output. Chapter 19 covers these extension attributes in detail.

You can also use `xml:space` within the XSLT stylesheet to get precisely the indentation that you want for a bit of code, by setting it to `preserve` as you would in the source XML.

Using Entities and CDATA Sections

Entities and CDATA sections both relate to the *physical* structure of an XML document, rather than its *logical* structure. Whether you use entities or CDATA sections within your XML document makes no difference to the XSLT processor — it still sees the same XML document. For example, the following lines of XML look exactly the same to an XSLT processor:

```
<email>Jeni Tennison &lt;mail@jenitennison.com></email>
<email><![CDATA[Jeni Tennison <mail@jenitennison.com>]]></email>
<email>Jeni&#x20;Tennison&#x20;&lt;mail@jenitennison.com></email>
```

An XSLT processor views all of these as an `email` element with a value of 'Jeni Tennison <mail@jenitennison.com>'. Similarly, you can use CDATA sections and entities within the stylesheet as much as you want to make it more readable and more reusable, but they are invisible to the XSLT processor and won't change what it outputs.

CDATA Sections Holding HTML

It's not unusual to see XML documents holding snippets of HTML within CDATA sections, as shown in the following:

```
<logo><![CDATA[<img src="logo.jpg">]]></logo>
```

Generally, XML language designers develop this kind of XML structure when they're taking HTML from a legacy database. XSLT processors can't see any structure in these snippets. As far as an XSLT processor is concerned, the preceding code is exactly the same as the following; the content of the logo element is just a string to the XSLT processor:

```
<logo>&lt;img src="logo.jpg"></logo>
```

You should avoid dealing with this kind of structure in a stylesheet and instead apply some processing earlier in the application so that the XML that the stylesheet works on is well-formed XML such as the following:

```
<logo><img src="logo.jpg" /></logo>
```

If that's not possible, you have to disable output escaping to output the serialized img element in the HTML you're generating. If you disable output escaping, the processor won't do its usual escaping of characters within the text, and instead output it as is. To output the serialized img element into HTML, you can use the disable-output-escaping attribute on xsl:value-of:

```
<xsl:value-of select="logo" disable-output-escaping="yes" />
```

You can't use this to generate XML or XHTML, as the result will be non-well-formed.

Using Entities in the Stylesheet

XSLT doesn't define any entities for its own use, so the only entities that it recognizes are the ones built into XML: &, <, >, ', and ". If you want to use any others, you need to define them within the DTD you use for your stylesheet, either internally or externally.

For example, you can make the entity   available within your stylesheet by adding an internal DTD with the following:

```
<?xml version="1.0"?>
<!DOCTYPE xsl:stylesheet [
<!ENTITY nbsp ' '>
]>
<xsl:stylesheet version="1.0"
                xmlns:xsl="http://www.w3.org/1999/XSL/Transform">
...
</xsl:stylesheet>
```

If you're dealing with a lot of characters that need entity definitions, you might find it useful to include the entities from XHTML by defining and using external parameter entities that point to those entity files within the DTD for the stylesheet:

```
<!ENTITY % lat1 SYSTEM 'xhtml-lat1.ent'>
%lat1;
<!ENTITY % symbol SYSTEM 'xhtml-symbol.ent'>
%symbol;
<!ENTITY % special SYSTEM 'xhtml-special.ent'>
%special;
```

These files are available as part of the XHTML1.0 Recommendation at http://www.w3.org/TR/xhtml1.

Outputting Character and Entity References

XSLT processors use character references to escape characters that can't be represented with the character encoding that you're using in the output. For example, ISO-8859-1 can cope with characters up to #xFF (#255) only — any characters that you use in your output with a numeric value above this will be output as character references.

The following example illustrates this further by generating some XSL-FO for a bulleted list. In the stylesheet, you could generate a bullet character using the decimal character reference • as follows:

```
<fo:list-item-label>
   <fo:block>&#8226;</fo:block>
</fo:list-item-label>
```

If you generate some XML using the UTF-8 character encoding (which can cope with any Unicode character) and look at the output in a Unicode-aware editor, the result looks like the following:

```
<fo:list-item-label>
   <fo:block>•</fo:block>
</fo:list-item-label>
```

If you view it in an editor that isn't Unicode-aware, the editor tries to interpret the bytes that make up the UTF-8 character as bytes for the type of encoding that it understands, such as ISO-8859-1 characters. In my editor, I see three characters instead:

```
<fo:list-item-label>
   <fo:block>♦¤¢</fo:block>
</fo:list-item-label>
```

Instead, you can set the output encoding to ISO-8859-1, using `xsl:output` as follows:

```
<xsl:output encoding="ISO-8859-1" />
```

The bullet character isn't part of ISO-8859-1, so it can't be literally output. Instead, it's output as a character reference, either decimal or hexadecimal:

```
<fo:list-item-label>
   <fo:block>&#x227A;</fo:block>
</fo:list-item-label>
```

If you're outputting using the HTML output method, rather than the XML output method, you may find that your XSLT processor uses entity references, rather than character references, for characters that have entities listed for them in HTML. The bullet character, for example, might be given as `&bull;`.

Some XSLT processors give you control over what type of character reference is generated, whether decimal or hexadecimal; or even further control, enabling you to use entity references in place of character references. These topics are covered in Chapter 19.

To make your output more readable for debugging, you might want to use an entity reference within your XML instead; generating the following output, for example:

```
<fo:list-item-label>
   <fo:block>&bullet;</fo:block>
</fo:list-item-label>
```

To do this, you need to declare the entity in a DTD, either externally or internally, as described earlier in this chapter, in the section "Adding DTD Information". You then need to create the entity reference. The entity reference uses an ampersand (&) character, which the XSLT processor would normally escape when outputting it in text. You need to disable this output escaping to generate the value that you want, using the `disable-output-escaping` attribute on `xsl:text`:

```
<fo:list-item-label>
   <fo:block>
      <xsl:text disable-output-escaping="yes">&amp;bullet;</xsl:text>
   </fo:block>
</fo:list-item-label>
```

You can use the same approach to generate entity references for external entities, such as separate documents to which you want to refer. If you are using a lot of entities, or using them repeatedly, you can make your stylesheet more readable by declaring entities for the XML that generates the entity reference. In this example, you could declare a `&bullet;` entity in your stylesheet's DTD to hold the `xsl:text` element that generates the `&bullet;` entity reference in the result, as follows:

```
<!ENTITY bullet
         '<xsl:text disable-output-escaping="yes">&amp;bullet;</xsl:text>' >
```

With this entity definition in your stylesheet, wherever you use the entity reference `&bullet;` in the content of an element in your stylesheet, you will create an entity reference `&bullet;` in the result. The preceding example is therefore simplified to the following code:

```
<fo:list-item-label>
   <fo:block>&bullet;</fo:block>
</fo:list-item-label>
```

You cannot disable output escaping in the content of an attribute that you create with XSLT. If you need to use an entity reference in an attribute, then you must generate the entire start tag and end tag of the element by writing the output you want as text, with output escaping disabled.

Outputting CDATA Sections

The point of CDATA sections is that they can contain less-than signs and ampersands without those characters having to be escaped with entity references. This is particularly helpful when you have sections of code or serialized XML within an XML document. For example, in an XHTML page, you might have the following:

```
<p>
   Here is an identity template:
</p>
<pre>
&lt;xsl:template match="@*|node()">
   &lt;xsl:copy>
      &lt;xsl:apply-templates select="@*|node()" />
   &lt;/xsl:copy>
&lt;/xsl:template>
</pre>
```

Rather than have the individual less-than signs escaped with <, you can wrap the entire content of the pre element in a CDATA section:

```
<p>
   Here is the identity template:
</p>
<pre><![CDATA[
<xsl:template match="@*|node()">
   <xsl:copy>
      <xsl:apply-templates select="@*|node()" />
   </xsl:copy>
</xsl:template>
]]></pre>
```

You can instruct an XSLT processor to use a CDATA section for the text nodes in particular elements using the cdata-section-elements attribute on xsl:output. If you were outputting the preceding XHTML from a stylesheet, you could tell the XSLT processor to use a CDATA section, rather than escape the less-than signs individually with the following xsl:output element:

```
<xsl:output cdata-section-elements="pre" />
```

 You can list as many elements as you like within the cdata-section-elements attribute, separated by spaces. If you have multiple xsl:output elements in your stylesheets, the values of their cdata-section-elements attributes are combined.

If you're outputting HTML, there are some situations in which the XSLT processor will automatically disable output escaping and output text as if it were in a CDATA section; namely, within the style and script elements of HTML.

Managing Namespace Declarations

XSLT processors are namespace-aware applications, which means that they conform to the *Namespaces in XML Recommendation* at http://www.w3.org/TR/REC-xml-names. Being namespace-aware means that namespace declarations (xmlns attributes and attributes with names of the form xmlns:*prefix*) aren't attributes as far as XSLT is concerned; instead, they define the scope of a namespace and what namespace nodes are where within the node tree.

Namespace Nodes

When an XSLT processor parses a source XML document, it assigns namespace nodes to every element, with each namespace node defining an association between a namespace prefix and its URI. Namespace nodes are added for every namespace declaration that's in scope for the element; that is, for every namespace declaration on that element, and for those on any of its ancestors (as long as the namespace declaration isn't overridden by one using the same prefix further down the tree). For example, consider the following XML document:

```
<bank:statement xmlns:bank="http://www.example.com /bank/statement">
   <bank:custInfo xmlns="http://www.example.com/person/details">
      <name>...</name>
      <address>...</address>
   </bank:custInfo>
   ...
</bank:statement>
```

Figure 16-3 shows the node tree for this document with the namespace nodes present on it. As you can see, there are namespace nodes on every element under the element holding a namespace declaration. There are also namespace nodes for the built-in XML namespace, despite the fact that this namespace isn't declared explicitly.

As described in the last section, the XSLT processor doesn't care about the physical structure of the documents that it deals with — it works on the document's logical format. The logical structure would be the same if there were repeated namespace declarations:

```
<bank:statement xmlns:bank="http://www.example.com/bank/statement">
   <bank:custInfo xmlns:bank="http://www.example.com/bank/statement"
                  xmlns="http://www.example.com/person/details">
      <name xmlns:bank="http://www.example.com/bank/statement"
            xmlns="http://www.example.com/person/details">...</name>
      <address xmlns:bank="http://www.example.com/bank/statement"
               xmlns="http://www.example.com/person/details">...</address>
   </bank:custInfo>
   ...
</bank:statement>
```

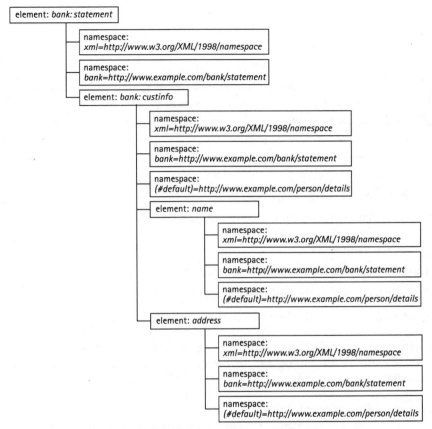

Figure 16-3: Example node tree, showing namespace nodes

As far as a namespace-aware application is concerned, the preceding XML would also be roughly the same if different prefixes were used for the namespaces. Whatever prefixes you used, the qualified names of the elements (the combination of namespace URI and local name) would remain the same. It would also be roughly the same if additional namespace declarations were added but not used within the document:

```
<statement xmlns="http://www.example.com/bank/statement">
    <custInfo xmlns="http://www.example.com/bank/statement"
            xmlns:p="http://www.example.com/person/details">
        <p:name xmlns="http://www.example.com/bank/statement"
            xmlns:p="http://www.example.com/person/details">...</p:name>
        <p:address xmlns="http://www.example.com/bank/statement"
            xmlns:p="http://www.example.com/person/details"
            xmlns:r="http://www.example.com/random">...</p:address>
```

```
      </custInfo>
      ...
</statement>
```

 Actually, an XSLT processor would treat these two documents slightly differently because the name() function on element names includes the original prefix for the namespace, and the namespace nodes would be defined with different prefixes.

Namespaces in the Stylesheet

The namespaces that you use within a stylesheet fall into four groups:

◆ The XSLT namespace

◆ Namespaces used for extension elements and functions

◆ Namespaces used in the source XML that you're processing

◆ Namespaces used in the result XML that you're producing

These namespace groupings may overlap. In particular, you may use the same namespaces in your result as you use in the source. For example, consider the following stylesheet:

```
<xsl:stylesheet version="1.0"
                xmlns:xsl="http://www.w3.org/1999/XSL/Transform"
                xmlns:exsl="http://exslt.org/common"
                xmlns:bank="http://www.example.com/bank/statement"
                xmlns:per="http://www.example.com/person/details"
                xmlns="http://www.w3.org/1999/xhtml"
                xmlns:math="http://www.w3.org/1998/Math/MathML">
...

<xsl:template match="per:address">
   <address>
      <xsl:apply-templates />
   </address>
</xsl:template>

</xsl:stylesheet>
```

This example includes six namespace declarations: the XSLT namespace; the EXSLT - Common namespace (which the stylesheet uses for extension functions); two namespace declarations for the elements used in the source XML; and the default XHTML namespace and MathML namespace that are required in the result.

It's good practice within an XSLT stylesheet to define all these namespaces on the xsl:stylesheet element, so that they're in scope throughout the stylesheet.

REMOVING NAMESPACE DECLARATIONS FROM YOUR RESULT

The main problem people encounter when it comes to managing namespaces is how to stop the namespaces in the first three groups from being declared in the result. When the XSLT processor generates the output, it takes the result tree and wherever it finds a namespace node for which it hasn't yet declared a namespace, it generates a namespace declaration. Removing namespace declarations from the output is therefore a matter of removing namespace nodes from the result tree.

Namespace nodes are added to the result tree in two ways: they can be copied from the source node tree, and they can be in scope when you create an element with a literal result element.

REMOVING NAMESPACE DECLARATIONS INTRODUCED BY XSL:COPY-OF   When you copy an element from the source tree using xsl:copy-of, the element, all its namespace nodes, all its attributes, and all its children are copied — you generate a *deep copy*. This means that any namespaces in scope for that element in the source have to be in scope for that element in the result. Because source XML often declares namespaces that you're not interested in, this can lead to unwanted namespace declarations.

You can remove these namespace declarations by using a recursive shallow copy, rather than the deep copy generated by xsl:copy-of. You can generate shallow copies recursively with an identity template, as shown in the following example:

```
<xsl:template match="@*|node()" mode="copy">
  <xsl:copy>
    <xsl:apply-templates select="@*|node()" mode="copy" />
  </xsl:copy>
</xsl:template>
```

The preceding recursive template doesn't copy any namespace nodes from the source XML. The only namespace nodes that are present in the result are those that have to be there because they are used by the elements and attributes that you're copying.

REMOVING NAMESPACE DECLARATIONS INTRODUCED BY LITERAL RESULT ELEMENTS   When you create an element using a literal result element in the stylesheet, the namespace declarations that are in scope for the literal result element are added as namespace nodes onto the element in the result tree, with a few notable exceptions.

The first exception is the XSLT namespace — the XSLT namespace is never output in the result unless you use a namespace alias in the stylesheet or explicitly generate elements or attributes in the XSLT namespace using `xsl:element` or `xsl:attribute`.

Chapter 17 describes how to use namespace aliases to produce XSLT elements.

The second set of exceptions includes any namespaces whose prefix you list in the `extension-element-prefixes` attribute on `xsl:stylesheet`. This attribute should hold the prefixes of the namespaces that you use for extension elements, attributes, and functions used in your stylesheet (which are often processor-specific). For the preceding example, you should include the EXSLT - Common namespace in the list given in the `extension-element-prefixes` attribute:

```
<xsl:stylesheet version="1.0"
                xmlns:xsl="http://www.w3.org/1999/XSL/Transform"
                xmlns:exsl="http://exslt.org/common"
                xmlns:bank="http://www.example.com/bank/statement"
                xmlns:per="http://www.example.com/person/details"
                xmlns="http://www.w3.org/1999/xhtml"
                xmlns:math="http://www.w3.org/1998/Math/MathML"
                extension-element-prefixes="exsl">
...
</xsl:stylesheet>
```

Part V describes how to use extension elements, attributes, and functions.

The final set of exceptions includes those namespaces whose prefixes you list in the `exclude-result-prefixes` attribute on `xsl:stylesheet`. If you find that you're getting namespace declarations for a namespace that you don't use within your result, then you should add the prefix of that namespace to this attribute value. Usually, these are namespaces that occur only in the source XML document. In this example, you should add the following bank and person namespaces to the `exclude-result-prefixes` attribute as follows:

```
<xsl:stylesheet version="1.0"
                xmlns:xsl="http://www.w3.org/1999/XSL/Transform"
                xmlns:exsl="http://exslt.org/common"
```

```
               xmlns:bank="http://www.example.com/bank/statement"
               xmlns:per="http://www.example.com/person/details"
               xmlns="http://www.w3.org/1999/xhtml"
               xmlns:math="http://www.w3.org/1998/Math/MathML"
               extension-element-prefixes="exsl"
               exclude-result-prefixes="bank per">
...
</xsl:stylesheet>
```

MOVING NAMESPACE DECLARATIONS IN THE RESULT

You can also use the `exclude-result-prefixes` attribute to make the XSLT processor place namespace declarations as far down the output as they can go while remaining in scope for all elements that actually need them. For example, with the preceding namespace declarations and the value for `exclude-result-prefixes`, you will get a result that has the XHTML and MathML namespace declarations on the document element. However, the MathML namespace isn't actually used until the `math` element later in the document:

```
<html xmlns="http://www.w3.org/1999/xhtml"
      xmlns:math="http://www.w3.org/1998/Math/MathML">
   <head>...</head>
   <body>
      ...
      <math:math>
         ...
      </math:math>
   </body>
</html>
```

You can add the MathML namespace to the set of excluded result namespaces by adding its prefix to the `exclude-result-prefixes` attribute in the stylesheet:

```
<xsl:stylesheet version="1.0"
               xmlns:xsl="http://www.w3.org/1999/XSL/Transform"
               xmlns:exsl="http://exslt.org/common"
               xmlns:bank="http://www.example.com/bank/statement"
               xmlns:per="http://www.example.com/person/details"
               xmlns="http://www.w3.org/1999/xhtml"
               xmlns:math="http://www.w3.org/1998/Math/MathML"
               extension-element-prefixes="exsl"
               exclude-result-prefixes="bank per math">
...
</xsl:stylesheet>
```

If you do this, the XSLT processor will delay emitting a namespace declaration for that namespace until an element uses that namespace. The result will therefore look like the following, with the MathML namespace declaration situated on the element where it's used:

```
<html xmlns="http://www.w3.org/1999/xhtml">
   <head>...</head>
   <body>
      ...
      <math:math xmlns:math="http://www.w3.org/1998/Math/MathML">
         ...
      </math:math>
   </body>
</html>
```

ADDING NAMESPACE DECLARATIONS TO YOUR RESULT

A growing number of XML vocabularies use qualified names within attribute or element values. In fact, XSLT is one example of this trend: the `method` attribute of `xsl:output` and the `data-type` attribute of `xsl:sort` are both examples of qualified names in attribute values, as are those attributes that set and refer to the names of variables, parameters, templates, decimal formats and attribute sets, and template modes. XML Schema is another example, where the type of an element is set using a qualified name. For example, the following piece of XML Schema indicates that the value of the `transaction` element should be a decimal number:

```
<xs:element name="transaction" type="xs:decimal" />
```

The value of the `type` attribute is set to `xs:decimal`, which is a qualified name. The `xs` prefix indicates that the decimal type being referred to is one from the XML Schema namespace, which has the URI `http://www.w3.org/2001/XMLSchema`.

You have to be a bit careful when dealing with these kinds of values because namespace awareness within XSLT doesn't include namespace awareness of values, only of element and attribute names.

If you have a source document that uses them, you need to manually retrieve the namespace associated with the qualified name. You do this by retrieving the prefix from the value using the `substring-before()` function and then getting the value of the namespace node whose name is that prefix. For example, with the current node being the `xs:element` element in the preceding example, you could retrieve the namespace used by the qualified name in the `type` attribute with the following:

```
namespace::*[name() = substring-before(../@type, ':')]
```

If you are generating a result that has qualified names within attributes, you may need to force the XSLT processor to output a namespace declaration for that namespace. As already shown, the XSLT processor will only output a namespace declaration if you create a namespace node for that namespace within the tree. You can create this namespace node by copying it from the source tree, by having it in scope when you create an element or by using it for an element or attribute.

If you know what namespaces you need to use within qualified name values, it's easiest to just declare them within the stylesheet and use a literal result element — the namespace nodes from the stylesheet will be copied onto the literal result element and you will get the namespace declarations that you need for resolving the value in the result.

If you use the namespace in the source XML but have a generic stylesheet and therefore can't hard-code the namespace in the stylesheet, you can copy the relevant namespace node from the source XML. For example, you could copy the namespace node that enables you to resolve the type of an element in an XML Schema using the following:

```
<xsl:copy-of select="namespace::*[name() = substring-before(../@type, ':')]" />
```

Finally, if you know the namespace URI and prefix, you can create a namespace node by creating a dummy attribute that uses that namespace. For example, given the following XML:

```
<type>
   <ns-uri>http://www.example.com/person/details</ns-uri>
   <ns-prefix>per</ns-prefix>
   <local-name>postcode</local-name>
</type>
```

you need to create an XML Schema declaration that looks like the following:

```
<xs:element xmlns:per="http://www.example.com/person/details"
            name="postcode" type="per:postcode" />
```

The closest you can get to this within the stylesheet is as follows:

```
<xs:element name="{local-name}" type="{ns-prefix}:{local-name}" />
```

However, using the preceding source will generate the following result, which lacks the namespace declaration; without the namespace declaration, the type attribute can't be resolved properly by the application that uses the result XML Schema:

```
<xs:element name="postcode" type="per:postcode" />
```

You don't know what the namespace will be in the stylesheet; the source doesn't have a namespace node that you can copy; and none of the elements in scope use the person namespace.

If you are prepared to use an extension function or your processor implements the XSLT 1.1, you could create a namespace node by creating an element in the namespace within a result tree fragment. You can convert the result tree fragment to a node set, and access the namespace node to copy it, as follows:

```
<xsl:variable name="namespacedElement">
  <xsl:element name="{ns-prefix}:dummy"
               namespace="{ns-uri}" />
</xsl:variable>
<xsl:copy-of
    select="exsl:node-set($namespacedElement)/*
                /namespace::*[name() =
                             current()/ns-prefix]" />
```

The only way around this situation with XSLT 1.0 is to create a dummy attribute in the namespace. Creating the attribute forces the XSLT processor to create a namespace node for the attribute's namespace, and thus a namespace declaration that will enable people using the result to resolve the qualified name in the type attribute. You can create this attribute with the following:

```
<xs:element name="{local-name}" type="{ns-prefix}:{local-name}">
  <xsl:attribute name="{ns-prefix}:dummy"
               namespace="{ns-uri}">dummy-value</xsl:attribute>
</xs:element>
```

Adding this attribute to the xs:element element will force the XSLT processor to add a namespace declaration, resulting in the following:

```
<xs:element xmlns:per="http://www.example.com/person/details"
          per:dummy="dummy-value"
          name="postcode" type="per:postcode" />
```

One of the requirements for XSLT 2.0 is an easier way than the preceding to dynamically create namespace nodes, probably with an xsl:namespace element that works along the same lines as the other result-generating instructions.

Summary

This chapter described some of the finer points of controlling the look of a transformation's result from within your stylesheet. You examined four areas in particular:

- ◆ Using DTDs to declare entities
- ◆ Adding and removing whitespace in your result
- ◆ Adding entity references and using CDATA sections
- ◆ Moving, removing, and adding namespace declarations in your result

Each of these areas controls what the output of a transformation looks like, rather than changing the logical content of the result. Avoid worrying too much about what the result looks like when it doesn't have any effect on the way that later processing will interpret it. Many of the controls described in this chapter are useful during debugging, but can be safely removed once you're satisfied that the stylesheet is producing the right kind of result.

Chapter 17

Enhancing XSLT

IN THIS CHAPTER

- ◆ Improving XPath expressions
- ◆ Improving the control flow in a stylesheet
- ◆ Making XSLT stylesheets easier to read

THIS CHAPTER DESCRIBES various ways to optimize your stylesheet to make it faster and use less memory, and to make it easier for you to read and maintain. The two goals of optimization and readability are usually somewhat at odds – it's up to you, on your particular project, to decide which is more important. In addition, optimization in XSLT is a tricky business. The best algorithm for a particular goal depends on the processor you're using and the optimizations built in to the implementer. It also depends on the particular data within the source XML you're using – how much there is, what kind of mix it is, and so on.

The only way to tell which solution is best in your situation is to try them with real data and a real processor. However, understanding the various ways of doing something and their potential performance benefits should at least help you focus your testing.

Rationalizing XPath

You can use two kinds of XPaths in XSLT:

- ◆ Expressions – to select nodes and to compute values
- ◆ Patterns – to match nodes

Rationalization of an XPath eliminates parts of the XPath that are unnecessary, which makes them easier for you to read and easier for the processor to parse, and often also speeds them up. Some methods for rationalization apply to both types of XPaths, but they do differ. Expressions move from the current node to pinpoint values or new nodes. Patterns, on the other hand, are a short way of testing the current node to determine whether it should be processed.

Patterns should never begin with '//'. The pattern

```
//transaction
```

matches any `transaction` element that is a descendant of the root node. Every `transaction` element in a document must be a descendant of the root node (*every* node in a document descends from the root node), so the preceding pattern matches the same nodes as:

```
transaction
```

Be aware, however, that when used in a template's `match` attribute, the first pattern has a higher default priority than the second, so changing the pattern may change which template is applied to a node.

Using Short Axes

The first step in rationalizing and optimizing XPaths is understanding the processing implications of each of the axes in a location path. Two axes always select a single node only (if they select a node at all). These axes are as follows:

◆ `parent` — selects the parent node of the context node

◆ `self` — selects the context node itself

These axes always take a certain amount of processing by the XSLT processor, but they are not dependent on the structure of the source XML. Other axes can involve more nodes. These axes are as follows:

◆ `child` — selects the children of the context node

◆ `attribute` — selects the attributes of the context node

◆ `namespace` — selects the namespaces of the context node

◆ `ancestor` — selects the ancestors of the context node

◆ `ancestor-or-self` — selects the ancestors of the context node and the context node itself

◆ `following-sibling` — selects the siblings of the context node that follow it in document order

◆ `preceding-sibling` — selects the siblings of the context node that precede it in document order

The amount of processing the processor needs to carry out when you use these axes depends on the source XML. If the context node has numerous children, the `child` axis takes a long time. If the context node is near the top of the node tree, the `ancestor` axis takes a short time.

The rest of the axes can involve substantially more nodes, though again it depends on the structure of the source XML. These axes are as follows:

- `descendant` — selects the descendants of the context node

- `descendant-or-self` — selects the descendants of the context node and the context node itself

- `following` — selects all nodes that occur after the context node in document order, aside from attributes and namespace nodes and the context node's descendants

- `preceding` — selects all nodes that occur before the context node in document order, aside from attributes and namespace nodes and the context node's ancestors

In general, it is best to avoid these axes if you can. If possible, you should point directly at the nodes you're interested in by stepping to them down the node tree, rather than by searching wildly for them among any descendants of the context node. For example, if `accountHolder` elements can occur only in `custInfo` elements that are children of the `statement` document element, rather than use the expression:

```
//accountHolder
```

you should use:

```
/statement/custInfo/accountHolder
```

If you select using the `descendant` axis, you end up testing every node under the context node. Usually, this is a lot less efficient than stepping down to the nodes you're interested in using the `child` axis for each step.

You can think of using multiple child steps rather than a single descendant step as a means of narrowing the search for the nodes that you're after to a particular branch of the node tree. The earlier that you can narrow the search, the fewer nodes that the processor will have to visit, and the more efficient the search will be. The same does not hold true of replacing a single ancestor step with multiple parent steps, on the other hand, because searching for an ancestor involves examining a list of nodes rather than a tree.

Patterns use steps as well, but rather than working through the path from left to right, journeying down the tree to select a node, patterns work through the path from right to left, taking a node and seeing whether it matches the pattern at each step. Consider the preceding XPath as a pattern rather than an expression:

```
match="/statement/custInfo/accountHolder"
```

Given a node to match, the processor will first look at it to see whether it is an `accountHolder` element; if it is, the processor will move to the node's parent to test whether it is a `custInfo` element; and so on up the tree to the root node. Thus, using the `child` axis in a pattern causes the same node traversal as using the `parent` axis in an expression.

Two other types of axis can be used in a pattern in their abbreviated forms: the `attribute` axis and the `descendant-or-self` axis (in the shorthand `//`). In terms of traversals up the tree, the `attribute` axis equates to finding the parent of the current node, while the `descendant-or-self` axis equates to finding an ancestor of the current node. As you've seen, nodes have relatively few ancestors, so unlike in an expression, using the shorthand `//` within a pattern to test for the existence of a particular ancestor will usually be no less efficient than specifying several steps to traverse from parent to parent.

The guidelines in this section assume a somewhat naïve XSLT processor. In fact, many processors optimize access to the axes that are commonly traversed, in particular the `child` axis, which can mean that accessing the parent of a node is more intensive than accessing its children. As always, it is best to experiment with your processor and your source XML.

Reducing the Number of Steps

The more steps you use, the more collection and testing of nodes the processor has to do. Reducing the number of steps in an XPath can make this more efficient. For example, if you know that the `custInfo` element is a child of the great-great-grandparent of the context node (a transaction's `payee` attribute), you can use the following:

```
parent::transaction/parent::transactions/parent::statement/custInfo[1]
```

This travels up the tree to the `statement` element before coming down again to the `custInfo` element, and (assuming that the `custInfo` element is the first child of the `statement` element) visits four nodes in total: the `transaction` element, the `transactions` element, the `statement` element and the `custInfo` element. Now consider the following path:

```
ancestor::statement[1]/custInfo[1]
```

Again, the processor must journey up the tree to the statement element before moving to its child custInfo element. The processor must visit exactly the same number of nodes in total, so is unlikely to be any less efficient. But the path itself is significantly shorter and more readable, both by you and by the XPath parser. Now consider the following path:

```
ancestor::transactions[1]/preceding-sibling::custInfo
```

Assuming that the transactions element is the second child of the statement element (the custInfo element is the first), this path visits three nodes rather than four: the transaction element, the transactions element and the custInfo element. The fact that it visits fewer nodes means that, all other things being equal, it is likely to be slightly more efficient than either of the preceding paths.

If you know that the statement element is the document element, another alternative is as follows:

```
/statement/custInfo
```

This path also visits three nodes: the root node, the statement element and the custInfo element.

The less you wander around the node tree, the fewer nodes that you need to test and the more efficient your XPath will be. Another consideration is that the fewer steps that you use in your XPath, the more readable it is for you and the easier it will be for an XPath processor to parse.

One step that you almost never need to make is from a node to its text content, for example:

```
transaction/text()
```

If an element contains a text node only, then its string value is the same as the string value of the text node. The only time you really need to select text nodes is when you're dealing with mixed content.

Traversing Each Axis Only Once

Another way to save processing time in locating nodes is to search along a given axis only once. This is particularly the case when the axis returns numerous nodes.

As example, consider a document that has a number of sections containing figures, which might be tables, diagrams, or screenshots. Within a section, a paragraph might contain a reference to one of the tables, figures, or screenshots according to its position within the section. Here is a snippet of the XML source document:

```
<section>
   ...
   <table>...</table>
   ...
   <para>
      This paragraph refers to the <ref fig="3">third figure</ref>
      in the section.
   </para>
   ...
</section>
```

Given that the current node is the ref element referring to the third figure in the section, how can you locate the third figure? You need to collect all the figures in the section—all the table, diagram, and screenshot elements descended from the section element—and then locate the third of these figures. You can gather the tables within the section by moving from the current node (the ref element) to the section element (its ancestor), and then finding all the descendant table elements:

```
ancestor::section/descendant::table
```

You can locate the diagram and screenshot elements similarly, and take the union of the three node sets to create a node set of all the figures within the section:

```
ancestor::section/descendant::table |
ancestor::section/descendant::diagram |
ancestor::section/descendant::screenshot
```

From this node set, you want the third element. The number 3 comes from the fig attribute of the ref element, which is the current element:

```
current()/@fig
```

Therefore, you can select the third element by finding the element whose position within the node set is equal to the fig attribute of the current node:

```
(ancestor::section/descendant::table |
 ancestor::section/descendant::diagram |
 ancestor::section/descendant::screenshot)
[position() = current()/@fig]
```

Using a number on its own inside a predicate is the same as testing whether the position of the context node is the same as that number. Therefore, an alternative to the predicate shown here is as follows:

```
[number(current()/@fig)]
```

Within this XPath, the processor has to go up to the `section` element and search all of its descendants three times: once for tables, once for diagrams, and once for screenshots. To make this more efficient, you want to take these steps only once; collect *all* the descendants of the `section` element, and filter those for any elements that are tables, diagrams, or screenshots. Use the following expression to collect all the descendant elements of the section:

```
ancestor::section/descendant::*
```

You can filter these elements for `table`, `diagram`, or `screenshot` elements by using the `self` axis within a predicate:

```
ancestor::section/descendant::*
        [self::table or self::diagram or self::screenshot]
```

The final filter to be applied is the one to retrieve the third of these figures:

```
ancestor::section/descendant::*
        [self::table or self::diagram or self::screenshot]
        [position() = current()/@fig]
```

XPath 2.0 may introduce a simpler form of this syntax that allows union operators within steps. With this form, you would be able to perform the following:

```
ancestor::section/(descendant::table |
                   descendant::diagram |
                   descendant::screenshot)
        [position() = current()/@fig]
```

Testing Only What Needs to Be Tested

You can often make assumptions about the source XML you're using that enable you to simplify the XPaths you use, particularly when using patterns. For example, if you *know* that all `li` elements must appear within either `ol` or `ul` elements, the pattern:

```
ol/li | ul/li
```

is equivalent to:

```
li
```

The same principle applies in location path expressions if the name of the element or attribute you're selecting is guaranteed by the structure of the source XML you are using. An example would be when your source XML has an element that contains a number of elements that are all named the same:

```
<list>
      <item>...</item>
      <item>...</item>
      ...
</list>
```

Given that the list element is the context node, you can get all the items in the list by selecting all item element children:

```
item
```

However, you *know* that the only elements within the list are item elements, so you can equally use the following:

```
*
```

A final example of this principle involves getting a node's parent. In the majority of cases, you know the name of a node's parent in advance. For readability, and to make explicit what you expect the source XML to look like, it can be helpful to specify the parent's name:

```
parent::list
```

However, you could let the parent's name remain implicit:

```
parent::*
```

You can go further than this, however. In the majority of cases, the parent of a node is guaranteed to be an element (the only exceptions are the document element and any comments or processing instructions that reside directly under the root node). Thus, again, you can implicitly specify that the parent is an element, and instead use either

```
parent::node()
```

or its abbreviation:

```
..
```

Making these kinds of changes within simple tests is unlikely to have a drastic effect on the efficiency of your processor, but the more tests you do, particularly if you start using predicates, the longer the expression will take to evaluate. In particular, you should avoid applying templates to a node-set that you select with a complex expression and then repeating that test in the match pattern of the template that's applied to them. For example, if you apply templates to elements with unique values in a grouping method, then you can guarantee that the template that matches those elements will only be applied to those with unique values – there's no need to test that again.

Another consideration to make when considering which assumptions to make explicit in your stylesheet is the way in which the markup language that your stylesheet handles is likely to change over time, and how you want the stylesheet to react to that. For example, the markup language might include room for extension – perhaps different types of items are allowed in the list, despite the fact that the markup language doesn't currently specify these extra elements. You need to choose whether to attempt to process the extra elements (in which case you can apply templates to all the children of the list element) or whether to purposefully ignore them (in which case you should apply templates to only the item elements).

Of course, it's a good idea to document any assumptions you make about the structure of the source to which a stylesheet is applied. If you can, include documentation that indicates a DTD or schema with which the source XML should comply. Otherwise, include comments or documentation each time you make one of these assumptions.

Using Numeric Predicates

Optimized processors will construct node sets on demand, getting the next node in the node set only when they need to. However, with the current state of XSLT processors, it's best to assume that a processor doesn't perform any optimization. In particular, if you don't need to construct an entire node set, you should avoid doing so. A typical instance is testing whether there are any nodes in a node set, for example, seeing whether there are any items in a list. You can do this by counting the number of items in the list and comparing it to zero:

```
count(li) = 0
```

However, this forces the processor to construct the entire node set so that it can count how many nodes are in it. Instead, you can tell whether a node set has any nodes in it by just seeing whether it has a single node in it – processors will usually stop after they find that one node:

```
count(li[1]) = 0
```

Of course, in a Boolean context, such as a test, a node set is converted to Boolean false if it doesn't hold any nodes, and to a Boolean true if it does. So you can use

```
li
```

to test whether there are any list items.

Using Implicit and Explicit Conversions

In certain contexts, a particular expression is interpreted in a particular way—implicitly converted to the required XPath data type. Often, you can simplify your XPaths by taking these implicit conversions into account. On the other hand, making the conversions explicit can make it easier for you and future maintainers of your stylesheet to understand why a particular expression is working in the way it is.

Expressions are interpreted automatically as Booleans in the following contexts:

◆ Within predicates, unless they evaluate to a number

◆ Within the `test` attribute of `xsl:if` and `xsl:when`

◆ When used as operands with operators such as `and` and `or`

◆ When used as an operand in an equality test (i.e., = or !=) and the other operand is a Boolean, unless the expression evaluates to a node set

◆ When passed as an argument to a function expecting a Boolean argument

There's no need to wrap an expression in the `boolean()` function if it's used in any of these situations.

Expressions are interpreted automatically as numbers in the following contexts:

◆ Within the `value` attribute of `xsl:number`

◆ When used as the operands of mathematical operators such as +, -, *, `mod`, and `div`

◆ When used as the operands of <, <=, >, or >=, unless the expression evaluates to a node set

◆ When used as an operand in an equality test (i.e., = or !=) and the other operand is a number, unless the expression evaluates to a node set

◆ When passed as an argument to a function expecting a numerical argument

In the preceding situations, there's no need to wrap an expression in the `number()` function. When node sets are converted to numbers, only the first node in the node set is examined, and its value converted to a number and returned. Therefore you do not need to add a [1] predicate to a location path to return only the first node from the node set when it is used as the argument to the `number()` function or in one of the preceding contexts—only the first node is chosen automatically.

Expressions are interpreted automatically as strings in the following contexts:

◆ Within the `select` attribute of `xsl:value-of` and `xsl:sort`

◆ When passed as an argument to a function expecting a string argument

◆ Often, when used as an argument to a function expecting an object, unless the expression evaluates to a node set (for example, the second argument of `key()`)

Expressions used in these contexts don't need to be wrapped in the `string()` function; similarly, as with the `number()` function, there's no need to add a `[1]` predicate to indicate that only the first node in a node set should be used. For example:

```
<xsl:value-of select="transaction[1]" />
```

has the same effect as

```
<xsl:value-of select="transaction" />
```

The latter is slightly shorter, but the former makes it clearer that only the first transaction's value is given.

Using Keys

If you are testing a particular property of numerous nodes multiple times, it's often wise to use a key, rather than to select the nodes with a plain XPath. For example, if you are collating transactions of different types by using several expressions such as

```
/statement/transaction[@type = 'SO']
/statement/transaction[@type = 'DD']
/statement/transaction[@type = 'CR']
```

it's worthwhile to create a key that matches the nodes you're interested in and uses the property of the node as the key value. In this case, you can use the following:

```
<xsl:key name="transactions-by-type"
         match="transaction" use="@type" />
```

The transactions can then be retrieved by using the following function calls:

```
key('transactions-by-type', 'SO')
key('transactions-by-type', 'DD')
key('transactions-by-type', 'CR')
```

The property you use to index the nodes can be anything you like: the value of one of its attributes, as shown here; the name of the node's third ancestor, the number of nodes it has underneath it, the first letter of its value — anything you can express in an XPath. The only limitation is that the use attribute can't contain a variable value.

It's worthwhile to declare and use a key only if you use it several times. When optimized, XSLT processors encountering a key being used for a particular document will build the equivalent of a hash table. All the nodes that match the pattern given in the match attribute are indexed by a key value. The key value is the value returned by evaluating the expression given by the use attribute, with the indexed node as the current node. Building the hash table involves going through the entire document to find the relevant nodes; therefore, if the key is used only once during the processing of the stylesheet, you may as well have used a path to find the nodes you were after. In addition, storing the hash table takes up memory, especially if many nodes are involved. In other words, it's never worth defining a key if you use it only once, and it's usually not worth it if you use it only twice.

Other than that, whether a key is worthwhile depends on numerous variables: the source XML; where and how the key is used; the processor's internal optimization of keys; and the platform on which you're running the stylesheet. I've run stylesheets using keys that have used so much memory that the computer ground to a halt. Clearly, there are situations in which the disadvantages of the additional memory requirement for keys far outweigh the speed advantages.

Testing Node Names

Often, you want to select or match nodes based on their names: names are one of the most important pieces of information about an element or attribute, and differently named nodes are treated differently within an application.

Specifying a node's name within a node test is the easiest way to select or match only nodes with that name. However, node tests for elements, attributes, and namespace nodes can be quite inflexible; they only enable you to select or match specific names that have to be hard-coded into the step. (Node tests for processing instructions are more flexible, as they enable you to specify the name of the processing instruction through a variable.) Instead, you can test node names by using the name() or local-name() functions, which enable you to test names against variable values or to construct names dynamically; or, alternatively, you can use the self axis.

How you should select or match nodes with particular names depends on the situation you're in. The rest of this section describes some general guidelines.

If you can, match or select elements, attributes, or processing instructions by name, simply by using the node's name in a node test.

The usual method of selecting or matching an element or attribute is through a basic node test, such as

```
doc:figure
```

to match an element named `figure` in the namespace associated with the prefix doc in the path's context, or

```
@customerID
```

to match an unprefixed attribute named `customerID`. Another alternative is

```
processing-instruction('include')
```

to match a processing instruction named `include`. XSLT processors are designed to process these expressions quickly and efficiently.

 TIP If you want to test whether the name of an *element* or *processing instruction* belongs to (or doesn't belong to) a distinct set of names, you should use the `self` axis.

Using the `self` axis enables you to write expressions and patterns that are short and readable, and can easily test the namespace of a node without fixing the prefixes within the XML source. For example, consider selecting the nearest preceding heading of the context node within an HTML document. Using the `name()` function, the expression is as follows:

```
preceding::*[name() = 'h1' or name() = 'h2' or name() = 'h3' or
            name() = 'h4' or name() = 'h5' or name() = 'h6'][1]
```

With the `self` axis, the equivalent expression is as follows:

```
preceding::*[self::h1 or self::h2 or self::h3 or
            self::h4 or self::h5 or self::h6][1]
```

This selects any preceding elements, filters that list to those elements that are themselves h1, h2, h3, h4, h5 or h6 elements, and finally picks the first of this list.

Similarly, the `self` axis can be used instead of the `name()` function when selecting elements that do *not* have a particular name. The following example matches or selects all elements that are children of the context node, aside from those that are del elements using the `self` axis:

```
*[not(self::del)]
```

The Dangers of Testing Node Names with name()

The `name()` function returns the qualified name of a node, with a prefix from the source XML (usually the one used for the node itself). In this example, we'll use the following XML:

```
<bk:book xmlns:bk="http://www.example.com/library/book">
    ...
</bk:book>
```

The `bk:book` element can be matched with the following:

```
*[name() = 'bk:book']
```

However, if another XML document declares the book namespace with a different prefix, such as in the following:

```
<book:book xmlns:book="http://www.example.com/library/book">
    ...
</book:book>
```

the preceding pattern won't match because the qualified names aren't the same. For this reason, you should avoid using the `name()` function and use the `local-name()` function instead. There are two exceptions to this. One, you might be able to guarantee the namespace prefix used in all the documents with which your stylesheet is used, perhaps because they're always generated using a particular process. Two, you might be matching nodes that are in no namespace (such as unprefixed attribute nodes), which never have a prefix.

If you want to test whether the name of an *unprefixed attribute* belongs to (or doesn't belong to) a distinct set of names, you should use the `name()` or `local-name()` function.

Unfortunately, you can't test attributes by using the `self` axis in the same way as you can elements or processing instructions. Attributes that don't have a prefix in the source XML document are always placed in no namespace, so you don't have to worry about testing what namespace they're in. For these attributes, both `name()` and `local-name()` produce the same result.

For example, suppose you have a variable called `$excludeAttrs` that holds a list of the names of attributes that you want stripped from your source XML document.

This list of attributes is held as a node set of `attr` elements, the value of each specifying a different attribute to be excluded. The original XML might look something like the following:

```
<attr>style</attr>
<attr>dir</attr>
<attr>onclick</attr>
...
```

To find those attributes on the context node whose name is not equal to one of the named attributes, the obvious expression is as follows:

```
@*[name() != $excludeAttrs]
```

However, the preceding expression will return all attributes whose name is not equal to *any one* of the excluded attribute names — in most cases, all attributes. To get the correct XPath, you need to rephrase what you want — those attributes for which it is not the case that the attribute name is equal to any of the excluded attributes. With this phrasing, the XPath looks like the following:

```
@*[not(name() = $excludeAttrs)]
```

Testing the Names of Prefixed Attributes

Prefixed attributes are associated with a particular namespace, but unlike elements, you can't use the `self` axis to test what namespace they're in. If it's important to test the namespace of the attribute (which it normally is — otherwise, it wouldn't be in a namespace), you need to test both its local name and the namespace URI with which it is associated.

For example, you can use the `local-name()` and `namespace-uri()` functions in combination to select all attributes on the context element node aside from `xml:space`:

```
@*[not(
    local-name() = 'space' and

    namespace-uri() = 'http://www.w3.org/XML/1998/namespace')]
```

A more cunning technique takes advantage of the fact that within a certain element, you can guarantee that there is only one attribute with the same namespace/local name combination. If you access *that* attribute, you can test whether it is the same as the attribute you're currently looking at. In this case, you can use

```
@*[count(. | ../@xml:space) != count(../@xml:space)]
```

TIP If you want to test the name of an *element* or *attribute* in *no namespace* based on a string held in a variable, a name constructed with XPath functions, or on some pattern in the element or attribute's name, you can use the name() function or the local-name() function.

To compare the name of an element or attribute to a string, you need to turn that name into a string, which has to be done with either the name() or local-name() function. If you're dealing with elements or attributes in no namespace, it doesn't matter which you use, as both will return the same thing, although local-name() may be slightly better as it enables you to move the XML into a namespace later without breaking the XPath.

For example, the following XPath selects, from the context node, the nearest preceding heading element within an HTML document that's been converted to XML (but not to XHTML, and therefore doesn't use a namespace). The path selects all preceding elements whose name starts with the letter h and has a numerical second character, and then selects the first of these to get the nearest heading element:

```
preceding::*[starts-with(name(), 'h') and
             number(substring(name(), 2, 1))][1]
```

The preceding XPath is somewhat more useful than specifying each of the heading elements individually, as it enables the HTML author to add extra levels of headings without breaking the XPath. If you wanted, you could add three more levels of headings, and the XPath shown would still select them accurately.

TIP If you want to test the name of an *element or attribute in a namespace* based on a string held in a variable, a name constructed with XPath functions, or on some pattern in their name, you should use the local-name() function.

You should test the names of elements or attributes that are in a namespace with the local-name() function to enable the path to work regardless of what prefix is used in the source XML documents. Often, a node test can be used to filter the nodes down to only those in a particular namespace before the actual name of the node is tested.

For example, suppose that the XHTML headings we're dealing with have been associated with the XHTML namespace within the source document. The following XPath will match any XHTML-like headings (h1, h2 and so on) in any namespace:

```
*[starts-with(local-name(), 'h') and
  number(substring(local-name(), 2, 1))]
```

In the preceding, all elements are selected, regardless of namespace, before being filtered for those whose local name matches the heading pattern. Elements from particular namespaces can also be selected; if the HTML namespace has been declared with the prefix html, the following selects all elements in the HTML namespace:

```
html:*
```

Therefore, the following selects all elements in the HTML namespace that follow the heading pattern:

```
html:*[starts-with(local-name(), 'h') and
       number(substring(local-name(), 2, 1))]
```

Don't use the name of a namespace node to match or select namespace nodes unless you can guarantee the prefix used for a namespace in the source and that your processor preserves them. Namespace prefixes are, by definition, changeable from document to document, so you are likely to miss namespace nodes if you rely on their names.

Namespace nodes are named after the prefix that is used in the source document. Aside from the XML namespace, which always has the prefix xml, it is usually possible for different source documents to use different prefixes. For this reason, you should match namespace nodes by their value (the namespace URI), rather than their name (the namespace prefix).

For example, you should use the following to locate a namespace node for the XHTML namespace:

```
namespace::*[. = 'http://www.w3.org/1999/xhtml']
```

rather than

```
namespace::html
```

which will only work if the XHTML namespace uses the prefix html in the source document — something you can't usually guarantee.

Testing Node Namespaces

It's a lot rarer to want to test a node's namespace than it is to want to test its name, but it does happen. This section shows you how to do so.

Again, you can select or match elements and attributes based on their namespace by associating a namespace prefix with the namespace within the path's context and then specifying this prefix as part of the node test. You can also test the namespace of a node through the `namespace-uri()` function or by using the `self` axis.

If you can, match or select simply by using the namespace of the element or attribute in a node test.

The usual method of selecting or matching elements or attributes in a particular namespace is through a basic node test such as

```
html:*
```

to match elements in the HTML namespace, or

```
@xml:*
```

to match attributes in the XML namespace. XSLT processors are designed to process these expressions quickly and efficiently.

If you want to test whether the namespace of an *element* belongs to (or doesn't belong to) a distinct set of namespaces, you should use the `self` axis.

The `self` axis enables you to combine simple node tests in logical expressions, but only for elements, rather than attributes. This is better than using the `namespace-uri()` function, as you do not have to include namespace URIs (which are usually quite long) in your paths: you can use the prefix associated with the namespace URI in the context that the path is used.

If you want to test whether an element or attribute is not in a namespace, you should test whether the `namespace-uri()` function returns anything.

If an element or attribute is not in a namespace, its namespace URI is the empty string. Therefore, if `namespace-uri()` for a node evaluates as `false()`, it is in no namespace. The following, for example, returns all attributes of the context element that are in no namespace:

```
@*[not(namespace-uri())]
```

Testing Namespaces for Prefixed Attributes

The `self` axis cannot be used with attributes. Instead, you can test the namespace of a prefixed attribute using the `namespace-uri()` function. For example, the following selects attributes of the context element that are not in the XML namespace:

```
@*[namespace-uri() != 'http://www.w3.org/XML/1998/namespace']
```

If you want to avoid specifying the namespace URI like this, you can also use set logic to test whether an attribute is part of the namespace. If an attribute is part of the set of all attributes of its parent element in a particular namespace, then it is in that namespace. Translating this into XPath functions, you need to union the set of attributes in that namespace with the attribute you're looking at. If counting the nodes in the resulting node set gives the same number as the count of attributes in the namespace, then the attribute is in the namespace. This gives you the following XPath:

```
@*[count(. | ../@xml:*) != count(../@xml:*)]
```

This method is much less efficient than testing the namespace URI directly, because the node sets have to be created and counted, which takes time. However, it does mean that you don't have to write out the namespace URI in the path.

If you want to test whether the namespace of an element is the default namespace, you should test whether there are any characters before the colon in its name.

Elements in the default namespace of the source XML document do not have a prefix. You can test whether an element has a prefix by checking whether there is any text before a colon in the element's expanded name. If there is text before a colon, it has a prefix; if not, it doesn't. For example, the following selects all elements in a document that are in the default namespace at the point where they are specified:

```
//*[not(substring-before(name(), ':'))]
```

The default namespace can change throughout a document, if it is redefined.

Rationalizing XSLT

Although rewriting XPaths can increase the efficiency and readability of a stylesheet, rationalizing the XSLT code that makes up the stylesheet can have just as much of an effect. The principles that apply here are the same as those that apply in any programming language, but certain special features of XSLT are worth looking at in more detail.

 One optimization that is likely to make a big impact on the efficiency of your stylesheet is using tail recursion within your templates. The chapters in the first part of this book demonstrate several tail-recursive templates, and Chapter 1 discusses both tail recursion and other methods of minimizing the depth of recursion.

Using Push or Pull Processing

A good way to optimize your stylesheet is to ensure that at each step you only process the nodes that you need to process. Each time you tell the processor to apply templates to a node, it has to search through all the available templates to find those that can be applied to it. Although good processors optimize this search, the less time you take to search for templates, the less time the transformation will take.

Processing only the nodes you need to involves adopting a *pull* method, rather than a *push* one. With push, the source XML drives the process — all the nodes in the source are processed and the templates determine what's done with them. With pull, the stylesheet drives the process by selecting only the nodes that are relevant at a particular point in the result tree.

Push processing is a far better method when dealing with source and result trees that are very similar to each other, such as DocBook to HTML, or when translating between order forms in English and French. Here, the nodes can generally be processed in the order in which they're found. Processing with pull is better when the source and result trees that you're after are very different, such as presenting an order form in HTML or building an index for a DocBook document. In these cases, the nodes are generally processed in a different order than the way they're arranged within the source XML.

If you're using pull, it's better to apply templates to only the nodes you're actively interested in, rather than to apply templates to all the nodes and only do something if the node is one of the ones you're interested in. For example, if you want to list only the credit transactions in a statement, you could apply templates to all the transactions, but do nothing with the ones you aren't interested in:

```
<xsl:template match="statement">
   <!-- apply templates to all transactions -->
   <xsl:apply-templates />
</xsl:template>
```

```
<!-- do nothing by default -->
<xsl:template match="transaction" />

<!-- do something with the credit transactions -->
<xsl:template match="transaction[@type = 'CR']">
   Credit: <xsl:value-of select="@amount" />
</xsl:template>
```

The processor would try to do something with every transaction it encountered. Given that credits, sadly, are less frequent than debits, most of the time it would end up doing nothing. A better alternative is the following:

```
<xsl:template match="statement">
   <!-- apply templates to credit transactions -->
   <xsl:apply-templates select="transaction[@type = 'CR']" />
</xsl:template>

<!-- only ever applied to credit transactions -->
<xsl:template match="transaction">
   Credit: <xsl:value-of select="@amount" />
</xsl:template>
```

Here, the processor tries to apply templates only to credit transactions; therefore, it has to locate templates much less frequently.

The match pattern for the `transaction`-matching template does not need to test whether the transaction is a credit transaction — it's guaranteed that it is because those are the only transactions to which templates are applied. However, this is an implicit assumption that is worth documenting in your stylesheet.

Similar situations appear within `xsl:for-each`. If an `xsl:for-each` has an `xsl:if` as its only child, then the test given in the `xsl:if` can instead be given as a predicate on the node set expression given in the `select` attribute on the `xsl:for-each`. For example, the following code:

```
<xsl:for-each select="transaction">
   <xsl:if test="@type = 'CR'">
      Credit: <xsl:value-of select="@amount" />
   </xsl:if>
</xsl:for-each>
```

is exactly the same as:

```
<xsl:for-each select="transaction[@type = 'CR']">
   Credit: <xsl:value-of select="@amount" />
</xsl:for-each>
```

The former will iterate over every `transaction` element, testing whether its `type` attribute is equal to `CR` and only creating content if it is; whereas the latter will iterate over only those whose `type` attribute is equal to `CR`. Although the two templates each involve the same number of visits to each node, the latter is likely to be done more efficiently because it is held with an XPath. The latter also involves fewer instructions, which means a slightly smaller stylesheet – a difference which is likely to make little impact in isolation, but can add up to a lot less typing and less parsing for the XSLT processor if there is similar code throughout your stylesheet.

The one thing that *does* change when you switch between having an internal `xsl:if` for `xsl:for-each` or a predicate on the match for `xsl:apply-templates` is the `position()` of the processed node. Consider, for example, a transaction that's the fifth transaction overall, and the second credit transaction in the statement. If all the transactions are selected, the `position()` of the transaction is that within the list of all transactions — it will have a `position()` of 5. On the other hand, if only credit transactions are selected, its `position()` will be within the list of credit transactions only — it will have a `position()` of 2.

Setting Variables to Primitive Values

Variables can store either result tree fragments (RTFs) or primitive values such as strings or numbers. Often, you'll only use a variable as a string or a number. In these situations, you should set it using its `select` attribute if you can, rather than using the content of the variable. For example, rather than use

```
<xsl:variable name="limit">3000</xsl:variable>
```

you should use

```
<xsl:variable name="limit" select="3000" />
```

Setting a value to a string or number rather than a result tree fragment makes it easier for the XSLT processor to store – it doesn't have to create a whole new result tree fragment just for that text node. A string or number is also easier than a result tree fragment for the XSLT processor to use – it doesn't have to convert the RTF into a string or number all the time.

Templates vs xsl:for-each

If you find yourself with `xsl:for-each` constructs that contain conditional statements based on some property of the node under consideration, consider using an `xsl:apply-templates` instead. This results in more modular code — it makes it easy to add another condition later, and the same template can be used from elsewhere in your stylesheet. On the other hand, using an `xsl:for-each` can be more efficient, because the processor doesn't have to search for a template that matches a selected node.

For example, you could process the transactions with the following:

```
<xsl:for-each select="transaction">
   <xsl:choose>
      <xsl:when test="@type = 'CR'">credit</xsl:when>
      <xsl:when test="@type = 'SO'">standing order</xsl:when>
      <xsl:when test="@type = 'DD'">direct debit</xsl:when>
      <xsl:otherwise>other</xsl:otherwise>
   </xsl:choose>
</xsl:for-each>
```

Alternatively, you could apply templates to the transactions and process them with a number of separate templates:

```
<xsl:template match="transaction[@type = 'CR']">credit</xsl:template>
<xsl:template match="transaction[@type = 'SO']">standing order</xsl:template>
<xsl:template match="transaction[@type = 'DD']">direct debit</xsl:template>

<xsl:template match="transaction">other</xsl:template>
```

Alternatively, of course, you could mix the two and have a single template that contained the condition:

```
<xsl:template match="transaction">
   <xsl:choose>
      <xsl:when test="@type = 'CR'">credit</xsl:when>
      <xsl:when test="@type = 'SO'">standing order</xsl:when>
      <xsl:when test="@type = 'DD'">direct debit</xsl:when>
      <xsl:otherwise>other</xsl:otherwise>
   </xsl:choose>
</xsl:template>
```

How you choose between the two latter forms depends on the amount of commonality between the outputs required from the different conditions. If there is a lot of commonality between them, a single template with conditions only around the changeable output is probably easier to maintain. If they are very different, on the other hand, splitting them into separate templates can make things easier to handle.

In general, it is also better to use

```
<xsl:variable name="variable-name" select="string(value)" />
```

rather than

```
<xsl:variable name="variable-name">
  <xsl:value-of select="value" />
</xsl:variable>
```

If you simply have several `xsl:value-of` instructions intermingled with text nodes as your variable value, then you should use `concat()` to concatenate the values and text that you want instead. For example,

```
<xsl:variable name="address">
   <xsl:value-of select="street" />
   <xsl:text>, </xsl:text>
   <xsl:value-of select="district" />
   <xsl:text>, </xsl:text>
   <xsl:value-of select="city" />
   <xsl:text> </xsl:text>
   <xsl:value-of select="postcode" />
</xsl:variable>
```

would be better phrased as

```
<xsl:variable name="address"
            select="concat(street, ', ', district, ', ',
                            city, ' ', postcode)" />
```

If you have to set the value of the variable to one of two strings, you can use one of the methods for choosing alternative strings outlined in Chapter 3, rather than use an internal `xsl:choose`.

Using Literal Result Elements

XSLT gives you four ways to add elements to your result tree: using literal result elements, using `xsl:element`, using `xsl:copy`, and using `xsl:copy-of`.

COPYING ELEMENTS

If you're copying an element — creating a result element with the same name and namespace as a source element — it often makes sense to use `xsl:copy`, or `xsl:copy-of` if you're also interested in all the attributes and content of the element. If you need to change the attributes or content of the element in any way, then you need a recursive copy, rather than simply `xsl:copy-of`.

However, copying elements copies their namespace nodes too. If you want a clean copy that doesn't include spurious namespace nodes, you might like to use the following equivalent:

```
<xsl:element name="{name()}"
             namespace="{namespace-uri()}">
  ...
</xsl:element>
```

If you use `name()`, rather than `local-name()`, to return the name of the element in the preceding example, you may get to keep the original namespace prefix. If you want to make that namespace the default, use `local-name()` instead.

For more information about managing namespaces, see Chapter 16.

USING XSL:ELEMENT

In general, literal result elements are a lot easier to use than `xsl:element`: they're smaller (both in their XML serialization and their node tree representation), they enable you to define attributes simply, and they're more readable.

There are only three situations in which you need to use `xsl:element` instead:

◆ When you need to determine the name of the element dynamically

◆ When you need to determine the namespace of the element dynamically

◆ When you need to create elements that would be interpreted differently if they were specified as literal result elements

In the first two situations, use `xsl:element` with attribute value templates as the values of the `name` and/or `namespace` attributes.

In the last case, rather than use `xsl:element`, you can declare a namespace alias that maps a meaningless namespace used within the stylesheet into a meaningful namespace in the result tree. For example, if you wanted to create an empty `xsl:copy` element in the result tree, you couldn't use the literal result element

```
<xsl:copy />
```

as this would create a copy of the current node. Instead, you could use

```
<xsl:element name="xsl:copy" />
```

Alternatively, you could create a new namespace that could act as an alias for the XSLT namespace, something like `http://www.w3.org/1999/XSL/TransformAlias`, and associate this with a different prefix in your stylesheet (something like `oxsl`). To tell the processor that this is an alias for the XSLT namespace in the result tree, use the `xsl:namespace-alias` element:

```
<xsl:namespace-alias stylesheet-prefix="oxsl" result-prefix="xsl" />
```

The `xsl:namespace-alias` element tells the processor to change the namespace URI that the elements that use stylesheet prefix in the stylesheet are associated with in the result. Some processors use the prefix specified by the `stylesheet-prefix` attribute in the result, others use the prefix specified by the `result-prefix` attribute.

With this namespace alias in place, we can now use the literal result element

```
<oxsl:copy />
```

to create a `copy` element in the XSLT namespace in the result tree.

USING LITERAL RESULT ATTRIBUTES

A similar distinction should be made between literal result attributes that are specified on literal result elements and attributes that are created with `xsl:attribute`. You should use a literal result attribute (with an attribute value template as a value if necessary) wherever possible, because it reduces the size of the stylesheet (both as serialized XML and as a node tree). In some situations, however, you do have to use an `xsl:attribute`:

◆ When the element to which the attributes are being isn't created with a literal result element

◆ When you need to determine the name of the attribute dynamically

◆ When you need to determine the namespace of the attribute dynamically

◆ When you need to create attributes that would be interpreted differently if they were specified as literal result attributes

◆ When you need to determine the value of the attribute dynamically and it's not possible to do so with an XPath

Chapter 6 discusses the various ways of determining attribute values dynamically.

One particular tip when generating attributes is to use the following method. Replace any occurrences that follow the pattern

```
<element>
   <xsl:attribute name="attribute-name">
      <xsl:choose>
         <xsl:when test="test">value-if-true</xsl:when>
         <xsl:otherwise>value-if-false</xsl:otherwise>
      </xsl:choose>
   </xsl:attribute>
   ...
</element>
```

with the following equivalent pattern:

```
<element attribute-name="value-if-false">
   <xsl:if test="test">
      <xsl:attribute name="attribute-name">
         <xsl:text>value-if-true</xsl:text>
      </xsl:attribute>
   </xsl:if>
   ...
</element>
```

If the attribute is added with an `xsl:attribute` when it is already specified as a literal result attribute, its value is overridden.

Removing xsl:text Elements

You only need to use `xsl:text` elements if you need to get rid of whitespace; other than that, it simply adds to the number of nodes in your stylesheet node tree and to the clutter in your stylesheet. In other words,

```
<title><xsl:text>Miss</xsl:text></title>
```

is exactly the same as

```
<title>Miss</title>
```

aside from the fact that the latter is longer, both in its XML serialization and its node tree representation. You can always get rid of xsl:text elements that directly abut tags both before and after. For example,

```
<blockquote
   ><xsl:text>"</xsl:text
   ><xsl:apply-templates
   /><xsl:text>"</xsl:text
></blockquote>
```

is exactly the same as

```
<blockquote>"<xsl:apply-templates />"</blockquote>
```

I think you'll agree that the latter is a lot easier to read. Where xsl:text elements abut a tag at one end but not at another, for example:

```
<blockquote>
   <xsl:text>"</xsl:text><xsl:apply-templates /><xsl:text>"</xsl:text>
</blockquote>
```

you may find it easier to read if you use the Allouche Method, which is named after David Allouche, who first introduced it. With this method, you use empty xsl:text elements instead:

```
<blockquote>
   <xsl:text />"<xsl:apply-templates />"<xsl:text />
</blockquote>
```

However, be aware of how the output that you're producing is going to be used. If you're producing HTML or FO, for example, viewers generally collapse white-space, ignoring line breaks and places where there are several spaces in a row — it rarely matters if there are a few extra spaces here and there. If you are producing XML according to some schema, then most simple data types involve normalizing spaces in some way, so it doesn't matter what whitespace is introduced.

In general, if you don't need to regulate spacing, don't use xsl:text.

Avoiding xsl:number

The xsl:number instruction is relatively complicated, and it can cause a lot of problems for XSLT processors because of the rules in the XSLT Recommendation regarding how to collect information about the number of a particular node. If you don't need to use it, avoid it.

Chapter 8 examines various ways of numbering nodes, including those that avoid using `xsl:number`.

Summary

This chapter described how you can adjust your stylesheets to make them more readable and/or efficient. You learned seven main tips to improve the XPaths that you use:

- ◆ Use axes that collect small numbers of nodes
- ◆ Use as few steps as possible
- ◆ Traverse each axis only once
- ◆ Test only what you need to test
- ◆ Use numerical predicates
- ◆ Use the implicit conversions between data types
- ◆ Use keys

Testing node names and namespaces are two XPath areas that offer numerous options. In general, node tests are the best way of testing node names and namespaces, but for complex tests, you may need to use either the `self` axis or the `name()`, `local-name()`, and `namespace-uri()` functions.

Improving processing efficiency also means performing the least amount of template matching as possible. Stylesheets that use the *pull* method, selecting only the nodes that they want to process, are likely to be more efficient than those that use the push method, in which all the nodes in the source are processed, and the templates determine what's done with them. Other alterations involve setting variables to primitive values, rather than result tree fragments; using literal result elements and attributes wherever possible; removing as many `xsl:text` elements as you can; and avoiding `xsl:number`.

Part V

Using Extensions

Chapter 18

Using Extension Functions

XPATH CONTAINS FUNCTIONS for most operations that you need to carry out. However, there are some things that XPath either can't do at all or doesn't support very well. Fortunately, XPath is extensible: there is scope for adding other functions to XPath as long as the names of those functions are in another namespace. Functions that aren't in the XPath namespace are known as *extension functions*.

 Neither XPath 1.0 nor XSLT 1.0 indicates how extension functions should be defined, just that they can exist and how you can use them. However, the XSLT 1.1 Working Draft and individual XSLT processors describe methods for doing so, and you'll learn how to define and implement your own extension functions in Chapter 20.

This chapter shows you how to use extension functions in your stylesheets. Unfortunately, using extension functions makes your stylesheet less portable — support for an extension function depends on the XSLT processor that you're using. Therefore, you'll also learn how to determine whether an extension function is available within your stylesheet, and examine which extension functions are supported by which XSLT processors, and how they work.

Using Extension Functions

Every extension function belongs to a non-XPath namespace. The namespace for an extension function is usually based on the processor that you use, although some namespaces are more general than that, such as the EXSLT namespaces.

To use an extension function, you first need to declare this namespace in the `xsl:stylesheet` element of your stylesheet. For example, to use the `exsl:node-set()` extension function, you need to declare the EXSLT - Common namespace as follows:

```
<xsl:stylesheet version="1.0"
                xmlns:xsl="http://www.w3.org/1999/XSL/Transform"
                xmlns:exsl="http://exslt.org/common">
...
</xsl:stylesheet>
```

You also need to ensure that this namespace isn't included in your output. Often, an extension function namespace is also used for extension elements, so it's best to prevent a namespace declaration from being output by indicating that the namespace is an extension element namespace, rather than by using `exclude-result-prefixes`:

```
<xsl:stylesheet version="1.0"
                xmlns:xsl="http://www.w3.org/1999/XSL/Transform"
                xmlns:exsl="http://exslt.org/common"
                extension-element-prefixes="exsl">
...
</xsl:stylesheet>
```

Once you have that set up, you can use the extension functions in that namespace wherever you can normally use an XPath function — in expressions or within predicates in match patterns.

Testing Function Availability

Declaring the namespace that's used for an extension function doesn't necessarily mean that the processor you're using supports that function. If you're writing stylesheets that rely on extension functions, it's good practice to test their availability before you try to use them.

You can determine whether a function is available during the particular run of the stylesheet using the `function-available()` function, passing the name of the function as the argument. For example, to see whether the processor supports `exsl:node-set()`, you can use the following:

```
function-available('exsl:node-set')
```

Calling an unavailable extension function is an error, and the stylesheet will halt. Thus you can't test the availability of a function with `function-available()` and use that function in the same expression.

Testing the Availability of Multiple Extensions

If you rely heavily on extension functions or elements that are available only in a particular processor, then you may want to determine whether that processor is being used. You can do this by retrieving the processor vendor details through the `system-property()` function. For example, if you're using numerous functions that you know are supported by Saxon, you could test whether the stylesheet is being used with Saxon using the following:

```
starts-with(system-property('xsl:vendor'), 'SAXON')
```

However, you should be careful about doing this. First, it's possible for a vendor to change the values that are returned from the `system-property()` function — in fact, the `xsl:vendor` string for Saxon changes with each version. Second, people might use your stylesheet with older versions of the processor, which still test to be the same processor according to `system-property()` despite supporting different extension functions. Finally, other processors might support the particular functions you currently use in the future, and so might be acceptable later even if they aren't now.

Recovering from Unavailable Functions

What you do if a function is unavailable depends on the function and what it does. Often, functions with the same functionality are available in a number of different processors. If it's not available in one, you can try using another. The `node-set()` extension function is a good example of this:

```
<xsl:choose>
    <xsl:when test="function-available('exsl:node-set')">
        <xsl:apply-templates select="exsl:node-set($rtf)" />
    </xsl:when>
    <xsl:when test="function-available('saxon:node-set')">
        <xsl:apply-templates select="saxon:node-set($rtf)" />
    </xsl:when>
    <xsl:when test="function-available('xalan:nodeSet')">
        <xsl:apply-templates select="xalan:nodeSet($rtf)" />
    </xsl:when>
    <xsl:when test="function-available('msxsl:node-set')">
        <xsl:apply-templates select="msxsl:node-set($rtf)" />
    </xsl:when>
    ...
    <xsl:otherwise>...</xsl:otherwise>
</xsl:choose>
```

Some extension functions are shortcuts for more complicated expressions or pieces of code. In these cases, if the function is unavailable, you can often call a template or use a pure XPath expression that does exactly the same thing. For example, if the `math:min()` function from EXSLT - Math is unavailable, you can use one of the templates described in Chapter 4 to determine the minimum value of a set of nodes:

```
<xsl:choose>
   <xsl:when test="function-available('math:min')">
      <xsl:value-of select="math:min($nodes)" />
   </xsl:when>
   <xsl:otherwise>
      <xsl:call-template name="minimum">
         <xsl:with-param name="nodes" select="$nodes" />
      </xsl:call-template>
   </xsl:otherwise>
</xsl:choose>
```

If there isn't an equivalent expression or template, you may have to use a default value instead. For example, there's no XSLT-equivalent template for the `date:date-time()` extension function, which gives the current date and time. If you're using this just to provide a date at the bottom of your HTML page, you don't want the transformation to fail solely because of the lack of that function. Instead, you can use a default value, perhaps passed in as a parameter:

```
<xsl:choose>
   <xsl:when test="function-available('date:date-time')">
      <xsl:value-of select="date:date-time()" />
   </xsl:when>
   <xsl:otherwise>
      <xsl:value-of select="$today" />
   </xsl:otherwise>
</xsl:choose>
```

Only when all else fails should the transformation halt as the result of a function not being available. In these cases, you should use `xsl:message` to terminate the transformation with an appropriate error message. For example, if your stylesheet requires the `exsl:node-set()` extension function in order to work and neither it nor its processor-specific equivalents are available, then you need the stylesheet to terminate:

```
<xsl:choose>
   <xsl:when test="function-available('exsl:node-set')">
      <xsl:apply-templates select="exsl:node-set($rtf)" />
   </xsl:when>
   ...
   <xsl:otherwise>
      <xsl:message terminate="yes">
```

```
            This stylesheet relies on exsl:node-set().
      </xsl:message>
   </xsl:otherwise>
</xsl:choose>
```

Converting Result Tree Fragments to Node Sets

The most common and most useful extension functions are those that convert result tree fragments to node sets. These functions are useful because they allow you to construct intermediate XML that you can use as the basis of further processing. We've seen examples of this functionality throughout this book; some examples are:

◆ When computing a sum, a minimum or a maximum based on a calculated value for a node

◆ When performing several transformations within a single stylesheet

◆ When numbering grouped nodes

Taking the first as an example, say that you wished to sum the values of a set of transaction elements, but their values have to be converted according to some exchange rate. It is simple to generate a copy of the transaction elements with converted values as follows:

```
<xsl:for-each select="transaction">
   <xsl:copy>
      <xsl:copy-of select="@*" />
      <xsl:choose>
         <xsl:when test="@currency = 'USD'">
            <xsl:value-of select=". * $exchange-rate" />
         </xsl:when>
         <xsl:otherwise>
            <xsl:value-of select="." />
         </xsl:otherwise>
      </xsl:choose>
   </xsl:copy>
</xsl:for-each>
```

Likewise, it is simple to sum the values of transaction elements with the sum() function:

```
<xsl:value-of select="sum(transaction)" />
```

However, you need a recursive function to do both of these at once. If you assign the copied transaction elements to a variable using its content, then the variable holds a result tree fragment:

```
<xsl:variable name="transactions-rtf">
   <xsl:for-each select="transaction">
      <xsl:copy>
         <xsl:copy-of select="@*" />
         <xsl:choose>
            <xsl:when test="@currency = 'USD'">
               <xsl:value-of select=". * $exchange-rate" />
            </xsl:when>
            <xsl:otherwise>
               <xsl:value-of select="." />
            </xsl:otherwise>
         </xsl:choose>
      </xsl:copy>
   </xsl:for-each>
</xsl:variable>
```

You cannot do any further processing on the result tree fragment without converting it to a node set. You can do the conversion with an extension function such as exsl:node-set(), and thence get the sum of the copied transaction elements as follows:

```
<xsl:value-of select="sum(exsl:node-set($transactions)/transaction)" />
```

Converting a result tree fragment to a node set returns the root node of the result tree fragment; you need to step further down the result tree fragment to access the contents of the variable.

Almost every XSLT processor in existence has its own function to convert a result tree fragment to a node set, such as msxsl:node-set(), saxon:node-set() and xalan:nodeSet(), as does the EXSLT initiative (exsl:node-set()). The XSLT 1.1 Working Draft does away with the concept of result tree fragments, so if you generate some XML as the value of a variable then that variable can be used immediately as if it was set to the root node of the generated node tree. It is also likely that XSLT 2.0 will also allow this implicit conversion.

However, as with any extension function, using an extension function to convert from a result tree fragment to a node set will tie the stylesheet to a particular processor, so if you do not have to use one of these functions, then you should not. For example, if you have some static XML that you use in your stylesheet, you should access it using the document() function rather than define it within a variable that you then convert to a node set.

Extension Functions

The rest of this chapter describes the functions that are available within EXSLT and in the major XSLT processors — MSXML, Saxon, and Xalan. For practicality, other processors are not covered here, although many of them have extension functions of their own.

It's the nature of extension functions that new ones are made available (or support is removed for old ones) as processors develop. Therefore, always check the latest version of your processor's documentation to see what extension functions it offers.

EXSLT Extension Functions

The EXSLT initiative (http://www.exslt.org) provides a set of extension functions in an attempt to supply a common namespace for common functions so that your stylesheets can be more portable across XSLT processors. The set of functions defined within EXSLT is constantly growing. Currently, three processors — Saxon, 4XSLT and jd.xslt — support the common functions.

The EXSLT site also provides third-party implementations for many of the functions. These can be used as the source in user-defined functions, which you cover in Chapter 20.

The EXSLT extensions are split into a number of modules that reflect the different types of functionality. The following sections describe only the core extension functions, which are the ones that have been discussed and implemented by the EXSLT community.

COMMON MODULE

The EXSLT - Common module (http://www.exslt.org/exsl) holds common extensions. The namespace for the Common module is

```
http://exslt.org/common
```

The extension functions in the Common module are described in Table 18-1.

TABLE 18-1 COMMON MODULE EXTENSION FUNCTIONS

Function	Description
node-set exsl:node-set(*rtf*)	Converts the argument result tree fragment to a node set
string object-type(*object*)	Returns the type of the object passed as an argument, giving a string value of 'boolean', 'number', 'string', 'node-set', 'rtf', or 'external'

MATH MODULE

The EXSLT - Math module (http://www.exslt.org/math) holds extensions relating to mathematical functionality. The namespace for the Math module is:

http://exslt.org/math

The extension functions in the Math module are described in Table 18-2.

TABLE 18-2 MATH MODULE EXTENSION FUNCTIONS

Function	Description
number math:min(*node-set*)	Returns the minimum value of the nodes passed as the argument
number math:max(*node-set*)	Returns the maximum value of the nodes passed as the argument
node-set math:lowest(*node-set*)	Returns the nodes in the node set that have the minimum value, as returned by math:min()
node-set math:highest(*node-set*)	Returns the nodes in the node set that have the maximum value, as returned by math:max()

SETS MODULE

The EXSLT - Sets module (http://www.exslt.org/set) holds extensions relating to set manipulation. The namespace for the Sets module is

http://exslt.org/sets

The extension functions in the Sets module are described in Table 18-3.

TABLE 18-3 SETS MODULE EXTENSION FUNCTIONS

Function	Description
node-set set:difference (*node-set*, *node-set*)	Returns the nodes that are in the first node set, but are not in the second node set
node-set set:intersection (*node-set*, *node-set*)	Returns the nodes that are in both the first and second argument node sets
node-set set:distinct (*node-set*)	Returns the nodes within the node set that are the first node in the node set with their value (the nodes with unique values)
boolean set:has-same-node (*node-set*, *node-set*)	Returns true if any node exists in both node sets; this can be used to test node identity
node-set set:leading (*node-set*, *node-set*)	Returns the nodes in the first node set that precede, in document order, the first node in the second node set
node-set set:trailing (*node-set*, *node-set*)	Returns the nodes in the first node set that follow, in document order, the first node in the second node set

DATES AND TIMES MODULE

The EXSLT - Dates and Times module (http://www.exslt.org/date) holds extensions relating to dates and times. The namespace for the Dates and Times module is

http://exslt.org/dates-and-times

The Dates and Times module relies on the date- and time-related formats specified in XML Schema - Datatypes at http://www.w3.org/TR/xmlschema-2/.

The extension functions in the Dates and Times module are described in Table 18-4.

TABLE **18-4** DATES AND TIMES MODULE EXTENSION FUNCTIONS

Function	Description
string date:date-time()	Returns the current date and time in xs:dateTime format
string date:date(*string*?)	Returns the date specified in the argument date/time in xs:date format; defaults to the current date
string date:time(*string*?)	Returns the time specified in the argument date/time in xs:time format; defaults to the current time
number date:year(*string*?)	Returns the year specified in the argument date/time as a number; defaults to the current year
boolean date:leap-year(*string*?)	Returns true if the year specified in the argument date/time is a leap year; defaults to the current year
number date:month-in-year(*string*?)	Returns the month specified in the argument date/time as a number; defaults to the current month
string date:month-name(*string*?)	Returns the name of the month specified in the argument date/time; defaults to the current month
string date:month-abbreviation(*string*?)	Returns the abbreviation of the month specified in the argument date/time; defaults to the current month
number date:week-in-year(*string*?)	Returns the number of the week specified in the argument date/time within the year; defaults to the current week
number date:day-in-year(*string*?)	Returns the number of the day specified in the argument date/time within the year; defaults to the current date
number date:day-in-month(*string*?)	Returns the number of the day specified in the argument date/time within the month; defaults to the current date

Function	Description
number date:day-of-week-in-month(*string*?)	Returns the number of the day of the week specified in the argument date/time within the month (such as 3rd Wednesday of the month); defaults to the current date
number date:day-in-week(*string*?)	Returns the number of the day specified in the argument date/time within the week; defaults to the current date
string date:day-name(*string*?)	Returns the name of the day of the week specified in the argument date/time; defaults to the current day
string date:day-abbreviation(*string*?)	Returns the name of the day of the week specified in the argument date/time; defaults to the current day
number date:hour-in-day(*string*?)	Returns the hour of the day specified in the argument date/time as a number; defaults to the current hour
number date:minute-in-hour(*string*?)	Returns the minutes specified in the argument date/time as a number; defaults to the current minute
number date:second-in-minute(*string*?)	Returns the seconds specified in the argument date/time as a number; defaults to the current second

MSXML Extension Functions

The latest version of MSXML is MSXML4. MSXML3 supplied `msxsl:node-set()` as an extension function. MSXML4 goes beyond this, offering access to XML Schema information as well as various extension functions for manipulating values in other ways.

 The information in this section is based on the MSXML 4.0 Technology Preview SDK documentation available from `http://msdn.microsoft.com/`. The function definitions may change as MSXML gets closer to a final release.

All the MSXML extension functions are in the following namespace:

`urn:schemas-microsoft-com:xslt`

The MSXML extension functions are summarized in Table 18-5.

TABLE 18-5 MSXML EXTENSION FUNCTIONS

Function	Description
Basic functions	
node-set `msxsl:node-set(`*rtf*`)`	Converts the argument result tree fragment to a node set
number `msxsl:string-compare` `(string, string, string?, string?)`	Returns -1 if the first string is "less than" the second string, 1 if it is "more than" the second string, and 0 if the two strings are equal; the third argument specifies the language used to compare the strings — it defaults to the local system language; the final argument determines how case is dealt with — the default behavior is case-sensitive, with lowercase first, `'-u'` specifies uppercase first instead, and `'-i'` specifies case-insensitive comparisons
XML Schema data types	
number `msxsl:number(`*string*`)`	Converts a string into a number in a similar way to `number()`, but correctly converts the strings `'INF'` (returns positive Infinity) and `'-INF'` (returns negative Infinity), and strings containing exponents. These numerical formats which are used in `xs:float` and `xs:double` data types in XML Schema (`number()` converts them into NaN)
string `msxsl:local-name(`*string*`)`	Returns the local name of the qualified name passed as the argument (the argument string is assumed to be in `xs:QName` format)
string `msxsl:namespace-uri(`*string*`)`	Returns the namespace URI of the qualified name passed as the argument (the argument string is assumed to be in `xs:QName` format); the prefix is resolved according to the namespaces in scope on the current node

Function	Description
string msxsl:utc(*string*)	Converts the date/time string passed as an argument, which must be in one of the XML Schema date/time formats, into a normalized date/time string in xs:dateTime format
string msxsl:format-date (*string*, *string*, *string*?)	Formats a date/time string as a date using the format pattern passed as the second argument; the third argument specifies a locale to be used in naming months and days
string msxsl:format-time (*string*, *string*, *string*?)	Formats a date/time string as a time using the format pattern passed as the second argument; the third argument specifies a locale to be used

XML Schema value types

Function	Description
boolean msxsl:schema-info-available()	Returns true if schema information about the context node is available
boolean msxsl:type-is (*string*, *string*)	Returns true if the context node is of the type specified; the first argument specifies the URI for the type, the second its local name; also returns false if no schema information is available for the context node
string msxsl:type-local-name (*node-set*?)	Returns the local name of the type of the first node in the node set; defaults to the context node
string msxsl:type-namespace-	Returns the namespace URI of the type of the first node in the node set; defaults to the context node

Saxon Extension Functions

The most recent versions of Saxon incorporate many of the EXSLT extension functions, but several Saxon functions offer functionality over and above that offered within the EXSLT equivalents. Saxon functions that are deprecated in favor of EXSLT are not covered here.

The information in this section is based on the Saxon 6.4.3 documentation available from `http://users.iclway.co.uk/mhkay/saxon/saxon6.4.3/extensions.html`.

All the Saxon extension functions are in the following namespace:

`http://icl.com/saxon`

Saxon has introduced a new object type, *expression*, which holds an XPath expression that can be dynamically evaluated. You can create an expression with `saxon:expression()`. Expressions are used in several of Saxon's extension functions to support higher-order functions.

The Saxon extension functions are summarized in Table 18-6.

TABLE 18-6 SAXON EXTENSION FUNCTIONS

Function	Description
Traversal functions	
node-set `saxon:before` (*node-set*, *node-set*)	Returns those nodes in the first node set that precede at least one of the nodes in the second node set
node-set `saxon:after` (*node-set*, *node-set*)	Returns those nodes in the first node set that follow at least one of the nodes in the second node set
node-set `saxon:leading` (*node-set*, *expression*)	Returns those nodes in the node set up to (but excluding) the first node for which the expression evaluates to false
node-set `saxon:closure` (*node-set*, *expression*)	Goes through the nodes in the node set and evaluates the expression for each to produce a node set; this node set is then used in the same way again, and the result of those are processed, and so on, recursively — all the nodes that are found along the way are returned; this function is particularly useful when dealing with flat hierarchies, in which parent-child information is stored through references, rather than within the XML structure

Function	Description
Dynamic evaluation	
object saxon:evaluate(*string*)	Dynamically evaluates a string as an XPath expression
expression saxon:expression (*string*)	Creates an expression object for use in other Saxon extension functions
object saxon:eval(*expression*)	Dynamically evaluates an expression object in the current context
Set functions	
node-set saxon:distinct (*node-set, expression*?)	Assigns each node in the node set a value by evaluating the expression with the node as the context node, and returns those nodes that are the first in the node set with each particular value; the expression defaults to the string value of the node, so if you use this without the second argument, you may as well use exsl:distinct( )
boolean saxon:exists (*node-set, expression*)	Returns true if the expression evaluates as true for any of the nodes in the node set
boolean saxon:for-all (*node-set, expression*)	Returns true if the expression evaluates as true for all of the nodes in the node set
boolean saxon:has-same-nodes (*node-set, node-set*)	Returns true if the two node sets contain exactly the same nodes
Math functions	
number saxon:sum	Sums the values of the nodes in the node set, where their values are calculated by evaluating the expression for each of them
node-set saxon:min (*node-set, expression*?)	Returns the minimum value of the nodes in the node set, where the value is calculated by evaluating the expression for the node; the expression defaults to the value of the node, so if you use this without the second argument, you may as well use exsl:min( )

Continued

TABLE **18-6** SAXON EXTENSION FUNCTIONS *(Continued)*

Function	Description
node-set saxon:max (*node-set*, *expression*?)	Returns the maximum value of the nodes in the node set, where the value is calculated by evaluating the expression for the node; the expression defaults to the value of the node, so if you use this without the second argument, you may as well use exsl:max()
node-set saxon:lowest (*node-set*, *expression*?)	Returns the first node, in document order, that has the minimum numerical value in the node set, where the value of a node is calculated by evaluating the expression for that node; the expression defaults to returning the numerical value of the node
node-set saxon:highest (*node-set*, *expression*?)	Returns the first node, in document order, that has the maximum numerical value in the node set, where the value of a node is calculated by evaluating the expression for that node; the expression defaults to returning the numerical value of the node
Conditional functions	
object saxon:if (*boolean*, *object*, *object*)	Returns the second argument if the first argument is true, and returns the third argument if the first argument is false; note that all the arguments are evaluated no matter what
boolean saxon:if-null (*external*)	Tests whether the Java object passed as an argument is null
Node-set generating functions	
node-set saxon:range (*number*, *number*)	Generates a node set of nodes with values ranging from the first number to the second number (inclusive)
node-set saxon:tokenize (*string*, *string*?)	Splits the first argument string into a set of nodes at any characters specified in the second argument string; the second argument defaults to whitespace characters

Function	Description
Debugging functions	
string saxon:path()	Returns a location path to the context node
number saxon:line-number()	Returns the line number of the context node in the source XML document
string saxon:systemId()	Returns the URI of the entity from which the context node comes
User data functions	
object saxon:get-user-data (*string*)	Returns the user data (set by saxon:set-user-data()) associated with the context node
string saxon:set-user-data (*string*, *object*)	Sets the user data associated with the context node for later retrieval by saxon:get-user-data()

Xalan Extension Functions

Xalan offers a range of extension functions, including a set of extension functions that support SQL access to a database.

 The information in this section is based on the Xalan-J 2.1.0 documentation available from `http://xml.apache.org/xalan-j/extensionslib.html`.

BASIC FUNCTIONS
The basic Xalan extension functions are in the following namespace:

`http://xml.apache.org/Xalan`

These functions are described in Table 18-7.

TABLE 18-7 XALAN EXTENSION FUNCTIONS

Function	Description
node-set xalan:node-set(*rtf*)	Converts the argument result tree fragment to a node set
object xalan:evaluate(*string*)	Dynamically evaluates a string as an XPath expression
node-set xalan:tokenize) (*string*, *string*?	Splits the first argument string into a set of nodes at any characters specified in the second argument string; the second argument defaults to whitespace characters
node-set xalan:difference (*node-set*, *node-set*)	Returns the nodes that are in the first node set but are not in the second node set
node-set xalan:intersection (*node-set*, *node-set*)	Returns the nodes that are in both the first and second argument node sets
node-set xalan:distinct (*node-set*)	Returns the nodes within the node set that are the first with their particular value (the nodes with unique values)
boolean xalan:hasSameNodes (*node-set*, *node-set*)	Returns true if the two node sets contain exactly the same nodes

SQL FUNCTIONS

The SQL support in Xalan uses JDBC to connect to and query a database. Most of the SQL extension functions use an external XConnection object, which can be created using the sql:new() function. The results of queries using these functions are node sets holding the root node of an XML structure in the following form:

```
<row-set>
   <column-header column-label="..." />
   <column-header column-label="..." />
   ...
   <row>
      <col>...</col>
      <col>...</col>
      ...
   </row>
   ...
</row-set>
```

The SQL extension functions are in the following namespace:

`org.apache.xalan.lib.sql.XConnection`

The use of this namespace illustrates how you can use Xalan to implement user-defined extension functions as a Java class; see Chapter 20 for more details.

These functions are described in Table 18-8.

TABLE 18-8 SQL EXTENSION FUNCTIONS

Function	Description
XConnection sql:new(*string, string, string?, string?*)	Creates a connection to a database; the first argument is the name of the JDBC driver, the second is the URL to the database; the third and fourth arguments specify the user name and password for accessing the database
node-set sql:query (*XConnection, string, string*)	Returns the node set resulting from the SQL query specified as the second argument on the database connection specified by the first argument
node-set sql:pquery (*XConnection, string*)	Returns the node set resulting from the SQL parameterized query specified as the second argument (question marks indicate the positions of parameters in the query string) on the database connection specified by the first argument; the third argument specifies a space-separated list of parameter value types
sql:addParameter (*XConnection, string*)	Adds the parameter value to the parameter list used when evaluating parameterized queries
sql:addParameters (*XConnection, node-set*)	Adds the values of the nodes in the node set to the parameter list used when evaluating parameterized queries
sql:clearParameters (*XConnection*)	Clears the parameter list used when evaluating parameterized queries
sql:close(*XConnection*)	Closes the connection to the database

Summary

Although XPath provides a good starting set of functions, it doesn't do everything. Extension functions can help you do things that otherwise require a lot of XSLT code (such as the various utility templates discussed in Chapter 1). They can be called from within attributes like the `select` attribute of `xsl:sort`, which can simplify your stylesheet. They can also enable you to do things that just aren't possible in XSLT, such as accessing databases or determining the current date.

This chapter showed you how to use extension functions in your stylesheet. You also learned how to use them while maintaining your stylesheet's portability. You saw how to use the most useful extension functions, which convert result tree fragments to node sets for further processing. Finally, you examined the various extension functions that are available in the main XSLT processors, as well as those defined in the EXSLT initiative.

Chapter 19

Using Extension Elements

AS DESCRIBED IN CHAPTER 18, extension functions plug the gaps in XPath. Extension elements, attributes, and attribute values likewise extend the functionality of XSLT. Extension elements and attributes can do all sorts of things; extension attribute values are used with attributes that are specifically labeled as extensible.

This chapter describes how to use these extensions, and discusses the extensions available in EXSLT and in various specific processors. Just as with extension functions, using extension elements can decrease the portability of your stylesheet. Therefore, you'll also learn how to check the availability of extension elements and how to ensure that other processors won't object to your stylesheet.

 Just as with extension functions, the XSLT Recommendation doesn't specify how you can define the extension elements that you use. Some processors — in particular, Xalan — allow you to implement your own extension elements and point to those implementations from the stylesheet; you'll learn how to do this in Chapter 20.

Using Extensions to XSLT

Three types of extensions to XSLT are described in this chapter:

◆ Extension elements – elements that control the processing of the source XML (rather than being output as part of the result)

◆ Extension attributes – attributes on XSLT elements (or on result elements) that control the processing of the source XML

◆ Extension attribute values – qualified names that are used as attribute values to provide extra control with certain XSLT instructions

Technically, any elements that you use at the top level of the stylesheet (children of xsl:stylesheet) don't count as extension elements, despite the fact that they can change the way that a stylesheet processes a document. The only elements of this type in the major processors are those that enable you to define extension functions and elements; these are covered in Chapter 20.

All these extensions use a non-XSLT namespace. As with extension functions, the namespace for any of these extensions is usually based on the processor that offers the extension (though some extensions use more general namespaces, such as those of EXSLT).

Future versions of XSLT may introduce elements in the XSLT namespace that aren't recognized by current XSLT processors. These elements would be treated in exactly the same way as extension elements.

Therefore, the first step in using these extensions is to declare the namespace(s) for the extensions that you use. For example, to use the exsl:document extension element, you need to declare the EXSLT - Common namespace as follows:

```
<xsl:stylesheet version="1.0"
            xmlns:xsl="http://www.w3.org/1999/XSL/Transform"
            xmlns:exsl="http://exslt.org/common">
...
</xsl:stylesheet>
```

The processor needs to recognize that the elements and attributes in this namespace are instructions to the processor, rather than things that should be output in the result. You use the extension-element-prefixes attribute on xsl:stylesheet to do this:

```
<xsl:stylesheet version="1.0"
            xmlns:xsl="http://www.w3.org/1999/XSL/Transform"
            xmlns:exsl="http://exslt.org/common"
```

```
                extension-element-prefixes="exsl">
...
</xsl:stylesheet>
```

When you've done that, you can use any extensions in that namespace; the XSLT processor will attempt to process the extension elements, and will use the extension attributes and attribute values if it understands them.

Checking Extension Availability

Different XSLT processors support different extensions. If you write a stylesheet that relies on a particular extension, it's good practice to verify that the extension exists, and to provide some kind of fallback behavior for the stylesheet if it doesn't.

Testing the Availability of Extension Elements

It's easy to test whether extension elements are available: XSLT adds the `element-available()` function to XPath, which works in a similar way to `function-available()`. If you pass it the name of an element, the `element-available()` function will return true if the element exists. For example, to see whether the processor supports `exsl:document`, you can use the following:

```
element-available('exsl:document')
```

The `element-available()` function doesn't indicate whether elements that you use at the top level of the stylesheet in a non-XSLT namespace are recognizable or not, only those that you use within a template.

Testing the Availability of Other Extensions

There's no built-in way to check whether a processor supports particular extension attributes or extension attribute values. Usually, this doesn't matter because the XSLT processor will default to using the basic behavior of the XSLT instruction without raising an error.

Sometimes, however, you might want to check whether the extension is available so that you can issue a warning that the stylesheet won't work precisely as advertised. Unfortunately, the only way of doing this is by checking the identity of the XSLT processor that's processing the stylesheet, with the `system-property()` function, which means that if you don't know about a processor that actually does support the extension, then you will generate the error message regardless. For example, if you're using an output method that you know is only supported by

Saxon, you could test whether the stylesheet is being used with Saxon with the following:

```
starts-with(system-property('xsl:vendor'), 'SAXON')
```

 You need to be a bit careful about using the vendor identity to determine what's available. Vendors might change the vendor information that they supply, or might change the availability of extensions in future versions. Moreover, other vendors may support the same extension without you being aware of it.

Recovering from Unavailable Extension Elements

You learned some of the ways in which you might respond to unavailable extension functions in Chapter 18. The same techniques for checking availability and acting accordingly if the extension is unavailable apply to these extensions as well as to extension functions.

You have an additional method of dealing with missing extension elements, however: the xsl:fallback element. If you use an extension element within a template but the XSLT processor doesn't recognize that element, it will search for an xsl:fallback element inside the extension element and process the contents of the xsl:fallback element instead.

For example, as described later, in the section "Creating Multiple Output Files," several processors offer elements for creating multiple output files from a transformation—saxon:output in Saxon, and redirect:write in Xalan, for example—and similar functionality is provided by xsl:document, introduced in the XSLT 1.1 working draft, and exsl:document from the EXSLT initiative. You can create a template that uses whichever of these is available using the xsl:fallback element as follows:

```
<xsl:template name="create-document">
   <xsl:param name="file" select="'out.xml'" />
   <xsl:param name="content" select="/.." />
   <xsl:document href="{$file}">
      <xsl:copy-of select="$content" />
      <xsl:fallback>
         <exsl:document href="{$file}">
            <xsl:copy-of select="$content" />
            <xsl:fallback>
               <saxon:output href="{$file}">
                  <xsl:copy-of select="$content" />
                  <xsl:fallback>
                     <redirect:write select="$file">
                        <xsl:copy-of select="$content" />
```

```
                <xsl:fallback>
                        ...
                </xsl:fallback>
                </redirect:write>
              </xsl:fallback>
            </saxon:output>
        </xsl:fallback>
      </exsl:document>
    </xsl:fallback>
  </xsl:document>
</xsl:template>
```

As you can see, when you have many alternatives, it's easier to test for element availability and use xsl:choose, rather than rely on xsl:fallback. The xsl:choose alternative is as follows:

```
<xsl:template name="create-document">
  <xsl:param name="file" select="'out.xml'" />
  <xsl:param name="content" select="/.." />
  <xsl:choose>
    <xsl:when test="element-available('xsl:document')">
      <xsl:document href="{$file}">
        <xsl:copy-of select="$content" />
      </xsl:document>
    </xsl:when>
    <xsl:when test="element-available('exsl:document')">
      <exsl:document href="{$file}">
        <xsl:copy-of select="$content" />
      </exsl:document>
    </xsl:when>
    <xsl:when test="element-available('saxon:output')">
      <saxon:output href="{$file}">
        <xsl:copy-of select="$content" />
      </saxon:output>
    </xsl:when>
    <xsl:when test="element-available('redirect:write')">
      <redirect:write select="$file">
        <xsl:copy-of select="$content" />
      </redirect:write>
    </xsl:when>
    <xsl:otherwise>
        ...
    </xsl:otherwise>
  </xsl:choose>
</xsl:template>
```

Some extension elements provide an easier way of achieving a goal that you may nevertheless be able to achieve with standard XSLT 1.0. In these cases, you can provide the XSLT 1.0 alternative within the fallback. If all else fails, you should use `xsl:message` to terminate the transformation with an appropriate error message. For example, if your stylesheet requires the `exsl:document` extension element in order to work, then you need the stylesheet to terminate if it's not available:

```
<exsl:document href="...">
   ...
   <xsl:fallback>
      <xsl:message terminate="yes">
         This stylesheet relies on exsl:document.
      </xsl:message>
   </xsl:fallback>
</exsl:document>
```

Creating Multiple Output Files

Many XSLT processors offer an extension element that enables you to create multiple output files with a single transformation, and the XSLT 1.1 Working Draft introduces an `xsl:document` element with the same aim.

Creating Frames

One situation in which creating multiple output files is helpful is when creating framesets in Web pages. Framesets have a single (usually static) page that specifies the layout of the frames and points to separate documents that hold the Web pages to be shown in each of the separate pages.

You can find information about creating framesets on the client side with MSXML in Chapter 14, and on the server side with Cocoon in Chapter 15.

For example, suppose you need to create a frameset that contains a menu frame on the left and a main frame on the right. The frameset document is the main output from the stylesheet. It refers to two separate pages: `menu.html` for the menu and `main.html` for the main part of the page. This is shown in Figure 19-1.

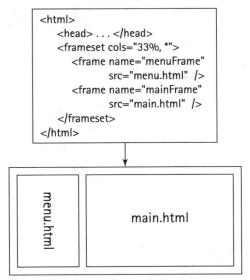

```
<html>
    <head> . . . </head>
    <frameset cols="33%, *">
        <frame name="menuFrame"
              src="menu.html" />
        <frame name="mainFrame"
              src="main.html" />
    </frameset>
</html>
```

menu.html

main.html

Figure 19-1: Stylesheet result creating a frameset referring to separate files

This is relatively straightforward with an element like `exsl:document`, which enables you to create several files at once. The main stylesheet process creates the frameset, and then you use `exsl:document` to create the content of the other files, usually by applying templates in different modes:

```
<xsl:template match="/">
   <frameset cols="33%,*">
      <frame name="menuFrame" src="menu.html" />
      <frame name="mainFrame" src="main.html" />
   </frameset>
   <exsl:document href="menu.html">
      <xsl:apply-templates mode="menu" />
   </exsl:document>
   <exsl:document href="main.html">
      <xsl:apply-templates mode="main" />
   </exsl:document>
</xsl:template>
```

The big advantage to creating frames in this way is that the content of the two frames is created in the same process. This saves processing because the stylesheet and the XML source only have to be parsed once, and you can reuse global variables and keys across the various documents that you're creating.

Importantly, it also means that the generated ID of a particular node will be the same during the generation of both documents, which means that you can easily set up links between them. For example, in that bank statement application, you want to link from a date to the first transaction with that date. Assuming that templates are applied only to these first transactions, you can have a template in `main` mode that generates an anchor for that transaction in the main part of the result using the generated ID of the transaction element:

```
<xsl:template match="transaction" mode="main">
   <tr>
      <td>
         <a name="{generate-id()}"><xsl:value-of select="@date" /></a>
      </td>
      ...
   </tr>
</xsl:template>
```

Meanwhile, in menu mode, you can have a template that generates a link to that anchor in the main frame:

```
<xsl:template match="transaction" mode="menu">
   <a href="main.html#{generate-id()}" target="mainframe">
      <xsl:value-of select="@date" />
   </a>
   <br />
</xsl:template>
```

Processing Multiple Files to Create Multiple Outputs

These extension elements give you the capability to create several files from the same transformation. The `document()` function also gives you the capability to access different XML files for use as the basis of a transformation. These two facilities combined mean that rather than performing batch transformations using several command lines, you can instead use one command to process a number of files to generate different results.

For example, my Web site is based on numerous XML files, but you can use a single transformation to generate the HTML from all of them:

```
<xsl:template match="/">
   <exsl:document href="index.html">
      <xsl:apply-templates select="document('index.xml')/*" />
   </exsl:document>
   <exsl:document href="contact.html">
      <xsl:apply-templates select="document('contact.xml')/*" />
   </exsl:document>
   <exsl:document href="cv.html">
```

```
    <xsl:apply-templates select="document('cv.xml')/*" />
  </exsl:document>
  ...
</xsl:template>
```

Again, this saves processing compared to multiple command lines because the processor only needs to be started once, and the stylesheet only needs to be parsed and loaded once.

 Being able to create a file and then read that same file in using `document()` breaks the "no side effects" rule of XSLT. Therefore, the order in which the instructions are processed can make a difference. For this reason, the `xsl:document` element from XSLT 1.1 (and hence the `exsl:document` extension element from EXSLT) both contain rules to ensure that the document is not created when the instruction is encountered, but rather at the end of the process, along with the main output.

Extensions in Different Processors

Different processors have different extension elements for creating multiple result documents, each of which work in slightly different ways. Of the major processors, MSXML does not currently have any built-in support for creating multiple output files (which is not entirely surprising given that it focuses on client-side transformation), although it does support user-defined extension functions, so you could write your own. Saxon supports `xsl:document` from XSLT 1.1 as well as `saxon:output` from its own namespace, which behaves in exactly the same way. The redirect extensions in Xalan work slightly differently.

 Chapter 20 describes how to use MSXML to define your own extension functions.

XSL:DOCUMENT, EXSL:DOCUMENT, AND SAXON:OUTPUT

These three extension elements work in the same way. `xsl:document` comes from the XSLT 1.1 Working Draft, which uses the same namespace as XSLT 1.0 (which is being merged into XSLT 2.0 and will never be a Recommendation).

The extension element `saxon:output` is Saxon-specific. Its namespace is as follows:

```
http://icl.com/saxon
```

The extension element `exsl:document` is from the Common module of the EXSLT initiative. Its namespace is as follows:

`http://exslt.org/common`

The attributes on these elements are mainly the same as the attributes on `xsl:output`, but can contain attribute value templates (so that you can set them dynamically). An `href` attribute specifies the location of the file to be created; the content of the element generates the content of the file. The attributes on these elements are described in more detail in Table 19-1.

TABLE **19-1** ATTRIBUTES ON XSL:DOCUMENT, EXSL:DOCUMENT, AND SAXON:OUTPUT

Attribute	Value Type	Description
href	String (attribute value template)	Specifies the URL for the file to be created
method	xml, text, html or a qualified name (attribute value template)	Specifies the type of output that is expected, and therefore the way in which elements, attributes, and characters are serialized (if they are at all); defaults to xml unless the document element of the result tree is called html or HTML
version	name token (attribute value template)	Specifies the version of the output method; if the output method is xml, it specifies the version of XML (default 1.0), if it's html, it specifies the version of HTML (default 4.0), and so on
encoding	encoding string (attribute value template)	Specifies the character encoding that should be used in the output file; defaults to UTF-8
omit-xml-declaration	yes or no (attribute value template)	Specifies whether the XML declaration should be given in the output; defaults to yes if the output method is xml
standalone	yes or no (attribute value template)	Specifies whether the result document can stand alone, without referencing external entities; this is added to the XML declaration in the output if it is specified

Attribute	Value Type	Description
doctype-public	string (attribute value template)	Specifies the public identifier for the document type of the result
doctype-system	URI (attribute value template)	Specifies the location of the DTD for the result
cdata-section-elements	space-separated list of qualified names (attribute value template)	Gives the names of elements whose content should be wrapped within CDATA sections; commonly, this holds the names of elements that contain code
indent	yes or no (attribute value template)	Tells the processor whether to make the output more readable by adding whitespace-only text nodes; defaults to no
media-type	string (attribute value template)	Specifies the content type of the output; defaults to text/xml if the output method is xml, and to text/html if the output method is html

Saxon adds a few further extensions to xsl:document and xsl:output (which has the same kind of effect, but for the main output of the transformation).

First, it adds a couple of additional output methods that can be used in the method attribute:

◆ saxon:fop — redirects the XSL-FO result of the stylesheet to Apache's FOP processor (if you have it installed) to create PDF

◆ saxon:xhtml — uses the XML output method, except that it follows the XHTML rules for compatibility with legacy HTML browsers

Next, it adds several extension attributes to provide finer control over the output (see Table 19-2):

TABLE **19-2 SAXON EXTENSION ATTRIBUTES ON XSL:OUTPUT**

Attribute	Value Type	Description
`saxon:indent-spaces`	number (attribute value template)	Specifies the number of spaces to be used when the result is output with indents
`saxon:character-representation`	if the output method is `xml`, can be `decimal` or `hex`; if the output method is `html`, must be a pair of values separated by a semi-colon — first value is one of `native`, `entity`, `decimal` or `hex`, second value is one of `entity`, `decimal` or `hex` (attribute value template)	Tells the processor how to output characters: as native characters, as entity references, or as decimal or hexadecimal character references (for example, a nonbreaking space might be output as a nonbreaking space, as or as in decimal or &#A0; in hex); for the HTML output method, the pair of values specifies the directive for non-ASCII characters, followed by the directive for those outside the character encoding
`saxon:omit-meta-tag`	`yes` or `no` (attribute value template)	If `yes`, tells the processor not to output a `meta` element in the head of the HTML document when the output method is `html`
`saxon:next-in-chain`	URL (attribute value template)	Specifies the URL of a stylesheet to be used on the result of this transformation

---

REDIRECT EXTENSIONS IN XALAN

Xalan supports a set of extension elements that deal with redirecting output to different files. These extension elements are in the following namespace:

```
org.apache.xalan.xslt.lib.Redirect
```

There are three extension elements in this namespace:

♦ `redirect:write` — writes its content to a file

♦ `redirect:open` — opens a file for writing

♦ `redirect:close` — closes a file for writing

The three elements each take two attributes: `select`, which gives an XPath expression to create a filename; and `file`, which specifies a literal filename and acts as a fallback if `select` isn't specified or if it evaluates to an invalid filename. Both `redirect:write` and `redirect:open` also have a `mkdirs` attribute, which will create the directories required for the file if set to 'yes' or 'true'.

If used alone, the `redirect:write` extension element works in a similar way to the other extension elements already discussed, creating a new file and writing the content to it. However, you can also explicitly open a file with `redirect:open`. If you do so, and then write to it, writing appends to the file, rather than overwrites it. The file can then be closed with `redirect:close`.

Extension Elements in Saxon

Saxon has gone further than most other XSLT processors in terms of the extension elements that it offers. The following sections briefly describe the most useful of them. All these extension elements are in the following namespace:

```
http://icl.com/saxon
```

Grouping in Saxon

As explained in Chapter 9, grouping is not straightforward in pure XSLT 1.0. The `saxon:group` and `saxon:item` elements in Saxon make it a lot easier to perform grouping.

The `saxon:group` extension element has two attributes: `select`, which is an expression that picks the nodes that you want to group, and `group-by`, which specifies an expression to be used to determine the value of a node and thus identify which group it comes from. Saxon takes the nodes that you select and sorts them according to any `xsl:sort` elements that are the first children of the `saxon:group` element. Saxon then goes through the nodes and uses the content of the `saxon:group` element to add content around any groups of nodes that have the same group-by value. Saxon processes the content of the `saxon:item` element within the `saxon:group` element to create a result for each of the individual nodes.

To illustrate this process, let's look at an example. A number of grouping problems of different types occur in Chapter 9, most of which could be handled easier using `saxon:group`. These examples used a set of transactions as a starting point:

```
<transaction date="2001-03-01" type="DD" payee="TV License">8.91</transaction>
<transaction date="2001-03-01" type="DD" payee="British Gas">22.00</transaction>
<transaction date="2001-03-03" type="CR" payee="Client">400.00</transaction>
<transaction date="2001-03-09" type="SO" payee="Rent">633.00</transaction>
<transaction date="2001-03-10" type="WD" payee="Cash">50.00</transaction>
<transaction date="2001-03-15" type="CR" payee="Interest">0.58</transaction>
```

GROUPING BY POSITION

Grouping by position involves collecting nodes into groups of the same size; for example, bunching the transactions into groups of four. With `saxon:group`, you can do this by having the `group-by` attribute select a value based on the position of the node being grouped. For example, the following groups the `transaction` elements according to the result of dividing their position by the size of the group that you're after:

```
<saxon:group select="transaction"
              group-by="floor((position() - 1) div $group-size)">
   <page no="floor((position() - 1) div $group-size)">
      <saxon:item>
         <xsl:copy-of select="." />
      </saxon:item>
   </page>
</saxon:group>
```

With the `$group-size` parameter set to 4, the result of this is as follows:

```
<page no="0">
   <transaction date="2001-03-01" type="DD"
                payee="TV License">8.91</transaction>
   <transaction date="2001-03-01" type="DD"
                payee="British Gas">22.00</transaction>
   <transaction date="2001-03-03" type="CR" payee="Client">400.00</transaction>
   <transaction date="2001-03-09" type="SO" payee="Rent">633.00</transaction>
</page>
<page no="1">
   <transaction date="2001-03-10" type="WD" payee="Cash">50.00</transaction>
   <transaction date="2001-03-15" type="CR" payee="Interest">0.58</transaction>
</page>
```

GROUPING BY VALUE

Grouping by value is done similarly, with the main content of the `saxon:group` element generating the group-level content, and the content of the `saxon:item` element generating the item-level content. When grouping by value, make sure that the nodes you're grouping are in the correct order, so that the nodes that you want grouped together form a contiguous group. You can do this by sorting the nodes with `xsl:sort`. You can also use `xsl:sort` to control the order in which the groups are processed, and the order in which the items are processed within the group.

For example, to group the `transaction` elements by type, and to sort the items within each group by value, you need two `xsl:sort` instructions — one to sort by type and one to sort by value:

```
<saxon:group select="transaction" group-by="@type">
   <xsl:sort select="@type" />
```

```
    <xsl:sort select="." data-type="number" />
    <h3>Transaction Type: <xsl:value-of select="@type" /></h3>
    <ul>
        <saxon:item>
            <li>
                <xsl:value-of select="@date" />: <xsl:text />
                <xsl:value-of select="." />
            </li>
        </saxon:item>
    </ul>
</saxon:group>
```

The result of this grouping on the preceding transactions would be as follows:

```
<h3>Transaction Type: CR</h3>
<ul>
    <li>2001-03-15: 0.58</li>
    <li>2001-03-03: 400.00</li>
</ul>
<h3>Transaction Type: DD</h3>
<ul>
    <li>2001-03-01: 8.91</li>
    <li>2001-03-01: 22.00</li>
</ul>
<h3>Transaction Type: SO</h3>
<ul>
    <li>2001-03-09: 633.00</li>
</ul>
<h3>Transaction Type: WD</h3>
<ul>
    <li>2001-03-10: 50.00</li>
</ul>
```

As you can see, using `saxon:group` for grouping problems of this kind results in cleaner and more understandable stylesheets. Grouping support is promised in XSLT 2.0 and may follow a similar kind of pattern.

Using a Procedural Style

By now, you've probably seen enough examples throughout this book to get an idea of what can be achieved using a declarative programming style. However, for those of you who aren't yet convinced, Saxon introduces a couple of extension elements that enable you to adopt a more procedural style: `saxon:assign` and `saxon:while`.

These extension elements break the "no side effects" rule of XSLT — using them means that the order in which the instructions in the XSLT are executed might make a difference to the result of the stylesheet and prevents the processor from executing the instructions in parallel.

The `saxon:assign` element works like `xsl:variable`, but unlike `xsl:variable`, it updates the value of an existing variable. To use it, the variable that you update must be labeled as assignable using the `saxon:assignable` extension attribute on `xsl:variable`. For example, you could use it to get the absolute value of a number:

```
<xsl:variable name="abs" select="$number" saxon:assignable="yes" />
<xsl:if test="$abs &lt; 0">
   <saxon:assign name="abs" select="$abs * -1" />
</xsl:if>
<xsl:value-of select="$abs" />
```

The biggest benefit of being able to assign a value to a variable becomes apparent when you use loops: you can update the variable within the loop, and it will be available with its updated value afterwards. Of course, you can use `xsl:for-each` for these loops, but Saxon also provides `saxon:while`. This enables you to continue looping until the condition in its `test` attribute (which must be based on an assignable variable in order to avoid infinite loops) becomes true.

For example, in Chapter 1, I wrote a recursive template to get the power of a number. With assignment and a while loop, you can do the same thing with a single loop:

```
<xsl:template name="power">
   <xsl:param name="number" />
   <xsl:param name="power" />
   <xsl:variable name="n" select="$number" saxon:assignable="yes" />
   <xsl:variable name="p" select="$power" saxon:assignable="yes" />
   <saxon:while test="$p > 1">
      <saxon:assign name="n" select="$n * $number" />
      <saxon:assign name="p" select="$p - 1" />
   </saxon:while>
   <xsl:value-of select="$n" />
</xsl:template>
```

Creating Internal DTDs

The final set of extension elements covered here involves creating internal DTDs in the result that you generate. Creating internal DTDs is especially useful if you want to use entity references in your output, and Saxon provides an extension element to create these entity references.

You learned how to create internal DTDs and entity references using pure XSLT 1.0 in Chapter 16.

CREATING DTDS

You can create an internal DTD in Saxon using the extension element `saxon:doctype`. This extension element has to precede the first element that you create in the result. The content of `saxon:doctype` should generate a number of elements in the following namespace:

    http://icl.com/saxon/dtd

These can be generated using literal result elements or using `xsl:element`, which gives you complete control over what you generate. The XML that you generate with `saxon:doctype` is interpreted when the result of the stylesheet is output, and Saxon generates DTD syntax from the elements. For example, if you create the following:

```
<dtd:doctype name="statement">
   <dtd:element name="transactions" content="(transaction+)" />
   <dtd:element name="transaction" content="(#PCDATA)" />
   <dtd:attlist element="transaction">
      <dtd:attribute name="date" type="CDATA" value="#REQUIRED" />
      <dtd:attribute name="type" type="(CR|DD|SO|WD)" value="'CR'" />
      <dtd:attribute name="payee" type="CDATA" value="#REQUIRED" />
   </dtd:attlist>
</dtd:doctype>
```

you will get the internal DTD:

```
<!DOCTYPE statement [
   <!ELEMENT transactions (transaction+)>
   <!ELEMENT transaction (#PCDATA)">
   <!ATTLIST transaction
      date    CDATA           #REQUIRED
      type    (CR|DD|SO|WD)   'CR'
      payee   CDATA           #REQUIRED>
]>
```

The elements that are interpreted by Saxon as defining a DTD are summarized in Table 19-3:

TABLE 19-3 SAXON ELEMENTS FOR DEFINING DTDS

Element	Content	Attributes
dtd:doctype	(dtd:element | dtd:attlist | dtd:entity | dtd:notation)*	name — name of the document element system — system ID (optional) public — public ID (optional)
dtd:element	EMPTY	name — name of the element content — content of the element
dtd:attlist	dtd:attribute+	element — name of the element
dtd:attribute	EMPTY	name — name of the attribute type — attribute type value — attribute value
dtd:entity	EMPTY	name — name of the notation system — system ID (optional) public — public ID (optional) parameter — yes or no (yes for a parameter entity) (optional) notation — name of the notation for an unparsed entity (optional)
dtd:notation	EMPTY	name — name of the notation system — system ID (optional) public — public ID (optional)

CREATING ENTITY DEFINITIONS AND REFERENCES

As already indicated, you can create an entity definition by generating a dtd:entity element in the content of a saxon:doctype element. Saxon also provides a saxon:entity-ref extension element for creating a reference to an entity. For example, you could create an internal DTD with entity definitions for the parts of a book:

```
<saxon:doctype>
   <dtd:doctype name="book"
            public="-//OASIS//DTD DocBook V3.1//EN"
            system="DTD/DocBook.dtd">
```

```
        <dtd:entity name="partI" system="partI.xml" />
        <dtd:entity name="partII" system="partII.xml" />
        ...
    </dtd:doctype>
</saxon:doctype>
```

This will produce the following DOCTYPE in the output:

```
<!DOCTYPE book PUBLIC '-//OASIS//DTD DocBook V3.1//EN'
                      'DTD/DocBook.dtd' [
  <!ENTITY partI SYSTEM 'partI.xml'>
  <!ENTITY partII SYSTEM 'partII.xml'>
  ...
]>
```

The entity declarations allow you to use an entity reference to pull in the external XML documents. It's difficult to create these in pure XSLT 1.0 because it means outputting an ampersand character without escaping it. The `saxon:entity-ref` gets around this problem. For example, to pull in the content of `partI.xml`, you can use the following:

```
<saxon:entity-ref name="partI" />
```

The `name` attribute holds the literal name of the entity, not an attribute value template for that name.

This will generate the following entity reference in the output:

```
&partI;
```

Summary

One of XSLT's greatest strengths is its extensibility. Extensions enable you to do things that you can't do in XSLT at all (such as create separate documents), or make it easier to do things that XSLT doesn't support very well (such as grouping). In this chapter, you learned how to use extension elements and, more importantly, how to ensure that your stylesheets remain as portable as possible when you do so.

You also learned about the extensions that are available in many processors for creating multiple documents, a capability that is extremely useful when generating several outputs for framesets or creating SVG documents. Because of the number of processors that support one, an element for directing output to a particular document is a very likely addition in XSLT 2.0.

Finally, you learned about some of the extension elements, attributes, and attribute values that are available in Saxon, both because it's a popular processor and because several of the extensions that it offers are in areas being targeted by XSLT 2.0. Therefore, you can expect to see similar functionality in XSLT in the future.

Chapter 20 examines a final major category of extension elements; namely, those extension elements that support the definition of extension functions and elements themselves.

Extending XPath Yourself

IN THIS CHAPTER

◆ Processor extensions for defining functions

◆ Writing extension functions in JavaScript

◆ Writing extension functions in XSLT

IN CHAPTER 18, YOU LEARNED about some of the extension functions that are available for XPath in specific XSLT processors. Although many processors offer a good set of extension functions, they can't cover everything, and often the functions that you need for a particular XSLT application are application-specific.

In this chapter, you'll learn how to define your own extension functions within stylesheets. Different processors use different methods to define functions, and support different languages for their definition. After learning how to use the major processors to define your own functions in languages such as JavaScript and Java, you'll learn how to use XSLT to define functions.

Defining Functions in Other Programming Languages

Many XSLT processors enable you to write extension functions using either Java or a scripting language like JavaScript and make them available in your stylesheet. These kinds of extension functions are particularly useful for two main reasons:

◆ Other languages have better access to the system environment than XSLT — you can't write an XSLT template to determine whether a file exists or to get the current date and time.

◆ Other languages have a wider range of objects and methods than XSLT — it's possible to write regular expression parsers in XSLT, but it's labor-intensive compared to using the existing ones in other languages.

There is a third reason to use extension functions; namely, they enable you to do things within an XPath expression for which you would otherwise have to use XSLT. However, if this is the only reason why you're using an extension function, you could use XSLT to define the function, as described in the next section.

Passing Arguments to User-Defined Functions

When you use XPath frequently, it's easy to get sloppy about the types of objects that you pass into functions. XPath functions tend to perform a lot of conversions behind the scenes — if you pass a node set to a function that's expecting a string, it will convert the node set to a string automatically. As discussed in Chapter 17, you can take advantage of these automatic conversions to make your XPath expressions simpler and neater.

With user-defined functions, on the other hand, the conversions have to take place somewhere, either within the XPath that calls the function or within the function itself. You can convert values in XPath to the primitive value types that it uses using the following functions:

- ◆ `string()` — converts to a string
- ◆ `number()` — converts to a number
- ◆ `boolean()` — converts to a boolean

The language that you use to define your function determines the way in which you carry out conversions between the string, number, and Boolean primitive types. However, the most common task here is to convert from a node set in XPath into a primitive value in the function.

When XPath converts a node set to a string, it takes the first node in the node set (in document order) and accesses its string value. Node sets in XPath are converted into DOM `NodeList` objects within other programming languages. Doing this with a `NodeList` involves accessing the first `Node` object in the `NodeList`, through the `item()` method. If the node is an attribute, text node, or comment, you can get the node's value through the `nodeValue` attribute; otherwise, you have to recursively step through the tree to calculate it, bearing in mind that the DOM object model includes things such as CDATA sections and entity references as distinct objects.

If you're using MSXML, you can use the `text` property on `DOMNode` to get more or less the string value of the node. (It's only more or less because MSXML normalizes whitespace when retrieving the text of a node.)

The XSLT 1.1 Working Draft sought to standardize the way in which extension functions are defined with an `xsl:script` element. Thus, as well as the various processor-specific methods of declaring extension functions, those processors that implement XSLT 1.1 also support `xsl:script`. The following section describes `xsl:script` first, and then examines the processor-specific methods for defining extension functions.

Defining Extension Functions in XSLT 1.1

The `xsl:script` element is put at the top level of a stylesheet. Each `xsl:script` element defines extension functions in a particular namespace and in a particular language. You can't have two `xsl:script` elements that use the same namespace and the same language at the same import precedence, which means that you have to be careful about including stylesheets. However, numerous `xsl:script` elements can use the same namespace but with different languages.

Just because a processor supports `xsl:script` doesn't mean it necessarily supports any particular language; it's not mandatory for an XSLT processor to support Java or JavaScript, for example. You should check your XSLT processor documentation to see what languages it does support. If you're using `xsl:script` but want to maintain the portability of your stylesheets, you should provide as many implementations of your extension functions in as many different languages as you can.

The `language` attribute indicates the language of the functions defined within the `xsl:script` element. The `language` attribute can be either a qualified name (with a prefix) or one of the following keywords:

◆ ecmascript

◆ javascript

◆ java

The special status of ECMAScript, JavaScript, and Java (over Python, tcl, or Perl, for example) was one of the more contentious aspects of `xsl:script`; this may be something that changes if `xsl:script` is incorporated into XSLT 2.0.

You indicate the namespace for the functions defined within an `xsl:script` element with the `implements-prefix` attribute. This attribute takes the prefix of the namespace in which the functions should be available.

For example, suppose you want to test whether a credit card number has the correct format: four groups of four digits separated by spaces. It's easy to do this in JavaScript with a regular expression. A `validCardNumber()` function in JavaScript would look something like the following:

```
cardRE = new RegExp("^([0-9]{4} ){3}[0-9]{4}$");
function validCardNumber(card) {
   return cardRE.test(card);
}
```

You want to make this function available in our stylesheet. It has to have a namespace (`http://www.example.com/bank/credit`), which you should define at the top level of the stylesheet for convenience. You should also declare that this namespace is a namespace for extension elements, despite the fact that you're only using it for extension functions:

```
<xsl:stylesheet version="1.1"
              xmlns:xsl="http://www.w3.org/1999/XSL/Transform"
              xmlns:credit="http://www.example.com/bank/credit"
              extension-element-prefixes="credit">
...
</xsl:stylesheet>
```

The `xsl:script` element you use to define the function has to indicate the prefix of the namespace in the `implements-prefix` attribute and the language for the implementation in the `language` attribute. Here, the content holds the implementation itself:

```
<xsl:stylesheet version="1.1"
              xmlns:xsl="http://www.w3.org/1999/XSL/Transform"
              xmlns:credit="http://www.example.com/bank/credit"
              extension-element-prefixes="credit">

<xsl:script implements-prefix="credit" language="javascript">
<![CDATA[
   cardRE = new RegExp("^([0-9]{4} ){3}[0-9]{4}$");
   function validCardNumber(card) {
      return cardRE.test(card);
   }
]]>
</xsl:script>

...
</xsl:stylesheet>
```

We use a CDATA section because it's good practice when embedding script in XSLT. Other programming languages tend to use < and &, and you don't want the XSLT processor to interpret them wrongly and claim that your stylesheet is not well formed; nor do you want to repeatedly escape them.

You can also use the xsl:script element to refer to external implementations of extension functions using the src attribute. The URI that you specify in the src attribute will be interpreted relative to the stylesheet. For example, you could move the function definition into another file, credit.js, and then refer to that file using the xsl:script element:

```
<xsl:script implements-prefix="credit" language="javascript"
          src="credit.js" />
```

You can also use the src attribute to refer to a Java class through the Java protocol. For example, to pull in the functions defined for the Java class com. example.bank.Credit, you could use the following:

```
<xsl:script implements-prefix="credit" language="javascript"
          src="java:com.example.bank.Credit" />
```

This latter method is somewhat cleaner than using the content of xsl:script — it keeps code that isn't XSLT separate from code that is. It also makes the functions more reusable, because you can refer to the same implementation file from several stylesheets (although you could always use a stylesheet wrapper that you include using xsl:include and xsl:import if you wish).

The final attribute of xsl:script is the archive attribute. This points to any number of resources that should be loaded before the function is executed.

IDENTIFYING FUNCTION IMPLEMENTATIONS

When the processor encounters an extension function in an XPath expression, it tries to identify a definition of that function. It will look through all the xsl:script elements that implement the namespace used by the extension function. It will then identify those that use a language supported by the processor. Within those, it will search for a function or method definition that matches the extension function call. How a processor determines whether a function or method matches an extension function call depends on the language of the implementation.

MATCHING FUNCTION NAMES   Generally, programming languages don't allow hyphens in names because they get confused with minus signs; XML (and XSLT), on the other hand, does allow hyphens in names, including function names. With Java, JavaScript, and ECMAScript, therefore, extension-function names containing hyphens are converted to camel case, with new words indicated by capital letters, by converting the letters after the hyphens into uppercase.

For example, in the preceding example, you defined the `validCardNumber()` JavaScript function with a camel case name. You could call this function within the stylesheet with any of the following calls:

```
credit:valid-card-number(string(@cardNo))
credit:validCardNumber(string(@cardNo))
credit:valid-cardNumber(string(@cardNo))
credit:validCard-number(string(@cardNo))
```

MATCHING FUNCTION ARGUMENTS In some languages, several methods or functions may have the same name, with different numbers or types of arguments. This happens in Java, for example, where you can overload a method by defining it several times. In these cases, the XSLT processor needs to determine which definition to use. How it does so depends on the language being used. I'll describe how it's done in Java because the XSLT 1.1 Working Draft has defined that; other similar languages are likely to use the same kinds of bindings.

With a Java implementation, the XSLT processor first looks for any public methods that have the right number of arguments. The "right number" here depends on the type of arguments. It includes those methods that have the following characteristics:

◆ They have the same number of arguments as you used in the extension function call.

◆ They have one more argument than you used in the extension function call, with the first argument for the method being an `XSLTContext` object.

◆ They have one less argument than the Java method, if the first argument in the extension function call is an instance, and the method is an instance method.

If there is more than one method with the right number of arguments, the XSLT processor starts looking at the types of the arguments to determine which method to use. The exact way in which it chooses is rather complicated, and it's best to look at the XSLT 1.1 Working Draft for a full description. In brief, the processor looks at each of the arguments in the extension function call and tries to convert them into the arguments defined for the methods. Some conversions are classified as more difficult than others. The method that's chosen is the one in which all the extension function arguments are more easily mapped onto that method's arguments than onto any other method's arguments.

Table 20-1 outlines the most natural conversion types. These mappings are also used to convert the return value of the Java method back into an XPath object.

TABLE 20-1 CONVERSIONS OF XPATH OBJECT TYPES INTO JAVA

XPath Object	Java Type
boolean	boolean, java.lang.Boolean
number	double, java.lang.Double
string	java.lang.String
node-set	java.lang.NodeList, java.lang.Node
external	object of the external type

 Because XSLT 1.1 eliminates result tree fragments, it doesn't define a conversion type from result tree fragments into Java.

If you use argument types that are more specific than these, the XSLT processor will try to convert the relevant extension function argument into the type that you declare. Some of these conversions may raise errors (for example, trying to map a string argument that has several characters onto a java.lang.Character argument in the Java method).

WRITING FUNCTION IMPLEMENTATIONS

The extension function implementations that you write have to be identifiable through the process just described. Once a processor finds a function, it runs with the relevant values as argument values. In Java, the extension function arguments are converted to the type indicated by the method arguments. In JavaScript, on the other hand, the function arguments are converted to the closest JavaScript value type: Boolean to Boolean, number to number, string to string, and node-set to NodeList.

Many functions that you implement in this way will stand alone, but some may require additional information about the context in which they are called. For example, many XPath functions use the context node as the default if no node set is passed as an argument. Others access information about the current node and the position of the context node in the context node list. This kind of information is made available to your function implementation using XSLTContext objects. The XSLTContext object holds the following information:

◆ contextNode — the context node

◆ contextPosition — the position of the context node in the context node list

- contextSize — the number of nodes in the context node list
- currentNode — the current node
- ownerDocument — a document that can be used for generating new nodes

It also has two utility methods:

- systemProperty(string namespaceURI, string localName) — returns the system property for the expanded name indicated by the arguments
- stringValue(Node node) — returns the string value of the node passed as an argument to it

In JavaScript, the XSLTContext object is available as a top-level object. In Java, you can access a context object if you have an XSLTContext object as the first argument to your method. For example, consider a method that would get the expanded name of a node in the format:

```
{namespace-URI}local-name
```

If you wanted the method to default to the context node if no node were specified as an argument, you could use the following Java methods:

```
public static java.lang.String expandedName(org.w3c.xsl.XSLTContext context) {
    return expandedName(context.contextNode);
}

public static java.lang.String expandedName(org.w3c.dom.Node node) {
    return '{' + node.getNamespaceURI() + '}' + node.getLocalName();
}
```

If you call the expanded-name() extension function with no arguments, the XSLT processor uses the first method because it is the only one with the right number of arguments (the XSLTContext object as the first argument of the method definition is ignored when counting arguments). If you call the extension function with a node set argument, the XSLT processor uses the second method, and converts the node set passed from the XSLT to a Node in the Java function by taking the first node in the node set.

STATUS OF XSL:SCRIPT

I've spent some time discussing xsl:script in depth for several reasons. One, it's likely that XSLT 2.0 will include something like it, and even if it doesn't, implementers might adopt func:script from the EXSLT initiative, which is very similar. Two, it's useful to see how xsl:script is designed because it highlights some of the strengths and limitations of the processor-specific approaches described in the rest of this section. Finally, although XSLT 1.1 will never be a Recommendation, you may want to play with some of the implementations available, in particular Saxon and jd.xslt.

Defining Extension Functions in MSXML

MSXML enables you to write extension functions in various scripting languages, including JavaScript and VBScript. To do so, you use the `msxsl:script` element, which, like `xsl:script`, lives at the top level of the stylesheet. The `msxsl` prefix refers to the following namespace:

```
urn:schemas-microsoft-com:xslt
```

The `msxsl:script` element is very similar to `xsl:script` — it has an `implements-prefix` attribute to indicate the namespace for the extension functions, and a `language` attribute to indicate the language in which the extension functions are written. If you don't specify the `language` attribute, MSXML assumes that you're using JScript to write the functions.

However, `msxsl:script` is limited compared to `xsl:script` in three ways. One, you can only define the implementations in the content of the `msxsl:script` element; you can't refer to an external file. Two, MSXML only looks for functions that have exactly the same name as the extension function that you use, so you can't use hyphenated function names. Finally, it doesn't have an `XSLTContext` object, so you can't access context information about the processing status. If you need that information, you have to pass it into the functions explicitly.

The following example shows the `credit:validCardNumber()` function defined with `msxsl:script`:

```
<xsl:stylesheet version="1.0"
                xmlns:xsl="http://www.w3.org/1999/XSL/Transform"
                xmlns:msxsl="urn:schemas-microsoft-com:xslt"
                xmlns:credit="http://www.example.com/bank/credit"
                extension-element-prefixes="msxsl credit">

<msxsl:script implements-prefix="credit" language="javascript">
<![CDATA[
   cardRE = new RegExp("^([0-9]{4} ){3}[0-9]{4}$");
   function validCardNumber(card) {
      return cardRE.test(card);
   }
]]>
</msxsl:script>


...
</xsl:stylesheet>
```

You can call the `credit:validCardNumber()` function with that name only, not with `credit:valid-card-number()`.

Defining Extension Functions in Xalan

Xalan enables you to define both extension functions and extension elements through the `xalan:component` and `xalan:script` elements. The `xalan:component` element defines the namespace in which the extensions are defined, and lists the extension functions and elements that are implemented. It can contain a number of `xalan:script` elements that hold or reference the implementations of these extensions in various languages. Both elements are in the following namespace:

```
http://xml.apache.org/xslt
```

This chapter does not go into detail about how to define extension elements using Xalan; you should consult the documentation at `http://xml.apache.org/xalan-j/extensions.html` for more details.

The `xalan:component` element takes three attributes:

◆ `prefix` — the prefix for the namespace that the extension functions/ elements are in

◆ `functions` — a space-separated list of function names listing the extension functions that are implemented in the component

◆ `elements` — a space-separated list of element names listing the extension elements that are implemented in the component

You must use exactly the same name for the extension function when you call it as you used in its implementation — hyphenated extension function names aren't converted into camel case for matching, unlike with `xsl:script`.

The `xalan:script` elements inside the `xalan:component` element use the `lang` attribute to indicate the language in which the function definitions are written.

For Java, the `lang` attribute is set to `javaclass`, and `xalan:script` takes a `src` attribute to indicate the Java class that implements the extension functions, using the `xalan` protocol. For example, to use the methods on the class `com.example.bank.Credit`, you would use the following `xalan:component` and `xalan:script`:

```
<xalan:component prefix="credit" functions="validCardNumber">
   <xalan:script lang="javaclass"
                 src="xalan://com.example.bank.Credit" />
</xalan:component>
```

For other languages, the `xalan:script` element holds the function definitions within the stylesheet itself. For example, you could add the JavaScript definition of the `credit:validCardNumber()` function to the `xalan:component` as follows:

```
<xalan:component prefix="credit" functions="validCardNumber">
   <xalan:script lang="javaclass"
                 src="xalan://com.mybank.Credit" />
   <xalan:script lang="javascript">
   <![CDATA[
      cardRE = new RegExp("^([0-9]{4} ){3}[0-9]{4}$");
      function validCardNumber(card) {
         return cardRE.test(card);
      }
   ]]>
   </xalan:script>
</xalan:component>
```

Xalan supports function definitions in various languages through the Java Bean Scripting Framework (BSF), including JavaScript, PerlScript, JPython, and Jacl.

Xalan approaches the sophistication (and complexity) of `xsl:script` in the way that it matches Java methods based on the number and type of arguments that are defined for them compared to those used in the extension function call. It also supplies an `org.apache.xalan.extensions.ExpressionContext` interface that provides information about the context of the extension function call. This interface enables you to access the context node and the context node list, and provides two utility methods for converting nodes to strings and to numbers.

Reusing Existing Java Methods

Both Xalan and Saxon offer a final method of defining extension functions, if you're using Java. In both, you can equate a namespace with a Java class using a namespace declaration. All the methods in that class are then available through that extension namespace.

For example, in Xalan, rather than use `xalan:component` and `xalan:script` as previously described, you could use the following:

```
<xsl:stylesheet version="1.0"
                xmlns:xsl="http://www.w3.org/1999/XSL/Transform"
                xmlns:credit="xalan://com.example.bank.Credit"
                extension-element-prefixes="credit">
...
</xsl:stylesheet>
```

If you glance back to Chapters 18 and 19, you'll see this in action for the SQL extension functions and Redirect extension elements that are available in Xalan. The namespaces of these extensions are actually pointers to Java classes.

Similarly, in Saxon, you can use a namespace declaration, this time using the `java` protocol to point to the relevant Java class:

```
<xsl:stylesheet version="1.0"
                xmlns:xsl="http://www.w3.org/1999/XSL/Transform"
                xmlns:credit="java:com.example.bank.Credit"
                extension-element-prefixes="credit">
...
</xsl:stylesheet>
```

As you can see, one of the disadvantages of this approach is that it isn't portable: if you define the namespace with Xalan's method for Xalan, you have to change the namespace declaration to use the same stylesheet with Saxon, and vice versa.

Defining Functions with XSLT

As described in the last section, different processors support different languages for defining functions, which limits the portability of your stylesheet unless you provide numerous implementations in a variety of languages. However, the one language that you can rely on every XSLT processor implementing is XSLT. For this reason, the EXSLT initiative has defined a `func:function` element that enables you to define your own functions using XSLT.

The `func:function` element actually only enables you to do in a function what you could otherwise do in a named template — it's still limited to what XSLT and XPath can do. If you need more functionality or an easier implementation, you may find that another language is better, as described previously.

The func:function element is a top-level element that works a lot like a named template, except that it can be called within an XPath, as an extension function, rather than through xsl:call-template. The name attribute of func:function specifies the extension function name (including the prefix); xsl:param elements declare the arguments for the function, and a func:result element defines the result.

As a simple example, look at the credit:valid-card-number() function as defined by func:function:

```
<func:function name="credit:valid-card-number">
  <xsl:param name="card" />
  <func:result select="number(substring($card, 1, 4)) and
                        substring($card, 5, 1) = ' ' and
                        number(substring($card, 6, 4)) and
                        substring($card, 10, 1) = ' ' and
                        number(substring($card, 11, 4)) and
                        substring($card, 15, 1) = ' ' and
                        number(substring($card, 16, 4)) and
                        string-length($card) = 19" />
</func:function>
```

The xsl:param element defines the argument for the extension function. Extension function arguments override xsl:param elements by position, so the first argument maps on to the first xsl:param, the second onto the second, and so on. You can't declare that a parameter is required using XSLT, so all arguments in extension functions defined with func:function are optional. When you're writing an extension function like this, therefore, you have to confirm that the user has actually passed in a valid value for the parameter.

Chapter 13 described how to test the values of the parameters that are passed into a template; you can use the same techniques for extension functions written in XSLT.

The result of the function call is defined by the func:result element, which works in a similar way to xsl:variable. You can use the select attribute to provide an XPath expression that is evaluated to generate the result of the function. The returned value type of the function is the same type as the value type of the expression's result. The func:function element cannot contain instructions such as xsl:value-of, xsl:element, or literal result elements — if you need a result tree fragment from the function, you can use the content of the func:result element. If no func:result element is processed while executing the function, the function returns an empty string by default.

This way of defining functions tries to keep within the general bounds of the XSLT processing model. Importantly, this means that processing doesn't stop when a func:result element is found—the func:result element doesn't return a value, but defines the result of the function. You can't process two func:result elements during the execution of the function, so you can't have something like the following:

```
<func:function name="stmt:transaction-type">
   <xsl:param name="transaction" select="." />
   <xsl:if test="$transaction/@type = 'CR'">
      <func:result select="'credit'" />
   </xsl:if>
   <func:result select="'debit'" />
</func:function>
```

In the preceding function, if the transaction type were 'CR', then the contents of the xsl:if would be processed, resulting in the string 'credit'. The processing would then continue to the final func:result. Because two func:result elements are processed, this leads to an error. Instead, the function has to be written as follows:

```
<func:function name="stmt:transaction-type">
   <xsl:param name="transaction" select="." />
   <xsl:choose>
      <xsl:when test="$transaction/@type = 'CR'">
         <func:result select="'credit'" />
      </xsl:when>
      <xsl:otherwise>
         <func:result select="'debit'" />
      </xsl:otherwise>
   </xsl:choose>
</func:function>
```

These rules mean that you also have to be careful about using xsl:for-each within function definitions, although it's fine to do so if you only select one node from it. For example, you can write a function to get the first node in alphabetical order using an xsl:for-each with xsl:sort, with an xsl:if inside that only selects one node during the iteration:

```
<func:function name="my:first-alphabetical">
   <xsl:param name="nodes" select="/.." />
   <xsl:for-each select="$nodes">
      <xsl:sort />
      <xsl:if test="position() = 1">
         <func:result select="." />
      </xsl:if>
   </xsl:for-each>
</func:function>
```

You can create reusable modules of these functions by importing and including stylesheets. Just as with named templates, you must not have two function definitions with the same name at the same import precedence, but it's fine to have more if they have lower import precedence.

Summary

This chapter has described three good reasons for writing your own extension functions:

◆ They enable you to do things within an XPath for which you otherwise have to use XSLT, which is very useful for things such as the select expression of `xsl:sort` or the use expression of `xsl:key`, where named templates aren't an option.

◆ They enable you to do things that you can't do in XSLT, such as gain access to the system environment.

◆ They make it easier to write code for complicated string manipulation with regular expressions or date calculations, because they allow you access to utilities available in other programming languages.

A final reason for writing an extension function, rather than a named template, is that it's a lot easier to call. However, because different processors use different methods for defining extension functions, you should have a good reason for using one if you care about portability.

This chapter described the methods used in implementations of the XSLT 1.1 Working Draft, MSXML, Saxon, and Xalan for defining extension functions in various languages, focusing on Java and JavaScript. You learned how to use the `func:function` extension from the EXSLT initiative to define functions using XSLT. With these methods in your arsenal, you can use XSLT to do just about anything.

Appendix A

XPath Quick Reference

This appendix contains a quick reference to the various object types, node types, axes, functions and operators that are defined within the XPath 1.0 Recommendation. There isn't space for a full reference, but the descriptions should be enough to remind you of the basics. At the end, there are a few XPath design patterns that you may find helpful.

Object Types

The six object types in XSLT 1.0 and XSLT 1.1 are as follows:

Object Type	Description
boolean	true or false
number	a floating-point number: a double-precision 64-bit format IEEE 754 value
string	a sequence of XML characters
node set	an unordered collection of nodes
result tree fragment (RTF)	the root node of a generated node tree
external object	an object created by an external application

Booleans, numbers, and strings can be converted to one another, as shown in the following table.

Object	Example	Conversion		
		Boolean	**Number**	**String**
boolean	`true`	`true`	`1`	`'true'`
	`false`	`false`	`0`	`'false'`
number	`NaN`	`false`	`NaN`	`'NaN'`
	`0`	`false`	`0`	`'0'`
	`-4`	`true`	`-4`	`'-4'`
	`350`	`true`	`350`	`'350'`
	`Infinity`	`true`	`Infinity`	`'Infinity'`
string	`' '`	`false`	`NaN`	`' '`
	`'false'`	`true`	`NaN`	`'false'`
	`'0'`	`true`	`0`	`'0'`
	`'sheep'`	`true`	`NaN`	`'sheep'`

Booleans, numbers, and strings cannot be converted to node sets, RTFs, or foreign objects — attempting to do so raises an error.

Node sets and RTFs can be converted to booleans, numbers, and strings, as follows:

Object	Boolean	Number	String
node set	`true` if the node set holds nodes; `false` if the node set is empty	the result of converting the string value of the first node in the node set to a number first	the string value of the node in the node set
RTF	`true`	the result of converting the string value of the RTF to a number	the string value of the RTF

External objects cannot be converted to any other object type.

Node Types

Nodes can be of the following types:

Node Type	Name	String Value
root node	-	concatenation of all text nodes in the document
element node	element name	concatenation of all text nodes descended from the element
attribute node	attribute name	attribute value
text node	-	text
comment node	-	text held within the comment
processing instruction node	processing instruction target	text in the processing instruction after the space after the target name
namespace node	namespace prefix	namespace URI

Node Tests

Node tests match different kinds of nodes, as follows:

Node Test	Description
node()	any node
*	any node of the principal node type for the axis
Name	any node of the principal node type for the axis with the given name

Continued

(Continued)

Node Test	Description
text()	any text node
comment()	any comment node
processing-instruction()	any processing instruction node
processing-instruction ('*name*')	any processing instruction node with the given name

Axes

Axes dictate the direction in which a step traverses the node tree, as follows:

Axis	Principal Node Type	Direction	Description
self	element nodes	–	the context node itself
child	element nodes	forward	the children of the context node
parent	element nodes	–	the parent of the context node
attribute	attribute nodes	forward	attributes of the context node
descendant	element nodes	forward	descendants of the context node
descendant-or-self	element nodes	forward	descendants of the context node, and the context node itself
ancestor	element nodes	reverse	ancestors of the context node
ancestor-or-self	element nodes	reverse	ancestors of the context node, and the context node itself

Axis	Principal Node Type	Direction	Description
following-sibling	element nodes	forward	siblings of the context node that follow the context node in document order
preceding-sibling	element nodes	reverse	siblings of the context node that precede the context node in document order
following	element nodes	forward	nodes (aside from attribute and namespace nodes) that follow the context node in document order and are not descendants of the context node
preceding	element nodes	reverse	nodes (aside from attribute and namespace nodes) that precede the context node in document order and are not ancestors of the context node
namespace	namespace nodes	forward	namespace nodes on the context node

Abbreviated Syntax

You can use several abbreviations in XPath expressions, as described in the following table.

Abbreviation	Full Equivalent	Description
.	self::node()	the context node
..	parent::node()	the parent of the context node
//	/descendant-or-self::node()/	supplies quick access to descendants of the context node
@	attribute::	shortens expressions that access attributes

Operators

The operators in XPath can be split into four groups:

◆ logical operators

◆ comparative operators

◆ numerical operators

◆ node set operators

The precedence of the operators (from lowest to highest) is as follows:

◆ `or`

◆ `and`

◆ `=, !=`

◆ `<=, <, >=, >`

◆ `+, -`

◆ `*, div, mod`

◆ unary `-`

◆ `|`

Logical Operators

The logical operators are as follows:

Operator	Description
or	true if either operand is true when converted to Booleans; the right operand is not evaluated if the left operand is true.
and	true if both operands are true when converted to Booleans; the right operand is not evaluated if the left operand is false.

Comparative Operators

The comparative operators are as follows:

Operator	Description
=	equal to
! =	not equal to
<	less than
<=	less than or equal to
>	greater than
>=	greater than or equal to

For the equal to and not equal to operators, the comparisons are defined as follows:

Object	Boolean	Number	String	Node Set
number	converts the number to a Boolean and compares	–		
string	converts the string to a Boolean and compares	converts the string to a number and compares	–	
node set	converts the node set to a Boolean and compares	compares the numerical values of all the nodes with the number; true if any comparison is true	compares the string values of all the nodes with the string; true if any comparison is true	compares the string values of each of the nodes in one node set with each of the nodes in the other; true if any comparison is true
RTF	converts the RTF to a Boolean and compares	converts the RTF to a number and compares	converts the RTF to a string and compares	converts the RTF to a string; compares the string values of all the nodes with the string; true if any comparison is true

For the other comparative operators, the comparisons are defined as follows:

Object	Boolean	Number	String	Node Set
number	converts the Boolean to a number and compares	–		
string	converts both to numbers and compares	converts the string to a number and compares	–	
node set	converts the Boolean to a number; compares the numerical values of all the nodes with the number; true if any comparison is true	compares the numerical values of all the nodes with the number; true if any comparison is true	converts the string to a number; compares the numerical values of all the nodes with the number; true if any comparison is true	compares the numerical values of each of the nodes in one node set with each of the nodes in the other; true if any comparison is true
RTF	converts both to numbers and compares	converts the RTF to a number and compares	converts both to numbers and compares	converts the RTF to a number; compares the numerical values of all the nodes with the number; true if any comparison is true

Numerical Operators

The numerical operators are as follows:

Operator	Description
+	addition
–	subtraction

Operator	Description
*	multiplication
div	floating point division
mod	remainder from a truncating division
unary -	negation

Node Set Operators

There is one node set operator:

Operator	Description
|	unions two node sets

Functions

The functions available in XSLT are described in the following table. For each function, I've provided the syntax and a description. Wherever a function expects an object of a certain type as an argument, the object passed to it will be converted to the expected object type according to the conversions outlined previously.

CONVERSION FUNCTIONS

Function	Description
boolean boolean(*object*?)	converts the object to a Boolean; defaults to the context node
string string(*object*?)	converts the object to a string; defaults to the context node
number number(object?)	converts the object to a number; defaults to the context node

NUMBERING FUNCTIONS

Function	Description
number last()	returns the context size (the index of the last node in the context node list)
number position()	returns the context position (the index of the context node in the context node list)
number count(node-set)	counts the number of nodes in the node set

NODE SET FUNCTIONS

Function	Description
node-set current()	returns the current node
node-set id(*object*)	retrieves the node in the current document with the argument ID specified as the value of their ID attribute; if the object is a node set, each node's value is interpreted as an ID and the nodes with those Ids are returned.
node-set key (*string*, *object*)	returns the nodes in the current document that have a key value equal to any of the values specified by the object in the key space named by the first argument; if the second argument is a node set, each node's value is interpreted as a key value.
node-set document (*object*, *node-set*?)	returns the root node(s) of the document(s) at the URL(s) specified by the object; if the object is a node set, each node's value is interpreted as a URL; if a URL is relative, it is resolved according to the base URI of the first node in the node set given as the second argument; the second argument defaults to the node holding the expression from which document( ) is called.
string unparsed-entity-uri(*string*)	returns the URI of the unparsed entity named by the argument in the current document

NODE TESTING FUNCTIONS

Function	Description
string name(*node-set*?)	returns a qualified name for the first node in the node set, using the namespace nodes in scope for the node; defaults to the context node
string local-name (*node-set*?)	returns the local name of the first node in the node set; defaults to the context node
string namespace-uri (*node-set*?)	returns the namespace URI for the first node in the node set; defaults to the context node
string generate-id (*node-set*?)	returns a unique ID for the first node in the node set; the node set defaults to the context node
boolean lang(string)	returns true if the context node's language (as specified with the xml:lang attribute) matches the string

STRING MANIPULATION FUNCTIONS

Function	Description
string concat(*string*, *string*+)	concatenates the strings
boolean starts-with (*string*, *string*)	returns true if the first string starts with the second string
boolean contains (*string*, *string*)	returns true if the first string contains the second string
string substring-before (*string*, *string*)	returns the substring of the first string that occurs before the second string or an empty string if the second string is not contained in the first string
string substring-after (*string*, *string*)	returns the substring of the first string that occurs after the second string or an empty string if the second string is not contained in the first string
string substring(*string*, *number*, *number*?)	returns the substring of the string starting at the (rounded) first number and ending the (rounded) second number of characters later; the second number defaults to Infinity

Continued

STRING MANIPULATION FUNCTIONS *(Continued)*

Function	Description
number string-length(*string*?)	returns the length of the string; defaults to the string value of the context node
string normalize-space(*string*?)	returns the string with leading and trailing whitespace stripped and any sequences of whitespace converted to single spaces; defaults to the string value of the context node
string translate(*string*, *string*, *string*)	returns the first string with all occurrences of the characters in the second string replaced by their corresponding characters in the third string; if there is no corresponding character, the character is deleted.
string format-number (*number*, *string*, *string*?)	returns the number formatted according to the pattern string specified as the second argument; the pattern string is interpreted according to the decimal format named by the third argument; the third argument defaults to the empty string and hence the default (unnamed) decimal format.

BOOLEAN FUNCTIONS

Function	Description
boolean not(*boolean*)	returns false if the argument is true and true otherwise
boolean true()	returns true
boolean false()	returns false

NUMERICAL FUNCTIONS

Function	Description
number sum(*node-set*)	sums the numerical values of the nodes in the node set
number floor(*number*)	rounds the number down to the nearest integer

Function	Description
number ceiling(*number*)	rounds the number up to the nearest integer
number round(*number*)	rounds the number up or down to the nearest integer; if the number is exactly between two integers, it's rounded to the even integer

PROCESSOR-RELATED FUNCTIONS

Function	Description
object system-property(*string*)	returns the value of a system property; built-in system properties are as follows:

◆ xsl:version — the version number of XSLT supported by the processor

◆ xsl:vendor — the name of the vendor of the XSLT processor

◆ xsl:vendor-url — a URL for the vendor of the XSLT processor

Function	Description
boolean element-available(*string*)	returns true if the processor supports the named (extension) element
boolean function-available(*string*)	returns true if the processor supports the named (extension) function

Design Patterns

This section describes some of the design patterns that you might find helpful within your XPath expressions. Most of these design patterns are used in the body of this book.

Testing Node Identity

Compare the generated unique IDs of the nodes:

```
generate-id(node1) = generate-id(node2)
```

Use set logic:

```
count(node1|node2) = 1
```

SET RELATIONS

Relation	Pattern
member of	count(*node*|*node-set*) = count(*node-set*)
subset of	count(*subset*|*superset*) = count(*superset*)
intersection	*node-set1*[count(.|*node-set2*) = count(*node-set2*)]
difference	node-set1[count(.|node-set2) != count(node-set2)]

CONDITIONAL VALUES

Object Type	Pattern
number	*false-value* + *test* * (*true-value* - *false-value*)
string	Organize the test so that the true value is the longer of the strings, and then use the following:

```
substring(concat(true-value, false-value),
          1 + string-length(true-value) * not(test),
          string-length(true-value))
```

If the false value is the empty string, use this:

```
substring(true-value, 1 div test)
```

node-set   *true-value*[*test*] \| *false-value*[not(*test*)]

See Chapter 3 for more details.

Maximum and Minimum Nodes

As long as the values that you want to compare are the values of the nodes themselves, you can use the following to get the nodes with the maximum value:

```
node-set[not(node-set > .)]
```

You can use the following to get the nodes with the minimum value:

```
node-set[not(. > node-set)]
```

You may find it more efficient to use recursion to do this for large node sets; see Chapter 5.

Unique Values

If the nodes that you want to test for unique values are siblings, use the following:

```
node-test[not(preceding-sibling::node-test = .)]
```

If you're testing the attributes on sibling elements, then you can use this:

```
element-name[not(preceding-sibling::element-name/@attribute-name =
                @attribute-name)]
```

You can use the same patterns with the `preceding` axis if the elements are scattered throughout the document.

It's usually more efficient to use a key to access unique nodes; see Chapter 9.

Appendix B

XSLT Quick Reference

THIS APPENDIX PROVIDES brief outlines of all the XSLT 1.0 elements and attributes: what they do, where they're allowed, and what values they can have. A set of design patterns for XSLT stylesheets is provided at the end of the appendix, which may help you construct your own stylesheets.

XSLT Elements

This section gives a general overview of the various XSLT elements, dividing them into functional groups, before looking at the elements in more detail in alphabetical order.

Element Types

The following table divides the XSLT elements into functional groups to help you identify the elements that you're looking for.

Document Elements

Element	Description
xsl:stylesheet	a document element for a stylesheet
xsl:transform	an alternative document element for a stylesheet

Modularity

Element	Description
xsl:include	includes the content of a stylesheet in another one, as if it were defined within it
xsl:import	imports the constructs of a stylesheet for use in another one, with lower priority

Input Control

Element	Description
xsl:strip-space	strips whitespace-only text nodes from the content of matched elements
xsl:preserve-space	preserves whitespace-only text nodes in the content of matched elements

Output Control

Element	Description
xsl:output	defines the way in which the result tree is serialized
xsl:namespace-alias	maps a namespace URI in the stylesheet to a different namespace URI in the result

Top-Level Definitions

Element	Description
xsl:key	defines a key for quickly indexing into nodes
xsl:attribute-set	defines a set of attributes that can be added onto elements
xsl:decimal-format	defines the significant characters in the format string used by format-number()
xsl:template	defines a matching or named template

Control Flow Instructions

Element	Description
xsl:apply-templates	applies matching templates to selected nodes in a selected mode
xsl:apply-imports	applies imported matching templates to the current node
xsl:call-template	calls a named template
xsl:for-each	iterates over a set of nodes
xsl:sort	changes the order in which nodes are processed
xsl:if	processes instructions if a condition is true
xsl:choose	carries out conditional processing
xsl:when	processes instructions if its condition is true and no previous xsl:when has been processed
xsl:otherwise	processes instructions if no xsl:when is processed
xsl:message	sends a message to standard error
xsl:fallback	defines processing to be carried out if the surrounding element is not recognized by the processor

Node Generation Instructions

Element	Description
xsl:element	creates an element node
xsl:attribute	creates an attribute node
xsl:comment	creates a comment node
xsl:processing-instruction	creates a processing instruction node
xsl:text	adds some text to the result
xsl:value-of	evaluates an expression and adds it to the result as text
xsl:number	constructs a number and adds it to the result as text

Continued

Node Generation Instructions *(Continued)*

Element	Description
xsl:copy	generates a shallow copy of the current node
xsl:copy-of	generates a deep copy of the selected nodes

Variable-Binding Elements

Element	Description
xsl:variable	binds a value to a variable name
xsl:param	declares a parameter and defines the default value for that parameter
xsl:with-param	passes a parameter into a template

Element Definitions

The rest of this section, arranged alphabetically, illustrates the syntax of each element.

XSL:APPLY-IMPORTS

This element applies imported templates to the current node. The imported templates may be from any stylesheet with lower import precedence; they don't necessarily have to be from stylesheets that are imported into the stylesheet in which the xsl:apply-imports resides, although it's better design if they are.

You cannot pass parameters to templates that are applied with xsl:apply-imports.

- ◆ **Situated:** anywhere in a template
- ◆ **Content:** empty
- ◆ **Attributes:** none

XSL:APPLY-TEMPLATES

This element applies templates to selected nodes. The nodes may be sorted with `xsl:sort`; these nodes become the current node list, and the processor goes through them, trying to find templates that match them in the mode specified by `xsl:apply-templates`. These templates may be passed parameters with `xsl:with-param`.

- ◆ **Situated:** anywhere in a template
- ◆ **Content:** any mix of `xsl:sort` or `xsl:param` elements, or empty

Attributes

Attribute	Value Type	Description
select	node set expression	selects the nodes to which templates are applied; if unspecified, defaults to all the children of the current node
mode	qualified name	defines the mode in which templates are applied

XSL:ATTRIBUTE

This element creates an attribute node. The content defines the value of the attribute.

- ◆ **Situated:** anywhere in a template, as long as it's not processed after content is added to the element; within an `xsl:attribute-set`; illegal as an immediate child of a variable-binding element
- ◆ **Content:** any instructions, as long as they generate only text

Attributes

Attribute	Value Type	Description
name	qualified name (attribute value template)	defines the name of the attribute; must be specified
namespace	URI (attribute value template)	defines the namespace for the attribute; if unspecified, the attribute is placed in the namespace indicated by the prefix used in the name, if there is one (otherwise, the attribute is placed in no namespace)

XSL:ATTRIBUTE-SET

This element defines a named set of attributes. When the attribute set is used, these attributes are added to the relevant element.

- ◆ **Situated:** top level of the stylesheet
- ◆ **Content:** xsl:attribute elements

Attributes

Attribute	Value Type	Description
name	qualified name	defines the name of the attribute set; must be specified
use-attribute-sets	space-delimited attribute set names	lists the attribute sets whose attributes should be included in this attribute set

XSL:CALL-TEMPLATE

This element calls a named template. The template may be passed parameters with xsl:with-param.

- ◆ **Situated:** anywhere in a template
- ◆ **Content:** xsl:with-param elements, or empty

Attributes

Attribute	Value Type	Description
name	qualified name	the name of the named template

XSL:CHOOSE

This element defines some conditional processing. It simply acts as a container for a set of xsl:when elements and an optional xsl:otherwise element.

- ◆ **Situated:** anywhere in a template
- ◆ **Content:** any number of xsl:when elements followed by an optional xsl:otherwise
- ◆ **Attributes:** none

XSL:COMMENT

This element creates a comment node. The content defines the value of the comment.

- ◆ **Situated:** anywhere in a template
- ◆ **Content:** any instructions, as long as they generate only text
- ◆ **Attributes:** none

XSL:COPY

This element copies the current node and, if it's an element, all its namespace nodes. The content will only be instantiated if the current node is an element.

- ◆ **Situated:** anywhere in a template
- ◆ **Content:** any instructions

Attributes

Attribute	Value Type	Description
use-attribute-sets	space-delimited attribute set names	lists the attribute sets whose attributes should be added to the copied element, if the current node is an element

---

XSL:COPY-OF

This element creates a deep copy of a set of nodes. This copy will include the attributes and children of nodes that have them.

- ◆ **Situated:** anywhere in a template
- ◆ **Content:** empty

Attributes

Attribute	Value Type	Description
Select	node set expression	selects the nodes that are copied; must be specified

---

XSL:DECIMAL-FORMAT

This element defines the significant characters that are used in a format string used by the format-number() function.

- ◆ **Situated:** top level of the stylesheet
- ◆ **Content:** empty

Attributes

Attribute	Value Type	Description
name	qualified name	defines the name of the decimal format; if not specified, the decimal format is used as the default when no third argument is used by `format-number()`
digit	character	declares the character used to represent an optional digit in the format string; defaults to #
zero-digit	character	declares the character used in place of a required digit in the number; defaults to 0
decimal-separator	character	declares the character used as the decimal point in the number; defaults to .
grouping-separator	character	declares the character used to separate groups of digits in the number; defaults to ,
minus-sign	character	declares the character used to indicate a negative number; defaults to -
pattern-separator	character	declares the character used to separate the positive and negative formats in the format string; defaults to ;
percent	character	declares the character used to indicate a percentage; defaults to %
per-mille	character	declares the character used as the per mille sign; defaults to ‰ or ‰
infinity	string	declares the string used to represent infinity; defaults to Infinity
NaN	string	declares the string used to represent a non-numerical number; defaults to NaN

XSL:ELEMENT

This element creates an element node. The content defines the content of the element.

- ◆ **Situated:** anywhere in a template
- ◆ **Content:** any instructions

Attributes

Attribute	Value Type	Description
Name	qualified name (attribute value template)	defines the name of the element; must be specified
Namespace	URI (attribute value template)	defines the namespace for the element; if unspecified, the element is placed in the namespace indicated by the prefix used in the name, if there is one (otherwise, the default namespace is used)
use-attribute-sets	space-delimited attribute set names	lists the attribute sets whose attributes should be added to the copied element, if the current node is an element

---

XSL:FALLBACK

This element provides alternative instructions if the parent (extension) element is not supported by the processor.

- ◆ **Situated:** anywhere within a template; usually as a child of an extension element
- ◆ **Content:** any instructions
- ◆ **Attributes:** none

XSL:FOR-EACH

This element iterates over a selected set of nodes. The nodes may be sorted with xsl:sort; these nodes become the current node list, and the processor processes the instructions held within the xsl:for-each on each of them in turn.

- ◆ **Situated:** anywhere in a template
- ◆ **Content:** any number of xsl:sort elements, followed by any instructions

Attributes

Attribute	Value Type	Description
Select	node set expression	selects the nodes that are processed; must be specified

XSL:IF

This element carries out a set of instructions only if a condition is true.

◆ **Situated:** anywhere in a template

◆ **Content:** any instructions

Attributes

Attribute	Value Type	Description
Test	Boolean expression	specifies the condition under which the instructions should be processed; must be specified

XSL:IMPORT

This element imports a stylesheet. The constructs in the imported stylesheet have a lower import precedence than those in the importing stylesheet and, therefore, can be overridden by them. The stylesheets that are imported last have a higher import precedence than those that occur before them.

◆ **Situated:** top level of the stylesheet

◆ **Content:** empty

Attributes

Attribute	Value Type	Description
href	URI	specifies the location of the imported stylesheet, relative to the importing stylesheet

XSL:INCLUDE

This element includes a stylesheet. The constructs in the included stylesheet are incorporated into the including stylesheet and treated as if they were defined in that location.

◆ **Situated:** top level of the stylesheet

◆ **Content:** empty

Attributes

Attribute	Value Type	Description
href	URI	gives the location of the included stylesheet, relative to the including stylesheet

XSL:KEY

This element defines a key. For each document for which the key is used, the processor builds a hash table linking all the nodes matched by the pattern in the match attribute to the string value specified by the use attribute. These nodes can then be quickly retrieved using the key() function.

◆ **Situated:** top level of the stylesheet

◆ **Content:** empty

Attributes

Attribute	Value Type	Description
name	qualified name	specifies the name of the key; multiple xsl:key elements may share the same name, in which case the hash tables are merged; must be specified
match	pattern (must not include variable references)	matches the nodes that should be indexed by the key; must be specified
use	expression	specifies the key value(s) that are used to index the matching nodes; if it evaluates to a string for a node, that key value is used; if it evaluates to a node set, the string values of each of the nodes in the node set are used as key values; must be specified

XSL:MESSAGE

This element sends a message to the user. How the message is provided to the user depends on the processor that you use to run the stylesheet. The content of the xsl:message element specifies the content of the message.

◆ **Situated:** anywhere in a template

◆ **Content:** any instructions

Attributes

Attribute	Value Type	Description
terminate	yes or no	determines whether the stylesheet should be terminated when the message is encountered; if yes, it should, if no, it shouldn't; defaults to no

XSL:NAMESPACE-ALIAS

This element maps a namespace used in the stylesheet to a different namespace in the result tree. This is particularly useful when using XSLT to produce XSLT as it enables you to use literal result elements without having them confused for XSLT instructions.

- ◆ **Situated:** top level of the stylesheet
- ◆ **Content:** empty

Attributes

Attribute	Value Type	Description
stylesheet-prefix	namespace prefix	specifies the prefix used for the (nonsense) namespace that's being used as an alias in the stylesheet
result-prefix	namespace prefix	specifies the prefix of the namespace that should be used instead, in the result tree

XSL:NUMBER

This element generates a number to be added to the result tree. This may be based on the position of the current node in the source XML or may be specified explicitly.

- ◆ **Situated:** anywhere in a template
- ◆ **Content:** empty

Attributes

Attribute	Value Type	Description
level	single, multiple or any	indicates the type of numbering scheme used if the number is generated; single produces numbering amongst siblings, multiple produces multi-level numbering, any produces numbering across the document; defaults to single; ignored if value is specified

Attribute	Value Type	Description
count	pattern	matches the nodes that should be counted if the number is generated; defaults to a pattern matching nodes of the same type and with the same name (if appropriate) as the current node; ignored if value is specified
from	pattern	matches the nodes at which the count should be reset; ignored if value is specified
value	numerical expression, whichshould result in a number greater than 0.5 and not Infinity	specifies the number to be formatted
format	string (attribute value template)	specifies the pattern for the number; alphanumeric characters indicate placeholders for numbers formatted in different ways, other characters are treated literally
lang	language code (attribute value template)	specifies the language used for alphabetic numbering
letter-value	traditional or alphabetic (attribute value template)	indicates whether a traditional numbering scheme (e.g., roman numerals) or alphabetic numbering scheme (e.g., a, b, c) should be used
grouping-size	number (attribute value template)	specifies how many digits should be arranged in a group when formatting large numbers
grouping-separator	character (attribute value template)	specifies the separator between digit groups when formatting large numbers

XSL:OTHERWISE

This element carries out a set of instructions if no xsl:when within its xsl:choose is processed.

◆ **Situated:** last child of an xsl:choose

◆ **Content:** any instructions

◆ **Attributes:** none

XSL:OUTPUT

This element controls the way in which the result tree is serialized into an output document.

- ◆ **Situated:** top level of the stylesheet
- ◆ **Content:** empty

Attributes

Attribute	Value Type	Description
method	xml, text, html or a qualified name	specifies the type of output that is expected and, therefore, the way in which elements, attributes, and characters are serialized (if they are at all); defaults to xml unless the document element of the result tree is called html with any case combination
version	name token	specifies the version of the output method; if the output method is xml, it specifies the version of XML (default 1.0), if it's html, the version of HTML (default 4.0), and so on
encoding	encoding string	specifies the character encoding that should be used in the output file; defaults to UTF-8
omit-xml-declaration	yes or no	specifies whether the XML declaration should be included in the output; defaults to yes if the output method is xml
standalone	yes or no	specifies whether the result document can stand alone, without referencing external entities; this is added to the XML declaration in the output if it is specified
doctype-public	string	specifies the public identifier for the document type of the result
doctype-system	URI	specifies the location of the DTD for the result
cdata-section-elements	space-separated list of qualified names	specifies the names of elements whose content should be wrapped within CDATA sections; commonly, this holds the names of elements that contain code

Attribute	Value Type	Description
indent	yes or no	indicates whether the processor should make the output more readable by adding white-space-only text nodes; defaults to no
media-type	string	specifies the content type of the output; defaults to text/xml if the output method is xml, and to text/html if the output method is html

XSL:PARAM

This element declares a parameter and sets a default value for it. If an xsl:param element occurs at the top level of a stylesheet, it is a global or stylesheet parameter; if it occurs within a template, it is a local or template parameter. The default value of the parameter is specified by the select attribute if it is specified, or the content of the xsl:param (as a result tree fragment) if the select attribute is not specified, or to an empty string if there is neither content nor a select attribute.

- ◆ **Situated:** top level of a stylesheet or as the first children of xsl:template

- ◆ **Content:** any instructions

Attributes

Attribute	Value Type	Description
name	qualified name	specifies the name of the parameter; must be specified
select	expression	gives the default value for the parameter

XSL:PRESERVE-SPACE

This element specifies the elements within which whitespace-only text nodes should be preserved. A whitespace-only text node that appears as a child of an element matched by a name test given in the elements attribute will appear in the source XML node tree.

- ◆ **Situated:** top level of a stylesheet
- ◆ **Content:** empty

Attributes

Attribute	Value Type	Description
elements	space-separated list of name tests (i.e., qualified names or *)	matches elements whose whitespace-only text node children should be preserved

---

XSL:PROCESSING-INSTRUCTION

This element creates a processing instruction in the result tree.

- ◆ **Situated:** anywhere in a template
- ◆ **Content:** any instructions, as long as they generate only text

---

Attributes

Attribute	Value Type	Description
name	unqualified name (attribute value template)	gives the name for the processing instruction

---

XSL:SORT

This element changes the order in which nodes in a node set are iterated over, either by xsl:for-each or by xsl:apply-templates. The processor assigns each of the nodes a sort value by evaluating the string expression held in the select attribute for that node. The nodes are then sorted by this sort value, which is interpreted as a string if the data-type attribute is text, or is converted to a number if the data-type is number.

- ◆ **Situated:** top level of a stylesheet
- ◆ **Content:** empty

Attributes

Attribute	Value Type	Description
select	string expression	gives the value by which the node should be sorted; defaults to . (i.e., the node's string value)
data-type	text, number, or a qualified name (attribute value template)	specifies the type of the value, whether it should be interpreted as a string or a number; defaults to text
order	ascending or (attribute value template) descending	gives the order in which the nodes should be sorted; defaults to ascending
lang	language code	specifies the language the processor uses to order the sort values
case-order	upper-first or lower-first (attribute value template)	specifies whether capitals should be sorted before lowercase letters; the default depends on the lang attribute

XSL:STRIP-SPACE

This element specifies the elements within which whitespace-only text nodes should be stripped. A whitespace-only text node that appears as a child of an element matched by a name test given in the elements attribute will not appear in the source XML node tree.

◆ **Situated:** top level of a stylesheet

◆ **Content:** empty

Attributes

Attribute	Value Type	Description
elements	space-separated list of name tests (i.e., qualified names or *)	matches elements whose whitespace-only text node children should be stripped

XSL:STYLESHEET

This is the document element for a stylesheet, holding all the other constructs. This can also be used as an element within another document to create an embedded stylesheet.

- ◆ **Situated:** document element
- ◆ **Content:** any number of xsl:import elements, followed by any top-level XSLT elements

Attributes

Attribute	Value Type	Description
version	1.0	specifies the version of XSLT used in the stylesheet; always 1.0 for XSLT 1.0; must be specified
extension-element-prefixes	space-separated list of namespace prefixes	lists the prefixes of namespaces that indicate extension elements that should be interpreted by the XSLT processor, rather than added to the result tree
exclude-result-prefixes	space-separated list of namespace prefixes	lists the prefixes of namespaces that should not be declared in the result unless they are used; typically, for namespaces that are used only in the source XML
id	ID	specifies an ID for the stylesheet, which is necessary to reference embedded stylesheets

XSL:TEMPLATE

This element defines a template, which can be applied (if a match pattern is specified) or called (if a name is specified).

- ◆ **Situated:** top level of a stylesheet
- ◆ **Content:** any number of xsl:param elements, followed by any instructions

Attributes

Attribute	Value Type	Description
Match	Pattern	matches the nodes that should be processed by this template
mode	qualified name	specifies the mode in which templates have to be applied in order to match this template
priority	Number	explicitly specifies the priority of the template when multiple templates match a node; the default priority is based on the complexity of the match pattern
name	qualified name	defines the name that can be used to call the template

XSL:TEXT

This element adds some text to the result tree. Whitespace-only text nodes within xsl:text are not stripped from the stylesheet tree, so you can use this element to add spaces or line breaks to the output.

- ◆ **Situated:** anywhere in a template
- ◆ **Content:** any text

ATTRIBUTES

Attribute	Value Type	Description
disable-output-escaping	yes or no	determines whether the text should be output without significant characters (such as < or &) being escaped; the default is no; some processors might not support disabling of output escaping

XSL:TRANSFORM

This element is an alias for `xsl:stylesheet`; see the definition of `xsl:stylesheet`.

XSL:VALUE-OF

This element evaluates an expression and adds the string value of the expression to the result tree.

- ◆ **Situated:** anywhere in a template
- ◆ **Content:** empty

Attributes

Attribute	Value Type	Description
Select	string expression	specifies the value to be added to the result tree
disable-output-escaping	yes or no	determines whether the value should be output without significant characters (such as < or &) being escaped; the default is no

XSL:VARIABLE

This element declares a variable. If an `xsl:variable` element occurs at the top level of a stylesheet, it is a global variable; if it occurs within a template, it is a local variable. The default value of the variable is given by the `select` attribute if it is specified, or the content of the `xsl:variable` (as a result tree fragment) if the `select` attribute is not specified, or to an empty string if there is neither content nor a `select` attribute.

- ◆ **Situated:** top level of a stylesheet or anywhere in a template
- ◆ **Content:** any instructions

Attributes

Attribute	Value Type	Description
name	qualified name	specifies the name of the variable; must be specified
select	expression	specifies the value of the variable

XSL:WHEN

This element carries out a set of instructions if its condition is true and no previous xsl:when within the same xsl:choose has been processed.

- ◆ **Situated:** within xsl:choose
- ◆ **Content:** any instructions

Attributes

Attribute	Value Type	Description
Test	Boolean expression	specifies the condition under which the instructions should be processed; must be specified

XSL:WITH-PARAM

This element passes a parameter value into a template. The value of the parameter is given by the select attribute if it is specified, or the content of the xsl:with-param (as a result tree fragment) if the select attribute is not specified, or to an empty string if there is neither content nor a select attribute.

- ◆ **Situated:** within xsl:apply-templates or xsl:call-template
- ◆ **Content:** any instructions

Attributes

Attribute	Value Type	Description
name	qualified name	specifies the name of the parameter; must be specified
select	expression	specifies the value for the template parameter

XSLT Attributes

The following attributes from the XSLT namespace can be added to any literal result element.

Attribute	Value Type	Description
xsl: extension- element- prefixes	space-delimited namespace prefixes, or #default keyword for default namespace	lists the prefixes of namespaces that indicate extension elements in the content of the literal result element
xsl:exclude- result- prefixes	space-delimited namespace prefixes, or #default keyword for default namespace	lists the prefixes of namespaces that should not be declared in the result unless they are used
xsl:use- attribute- sets	space-delimited attribute set names	lists the attribute sets whose attributes should be added to the literal result element
xsl:version	1.0	indicates the version of XSLT being used within the literal result element; this is required on the document element in a simplified stylesheet

Design Patterns

This section describes some of the common patterns of definitions and templates that you can combine to achieve common goals.

Identity Template

If you use an identity template, all nodes are copied to the result tree unless you override this template with a more specific one:

```
<xsl:template match="@*|node()">
   <xsl:copy>
      <xsl:apply-templates select="@*|node()" />
   </xsl:copy>
</xsl:template>
```

Recursive Templates

There are three main models for recursive templates. Each has a parameter, a test of that parameter that determines whether more processing is required, and a revised value for that parameter. Different types of recursion have different sets of these attributes, as the following table shows.

Type	Process	Test	Next
delimited strings	substring-before ($string, $delimiter)	contains($string, $delimiter)	substring-after($string, $delimiter)
fixed-format strings	substring($string, 1, $length)	string-length ($string)	substring ($string, $length + 1)
node set	$nodes[1]	$nodes[2]	$nodes[position () > 1]
sibling nodes	$node	following-sibling::*node-test*[1]	following-sibling::*node-test*[1]
parent nodes	$node	..	..

Continued

(Continued)

Type	Process	Test	Next
keyed nodes	`$node $value)`	`key('key-name',`	`key('key-name' , $value)`
counting up	`$count`	`$max > $count`	`$count + 1`
counting down	`$count`	`$count > $min`	`$count - 1`
base conversions	`$number div $base`	`$number mod $base`	`$number mod $base`

You should use the first type of template when the processing doesn't use the parameter value, or doesn't depend on the same property of the parameter value as is used to test whether to iterate again:

```
<xsl:template name="template-name">
   <xsl:param name="param-name" select="default-value" />
   <!— do some processing —>
   <xsl:if test="param-test">
      <xsl:call-template name="template-name">
         <xsl:with-param name="param-name" select="revised-value" />
      </xsl:call-template>
   </xsl:if>
</xsl:template>
```

You should use the second type of template when the processing uses the parameter value and the process depends on the same property of the parameter as is used to determine whether to continue recursing:

```
<xsl:template name="template-name">
   <xsl:param name="param-name" select="default-value" />
   <xsl:choose>
      <xsl:when test="not(param-test)">
         <!— do some processing —>
      </xsl:when>
      <xsl:otherwise>
         <!— do some other processing —>
         <xsl:call-template name="template-name">
            <xsl:with-param name="param-name"
```

```
                             select="revised-value" />
            </xsl:call-template>
         </xsl:otherwise>
      </xsl:choose>
</xsl:template>
```

You should use the third type of template when the processing combines the parameter value with the result of calling the template on the remaining value:

```
<xsl:template name="template-name">
   <xsl:param name="param-name" select="default-value" />
   <xsl:param name="partial-result-name" select="null-value" />
   <xsl:choose>
      <xsl:when test="not(param-test)">
         <xsl:value-of select="$partial-result-name" />
      </xsl:when>
      <xsl:otherwise>
         <!-- do some other processing to combine the partial result
             with the result from this recursion -->
         <xsl:call-template name="template-name">
            <xsl:with-param name="param-name"
                            select="revised-value" />
            <xsl:with-param name="partial-result-name"
                            select="revised-partial-result" />
         </xsl:call-template>
      </xsl:otherwise>
   </xsl:choose>
</xsl:template>
```

Iterating: The Piez Method

You can iterate a set number of times with `xsl:for-each` if you collect the right number of nodes. You can access differently sized sets of random nodes with (in increasing size) the following:

- ◆ `document('')//*`

- ◆ `document('')//node()`

- ◆ `document('')//node() | document('')//@*`

- ◆ `document('')//node() | document('')//@* | document('')//namespace::*`

The `xsl:for-each` then looks like the following:

```
<xsl:for-each select="$random-nodes[position() &lt;= $number]">
  <!— repeated process —>
</xsl:for-each>
```

The content of `xsl:for-each` can reference `position()` to get an increasing count.

Grouping: The Muenchian Method

With this grouping method, you must first define a key for the nodes that you want to group. The name can be anything. The `match` attribute must match the nodes that you want to group. The `use` expression is evaluated for each matched node to calculate a grouping value. The `xsl:key` element looks as follows:

```
<xsl:key name="key-name"
         match="node-matching-pattern"
         use="value-expression" />
```

You can then get the unique values with the following:

```
$nodes[count(.|key('key-name', value-expression)[1]) = 1]
```

Apply templates to these nodes in `group` mode. Write a template that matches them, provides the group-level output, and applies templates to the other nodes in the group in `item` mode:

```
<xsl:template match="node-matching-pattern" mode="group">
  <!— group-level output —>
  <xsl:apply-templates select="key('key-name', value-expression)"
                        mode="item" />
  <!— group-level output —>
</xsl:template>
```

Finally, write a template that matches these nodes in `item` mode, to generate the item-level output:

```
<xsl:template match="node-matching-pattern" mode="item">
  <!— item-level output —>
</xsl:template>
```

1

Index

continued

continued

continued

continued

continued

continued

What Makes This Book an Unlimited Edition?

find out at www.unlimited-edition.com

You may have noticed that this book is an "Unlimited Edition." This means that we continue to update the book with new material even after it's printed. As the owner of this book, you get special access to the new material as soon as it's ready. Visit our Unlimited Edition Web site to sign up.

At the Unlimited Edition Web site you'll find:

- Online access to every chapter of the book, so you can get the answer you need even if you left the book at the office.
- Brand-new content written just for owners of the book! New material gets posted to the site for up to a year after the book publishes, or until a new edition becomes available.
- Downloadable updates and new articles in pdf format for your offline perusal.

FIND YOUR ONLINE EXTENSION OF THE BOOK AT WWW.UNLIMITED-EDITION.COM